Coming Home to Lemuria

ISBN: 0-9831-4331-5
ISBN-13: 9780983143314

Coming Home to Lemuria

An Ascension Adventure Story

Phillip Elton Collins

Phillip E. Collins

Angel News Network

2011

Dedication

To Mount Shasta, there have been many stories and legends about you. Once in a while, another story like this one surfaces and you reveal more of yourself.

To Adama, High Priest of Telos, Lemuria, our guide to another dimension. This book is a continuation of you being heard and of our two worlds soon joining together.

To Michael, an archangel, who created this sacred journey after I was led to initiate it.

To my fellow proxies, Jeff and Joel, who encouraged me and insisted this was my story to tell.

To the modern-day Lemurians, Dianne and Ashalyn: Dianne made the physical journey possible. Ashalyn became the sixth point on our star.

To my husband, James, who teaches me how to receive love each day and, through that love, makes this work possible.

Contents

Acknowledgments

I would like to express my gratitude to my parents, Joyce and Bob Collins, who knew from the get-go that one of their twin sons was decidedly different from the other (and others), and encouraged and supported my difference. My deep appreciation extends to my Lemurian brothers and sisters, who made themselves known to me at a point in my life when most have lost their purpose; to the archangelic realms of Gabriel, Michael, Raphael, and Uriel, who taught me all I think I know; and to the ascended masters leading us all lovingly back home. Thanks also to my light ascension teacher, Robert Baker, who created the foundation for all I am today.

Heartfelt thanks to my fellow proxies, Jeff Fasano, Joel Anastasi, George Ganges, and David Wheeler, for joining the journey and making it perfect; and to Dianne Robbins and Ashalyn, who made the journey possible.

I would like to acknowledge my editor/muse, Stephanie Gunning, who took a huge manuscript that fell out of me and brought her talent and consciousness to it.

Last, but not least, I am grateful to my husband, James Gozon, who is just always present being a present.

With deep love and gratitude, I thank you all for being in my life.

The events depicted in this book solely represent my memories and experiences. Other members of the mountain journey may have experienced or remember these events differently. My depiction of my fellow proxies is intended to portray their perfection in serving humanity, not in any way to reflect negatively on anyone's individual character. Channels other than me may have had similar information about Lemuria come through them. In our current era of humanity's awakening to the consciousness of higher-frequency energy, all of us are needed; and it is my belief that channeling shall soon become a commonplace event.

Preface

We live in an era of transformation. It is essential to understand what is going on energetically and physically within and upon our planet, as it evolves at this time. Earth is in an ascension process of moving to a higher frequency of consciousness and existence. So is humankind. More than ever before, there is a need to embrace our ascension and for each of us to awaken to our purpose. Today we have a window of opportunity to heal and grow in wisdom. We have all been asleep for a long time, and this has brought us much pain. But we can now remember...

The purpose of this book, *Coming Home to Lemuria,* is to reveal that an unseen civilization co-exists with ours on this planet, and explain the purpose of its inhabitants in relationship to us. For a very long time, humankind has not been told the entire truth of who we are and our history. Thus, much of what we think is true about the world and ourselves is not. Our belief systems are based upon untruths. The truth we have received has been received through myths, legends, and fiction (and often good fiction is based upon the truth). Possibly this was the only way we could receive the truth. But it is now time to tell the truth directly through the truth.

Are you ready? Can you handle it?

Can the world handle it?

Truth is, we are not children being controlled by unseen forces. Nor is ascension a process in which the few can control the many. If each of us can discern the truth of our own vibration—not to judge it or shame it, but to accept it and raise it—and if we dissolve the illusion of separation and duality within us as individuals and among us as a race of spiritual beings, we can begin to more clearly see the beauty and common energy that runs through everyone and connects us with Earth. The time has come for us to shed our many erroneous beliefs about ourselves, our planet, religions, governments, and the universe that have kept most of our kind trapped in varying degrees of lack and limitation. We alone can do this through connection with our divine essence.

Coming Home to Lemuria is an adventure story about a small group of travelers who made a sacred journey to Mount Shasta in Northern California under the spiritual guidance of a talkative archangel, Michael, and a very wise high priest from Lemuria, Adama. It's all right with me if you do not believe everything I am about to tell you. I don't need you to believe me (but please do enjoy the adventure). Some people already know portions of what we learned before and during our adventure, so many readers will know that what is described is true. Please know there is no need in me to convince you. That would be to try to control you, which I have no need to do. In my heart and from direct experience I know that everything I share in this book is true, even if the mind cannot always accept that it is. The mind believes; the heart knows.

I am a latecomer to learning about the Lemurian civilization. Individuals, such as Dianne Robbins, Aurelia Louise Jones, and members of different Lemurian and Telos organizations throughout the world have dedicated their lives to disseminating the wisdom of Lemuria. My predecessors, I salute you! I only ask that you kindly allow this newcomer to join you.

Many sacred journeys are taking place worldwide that support the good of humanity and the planet. I acknowledge everyone who does energy work of this kind. It is incredibly significant. I have also participated in sacred trips of this kind over the years. The journey you will read about in these pages may be one of many, but it is also like no other. And it is mine to share because it is the story of a remarkable adventure that I had with a small group of dedicated light workers.

There are many tools, teachings, and messages peppered throughout this book that can further assist both you and me in choosing to shift to a higher form of existence. Please take them and utilize them if it feels right to you. Enjoy the journey...

Part One
First Contact Occurs

Chapter 1
A Dusty Old Thrift Shop

The higher beings who are central to this story suggested that I start at the beginning. While the beginning may feel a bit like a cliché, I assure you it is the only thing about this story that is.

You see, I was in a dusty old thrift shop, the type of place that is primarily defined by its smell. For me, shopping in such a place meant escaping the American retail industry with its inflated prices and lack of customer support. Also I loved the idea that the clothes and books I would buy there, if I did, had a history—one that might continue after me. Or maybe I was just being cheap. Over the years I have bought some great stuff in thrift stores for little money.

On this particular day, I went to this "other people's things" store to look for a warm jacket since South Florida, the area encompassing Miami, Fort Lauderdale, and Palm Beach, was having the coldest winter on record. Ever since retiring from the business of film making, I have spent summers in New York City and winters in Fort Lauderdale, and I had left most of my winter garments in my apartment up north. I didn't want to replace my entire wardrobe; I wanted something inexpensive, yet effective, to get me through the cold snap. Suddenly, an inner voice—not my own—directed me, "Go check out the used book section."

Well, hello there! I wasn't that surprised to hear a voice speaking to me. My current profession is as a practitioner of healing arts and I've had training over the years in various modalities from Reiki and light ascension therapy, to acupuncture and homeopathy. As an intuitive counselor, I am receptive to communication with angelic beings, which I sense as different frequencies of energy. However, this unfamiliar voice was none I could recognize. An energy of unknown origin, it was speaking to me uninvited and without introduction.

Honestly, what surprised me most was that I knew, from past experience, how chaotic the used book area of the store was. Why was I being led to sort through hundreds of books stuffed into boxes on the floor and haphazardly spread across the shelves like peanut butter on toast?

Then I remembered it was my friend Joel's birthday. A book would be a meaningful gift for him, but I wasn't convinced the literature he enjoys could be found in a thrift store. Furthermore, I doubted that I could survive the smell long enough to sort through a bad case of the book piles. Nonetheless, acceding to the guidance I'd received, I took a deep breath, stepped away from the clothing racks that I was rummaging through, and headed over to the used books section in an attempt to accomplish this seemingly impossible mission.

Once among the boxes of books, the same inner voice as before directed me to search a specific book shelf. Feeling like a hound dog hot on the trail of its prey, I knew exactly where to look and exactly what book I would find there. Joel is fascinated by the physical appearances of the Virgin Mary in Eastern Europe and he has visited Megjugorje in Croatia twice. In an instant, my fingers landed on a book of the history of Mother Mary visitations. I couldn't believe it—or maybe

I did. The voice that had drawn me to look in this spot had been so definitive.

I pulled the book off the shelf, considering myself very fortunate, and was in the process of turning toward the front exit when my find slipped from my grasp as quickly as it had appeared. While I was shuffling around trying to relocate it, three other books from three different shelves spontaneously fell right at my feet. Although the titles of these paperbacks had no meaning to me, they had something in common; each said something about "Lemuria." (What in the world was that?) I quickly returned them to their points of departure and found the Mary book.

After grabbing a warm jacket off the rack in the men's clothing area, I felt my mission was complete. I paid the cashier, walking out of the store with my prizes in a musty plastic bag.

Since I haunted this particular thrift store on a regular basis, in only a couple of weeks I was back again for another nasal assault and bargain hunt. Interestingly, the very same inner voice I'd heard before greeted me as soon as I entered the shop's soiled doors. "Go immediately to the used book section," it said. But I was there to find a warm shirt since the cold winter weather was continuing. I was inclined to ignore the suggestion that was being made to me. "Never mind the clothes," the voice insisted, "you are not here for that. Go to the books."

Okay, then! Like an ancient warrior following orders, I placed myself in front of the same bookshelves as on my visit two weeks prior. "Why am I here?" I asked myself as well as the inner voice. As if in reply, and without me touching the bookshelves, the exact same three books I'd knocked off the shelves before began to fall in succession directly onto my feet from three different shelves...thud, thud, thud.

That was strange—and, *ouch,* I was wearing open-toed sandals!

Seriously, hearing inner voices has become a regular occurrence in my life since I became a healer. But flying objects?

"Okay, I get it," I said. "I'm supposed to read these books...but *why?*"

Then, oddly, I began to feel as if the inner voice I had heard was literally speaking to me from inside the books. *(Whose voice was this?)* None of it made sense. How could three books fall from three different shelves, without assistance? And hit me two weeks in a row? Wow, somebody or something must have really wanted me to read these books!

Looking down at the first book, I saw that there was a picture of a mountain on the cover. I recognized it as Mount Shasta in California. Ten years earlier I had been to Mount Shasta with Joel, the friend for whom I had bought the birthday book about the sightings of Mary. That had been a wonderful vacation. The title of the book read *Telos.* Okay. But this was a bit confusing. The word "Telos" had no connection to the trip I'd taken to Mount Shasta or to my life in the present. Furthermore, I was unfamiliar with the name of the book's author, Dianne Robbins.

Continuing my investigation, I saw that another word, "Lemuria," appeared on the cover of one of the other two books. I vaguely remembered from my metaphysical training that Lemuria was a possible ancient civilization. I'd taken a trip to Egypt led by one of my spiritual teachers. In Luxor, outside the famous temple of Karnak, there sits an enormous boulder that my companions told me was a crystal remnant from Lemuria. I hadn't learned too much from them, except that Lemuria was supposed to have disappeared like Atlantis.

A thrilling emotion came over me; every hair on my body was standing on end. Somehow I knew I was about to begin an amazing adventure...

I gathered the books off the floor and held the three volumes next to my heart, feeling like I had just found the proverbial goose that laid the golden egg. I rushed to the checkout counter to pay for them. They cost seventy-five cents each. "A treasure for pennies," I thought without knowing why.

When I got home I became consumed with reading the three books. My speed-reading skills from high school sure came in handy. I zipped through all three in a day or two, and then read and re-read Dianne Robbins' book again and again, feeling mesmerized. Somehow the amazing things I was reading felt like a distant memory being awakened. Her book began with comments from a spokesman named Adama, who started out by saying that he and others living in a hidden world on Earth were bringing humankind the "memories of Lemuria." (Was this Adama *Adam* from the story of Adam and Eve? Was Lemuria *the Garden of Eden?*)

Adama, a being from Lemuria who was channeled by Robbins, went on to explain that even though human memories of his extraordinary civilization have been lost for millennia, it is time for our two civilizations to become united. (Where was this unseen world? Why was this information coming forward now?) Even though none of this remarkable commentary made sense, it felt true. It resonated with me on a very deep level.

So I continued my studies...

The first thing I learned from Robbins' book, *Telos* (Trafford Publishing 2008), which is subtitled *Original Transmissions from the Subterranean City Beneath Mt. Shasta,* was that Lemuria is located inside the Earth. Now how was that possible? Everyone knows that the interior of our planet is molten rock! Who or what could possibly live there?

At first glance, this book came across to me like the recollection of a sci-fi adventure story about an expedition to the interior of the Earth. It sounded like a Hollywood script. And I should know, as I worked in Northern California for many years for George Lucas of *Star Wars* fame.

My mind began to discount the event in the bookstore and to challenge the entire experience that was unfolding as I read the book. "This is crazy. You are *literally* going crazy," I told myself repeatedly. But my heart would not let the idea of Lemuria go. Who was it that said, "The heart knows and the mind believes"? The feeling I got from my heart kept saying, "Trust this, it is true. You are supposed to know this information for a reason that will be revealed." I thought for a few seconds to set the books aside and forget the entire matter. But I could not.

"Stay open," the inner voice of my unseen companion commanded me.

I decided to Google Lemuria. All I could find out was that through legends we were told it was possible that a huge continent that existed some twelve thousand years ago was lost after submerging off the coast of California. This idea had been circulated by the Rosicrucians, and the acclaimed seer Edgar Cayce apparently had a few dreams about it. There seemed to be little physical evidence that this place or other places of this kind, like Atlantis, ever really existed.

I have worked with the human condition in clinical settings for many years. The relationship between the human mind—our thoughts and emotions—and the physical body is central to my work as a healing arts practitioner. I know what delusion is, and denial. But somehow, perhaps since I felt such a strong connection to this new world coming into my life, I trusted in its reality. If I was crazy that would be revealed in time to me and others. It was now appropriate to let go of my concerns and enjoy the journey of discovery.

If madness felt this good, then bring it on! I had never felt this happy in my entire life. Even though my life was already filled with love, happiness, and personal and professional fulfillment, in some not-so-strange way I felt I was coming home to an exceptionally more evolved home—an unseen reality—than the world we live in and ordinarily recognize as real.

There was a quality to the voice I was hearing that was different from the angelic voices I had previously channeled, a quality that led me to believe that the voice speaking to me was this same guy, Adama from Lemuria, who Robbins had channeled for her book. Recognizing that it was time to establish direct communication between us, I decided to ask. "Are you Adama?"

"Yes, I am," he confirmed. "Through me, our world can be revealed to yours. You will come to know the truth of Lemuria."

Chapter 2
Conversations with Adama

My inner-voice guy, the spokesman from Lemuria called Adama, explained the things he wanted me to know through an experience you might call "downloading." I would sense his energy stirring through my body, this would be translated in my head so that I sort of heard his words, and then I would write them down. He became like my new best friend, or an older brother—the kind everyone always wants as a kid. But this brother seemed connected to everything. We had an initial series of conversations that took place over the course of a week or two.

The first thing Adama communicated to me was that Lemuria was a nation that existed approximately twelve thousand years ago on a large continent that extended from what is now the coast of California far out into the Pacific Ocean. It was much larger than North America is today. The entire continent had been sunk due to warring with another nation called Atlantis that had existed at the same time on the other side of the globe. It seems these two powerful nations had major disagreements about how life should be and who should be in control of the world. (Sound familiar?) Since they had advanced technology at their disposal, technology that was much more advanced than anything we presently possess, it was fairly easy for the one culture to dispose of the other. Around 350 million people were killed overnight when

Lemuria sank. The remaining inhabitants survived only by designing a home for themselves in the center of the earth. Through civil war, some two thousand years later, Atlantis also destroyed itself.

I guess the moral of the story is that when you develop the ability to destroy one another it is a good idea to learn how to get along. If you don't, the consequences can be severe. As I learned about the destruction of Lemuria from Adama, mythology began coming to life as history. I had always been told that myths were based upon truth. But I had never suspected how much.

"Okay, but how do we get from then to now?" I wondered. "If Lemuria was destroyed millennia ago and I am being told that Lemurians still live inside the core of the Earth, how is it possible?" It didn't seem as if there even could be a rational explanation.

Adama went on to explain that there are many frequencies of reality within the universe. Those of us on the surface of the Earth live in the third dimension. But both when we go to sleep and when we die we enter into another frequency of existence, the fourth dimension, which is a slightly higher frequency than the third. The Lemurians themselves actually live in the fifth dimension, a frequency much higher than ours, one that few humans yet can see or visit.

The only Fifth Dimension I had ever known was a musical group. What Adama was telling me reminded me of the way animals can hear things we can't—taken to a new extreme.

"Okay, so why does this fifth-dimensional culture live inside the Earth and not on the surface?" I asked.

Adama told me that most of the surface of the planet had not been fit for his people to live on due to the many years of fighting wars. The only habitable place available to the Lemurians after the destruction was inside the Earth. But this required them to shift to another frequency of existence than the frequency of dwellers on the surface. Apparently, most planets in the universe are inhabited in their cores rather than on their surface. In my head I heard the words, "You live inside a house, not on its roof, dear one."

I immediately thought, "Is that the reason we don't see life on the surface of other planets in our solar system? Maybe everybody else is living at a frequency we cannot yet see. *Hmmm.* Physics is explaining new realities all the time..." This was food for thought. If this was true, our world was certainly turning out to be more complicated than I had imagined.

Adama continued the fascinating story. His people, survivors of a mighty civilization that once lived on the surface like us, are real and they live underneath Mount Shasta in California. Since we are at an important transitional moment in our evolution, they now want to know us.

"My God," I thought, "California is known for being exotic, but this is really pushing things—even for California! Even when I was working for George Lucas I never heard a story like this one." Many of the plots of George's films were drawn from mythology—Joseph Campbell was one of his influences—and the experience of speaking to Adama felt similar to watching and being drawn into one of those epic science fiction adventures. But something more was happening within me. As these conversations went on, I was beginning to connect the dots about my own role in this emerging drama. Until then, I had never seen a link between my work as director of marketing in the film industry and the healing arts I practiced. Perhaps there is a greater purpose for why I had made my career transition years ago. It had led me here.

Seeing my response, and the many thoughts it was provoking in me, Adama encouraged me to process the entire unique experience through my heart. "Your mind will never accept or believe all I am about to tell you. But your heart actually has access to memories of the entire experience, since you, like many other human beings, were actually on Earth when these events took place," he reassured me.

This was exciting! As a small boy, I often thought that there had to be more to life than one lifetime. One shot at being here never made sense to me. Thus, long ago, I had come to believe in reincarnation, even though I had no evidence other than supposition. What Adama was telling me seemed to be the proof I had been looking for my entire life. "But will anyone else believe it?" I wondered. Then, as quickly as I thought this, I realized that the opinions of others did not matter. What mattered was to know the truth.

"The time has come for our two civilizations to unite and you can assist this in happening," my unseen friend explained. "We are planning to come among your people soon to join with those of you who are ready in a world of equality, harmony, and balance."

Boy, this really was sounding more and more like one of George's films.

"It is our deepest wish to teach you all that we have learned since the sinking of our continent and to support you in creating the type of paradise we created for ourselves in Lemuria," Adama whispered.

Could it really be that there is a paradise somewhere in our troubled world? Wouldn't it be amazing if it was right under our feet, unseen? Does the Garden of Eden exist in another realm, another dimension within our planet? Is this what string theory is teaching us? Are there many realities all happening at once? Are the quantum physicists right? Questions were flying through my mind, so I tried hard to return to my heart and quiet my mind. "Breathe deep," I reminded myself.

"The truth lies within the breath and the heart, not the mind" became my mantra.

"I ask you to take the information you are receiving now into your heart," Adama requested, "and make a conscious effort to create a bridge of communication and love between our two civilizations. We have the same basic genetic makeup as you; in effect we are one. The wisdom we Lemurians are about to share with humanity can prevent you from making the same mistakes we made so long ago. This will allow you to move into a destiny much different from your past and present," Adama continued.

Whoever this guy was, he really knew how to get my attention.

Mount Shasta is a spectacular volcanic mountain in a range of mountain peaks some forty miles south of the California-Oregon border. The peak is at fourteen thousand-plus feet, so you can see it from over a hundred miles away. It is the second largest volcanic peak in America and, indeed, a force of nature. It was considered a sacred place for centuries before European settlers arrived, a magical power source. Throughout recorded history, Mount Shasta has been recognized as a place of angels, masters from other realms, spaceships, and spirit guides. I'm not surprised now to know it is also the home of the survivors of ancient Lemuria. It seems appropriate that an advanced civilization selected such a special spot for their homeland.

Even if you cannot comprehend or do not agree with what is being stated here, if you were standing before this massive being of a mountain you wouldn't be able to help but feel there's more here than meets the eye. Strange lights and sounds are often seen or heard around the mountain. Unusual stationary clouds called lenticulars, which look like lenses, form above it. Extraordinary sunsets complete the mix of this being a mystical, otherworldly destination.

Adama gave me an explanation for why such phenomena occur. "This place has many openings into the fifth-dimensional cities and homes of the present-day Lemurians who are the survivors from the sinking of the continent so very long ago. You on the surface are currently shifting your frequency from third- to fourth- to fifth-dimensional reality. These other frequencies exist around you, although most of you do not yet have the awareness to see them for what they are. But this will soon change," my mentor downloaded to me.

The Lemurians knew well in advance of the impending demise of their world. Thus, they were able to use their crystalline energy-mastery technology to create a massive underground city where they could preserve their culture not only for themselves, but also for those of us who would live in the Earth in the future. Without their efforts at preservation, those on the planet's surface never could return "home" to a higher frequency of existence.

Needless to say, this part of Earth's history was lost to humankind. Until recently, very few of our kind knew or suspected anything about it.

About twenty-five thousand Lemurians managed to migrate to the interior of Mount Shasta before the Atlanteans destroyed their home on the surface. Adama told me, "We currently exist in light bodies that are not constrained by the limitations of your physical world. Someday you will join us in this fifth-dimensional reality. Your Mother Earth has already begun to shift her frequency; and all things within and upon her body also will shift. This is your destiny."

I don't know about you, but I am willing and ready to make a shift from the world we live in. If the blueprint necessary to do that already exists here and now, so be it...

Adama reported that the Lemurian civilization existed on the surface literally for millions of years. They mastered electron energy and telepathy eons ago. "We have technological abilities that make your 3D abilities look like child's play. We control most of our crystalline and amino acid technologies with our minds. We can travel through space and have the ability to make our spaceships invisible and soundless to avoid detection by your military. Many of your world leaders know we exist, however they are keeping this fact from you. Although we are physical beings, we can shift our energy fields from the third to the fifth frequency and be visible or invisible at will." Adama added, "This will prevent the inhabitants of your world from harming us until the time when you are ready to know and accept us."

This definitely was science fiction coming to life!

Chapter 3
Visiting Telos

One morning I was woken at 3:30 a.m. with a sense of urgency to get to the computer. This felt like the jolt you get from having a cup of coffee, so it got me up and out of bed.

I had become accustomed to waking in the wee hours to communicate with my new Lemurian friend. After rising, I would dress quietly and tiptoe out of the bedroom, then carefully close the door behind me and go into the office so as not to disturb my sleeping husband while I typed Adama's messages. This was a private time for me, quiet, intimate, with no one else stirring inside or outside the house. Later, I would go back to bed and rise at a normal hour.

This day was different. When Adama began to communicate with me telepathically, I asked for permission to make a visit to Lemuria. Eager to know what it was like, I said, "I'd like to go." My eyes were closed and I dropped into a trance, at which point I became aware of the presence of two guides from Lemuria who were there to serve as my spiritual escorts. Instantaneously, I passed through an energetic conduit to the fifth dimension and found myself—or rather, my light body—standing in the city of Telos. The funny thing, and I understood this right away, is that in this frequency of being there is no unknowing. I knew exactly where I was and what to do.

I would like to take a moment to explain how direct connection with the Lemurians is possible. We all know a little about astral projection (moving through different frequencies) and telepathy (communicating through thoughts without the limits of time and distance). Actually, all people use these abilities when we access our intuition, although not everyone is aware of doing so. When I wish to connect with Adama (or another higher-frequency being), I clear an energetic space for him by saying, "This is not about me. I release myself from myself and let go." Then I allow his presence, his energy to come into me—to merge with mine. He is able to project his thoughts telepathically wherever he wishes and I consciously choose to receive them.

Practice makes perfect. This is how every communication described in this book took place. It is also how I am able to channel angelic energy, such as the frequency of Archangel Uriel, which is something I began doing a few years before the events I am recounting. There are two types of channels: conscious channels who stay awake when higher energy comes through them (people like me) and trance channels whose consciousness leaves their bodies (people like Edgar Cayce). Everyone has the ability. Being able to do it really is nothing special. Try it yourself. It's like going to the gym; if you work a muscle, it will grow. The more you practice channeling, the better you become at it. More individuals in our dimension are now receiving messages from other dimensions to assist us in the shift of consciousness that we of our world need to make.

Can you imagine if things stayed the way they are now? We probably would be destroyed like the Lemurians of old. They don't want to see this happen to us for reasons that will become clear in this book. The times are changing and we are receiving assistance. But rest assured, there is nothing to fear; we have freedom of choice. No being can make us be and do anything. Each one has to choose. As more individuals on the surface of the Earth open our hearts, more of the truth will come out. Since I have chosen oneness, I am able to accept and receive these messages.

Additional details about this development will be explained further on, for now I just want to express that it felt natural for me to leave my physical body and travel in an astral state to Telos.

Telos, which is located in the fifth dimension, is a much different environment than our own. Nothing is as dense as it is here, although being there feels similar. Although I experienced myself as having a body with senses and a physical reality around me, I also had added senses. Most significantly, at this frequency, everything is known. Questions are answered at the moment of being asked.

I immediately understood that in order to sustain an extended stay within this higher frequency, certain things are required. The foremost of these is that we are asked to love ourselves and others unconditionally. Self-love is primary and necessary for other-love. As the only relationship we are ever really having is the one with our self, this relationship is mirrored outwardly in our relationships with others. Our unconditional love must include all aspects of Mother Earth, including her plant, animal, and mineral kingdoms, the air, and water, if we are to sustain form at the higher frequency. So I knew my visit would inevitably be a brief one.

Another requirement for sustaining a fifth-dimensional existence is to ensure that your relationship with the masculine and feminine energies that are interwoven in your energetic field includes equality, harmony, and balance. There can be no intention to harm anyone or anything. It is necessary to cleanse yourself of negative emotions and thoughts—shame and blame related to the past, present, and future—towards yourself as much as others. Unfortunately, balance and harmony are still major issues for those of us who live on the surface of the planet.

These requirements make the high-frequency civilization of Lemuria possible. It is the higher frequency of Lemurians that makes them invisible to those of us who live at a denser frequency.

Interestingly, in Lemuria thoughts and emotions of any frequency denser than the Lemurians' own are magnified many times over. Thus, they can cause trauma for third-dimensional beings like us, which means surface dwellers can be allowed only a brief stay among them. We would have to go through many initiations if we desired to live in Lemuria for good.

Through advanced technology, astral projection, telepathy, and higher consciousness, the Lemurians have been able to replicate details of the environment on the surface of the Earth inside the Earth in a perfected Utopian fashion. That which they pay attention to, and intend is created. They have created a sun by drawing electrons from another galaxy. Their air is pure. Their water is alive and provides vital nourishment to those who drink it. The entire population is vegetarian. Fruit and leaves are consumed, but not roots. No being—animal or plant—is ever killed.

When I arrived, it was a spectacular day. I found that the Lemurian sun is suspended in a perfectly blue sky and the weather is held at 72 degrees with no storms, except when the water needs to be replenished by rain. It turns out that consciousness creates weather patterns. The harmoniousness of Lemurian consciousness creates consistently pleasant conditions.

Everything around me seemed to have a life of its own: The sun, the sky, the trees, the colors, the smells, the sounds, the plants, and the animals all were alive with their own consciousness—and I could communicate and connect with them! I felt like Dorothy in *The Wizard of Oz* on steroids. I understood the connectivity of everything all at once. What affects one affects all. Now if I could only bring this awareness and truth back to the third dimension!

The average Lemurian is seven-foot tall, beautiful, and—barring destructive forces like the attack from the ancient Atlanteans, accidents, and personal choice—is immortal. They do not suffer from illness and fatigue as we do. Their day begins in meditation, prayer, and expressions of gratitude. As I moved among them freely and unattended, I could sense their heightened state of consciousness, which contrasted favorably to the consciousness of the 3D world.

Present in this frequency, I found myself able to expand consciously to connect with Mother Earth and all the living things on her body. *Sunlight and love make all things possible!* I suddenly realized. I had often heard this, but in this higher frequency I knew what it meant and experienced the power of the message. I felt love for humankind on the surface like I had never felt before. Without being told, I understood that the light I was sensing would allow necessary changes on the surface of our planet to take place. All life on the surface was going to change its frequency to match the vibration of the light I was experiencing within and without me. This is the same light from which everything is made. This light is love, and it is the building block of everything.

I was invited to step inside one of the many spherical, crystalline homes as I passed by. Interestingly, the structure of their homes allows Lemurians to see everything outside, although those outside cannot see inside a home. From the inside, there is no separation between the world inside and outside the home; it feels like a single environment. This mirrors their social order. In Lemuria, all that is created is shared between households. No one goes without. It is understood that there is enough for everyone. Lemurians view themselves as one big, extended family. You can feel the knowingness they have of oneness. Sharing and exchange allows everyone the opportunity to visit and be together more often. Isolation and exclusion do not occur.

Almost everything the Lemurians need can be manifested through intentions and thoughts. Thus, nothing is created in excess and there is no waste. They have no need for money. They even create their homes through sustained focus. Whatever they pay attention to, and intend they can manifest. The formula is attention plus intention equals manifestation. "Wow, I look forward to that," I thought to myself. "No more contractors or budgets."

I noticed that there were no police patrolling the streets and no locks upon the doors. "Since we are all connected to one another, there really is no need for protective services or devices," a handsome passerby explained. "When you know you are brothers and sisters connected to the same Source, there is no fear. We experience none of the danger that exists on the surface."

Adama joined me to be my guide and offer further explanation. "We intend to be loving and tolerant to all with whom we come in contact no matter now different they appear to be, for beneath the exterior, inside our essence is the same. We are the Creator experiencing itself. When seeing one another, it is the eyes of the Creator we see, and it is the Creator's heart we feel through when caring for one another and sharing. This is the truth those on the planet's surface have lost, which is still causing your wars and is the root of your greed. But you will recapture this understanding. The pain of separation from one another will be coming to an end soon.

"Achieving immortality is also important for those who reside on the planet's surface, but not for the reasons you might think. Once you achieve immortality, you will be able to put all of your wisdom to use so that you can truly experience a life of joy and creativity. Right now you live a life of a few decades, you die, and you come back to life—but you forget that which you have learned. It's essential for this cycle of life and death to end in order for you to advance as a race of sentient and luminous beings.

"The Lemurians shall soon surface to show humanity the way. In spite of how things may appear on the surface, many of you are ready to make the changes in your world necessary for us to come forward," Adama assured me. "Be patient. It is happening,"

He went on to tell me that humans have each had thousand of lifetimes on our planet—and sometimes elsewhere (though we don't remember these due to the frequency in which we live). However, when we are in the frequency of the Lemurians we begin to remember our lifetimes, to awaken. The awakening that many religions encourage is actually the process of remembering who we are, why we are here, and where we came from. "Ancient memories of being in Lemuria during past lives are present in your cellular memory, and they are being activated at this time," Adama said, adding, "That's what 'coming home' really means.

"Human beings originally came from the higher dimensions. Now it must be your intention to remember your essence, to know your purpose, and reconnect with Source."

Listening to Adama, I could not help imagining what it would be like for us if it was part of our education as young children to learn this information. Ours would be a decidedly different world. Whenever I see people who know their purpose, they are usually changing the world for the better.

As we continued to walk around Telos, we saw many Lemurians enjoying one another's company and relaxing. Work is not the highest priority of their civilization, although everyone makes a contribution that supports the community. I learned that the city is divided into various elevations that serve different functions. We visited an elevation that held nature preserves and parks used for hiking. The lakes and waterfalls we walked past dazzled me with their pristine beauty. There was an intense felt connection to Earth since we were so close to her heart. At the same time, I was acutely aware that we were connected to the cosmos above.

It felt like a perfect spring day, filled with magic. Warmth was in the air. Spring is the time of the year when a force within the earth awakens the plants, animals, and us. Have you ever wondered where this force comes from? In Lemuria I learned that it is created and maintained in high-frequency areas like this one. The flowers, plants, and trees in Telos have a visible life force that radiates from their leaves and branches, and is spread through their fragrance. There were colors and smells coming from the flowers we encountered that I had literally never experienced before. Everything living around me was actually communicating with me through its innate frequency. I had never felt so connected to anything or anyone, including myself.

I had entirely lost my awareness that I was inside a planet until Adama led me on an exploration of Telos' amazing tunnel system. Each tunnel was brightly lit, so there was no sense of being in a confined space. Electromagnetic vehicles were zipping around us. These apparently can quickly carry you anywhere you want or need to be. They are silent and much faster than any mode of transportation that we presently have on the surface.

I observed many temples, which I knew were dedicated to forces, known as "flames" or "rays," that allow Lemuria to exist. At the temples, I was told that they have tended these flames for eons to sustain their own lives, and also so that the flames would be available to us when we were ready to make our way back home. Without the flames, apparently we would be stuck at our current frequency in the third dimension. Tending the flames demonstrated to me how much the Lemurians love us and how closely intertwined they perceive our two races to be.

As I was shown around Telos, the city appeared to be in a constant celebration of life. I saw people freely and openly showing sincere affection for one another. They were not just dashing from one place to another. They were clearly a gregarious and social people who wanted to share life's joy. Anything less than joy did not appear to factor into their consciousness.

Adama affirmed, "We wake up with our hearts filled with love and we go to bed at night knowing we have been in constant service to each other. Very soon, my beloveds, you on the surface will ascend into a higher state of consciousness and begin openly showing your love for one another as we do. You will begin to look deeply into each other's eyes and recognize the soul behind the look and know that it is you."

Everywhere I went, Lemurians telepathically added to my understanding of their civilization. They wanted me to know that they celebrate their holidays with friends and family just like us, gathering in their thought-created homes, feasting and expressing gratitude to the Creator for all the abundance on and within the Earth. I understood that gratitude is the essence of abundance.

Adama specifically wanted me to know that since thoughts create reality, the key to the Lemurians success in transforming into fifth-dimensional beings—their success in *ascension*—was a direct result of high intentionality and their love for life itself. "You, too, will soon evoke the power of love and intentionality in creating a new world paradigm on the surface."

As my brief visit was nearing its end, Adama mentioned that the time is coming for our two civilizations to merge. Once we raise the frequency of our consciousness and we are peaceful, they can share advanced technology with us that is capable of healing the planet. But we're not ready yet. It's ironic that we don't understand that the planet is a living being we need to honor in order for us to survive. I felt relief that despite the damage we have caused to Mother Earth, there is a way it could be repaired, a way to live safely and happily on the planet's body

Adama also wished me to know, "You and your brothers and sisters on the surface can come to Telos in your 'light body' at night when you sleep." He concluded, "Just telepathically call upon me and I shall welcome you."

In other words: *Mi casa es su casa.*

Chapter 4
Deeper Understanding

"Since the Lemurians are so advanced, why don't you do something about the mess on the surface of this planet? No one seems to be able to get along, much of the world is at war, and new diseases are spreading. The few still control the many and the resources of the planet are not shared. There is little equality. Why don't you step in and help us? " I asked.

Adama explained: "We moved into the interior of the Earth so we would be unencumbered by negativity from above and below. We have seen clearly what was happening on the surface. We intentionally isolated ourselves from it so we could evolve more rapidly. Both cultures, yours and ours, are experiments. In the case of humanity, you chose to see how far from Source you could go before returning to it. In our case, we chose to see how much we could evolve if we did not engage in the energy of inequality, imbalance, and disharmony. Becoming involved with life on the surface would have defeated our Inner Earth existence, for we surely would have brought your negative aspects underground with us.

"We hope you can understand our decision. Each culture has a divine plan with which the other is not to interfere. If we had attempted to assist you in the past, we would have risked being destroyed ourselves. Often humans destroy what you cannot understand, accept, or control.

"The universe knows that we Lemurians had enough of wars and strife, and need to focus on our own spiritual growth. We lost more than you can imagine, so we are attempting now to assist you in avoiding learning the lesson we learned in the

way that we learned it. We actually have done what we did—
isolating ourselves—for the benefit of both of our races. Had
we not done this, our wisdom, truths, teachings, culture, and
lives would have been destroyed and you would not have access to them. We could not allow this to happen. We are your
only way back home to connection with Source.

"Please know that we understand how you may feel regarding our absence. We truly wish it could have been otherwise. It was simply not meant to be. However, the consciousness of your race is now reaching a critical mass. Energies on
the surface of the planet are shifting. If this continues, very
soon we can come to the surface and mix and mingle with the
light workers among you who are able and willing to understand and accept us."

A New View of Earth History

Adama felt it was appropriate to begin to share with
me an alternate history of how things started on our planet.
What you are about to read, therefore, is quite different from
any history book I've so far read. I have paraphrased his words
as best as I could in the material that follows.

There have actually been civilizations on this planet
for millions of years, not thousands. Most of these were colonies of beings from extraterrestrial worlds, whose inhabitants
came to enjoy the beauty of our planet and take advantage of
the natural resources. The details of these civilizations were
lost when the Great Library of Alexandria was destroyed.
They were destroyed on purpose so that another version of
events could be told. Luckily, most of the wisdom from the
library was transported to the Lemurian library in Telos prior
to the destruction of Alexandria. Few of the true facts of the
long history of Earth exist anywhere in our world today. The
records that did survive in the third dimension were hidden

or eventually destroyed in one way or another and for various different reasons by people who held power.

Millions of years ago, the first Lemurians came here from a planet called Lemur in the Dahl Universe (a parallel universe to ours). At the time, Earth was a paradise and considered the most wonderful planet in the entire universe, a blue-green jewel. This perfection was maintained for millions of years, attracting other races from twelve other star systems, which came and joined the pioneering Lemurians. All the extraterrestrials mixed their genetic codes and became like a "super mutt" race. Humans are their descendants. Lemuria, the Motherland on Earth, became the most enlightened civilization among all of them. Many other civilizations on our planet were born from the Lemurian civilization. But the civilization of Atlantis and the origins of human history as a separate race from the Lemurians came much later, only after an eventual fall from unity took place.

Eventually the entire huge continent of Lemuria was populated. It was an immense area, which filled the area we now call the Pacific Ocean and extended beyond it. Before the destruction of Lemuria through its warfare with Atlantis millions of year later, all of Earth existed in a higher frequency at one with the Source. The Lemurians lived mostly in the fifth dimension, with the ability to become denser (fourth- or third-dimensional), if they so desired. There was a gradual lowering of frequencies over eons, until eventually this marvelous race and many of the others that were its companions lost unity with the Source. What caused their fall? The very same negative forces that are in place in our world today: separation, corruption of truth, greed, and lack of equality, balance, and love.

Since things were good for so long in Lemuria, it is important to discuss the physical ending of this magnificent civilization. Maybe we might just learn a few things from an enlightened civilization's demise (even knowing they have survived and rejoined the fifth dimension). It's sad to think that so many great cultures have come and gone on Earth without learning why or applying lessons learned to sustain our own. Their survival teaches us that we are able to return to a higher frequency if we so choose. Maybe this time we won't have to end civilization...we can just keep growing and expanding... ultimately joining the Lemurians and others.

All data in Lemuria is stored in a crystalline form. If you want to know something, you simply sit down and connect with a crystal to experience an entire subject in a moment. Maybe we would not continue to choose war if we experienced the previous ones humanity created.

The Lemurian Era on the surface of this planet began about four and half million years ago. As mentioned earlier, it ended about 12,000 years ago. At the time of this calamity, seven large continents existed on Earth, including the continents of Lemuria and Atlantis. What physically remains of Lemuria today includes the land masses of Australia, New Zealand, Hawaii, the Easter Islands, the Fiji Islands, Madagascar, California, and British Columbia. No wonder they chose Mount Shasta as their fifth-dimensional home. It was part of their ancient homeland.

There is little physical evidence remaining of their existence on the surface of the planet since the Lemurians existed in a higher frequency that was less dense (less material) than ours. This may seem confusing. But the field of quantum physics is now allowing us to understand different frequencies of reality. Believe it or not, someday soon, this understanding will seem old hat. "We are merely being way showers for humankind," Adama explained to me.

Lemuria Today

When Lemuria was physically (but not energetically) destroyed by the Atlanteans, it resulted in the death of 350 million Lemurians in a scene of the greatest devastation the world has ever known. Adama expressly wished for me to know that the pain and trauma of these events so long ago still reside in the cellular memory of humanity, as well as within Mother Earth herself. This pain is so great that we choose to bury it deeply and not remember it. Repression of knowledge is a powerful mental defense we humans use. We aim to forget that which feels too painful.

"It will be our re-connection with you and your new awareness of our existence that will assist in the final healing of the pain that has been passed down unconsciously from generation to generation," Adama explained. "Throughout your Earth's history, this pain has expressed itself in many ways: through lack of self-love, lack of trust (separation), creation of wars, and loss of oneness. Now the unexplained pain and healing can begin by raising your awareness, and through your prayers and meditations. The possibility that an advanced reality (not an escape) exists may be enough for some to heal their carried pain and trauma."

We Are Truly One

I've heard the expression "We are one" many times in my life and during my studies. Sometimes I can grab hold of this truth for a moment or two, other times it becomes lost for long periods of time. Working with Adama began to give me a greater understanding of this concept, the reality of oneness. Adama shared with me that through their advanced technology and amino acid computers they can actually measure humanity's level of "oneness." It seems that our frequency had been going up on a daily basis, which is why the Lemurians have made contact. Apparently, the Lemurians' wisdom, spiritual truth, and advanced technology give them the capacity to assist those of us living on the surface of the Earth in the third dimension to shift our vibrations. Shifting would allow us to create a new world of equality, harmony, and balance, which would lead us to connect directly to the Source of all there is (call it what you may).

As I connected with the Lemurian energy and transported my light body there I felt the freedom of 5D reality and wondered why I have to come back to 3D. Adama explained that the transition for humanity from 3D to 4D and then 5D must be done step by step, and there are no short cuts we can take. "We achieved our new reality very much the same way you will," he told me. "Be patient. We are assisting you. The path will be much easier for you than ours was for us, and the timing accelerated, if enough of you choose. There is a window of opportunity like never before available to humankind. The question is: Do you want to take advantage of it?"

In the days that followed, my connection with the Lemurians filled my heart with gratitude and gave new meaning, value, and purpose to my life. I realized that many others were experiencing the same thing as me. For certain, I was not alone. In fact, as Adama explained to me, the Lemurians and other advanced beings were already in contact with various government and spiritual leaders around the world doing their best to assist in effecting necessary changes. Some of those outreaches were more successful than others.

Perhaps the most surprising and exciting revelation Adama made was that our genetic code, our human DNA, and the Lemurians' genetic code are essentially the same. Remember, they once lived where we do. He told me, "Since you are still trapped beyond the veil of the third dimension, you are probably curious about this. Since our DNA and technical makeup is the same as yours, you might say that we are an updated, improved model of you. We are taller and somewhat sturdier than you are now. But you were once taller, like us.

"Furthermore, human death is a mere inconvenience that you can choose to end soon. Having achieved fifth-dimensional vibrations, we are now immortal. We take the same bodies with us through all of our evolutionary adventures. Even when we reach several thousand years of age, we remain youthful. According to what we choose, we can look anywhere from twenty-five to forty-five in the human lifespan. We literally never achieve any of the signs of growing old once we are past childhood. This may appear unusual to those of you who live on the surface, but soon you will learn to achieve this yourselves. It's easy to get used to being youthful and immortal. And as you know, there's not much that's fun in your degenerative aging process."

It was only possible for me to travel to Lemuria in my light body. But when I stood in the presence of the eternal beauty and youth of the inhabitants, the feelings were overwhelming. My eyes filled with tears of joy in knowing that we can be released from our karmic cycle of life and death and the pain that often accompanies it. Adama took my hand and connected it to his heart, saying, "One day this pain will all be behind you." A feeling of peace and relief came over me.

Sacred Geometrics

"Most things in our lives revolve around sacred geometrics," Adama explained to me. "The study of these geometrics is a science. For the moment, please know that the universe is in perfect order due to these designs." Since sacred geometrics are at play in Lemuria, most of the homes are circular, which is the symbol of unity and oneness. I knew that special crystals are grown for the purpose of building them. But as there is a huge gap between the third dimension and the fifth dimension, I asked Adama to give me a step-by-step description of building a home.

He said, "Our physicality is filled with so much light that it has lost much of its density and would not be visible to your awareness. That's why so little of Lemuria remains in physical form today. Nonetheless, our dimension feels as real to us as yours does to you. This you need to try to understand before we begin building. As you know, our homes are built from crystals that radiate light and are amazingly beautiful."

Adama continues, "Now let's build a cozy, circular home...The first thing I pay attention to is the location of the home and its size. Second, mentally, through my intention, I start seeing a detailed blueprint of the structure I wish to manifest. One must be very specific at this time. The universe delivers exactly what you ask for. Being impeccable with my thoughts is the key. Having the mind be in service to the heart (and not vice versa) is important to what I intend to create. I next begin to imagine each crystal executing the design in the right place. At this juncture, things are still an energetic outline, not dense yet. But since there's really no time where we are, this happens instantly. In your frequency, it takes about forty-five minutes.

"Third, when my heart is filled with joy and I know my creation is fulfilling my intention, I begin to flood each stone with a concentration of crystalline light and bring more density into the structure. As I apply my attention, my new home fills with light and love and is complete. Love and light are the building blocks of the universe, so all of the interior elements of this home will also be built with love and light."

Lemurian Government

There are no real governments of the people, for the people in the third dimension, not even in our so-called democratic nations. Through deceit and denial, there is sometimes an illusion of such. But it's ironic, because the governments we have are a reflection of the people in our different countries who are giving their power away. In Lemuria only highly-evolved individuals are allowed to govern. And since everyone is connected through oneness, the main purpose of government is really to maintain the laws of the universe. These laws come from the Source of all creation and are greatly enforced in order to maintain equality, harmony, and balance. Human-made laws usually serve the people who create them. The difference is this: If a law is not supporting the highest good of all things, it is not a universal law.

In Lemuria, there are two forms of government: The first is the rule of a king and queen, but these are unlike any of the monarchies of our world. I actually hesitate to use the words "king" and "queen" because of the associations these words have on the surface of the planet. There has been so much abuse of power through this form of government. But such abuse is impossible in Lemuria. The king and queen of Lemuria are highly inspired individuals who have had many years of spiritual training in following universal law completely. And such monarchs, if we can call them that, are always paired—twin flames balancing male and female energy. In fact, Adama explained, their sole purpose is to enforce universal law.

The king and queen introduced themselves to me using the Lemurian language, which is called Solara Maru, as Ra (the king) and Ranu Ma (the queen). Their language sounded more like singing than anything else to my ear. But they also apparently spoke English perfectly well, which is the tongue in which the remainder of our conversation took place. Everywhere I went, people communicated with me in English telepathically, so it was easy to communicate.

Ranu Ma and Ra told me they are from the Land of Mu in the Dahl Universe. They are considered "ascended masters," meaning they have chosen for many millennia to do their very best to elevate their consciousness and serve the world. Because of their enlightened wisdom, they usually have final word on matters.

As I stood before the royal family of Lemuria, I felt the benefit of being immortal. These individuals have thousands of years of experience to draw upon in their decision making. It's not six to nine decades of life and then sinking back into forgetfulness as you are reborn into a new incarnation, as it is for human beings. They have much knowledge upon which to draw.

Ma and Ra took me on a tour of their magnificent palace, which was made of precious minerals in the shape of a golden pyramid. There were various chambers in the palace honoring similar energies as the temples of wisdom, healing, and love located throughout Lemuria. These were dedicated to emotional, mental, and physical healing. We paused so I could receive a healing in the chamber of my choice. I choose emotional healing.

The second form of government in Lemuria is the Council of Twelve, whose members represent the twelve star systems that seeded our planet four and a half million years ago. Again to balance masculine and feminine energy, the Council is composed of six men and six women. My spokesman, Adama, was serving as a thirteenth member, as the high priest of Telos. Again, as with royal titles, I hesitate to use the word "priest," due to connotations that come from the abuse of such roles in our world. Keep in mind, or should I say in your heart, that any abuse is impossible in Lemuria due to the evolution they have undergone as a race. Adama acts as the leader of the Council of Twelve and casts the final vote if a tiebreaker is necessary.

Maturity, innate qualities, authentic expertise, and true spiritual attainment are the criteria for being selected as a council member. There is no candidate financing or voting in Lemuria. When a member feels his or her service is complete, the opportunity to assume a council seat is made known to the people, and anyone may apply as long as balance of energy is maintained. Before a new member is invited to join, all applicants are carefully considered by the Council of Twelve, by Lemurian spiritual leaders, and the king and queen have final word.

Telos

Two million Lemurians live in the city of Telos. When you walk the streets, your heart is filled with love and joy. Everyone and everything resonates with interconnectivity. This is a huge contrast to my experience of walking in New York City or driving in Southeast Florida, where people appear self-contained and disconnected from others and the environment. I've always been puzzled by the fact that we largely do not see our planet as a living being and do not seem to understand the relationship of all the Earth's elements (air, water, minerals, oil) to the planet herself. The Earth is our mother and these elements are vital to her survival. She cannot be raped and robbed for individual gain without a dramatic consequence. Telos, like other large cities in Earth's core, is divided into smaller hamlets with local governments.

The city proper has five main elevations that are divided according to their contribution to the whole. Elevation one houses several main temples, other public buildings, and the city administration. Most people live in this section. Elevation two is where most manufacturing and production for the city takes place, as well as adult education and children's schools.

Elevation three is where food is grown, mostly hydroponically and entirely organically. No plant is ever killed. Only the leaves and fruit are eaten. Due to advanced technology, production is effective and efficient. Lemurians do not need to eat in the way we do since they also absorb energy directly. Elevation four contains public parks complete with lakes and fountains, and some gardening and manufacturing facilities.

Elevation five is dedicated to Mother Nature. There is an amazing contrast to the nature we experience on the surface. Animals do not eat each other. All beings are vegetarian. It is a world without fear and aggression. Can you imagine our world like this? We have always thought of nature as "eat or be eaten." For myself, I grew up in a family of hunters who were able to kill animals at will. I could never justify killing animals, not even for sustenance. I guess you could say I did not inherit the killer gene. At heart, I've always been a Lemurian.

Lemurians travel from one section of Telos to another by high-speed electromagnetic metros, moving sidewalks, and inter-sectional elevators. One vehicle I rode exceeded a speed of 3,000 miles per hour. With a different density level and advanced technology things can really fly while staying on the ground (or in this case, within the ground). I loved the silence associated with the technology. In 3D reality we seem so attached—almost addicted—to noise. The only vibration or sound I heard, even when going over 3,000 m.p.h., was one of peace and harmony.

Since we are discussing underground cities, I must remind you Lemurian abilities include major tunneling techniques. Much of this electromagnetic ability, I was told, will soon be shared with us. This would mean free power for everyone and forever! What will this do to corporate profits? Eliminate the need for them? Imagine that! Apparently, this is possible.

We and the Lemurians Are not Alone

Just when I was getting used to the idea of an advanced civilization within the Earth, Adama told me the Lemurians are not the only ones there! Briefly, these other Inner Earth civilizations form something called the Agartha Network. This network's members consist of many ancient civilizations that long ago came from other galaxies, including the civilizations that seeded this planet. They live in multi-dimensional awareness, and fifth-dimensional and higher frequencies. Their homes are located under Northern Brazil, the Himalaya Mountains in India, and China. North America isn't the only continent to house underground frequencies.

The Noah's Ark Connection

I made another visit to the thrift shop where this adventure began. Remember, in this place you have to adjust to a musty smell and secondhand clutter and visual input. Somehow, I was beginning to realize this unlikely place was some kind of a portal to Lemuria. Sure enough, as soon as I walked in, there was a print of a Noah's Ark painting lying on a worn sofa—five bucks. I felt drawn to the picture and picked it up. My judgmental ego started in, "You don't need that; put it down." I sat it down and walked away. But the painting kept calling me back. I circled it several times. Then I knew I was supposed to have it, without really knowing why.

When I got home, I lovingly repaired the frame and cleaned it. As I focused on the animals going two by two into the ark, I flashed back to the night Lemuria sank! My heart almost stopped. "Breathe," I said to myself, "or you'll pass out." From that memory, I knew I had been there. Maybe you were also. This painting was my reminder of all the Lemurians had gone through and suffered. It made me fully aware of the gift they were attempting to give us. In full devotion, I hung the painting over my bathroom tub so I could remember...each time the water hit...the gift I was receiving from Adama and the other Lemurians.

As Adama subsequently taught me, the Lemurians built their Inner Earth world to save their way of life and all their magnificent advancements once they knew their continent was going under, but it was also to save the lives of the creatures living on the planet's surface. Really, the myth of a great deluge that has survived in our ancient sacred texts is the story of the sinking of Atlantis. The Lemurians' own version of Noah's Ark involved saving members of every animal species alive on their continent in that era, including so-called mythical creatures like dragons and unicorns. The Lemurians have many of the same animal species that we have on the surface, but they are larger than ours, like the Lemurians themselves. They have never been exposed to any violence or abuse of any kind. They are all vegetarians, like the Lemurians, and do not eat one another. So you can safely play with any of them even though they are rather large.

The way the Lemurians honor animals is beyond our comprehension since they fully experience the connection of the Creator's Being of Light, which the animal kingdom represents; they are another aspect of God's divinity, even as we and they are aspects of that divinity. While there are those on the surface who know that animals are an important aspect of the whole of the universe, in Lemuria, animals are quite different from the animals of our awareness. "They have vast intellect, and some rule planets and other galaxies and live in multiple dimensions," Adama explains. "Animals have higher selves like us, and are a different kingdom of being in their divinity. Animals have chosen to share our planet and experience the third dimension like you. Because they come in a different body, does not make them less than you. They are here to teach and assist humankind to learn love. And they have as much right to be here as you."

It was further explained to me that the only way we on the surface can move forward in our evolution is to unconditionally love all the life forms on our planet, including ourselves. Right now, most humans believe that the animals, plants, minerals, and other natural resources on Earth are here for the taking, and to make a profit. In some ways, this is a reflection of how we feel about ourselves. Our Lemurian brothers and sisters warned me that Mother Earth has had enough of our plunder and rape. There will be consequences if this behavior continues. She is bigger than us, and is intent on surviving whether or not we are here. "The only ones who will remain are those who choose to honor their home and all who dwell within and upon it. Once Earth's dimensional shift is fully underway, the others will be relocated elsewhere, so they can take whatever additional time they need to wake up."

In other words, he was informing me, this planet is moving forward in consciousness and we shall be joining forces with the Lemurians soon. It is the divine plan of our planet to return to the light and our time has finally come to shine!

Chapter 5
Sharing with Friends

I had been in daily contact with my newfound friends inside the Earth for several weeks when I finally gathered the courage to share details of this experience with a colleague. I often exchange healing sessions with other therapists and I thought it would be healthy for me to bounce my thoughts about the Lemurians off of someone else. Immediately, I thought of my pal Mary Liz Murphy in New York. We had worked together on some pretty far out stuff over the years, so I felt confident she would not call the folks at the Bellevue Psych Ward to come get me—at least not right away. Admittedly, the healing arts that I practice often involve conferences with sources not on the earthly plane, such as angels and spirit guides. But beings within the interior of the planet were new to me. Although I was connecting directly with them and resonating with the experience, gaining an objective perspective on the situation would be helpful.

I picked up the phone and dialed Mary Liz. "Hello, this is Phillip in Fort Lauderdale," I said, cutting to the chase, "Ever heard anything about a race called the Lemurians that just happens to live in another dimension in the core of the Earth?"

Obviously I had called the right person. Without taking a beat, Mary Liz said, "Sure. I don't personally relate to their frequency, but I know someone who does: Dianne Robbins. You should contact her. She channels the Lemurians and has written several books about them." This was an incredible synchronicity. Of course, Dianne was a real, live person with whom I could connect!

"Funny you should mention those books, as I've been reading them," I told Mary Liz. "And what you're describing is exactly what I've been doing. I've been connecting with the Lemurians and writing down what they say." Then I recounted the story of going to the thrift shop, hearing Adama's voice, and having the books project themselves at me from the shelves. She listened closely as I described my visits to Telos. It felt great to be able to let someone else know what I had been going through. Even better, she didn't respond as if I had gone bonkers.

At the conclusion of our call, I asked, "Mary Liz, is there any chance that you have Dianne's email address or phone number?" Fortunately, she did. It really was amazing. Now I was being introduced to the woman who had previously channeled these high-frequency beings and published her findings. I felt a real calm and relief come over me.

That night I sent an email to Dianne, who lived in Mount Shasta, telling her about my Lemurian experiences. When you are having this type of unusual experience, it's nice to meet others who have had a similar experience. It helps you maintain your sense of sanity.

Dianne immediately wrote back: "My dear Phillip, welcome to our Lemurian family, I am so delighted you have connected with the Lemurians and especially Adama. Let us talk soon."

The next day, as soon as our respective time zones would allow, I phoned Dianne. After a few rings, a calm, sweet voice answered, "Hello." Following my story of the Lemurian books presenting themselves to me, Dianne remarked, "Yes, that's the way it often happens."

"Dianne, would you please send me anything else you have written about these people from your original transmissions?" I asked. Several days later, a couple more books joined my Lemurian library. Along with what I was receiving directly and had experienced in my visits to Telos, after speaking with Dianne and reading these additional volumes my knowledge seemed more complete and I felt much more secure in my relationship with the Lemurians.

After developing an even stronger connection with Adama, I felt braver about sharing my knowledge of the Lemurians with other acquaintances besides Mary Liz and Dianne. I had been a member of a metaphysical group in New York City for several years. Five men from this group had taken to meeting in the living room of my apartment on West 57th Street, where one would do channeling sessions for us so that we could speak with the Archangel Michael. Many enlightening messages and spiritual tools had come out of those sessions. It therefore crossed my mind that they should be brought up to speed on what I had been experiencing.

Also, I had just learned from Adama that Archangel Michael had played an essential role in the establishment and development of the Lemurian culture on earth...another part of my life was connecting me strongly to the Lemurians. All roads seemed to be leading to Lemuria.

Chapter 6
My Background

My entire life, at essence, has been about love and light, which are the most basic building blocks of creation. My twin brother, Bill, and I were brought up in a prosperous, loving family on the west coast of Florida. I would be hard pressed to say anything negative about my privileged childhood. The Sunshine State delivered beautiful, warm sunlight all year long. But when my parents took me to New York City for the first time at the age of twelve, I knew I would live there when I grew up. After college, where I got a degree in journalism, and a stint in the navy, I moved to Manhattan with $250 in my pocket and no job prospects. My parents would have preferred that I go into the family business, so they made no attempts to support me. Although in their hearts they knew I had to go, they hoped I would return home. That was forty years ago and, as I've said, to this day I keep an apartment in New York.

After unsuccessfully attempting to go into journalism and then the theatre, I was able to talk my way into a trainee position at Young & Rubicam, the leading advertising agency on Madison Avenue. The pay was $3,500 a year. I hung a sign in my office reading: "This is a great place to work if your family can afford to send you here." What the agency lacked in startup salaries was more than compensated for by the opportunities it provided, however. As the most prestigious agency in town, it had top clients. The experience was priceless. Of course, you can't eat "priceless," so I ate a lot of peanut butter and jelly sandwiches in those days—unless I was working overtime. Then meals were included.

My first apartment was an expensive, illegal sublet, which eventually became mine when the owner moved to the West Coast. A young Barbra Walters and choreographer/director Michael Bennett, and many Radio City Rockettes also lived in the building. It was there that the Broadway show "A Chorus Line" was conceived.

Eventually I got away from the business side of advertising and landed in the art department where I belonged. This was where I began to love my job. The creative output of the agency was terrific and our budgets allowed us to work with top photographers, like Richard Avedon, and film directors, like Ridley Scott. I was immersed in a world of light and beauty. It was the '60s and I was living the heyday of Madison Avenue. I had also fallen in love and was having the first full love affair of my life. My partner worked at The Film Society of Lincoln Center, which produces the New Film Festival and holds a spring gala every year to honor the who's who of the film world. This relationship allowed me to spend quality time with some of the world's most talented directors, actors, and producers, among them Bette Davis, Audrey Hepburn, Jack Lemon, Charlie Chaplin, Elizabeth Taylor, Paul Newman, Joanne Woodward, Ginger Rogers, and Mike Nichols. For twenty-eight years, we would pick them up at the airport and make sure their stay in our city was pleasant. It was thrilling for a young man. Later, this experience would also help me greatly in my film career. Knowing how to handle talented people is vital.

After several years, the agency and I agreed we were not a perfect fit. I had learned a lot and was ready to leave. I didn't need "Big Daddy' taking care of me anymore. I was motivated by the unfortunate accidental death of my twin brother at age 29 in a motorcycle accident. Looking down at his tombstone and seeing my birthday chiseled there put my mortality in perspective. I decided that I had to follow my own path and began to study film at New York University and move into that side of the industry. Some of the most talented (now famous) young directors were teaching there. The streets of the city were our back lot. I learned more about lighting than I ever had in my undergraduate photography courses and I loved being behind and in front of the camera.

My first break in film production was working with Jeffrey Metzner, a well-known art director turned film director. Jeffrey had a great sense of design and casting abilities. The lighting of his films was very real and natural. His wife, Sheila Metzner, was just getting her still photography career going. Her work looked more like paintings than photography, very impressionistic. Today she is considered one of the world's top photographers. The Metzners and their five children soon became my New York family. So again, my life was filled with love and light.

A turning point in my life happened when the Metzners introduced me to their family doctor, Dr. Herbert Fill. He was a rare mix of a psychiatrist and an acupuncturist, having trained in both Germany and China. He focused on alternative medicine, utilizing anthroposophy (the study of body, mind, and spirit), a deeper form of love and light. Soon I transformed from a patient into a student of acupuncture and homeopathic pharmacy. This was the beginning of my healing arts training.

Everyone who goes into healing arts has a personal reason they are directed towards it. Once they learn to heal themselves, they are able to teach and work with others. This is the ultimate conduit that creates all healers. People start out with a personal experience with cancer, HIV, an accident, or another life-threatening situation that causes them to focus on healing themselves, and in the process they accept that they have a divine mission to heal help others to heal themselves. Working in the film industry, I was often jokingly called Dr. Phil (long before there was *the* Dr. Phil on TV). People would line up outside my door waiting for a chance to ask my opinion on a homeopathic remedy for an ailment. More and more I was resonating with healing.

In the early days of the AIDS crisis, before it was known how the HIV virus was passed around, I picked it up along with hundreds of my friends and colleagues. Over the next few years, all told I must have gone to hundreds of funerals and memorial services. This was before the so-called "cocktail" of medications was developed by doctors and scientific researchers. The entire industry literally was decimated and it was like a horror show—and so, so sad for the survivors. We saw camera operators, directors, makeup artists, actors, costume and set designers, writers, and producers, and on and on and on, getting sick and dying around us. For myself, I feel truly blessed that I've never had a symptom. My interest and focus on alternative healing was born during those years, partly from a desire to maintain my physical health and handle my grief, as well as to support others in managing their wellbeing physically, emotionally, and spiritually.

While working at my first motion film gig, I was also serving on a trade film board. All independent film companies throughout American were represented in this trade association. I was considered an ambitious, talented young man and some saw promise in me. One of my colleagues on the board approached me one day and asked, "How would you like to start a new, international film production company with some of Europe and England's most talented film directors?" Even though I felt loyalty to Jeffrey Metzner, this sounded like an opportunity I had to check out. The backer was in Paris. The company would be based in New York and Los Angeles with offices in London and Paris. "When can you leave for Paris to meet the man who wishes to finance this company in America?" my colleague asked. I definitely saw light in the form of stars at that moment, and I felt so much gratitude to be offered the opportunity.

Untidy in appearance and overweight, the aristocratic Frenchman I met came from the lineage of a long-standing royal family with business and financial connections that only wars could accumulate over centuries throughout Europe and England. At first glance, he reminded me of the Orson Welles I had worked with long ago in advertising when Orson was doing voiceovers for Eastern Airlines; brilliant, but somewhat scary. "I have a long-term working relationship with the greatest directorial talent over here and I have always had a dream to create an American production company with them," he said introducing himself. "Most people don't like me and are scared of me," he continued. I could see why. "I need a skilled, talented man to bring my dream to life in America," he panted. "You come highly recommended from a trusted colleague in New York and seem to present a persona I do not possess."

When he started revealing the directorial talent he had at hand, I could not believe it. It was the who's who of the European and British film world. The American advertising industry was in somewhat of a crisis, reflecting one of the country's many economic downturns. "Fresh talent might be just what the industry needs—and a real opportunity to start a new film production company," I thought. But it felt a little like getting into bed with the devil. Could I trust this guy? Did he really need someone like me? I had never started a company before. Could I do it? My mind did its usual sabotage routine. I flew back to New York to think about this grand dream.

It was one of those decisions that are already made before you have time to think about them. How could I not do this? I had nothing to lose but my pride. This guy was going to put up all the cash and give me the greatest opportunity of my young career. After several trips to Paris and rounds of negotiations with my silent partner, who I came to think of as Tricky Dick, we reached an agreement and I was given the finances to start a large film company in New York. My task was bringing twenty international film directors into the American commercial film market. I named the company Fairbanks Films to reflect the history of American film even as we brought foreigners into it.

Since America had taught the world film production, the company represented the student teaching the teacher. The American directors had gotten greedy. They had lost their passion for lighting and had given editorial control over to others in order to be able to move on to the next job. Like locusts in a fresh field of corn, my European and British film directors with their crisp lighting style and desire to deliver edited films soon ate up the commercial film production market in the United States. Within less than a year, we were the number one company in America and held that position for a decade. It all had to do with lighting. It was these directors' love of lighting and the freshness it brought to the look of their films that made it happen.

Everything on our planet seems to have a cycle of life, death, and rebirth, including my career. When Fairbanks Films split into ten different companies it was time for me to look for my next "love and light" opportunity/experience. It came roaring into life with unexpected gusto. My film company had caught the attention of many in the film world, including the people running George Lucas' Industrial Light & Magic. Lucas had invented and created a whole new way to tell his *Star Wars* stories through a new, synthetic filmmaking process using computer digital images. He had put these stories, inspired by mythology, in his back pocket as a young man, waiting for the technology he needed to make them a visual reality. He had developed a whole new way to create light and motion. It was the passion and love behind this new media that powered it forward. At the time, I sure was not a techie—and I am not to this day. My soul's plan was drawing me closer to these other worlds being revealed in Lucas' stories and films. I became the director of marketing for his commercial division.

Audiences thrilled to see the otherworldly creatures and places Lucas was showing them on screen. They longed to know we were not alone in the universe. I know now that much of what is presented in Lucas's stories is based on truth. Galactic organizations and *Star Wars*-like activities really do exist. The Lemurians have confirmed it. Lucas gained much from his relationship with mythologist Joseph Campbell. Myths often contain fragments of memories of the distant past. So Lucas's stories resonate with the truth of the ancient world.

When film director Ridley Scott and I were working together in London, Paris, and America, I never envisioned that the world of light I see today as possible, and even inevitable, would be so different from the dark version of the one he foretold in *Blade Runner* and many of his other films. But when we produced the 1984 Apple Computer commercial, we launched the ether-net and light computer technology to the world. The speed of light would now rule communication. Today, this commercial is considered the most famous commercial of all time. The Lemurians are giving us hope of living in a world that's joined together in love and oneness, rather than of living in a world that's an exaggerated version of what we currently have.

Now my film career was putting me directly in touch with other frequencies of reality. It was time to make these energies a focus in my life. Halfway through my life, a shift began inside me to more fully embrace who I am and why I am here.

Around this period, I reconnected with Joel Anastasi, an old friend. Being a master of many talents, Joel is a fascinating guy. He completed a master's degree in journalism at Columbia University (the same subject I studied in college) and when he realized he couldn't make any real money in journalism (same thing happened to me) he departed for the "belly of the beast." He became a stockbroker and financial adviser. From there he developed management and employee development workshops, travelling the world teaching equality and balance in the workplace (although I don't think he ever found or created it). Joel's heart yearned for something more.

Joel and I met each other again on Fire Island, the longest thirty-five miles in the world away from Manhattan. His long-term partner had just died. My partner of twenty-eight years had just walked out on me without bothering to explain why. Thus, we were both at major crosswalks in our lives when we renewed our friendship. From the beginning of our reconnection our shared focus was always on spiritual growth. His spirituality had been expressed through Catholicism initially; mine through a combination of Native American hedonism and Celtic Irish folk traditions. Soon these two different backgrounds would merge into one combined mission.

One weekend Joel and I went up to The Omega Institute, a spiritual retreat center in Upstate New York, to do a workshop with Neale Donald Walsch, author of the *Conversations with God* book series. We both had read all five of his bestselling books and were impressed with their messages. After a couple of days in the workshop, the three of us bonded like hot glue. Neale was impressed with our professional backgrounds and wanted us to become involved in running his worldwide foundation on the West Coast. We felt this was a natural next step in our spiritual growth: to be working with a modern Moses. After spending time in Ashland, Oregon, and taking several more meetings in New York, we were ready to give this new venture a go. But then, after spending time visiting the internal organization, we came to know this enterprise was not the right fit. So we were still looking for a place to make a contribution.

Then, I was attending a Unity Church retreat in Connecticut one weekend when I met an African-American woman who would change my life forever. She was something called a Reiki master therapist. I had no idea what that was. She explained that Reiki, which means "universal life force energy," is a hands-on healing technique that balances the mind, emotions, and body. She knew how to connect with this energy and pass it on. She explained this was an ancient therapy that had come into the West through the East. "The thing to do is to experience it," she said. So the next thing I knew, I was lying on my hotel bed with this woman's hands on me.

During this session, my body immediately relaxed and I felt all my stress leave me. I went into deep sleep. I awoke feeling refreshed and balanced in an unfamiliar way. A voice inside me told me, "This is your next step. You are to become a Reiki therapist." How could this be? I barely knew what it was. Why did I feel so strongly this was to be my next step? Then I remembered hearing stories of my paternal great-grandmother, who was a healer, and how people walked miles to get to her in rural Alabama before there were cars because she could work miracles. That was the Celtic side of my family, the Irish side. My mother's side of the family was Native American. I have two 'I's" in my background: Irish and Indian. Both lines of my cultural heritage have strong, ancient healing traditions.

"Hmm," I thought, "maybe that's where this is coming from," as I attempted to explain to myself what was happening. I figured, "It's in my DNA."

When I got back to New York, I began the search for someone to teach me Reiki. Every attempt failed until I connected with a Reiki master teacher named Robert Baker. Robert was a boyish, curly-haired blond man, slight of figure with deep blue eyes. He said, "You are fortunate. I rarely have openings in my classes, but a beginner's class is starting now and you can join it." Both Joel and I enrolled in the course. Not only did I not know what Reiki was, I also did not realize that the two years of training to become a Reiki master would involve the most intense self-examination I had ever done. In addition to his training program, Robert required that I commit to personal processing work with him since the training would bring up a lot of feelings.

Very few Reiki master teachers possess the skills to offer this type of metaphysical psychotherapy in combination with the training. I was fortunate indeed.

I found myself in a whole new world, one where it was natural to connect with the energies outside and within me and the powers within them. I didn't know it at first, but soon found out that Robert was a trance channel for the Archangel Gabriel. In fact, most of my training would come from Gabriel's teachings, rather than Robert's mind. "Being trained by an angel, that's a blessed experience," I mused. All of my belief systems would be challenged and shifted.

"Focus on the message if you cannot accept the messenger, and apply it if it resonates. If it doesn't resonate, throw it out the window," Robert would repeat over and over. He knew that because many people cannot accept messages from other realms they lose the value by "killing the messenger." The mind often has trouble accepting what it cannot prove at the moment, when the heart already knows it. But it can be trained to accept inspiration, genius, and prodigy without asking where these come from. I was learning to "think with the heart."

Led by Robert and his colleague Ron Baker (who was not a relative), some of the members of our spiritual center, called Children of Light, took sacred journeys all over the globe. These trips were usually initiated by Archangel Gabriel, who set up specific rituals and intentions associated with each trip. I went on several such trips. An in-depth, on-site spiritual journey is an extraordinary way to see distant parts of the world. Egypt was a favorite destination of mine. Archangel Gabriel and other beings Robert channeled for us on the trip explained who actually built the pyramids, sphinx, and temples, and why. That was where I had first heard of Lemuria. It seems that when Lemuria was destroyed, many Lemurians went to Egypt with their advanced technology. We had some remarkable initiations and rituals, including one that took place inside the King's Chamber of the Great Pyramid in Giza, located near Cairo.

Upon completion of my total emersion into Reiki master training (it felt like I had done all of it before), I elected to continue into advanced healing arts studies called light ascension therapy. This was a deeper program of self-mastery and the ability to teach spiritual truths to others. These studies drew upon thousands of years of humankind's experiences upon this planet. It would require another book to explain the teachings of light ascension. Suffice to say, it prepares one for the changes in consciousness this world is making to return to love and light.

On Sunday nights, a group would gather at Robert's Manhattan apartment to listen to live channeled messages from Gabriel. This "bandwidth of consciousness," as Gabriel called himself, this field of energy, was like a database of information. The first time I heard a channeled message, my mind and heart resonated with its truth. I felt blessed to be in the presence of such wisdom. I understood, accepted, and honored that there would be those who could not accept this way of learning. It does not resonate with everyone. But I kept asking myself, "How can I help bring this extraordinary wisdom out into the world?"

Gabriel would broach any and all topics concerning our world. He was an equal opportunity offender when it came to truth...religions, governments, corporations—none was excluded from his profound examination. This wasn't just some sweet angel singing love songs. He wanted us to be aware of what was happening in the world and why. It changed my view of angels forever! It also opened my heart to a desire to connect directly with other frequencies of consciousness myself.

Over the years since my brother's death, he had appeared to me three times. A special guy during his life, Bill had gone to Vietnam and become a highly decorated war hero, come home, married his sweetheart, and had two young children. We were fraternal twins, not identical. Twins share a soul and, in our case, we must have split abilities too, for we couldn't have been more different from one another. He was an accomplished athlete and quiet. I was an extrovert and verbal, his intellectual counterpart. It was like we were one persona—my twin, the physical, and me, the mental. His visitations, which were not frightening to me, but unconditionally loving experiences, included requests that I stay involved in his kids' lives. The third time, he came to say goodbye and told me that I would not see him again. I suppose the possibility of channeling higher frequencies of energy has always seemed natural to me because of our connection following his departure from the third dimension.

This is the background that made me ready to connect with the Lemurians.

Chapter 7
The Michael Group

Through my healing arts training in Reiki and light ascension therapy with Robert Baker, I befriended several men who were also ready to go out into the world with their spiritual talents and gifts. One of the guys, Jeff Fasano, is a trance channel for the Archangel Michael. While Gabriel focuses on information, Michael's messages are designed to assist humankind in moving from the mind (that believes) to the heart (that knows). His purpose is to teach us how to think with our hearts. Rather organically and easily, five of us formed a metaphysical group and named it Children of the Awakened Heart. Michael spoke to us and gave us exercises to support us in answering two primary questions: "Who am I?" and "Why am I here?"

Jeff often traded healing sessions with me. We never knew which energies would pop up during these hands-on sessions. Jeff was like a broadband radio picking up signals from all over the universe. During one session when he was working on me, the Archangel Uriel came in and spoke to me, saying, "You have been chosen to be a channel for this realm of consciousness. Get out your calendar and mark down fifty days. At the end of those fifty days, let us know if you chose to be this." I wasn't even sure who Uriel was, but I was excited to be chosen!

During my fifty-day grace period, I researched the subject of archangels as thoroughly as I could. I discovered that four main archangels guide humanity: Gabriel and Michael, of whom we have spoken; Raphael, whose focus is health and healing; and Uriel, whose focus is the interconnection of all things within and upon the planet. Frankly, I already knew what my choice was: Of course I was going to be a messenger. My entire life had been a preparation for that moment. Communicating messages from Archangel Uriel was the beginning of my channeling. I had no idea then that there would be many other channeled connections to come.

Uriel speaks a great deal about the conditions of the planet and how people are treating the Earth. He talks about the way this is a reflection of our individual relationships with our selves. Since the frequency of Uriel is completely involved in interconnectivity, he generally explains how things relate and describes how what affects one, affects all.

When the Michael group formed, it naturally included Jeff, who, besides being a channel, is a gifted photographer. There is no wonder that Jeff was chosen by the Archangelic Realm of Michael to be an important messenger. Michael is about the heart and so is Jeff. I don't think I've ever met a man with a more open, loving heart than he. Yes, he had some issues in his life, but we all had our issues to heal. That's why we were together, to support and love one another in those healings, right? Jeff is a soulful photographer. That's how he pays his rent. But it's more than that. He captures on film the soul essence of those he shoots. His photography is stunning. And I'm giving myself permission to say that after having worked with some of the world's top photographers when I was in advertising. He especially loves to make pictures of musicians and actors. Jeff has also published a book of Michael's messages, *Journey of the Awakened Heart*.

My longtime friend Joel Anastasi was the eldest member of the Michael group, and perhaps the most experienced due to extensive professional and life experiences. A couple of years ago, I encouraged Joel to interview Archangel Gabriel for a book. Gabriel's channel, Robert Baker, who had been our healing arts master teacher agreed to lend his presence to this process. For the book, Gabriel being neither your basic sweet angel, nor what most would expect, took on the major issues of the day, as well as offering cosmic explanations of human existence. Joel used his investigative reporter skills and began interviewing Gabriel with hot topic questions. Today, Joel, Robert, and Gabriel's book, *The Second Coming*, is considered one of the most profound messages to come out in print in recent times. Joel has been called the Messenger of the Messages.

Eventually, all of Joel's experiences had solidified his readiness and commitment to create an organization that would support equality, harmony, and balance. He joined the Michael group as one of its forbears. While he may have been physically oldest in the group, his handsome, well-kept appearance and energy were those of a man many years his junior.

I first met George Ganges when Robert Baker moved his business out of his living room and into the Children of Light Wellness Center on Broadway in uptown Manhattan. A personal trainer, George had recently taken up his spiritual path. He was a dedicated student, applying to this new endeavor the same discipline and focus that made him excellent in the field of fitness and bodybuilding. When he was not working with clients, it seemed he hardly ever left the place. He took full advantage of all the advanced metaphysical training Robert and his partner Ron were offering. The work they were doing changed people's lives. The light ascension training George and the rest of us received at their center was the foundation of everything we did later. That some members of our group have ourselves become channels simply would not have been possible without being influenced by their commitment to spiritual truth. Our basic training was done through angelic as well as human instruction. Archangel Gabriel's teachings were the foundation of everything, and George absorbed them all like a sponge.

It became obvious that George's divine soul plan had led him to the Michael group to begin to awaken the healer, mystic, and teacher within himself. George was still in process on this one. When George was standing in his power, there was no equal. He had developed and awakened major tools in himself to assist others. But it seemed to me that as a result of not fully embracing himself, control factors were preventing him from standing in his divine empowerment. It was this aspect of George that often kept me in separation from him. But he was always a can-do guy, taking responsibility. We founded the Michael group right after the close of the Children of Light Wellness Center a couple of years after it was founded. I felt that George was taking on a large portion of our group's administrative work in an effort to gain validation.

I also met David Wheeler through Robert Baker's wellness center. He had been a student of Robert's for many years and was completely committed to the teachings and personal process work of Archangel Gabriel. Energetic healing and feelings appeared to be the focus of David's life. He was a sensitive, beautiful child of God who knew how to use his gentleness as strength. A professional actor, first and foremost, David was trained to embody the truth of the different characters he portrayed, to become them fully, thus revealing their inner conflicts, desires, and motivations. He was passionate about acting and incorporated much of his metaphysical wisdom in his artistic process. Audiences who see him perform on stage are fortunate, indeed, for he is giving them much more than entertainment, he is teaching them the essence of life.

Before the Michael group was formed, David himself was channeling Mother Mary and other energies. The messages he receives are always profoundly sweet and powerful, like David. But one key issue David seemed to be working through was an attachment to receiving messages from archangelic realms. More and more it seemed to me that he was realizing that all he needed lay within him, not outside of himself.

Throughout the first year after forming Children of the Awakened Heart, Archangel Michael put the five of us, along with others, through a series of specific healing processes aimed at helping us heal on every level of our being and lives. He asked us to make a soul pact with him called the Five Agreements. These were also agreements we made with ourselves to raise our consciousness and awaken the truth in our hearts. As developed into a mission statement, these were to:

Agreement 1: Commit to world service. World Service is our mission and the foundation of our work. It is an agreement to use our gifts and talents to raise the level of resonance and vibration in the world in order to create a new world of community, harmony, and equality.

Agreement 2: Commit to a personal process. Moving our consciousness from "me" to "we," naturally, requires moving the me out of the we. This requires releasing the old narcissistic me that holds us in the old. The old is all about me and needing to be validated, gratified, and getting something, so we can continue to survive rather than live life.

Living life requires knowing who we are and having a strong sense of self so that we can begin to move into the unknown and serve the world with our talents and gifts. Instead of it being all about me, we create a balance of giving and receiving.

Doing this requires a willingness to process our personal issues that holds us in a sense of lack and limitation because of old patterns, attachments, and behaviors. It involves an agreement to take responsibility for ourselves by processing the me as an individual so that we can honor, value, and love ourselves in order to realize our own divine plan and enter into world service.

Agreement 3: Focus on "what is" in our lives. This is an agreement to focus on what is in our lives as opposed to what we perceive is *not* there. Focusing on *what is* raises the level of resonance and vibration in our lives. Focusing on what we think is *not* there traps us in a cycle of perpetual discontent, forcing us to look outside of us for what we think we lack. It reduces the level of resonance and vibration in us and squanders our energy.

Agreement 4: Develop a sense of self. This is an agreement to move into the depth of our hearts to honor, value, and love our selves. When we know, love, and honor ourselves we can offer our gifts and talents in service to the world. It is the deep love of the *self* that allows us to *be* who we are, access our talents and gifts, and discover our individual divine plan.

Agreement 5: Receive love. Loving ourselves powers our ability to be who we are. So we must open our hearts by honoring and *receiving* love from ourselves. In order to give love with the intention for another to receive, we must know how it feels to receive love. When we come from love, we give of our talents and gifts from that place. We no longer need to look outside of ourselves for love and make others responsible for loving us. We can then be the person we choose to be and create the world we say we want.

It was with the four other guys of this Michael group that I introduced the idea of taking a sacred journey to Mount Shasta. In the past, all the sacred journeys the five of us had taken with Robert Baker were initiated by the archangelic realm, not by human beings. Archangel Gabriel had planned out each and every trip down to the exact date we would leave and designed the rituals that would be performed on the trip. It felt strange to be saying that the idea for this new trip came through me. But when I introduced it to the five guys, they jumped on it right away. Everyone thought it was nice that the location was on this continent, not half way around the world. "Let's talk to Michael about this and see what he says," I said, feeling I needed his endorsement to make it real.

When we had our next session with Archangel Michael, I asked him about the merits of taking a sacred journey to Mount Shasta. There was almost a non-response, which confused me. I kept pushing for clarification. "Is this something we are supposed to do, Michael?" I asked.

Still I was not getting much of a response from this usually talkative angel. So I pushed again, "Michael I am aware of your connection with the Lemurian civilization; you helped them begin their civilization on this planet when they came here from their home planet Lemur."

He dodged and worked around the question, asking me, "How do you feel about it?"

Huh? Boy was I confused. "Michael, is yours the right frequency for this trip? And is Jeff the right channel to help guide us?" I asked, as I tried to understand his reluctance. It crossed my mind that I could take the journey elsewhere, to another group of individuals, if need be. Perhaps it was a trip my soul needed to take that the souls of the others didn't. I could feel my colleagues in the room listening intently to this exchange.

Finally, I could feel the energy in the room shift and crack.

Then Michael broke his silence and began to support the idea of our group making such a journey. "Yes, dear ones, there is a very important mission to be accomplished on Mount Shasta, and the five of you will serve as proxies for humankind to achieve that mission. When you are there you will open a gateway between the Lemurians below ground and those of us in the fifth dimension above. This event will assist in balancing the feminine and masculine energies on your planet; it will enable you to balance receiving and giving. The planet is shifting into balance and everything within and upon her body must also shift."

Wow! My heart was beating faster.

This was beginning to sound like an important mission.

Chapter 8
Confirmation from Lemuria

The next day, the following message came through from Adama.

"The time has come for us to connect directly. Each one of you brothers of the awakened heart are being prepared to do so, if you so choose. You have connected with the Lemurians through the heart energy of your beloved Michael. For only through your hearts can you connect with the fifth dimension. Situations are happening faster than even we Lemurians thought possible. Much is in the process of being revealed to your world. Other worlds and realities are coming forth, and humankind is almost ready to receive the truth. We dwell in your inner planet, safe from your density and separation. We are assisting in your awakening to the truth of your being from below and from above, from your archangelic and star realms. The above and below are meeting in your hearts, dear ones, bypassing your minds.

"This change is more change than your world has ever seen from the unseen. For it is time. The time has come for humankind to know who you are and why you are here, and this begins with each and every one of you individually. Your beloved Michael is teaching you this, as this realm created and taught us. You are finally awakening to the divinity within you and to remember that you are eternal life force light connected to the Creator.

"Your impending sacred journey to our inner home Mount Shasta is a journey the five of you are being guided to receive by us and Michael...others shall follow. During this trip we shall reveal ourselves to you so that you may fully know that we exist and prepare others for this truth. You have prepared for this journey your entire life—and even before. The work and exercises that you are presently involved in doing with Michael are essential prior to this trip. That is why Michael is guiding you to do them. Only through the healing of yourself can you heal your world and receive our reality, the new world order.

"This is a precious opportunity for your world that shall not come again soon. You chose to be here now to assist in the necessary shift. Again, it is essential that you do the work on yourself, to remove yourself from yourself, in order to move into the 'we.' The world Lemurians live in is all about the 'we.' For the 'we' is all there is. Your veils are being lifted to see us and the truth. You are beings of light and must return to the light. Your planet has already done so. Thus, all things within and upon your planet must do so also. Those who choose otherwise shall dwell in another reality elsewhere, if necessary.

"We love you beyond your present love of self and are as anxious to meet you, as you are to meet us. But you must be ready. Are you ready? We must meet at a similar frequency, and that requires you coming to us. We await you."

After receiving this message from Adama, I realized that the trip had already begun (no matter what). The five of us agreed to meet once each week with Michael to receive both his messages and his specific instructions for the journey.

The five members of our group ranged in age from forty to seventy. In some ways, we appeared similar: We were male, Caucasian, American, and spiritually-minded. However, in many ways we probably could not have been any more different from one another. As a result, our attitudes were not always harmonious. I believed in divine perfection, but this didn't feel like it yet. The one thing we always seemed to be able to agree upon, however, was serving a higher purpose. But there was a catch: You had to know what your purpose was within the higher purpose. Michael, thus, was to repeat a couple of years of teaching in a few months. He decided to give us a crash course self-mastery review of everything he had taught us. This was to prepare us to meet our higher-frequency brothers and sisters beneath (and yet above) us.

We would now experience the teachings—and sometimes non-application of them. Right away it felt like a power struggle began between different members. But there wasn't true opposition since our individual soul plans were connected to the mission. There were feelings about needing to be in control of our activities and preparing to meet a more advanced civilization. But our higher selves knew that we were the perfect proxies for humankind and our differences were only a reflection of that truth. Our struggling was often confusing and sad. Was this to be a mini-version of what the Lemurians and Atlanteans had experienced? Was this another cosmic course of learning? Or was it just another example of the separation and duality in our present world, and a reminder of that which causes it: Our unhealed wounds preventing us from experiencing true intimacy with each other.

Since the idea for the trip came through me, I felt my best position, in regards to my fellow proxies, was one of neutrality. I was to surrender and let events unfold, and not appear to be or attempt to be in control. But deep inside I did feel to an extent that this was my journey and I had a right to be in control. I was clear on my mission: I was to go home to Lemuria and reveal the Lemurians to the world. Fortunately, my being in Florida and the other guys being in New York gave me needed space from some of their unhealed behavior and a place to process my own.

Suddenly one day, I remembered hearing about an ascension initiation that occurs within a Lemurian temple. You are put in a room with all the people in your life with whom you have difficulty being. Those who ascend to the next level of ascension are the ones who choose love and are able to love and be with their "difficult" ones. They are able to find a way to accept, with compassion, and forgive the others and themselves, able to see the mirror of themselves in those others. From then on I was seeing the divine perfection of me bringing this trip to this group.

Weekly Conference Calls

Each week the five of us came together, religiously, to share where each of us was in our individual personal process. We had all done the work in previous years, but now we were being asked to go deeper and revisit the lessons with a mission in mind: Lemuria or bust.

I recognized early on that the other four did not have the same exact connection I did to Lemuria. But for some divine reason we were supposed to be together and do this sacred journey together. The others didn't necessarily resonate with the Lemurian energy or with my knowledge of them. But that didn't matter much. What mattered most was their commitment to the journey. Their respective divine soul plans knew they were supposed to go. And so they were going. Each one of us was at a different point on our paths, but eventually we had ended up in the same place.

Having a long-term healing arts practice allowed me the opportunity to use the lessons our group was revisiting personally on a daily basis through clinical experience. My clients were a fantastic mirror, and often I saw myself in them.

Michael was reminding us we had to get our unhealed aspects out of the way prior to meeting the Lemurians. They could not come entirely down to our dense vibration; we had to raise ours up in order to communicate with them.

Fortunately, I had a firm fix on who I was and why I was undertaking this mission. I also was resonating sufficiently with the Lemurian energy that I was able to continue making nocturnal visits in my light body to Telos upon occasion. It was effortless to apply my talents and skills towards this journey. I felt blessed to have cleared most of the major issues in my life to be who I was right then. Nothing in my life ever felt any more right than this, even if I didn't always resonate with everyone in the group in each moment. I decided to focus on the two with whom I did share a connection (focusing on "what is," rather than on "what is not").

As we continued our meetings with Michael, he gave us the following mantra to recite three times each night before we went to bed. We would do this for several months.

We now clear this area of all low-vibration energies that no longer can support the highest good of the connection to the Lemurian subculture, in order to open the gateway for those who are ready to live their purpose in this third-dimensional realm, for those who are ready to connect with the energies, messages, vibrations, and resonance of the Lemurian subculture that will assist and guide the light workers on their paths to create the new world of community, harmony, and equality.

Some nights when I'd forget to say the mantra, I'd be awoken and reminded by Adama. A delightful feeling of love and belonging would come over me.

"We're really going home," I would think with joy.

Chapter 9
Trip Preparations

Over the next several months, Michael began to prepare us individually and as a group for the trip. We met with him each week as he outlined specific rituals and detailed events that would take place on the mountain. The five of us were extremely committed to taking ourselves through Michael's personal process work again. It had taken Michael a couple of years to complete the teachings we were reviewing. Every aspect of the self was being reexamined in order to uncover unhealed items that were preventing us from having entirely loving relationships with ourselves. We were digging deeper into the questions of who we were and why we were here on earth, increasing our understanding of our talents and skills, and realizing more of what it means to move from the narcissistic "me" into the energetically balanced "we" of world service. We understood that if we couldn't love ourselves fully we could neither love others, nor enter the higher frequency of existence where the Lemurians live. Even when we had done this work earlier, without the urgency of a pending trip in the air, we knew that the personal process Michael gave us was a powerful, essential path to self-mastery.

In truth, the only relationship any of us is ever having is the one with our self. All others are mirrors of this primary relationship. Love is the highest vibration of energy there is; anything else is too dense to be sustained in the fifth dimension for long. Love is the glue that holds together every advanced civilization, including our own. We just don't recognize this on Earth. The third dimension is a dense frequency that is largely filled with separation and duality, reflecting the relationships that individuals are having with themselves. People in our third-dimensional reality frequently lack self-love. The fifth dimension is a higher frequency that reflects a healed relationship with the self, which allows individual connection to all. Underlying this reality there is a cognizance of the unity of every life form and ecosystem, including stars and planets.

The inhabitants of every dimension go through an ascension process that allows them to grow and expand infinitely as a collective. Ascension never stops. Earth is ascending along with humanity. The Lemurians are ascending. It is our divine destiny in the third dimension to move to a higher frequency, just as it is their divine destiny in the fifth dimension to move to a higher frequency. There is nowhere else to go but up, for any of us. Of course, the concept of "up" is really a misnomer, as frequencies coexist and overlap one another. Being in a transition now, the barriers between dimensions are dropping away and beings are crossing over.

Most of the work we in Children of the Awakened Heart were doing individually involved reviewing numerous exercises and teachings of Michael daily. Standing in front of a mirror naked and making eye contact with every part of my body was one of the toughest ones for me. Listening to the voices in my mind judging and shaming me (and often remembering where that learned behavior had come from) was uncomfortable, even as it freed my stuck energy and opened my mind.

Michael had said that yes the trip would happen and we had set a date, but he still had not given us many details about it. We were told to continue our weekly conference calls and in due time all we needed to know would be revealed. Thus, it was a mystery unfolding. Our weekly conference calls were keeping the five of us connected and aware of ourselves. Other than that, we also had the message from Adama saying the trip was on and why it was necessary. For the moment, we had to surrender to not knowing and to allow different possibilities to be revealed. Bottom line, we knew where we were going; we just had no idea what we would be doing when we got there.

Our weekly conference call allowed us to check in with each other and ask Michael for direction. We were allowed to ask questions about the trip, but most were not being specifically answered. He would respond, saying things like: "Release the vision of the outcome. It is not a vision for the outcome you need. It is an intention for what you are giving to the world. It is not a vision of where it will land, or how it will sound, or where it will be. That is not a vision; that is control. The vision is a broad spectrum of possibility and probability that will unfold along the journey based upon expressing who you are, your talents and gifts, and your purpose in this lifetime."

Well, I knew what my vision was and what I wanted to give to the world. I wanted to come home to Lemuria and share their advanced teachings with our wounded world.

The Preparation Continues

Among ourselves we had agreed on a late May arrival date in Mount Shasta, which we confirmed with Michael. Initially we worried about facing snow at higher elevations, and then we decided the date was perfect since it meant we would finish our work on the mountain the day prior to the Buddha's birthday. That seemed auspicious. So the date was set.

As the weeks passed and the time grew closer to our need to be there, Michael's messages began to be somewhat more specific. "This is a crucial journey, important because you will be refining and defining yourself, your gifts and talents, and the purpose for your life to come after the journey ends," Michael explained.

I did not know at the time exactly what that meant, but I was intrigued to learn more. The dots were beginning to connect. In future meetings Michael went on to say, "It is time to move deeper within yourself to reveal the essence of you. Before you plan your outer journey to Mount Shasta, it is important to have the inner journey within yourself." That comment resonated with me. I was connecting to the reality that I could choose love no matter what the circumstances. I might forget in the moment, but I saw that I did have the capacity to choose it in the end. My inner journey was to determine if I could now love myself enough to choose love no matter what the outside appearances were. Yes, I knew I could.

Michael explained that as "way showers" to the world of the self-mastery work we were doing in preparation for the journey we would be given "more than you have ever known." I was already feeling this to some degree as I stepped back and let others in the group be in control or have their way on different matters. Only through my giving would I receive anything, because giving equals receiving. But giving and receiving would only be balanced if I truly wasn't giving to get. As Michael said, "That lesson and the work you do will take you to a higher plane."

The self-examination work we were being asked to do was profound and healing. Some of the exercises Michael gave us were as follows. We spent a week focusing on each one.

> · *Exercise 1.* List what you accept with compassion in each and every moment of the now. What are you committed to? Where are you committed? Where are you combining acceptance, compassion, and commitment?

- *Exercise 2.* Which of your old patterns (comfort zones) no longer serves you? What do you need to change? Where are you resisting or avoiding your feelings? Which of the things in your life that no longer serves are you willing to change?
- *Exercise 3.* Can you surrender and accept your heart? What are you attached to where you seek validation and gratification outside yourself? Where are you not standing in your power by expressing your truth, needs, and boundaries?
- *Exercise 4.* Can you be alone without being lonely? Where can you make different choices based upon discernment? Do you have total freedom to make choices? Can you remove yourself from a situation while letting go of any outcome?
- *Exercise 5.* Is giving and receiving in equal balance in your life? Are you applying breath, sound, and motion (creation) in your daily life? What is your definition of love?
- *Exercise 6.* Who and what do you trust? What in the past ten days have you created for yourself? Open your eyes and see the greatness of you! Where are you impeccable with your word?
- *Exercise 7.* Allow yourself to connect with multi-dimensional realms of energy/consciousness through your intuition. Write down what is important to you. What are your intentions?
- *Exercise 8.* Are you committed to these teachings and to moving toward being the master teacher and leading others? Write down details of the relationships that have supported you through this process.

- *Exercise 9.* Where do you focus your attention and intention, knowing that attention plus intention equals manifestation?
- *Exercise 10.* What positive factors in your life have allowed you to move to the place where you are now? What are your accomplishments? Write them down.
- *Exercise 11.* Why are you in the relationships you are in? Do you matter? Do you matter to yourself? Are you being in your life and fully having it? Are you honoring and valuing all of your gifts and talents? What do you shame and judge in yourself and others?
- *Exercise 12.* Why is "drama" still pervasive in your life? What is so important about this "drama" that you are attached to it? Where is your fear? What are your top five fears?
- *Exercise 13.* Who are you? Are you loving yourself?
- *Exercise 14.* Look around at what's happening on your planet and be aware. Feel the depth and breadth of others. Nothing can be controlled and yet control is a pattern for some people. Are you feeling "out of control"? If you are, the reason is that you are not compassionately accepting the feeling of "not being good enough." Allow yourself to move into the unknown with your being intact, trusting your ability to respond as you face the unknown.
- *Exercise 15.* What do you need? What are the five most important aspects of who you are that you love? Write down what your future looks like, based upon self-love. Move into silent gratitude and be grateful for your life.

"Each of you is unique; you forget that. You're not the same, yet all of you are one," Michael mused to us during one of our meetings. I was beginning to see even more clearly how we were really different versions of human being, coming from the same Source, and learning to love ourselves, thus one another. Adama had spoken to me about how our small group would serve as proxies for humankind. The purpose of this trip, he said, would be for us to open a gateway to connect energy from Lemuria inside Earth with frequencies above the planet. Performing specific actions would empower us to assist the planet and the rest of humanity to shift to a higher frequency of energy. That was why it was essential to raise the level of our resonance.

"The one you call Adama will be the so-called overseer for your journey. He will be holding space and ushering you to a gathering place on Mount Shasta," Michael later explained. I was glad to know our friend Adama was coming into the mix. Michael added, "In this gathering place, there will be a large amount of giving and receiving, and a large amount of energy that will allow you to come fully to the realization of why you are here."

By this point, I pretty well knew why I was here: to go home. For me "home" meant Lemuria. But I also suspected that my body would die. For several weeks I'd had a feeling that I would not physically return from the journey, but would make a transition into fifth-dimensional reality while on Mount Shasta. I even put my affairs in order and told my husband farewell. It felt very strange explaining to someone I loved that I would not be coming back, knowing he would not be able to fully comprehend what I was saying, nor why I said it—and possibly causing him to feel like he had married a crazy person.

In preparation for the trip, it seemed a good idea to cleanse my body. I decided to work with a couple of gifted and powerful healers at the wellness center where I teach and co-direct a mystery school. Even though I am HIV-positive and have been carrying the virus probably ever since it was introduced into the American population, I have always considered myself healthy and strong. I've never had any side effects from medications I take or symptoms from the virus itself. In this regard, I am blessed. The two therapists I chose to work with agreed that for an ascension journey like ours, a powerful cleansing was in order. So I went on a full-throttle regimen of detoxifying supplements, biofeedback, quantum cold laser therapy, and energy therapy. I felt great for a couple of weeks and then was hit (as if running into a stone wall) with a healing crisis the likes of which I had never experienced. It felt like death. My auric field photos appeared bright red, and my body was tired and achy in the extreme. Apparently too much of the HIV medication I'd taken for years, which was stored in the tissues of my body, was being released at once. While the intention to clear and cleanse my body was a good one, I did not want it to kill me. So I also announced to my journey partners that unless I got much better soon, I most likely would not be able to make the trip.

I held the belief I would be dying for weeks, until Adama explained to me that I would physically return from the trip, but many aspects of my old self were dying. My DNA and genetic code would be reconfigured and healed on the mountain.

Cancel the reading of my will.

Michael's personal guidance and his hints about our mission, which were coming forth in our Children of the Awakened Heart meetings, had created the beginning of a blueprint for our journey. Michael revealed, "In many ways, this journey will be a culmination. For some, in many ways it is an ordination, and for others it is a graduation. You all have a unique and specific mission and connection in the depth and breadth of your heart space with various multi-dimensional energies, and so you will form important spokes on a wheel."

Frankly, the journey had begun the moment we said yes to doing it. Everything that was happening then felt like a culmination of all that had come before it. I knew my connection to the Lemurians and I knew that certain ordination ceremonies would take place on the mountain. From these I would graduate (once again) as a true, multi-dimensional Lemurian.

Michael explained that we would meet like-minded individuals to whom we could fully reveal ourselves during our trip. Some would become members of our new soul family. "It will be up to you, if you choose and it is in their souls' divine plans, to meet others and tell them who you are: 'These are my talents and gifts and I am now here to give to you.' You will be coming as true brethren for the greater good of the world of community, harmony, and equality." The purpose of forming a new soul family is to join in raising the resonance and vibration of the new world. This concept was very much in keeping with what Adama had shared earlier. With these words, I felt Michael and Adama working in concert.

"You will be connecting with energies in the fifth dimension so you can live in fifth-dimensional reality even as you move through your experience in human form," Michael explained, adding, "On the journey, allow each and every moment to be what it is so you can respond utilizing the tools you have acquired through doing the self-mastery work."

Michael reminded us, "This journey is about relying on the depth and breadth of who you are (your talents and gifts) and giving of this to the world. It is time to release trying to get something outside of yourself to fill up some mythical emptiness within you. Doing the self-mastery work again will show you that what is inside of you is already filled."

There are so many seekers in the world today, people constantly looking out for the next workshop or truth to come to them when it is already there. Everything we need to know is already within us. We just need people around us to remind us to look inside. We seem finally to be reaching a point as a civilization where we can understand the necessity of equality and harmony. It has to be for everyone or none of us is going to have it.

Constantly focusing us, Michael defined our mission. "Each of you will organically know your purpose for going on this journey, and it will be different for each of you. The reason you are going part and parcel to the vortex on this mountain is to impart the principles of community, harmony, and equality first within, to yourself, and then within the group known as Children of the Awakened Heart, then within the new soul family, and then to the world as a whole. This is the reason you have chosen to undertake this journey at this point in time."

I was certain that my purpose was to go to Mount Shasta and connect directly with the fifth-dimensional Lemurian energy so I could bring back their principles of true community and share the way they live with my brethren. I wanted the rest of my life to be a testament to that.

Michael revealed, "You are at the final stages of releasing old karmic patterns within the five of you. These old patterns have been present for many lifetimes and you are moving through the self-mastery process for this purpose alone, so you can release the final residual aspects of group karma that lie within your heart space." The five of us were so different and we had been having our ups and downs, but we all knew we were blessed to receive Michael's wisdom. Knowing we were proxies for the rest of humanity made it easier for me to get along with the other members of the group—granted, not always in the moment. I took Michael's comment to mean that we might separate once the trip was done. When you choose love, karma is burned away forever.

"Your journey to Mount Shasta in many ways will be a dress rehearsal for what is to come later in a larger arena. This is why the five of you are doing this trip as the five of you. The larger arena will come to fruition for each of you individually and will take place organically on your specific aspect of the new journey. In your heart, you will feel where you need to be and take your talents and gifts." Michael assured us, "You will know the arena in which to do this."

Through the weekly meetings Michael forged us on, "Each of the five of you has unique talents and gifts. These will be utilized on this journey. Then, you will be open to receive love. In the future, you will be stating your needs and setting boundaries with those you have never met, so it is important that you know what you need. As you feel your feelings and discover more specifically what you need, you can state your needs to others. This will also make it easier to respond to the needs of others using your talents and gifts when they come to you."

I knew my talents and gifts had led me to initiate the journey ahead and that my most urgent need was to reunite with the Lemurian civilization on the site where it makes its home on Earth.

Michael continued teaching us what would happen at Mount Shasta, "Multi-dimensional energies will move down through the vortex on the mountain as Lemurian energies move up from Inner Earth. In your hearts, you will combine an equal measure of feminine and masculine energy, a balance of these energies. What will be revealed is where you have an excess of either. The journey will balance these energies with-in you. It will bring up acceptance and compassion. Some will be learning to assert themselves, and some balancing accep-tance and compassion."

Now Michael was really beginning to get specific about our purpose! We would be balancing the masculine and femi-nine energies, and giving and receiving by helping to merge different frequencies from higher dimensions. Then we were to take what we learned and our understanding of what we needed individually and apply this to our lives and our service in the world. I got it!

Michael reminded us of the reason for doing self-mas-tery work: "to declare yourself into the world based upon be-ing fully individualized and self-contained by containing your energy." He also cautioned us, "Release trying to control what might happen, what could happen, and what you think will happen on the journey. Remain with your intuition intact. It is most important on this journey that you begin to trust you. We ask you to move into moment-by-moment existence; do this as best as you can. Trying to control everything is coming up for each and every one of you, and you are wondering what the results of the trip will be. Release the mental body. Guide yourself into the depth and breadth of your heart where your intuition lies—as does your connection to your soul's divine plan. Each of you will connect to whomever you are supposed to, and to whatever energy you are supposed to be connected with on the journey."

Control sure was becoming an issue for some of our five-some. I relied on my intuition to help me remain neutral in the face of imbalances, and when I found my ego defenses being activated I would remind myself that just as we were serving as proxies for humankind. "This trip isn't about me," I told myself, even though at times it felt that way.

Michael taught us, "You are beginning to refine and define who you are and to unburden yourself from the seeming necessity of having to prove who you are by releasing the mask from around your heart. You are realizing that it takes less energy to be you than it does to hold this mask in place." He also reminded us that the process of doing the exercises he had given us was bringing us closer to ourselves. "You are accepting you, loving you, and allowing yourself a choice of world service."

Explaining the journey in more detail, Michael explained, "You are poised to connect with those who will be forming your new soul family. For each of you that family could be different. To find your soul family, first look at the relationship you are having with yourself. Moving through the self-mastery work reveals this. Then see where you are beginning to understand or even to know your purpose and mission in this third-dimensional realm."

He continued, "Your new soul family will join with you in a common purpose, moving together in service to the world, and in this way contributing to the creation of a new world of community, harmony, and equality. Although each of you might be creating a soul family that does not include the others, each of you is ready to move into a higher vibration. Your resonance will determine your purpose, why you are here, and the formation of your new soul family. This family will begin to form when you begin to see, understand, and know what your purpose is."

I knew in my heart that my soul family could only be found among those who truly knew their divine purpose. I would accept those with compassion who did not yet know, but move on from them when our paths crossed. It was clear to me that my purpose was to bring truth into a world that does not always want to hear or accept it. My private practice in the healing arts had changed many people's lives over the years, and my work was growing and expanding.

One of the final instructions Michael gave us before going into the specifics of our journey was: "Pay attention to joy and what brings you joy. Allow joy to be your guide. Part of the intention of every fifth-dimensional being who visits your earthly plane is to create joy with you. This already exists in you; it is the joy of the inner child. A child comes into your world joyfully. A child only knows love and joy and peace and community and harmony and equality. You are moving back into your heart to connect with that child who knows all of these." And he gave us a great visual, "As your adult self, take that child's hand in yours and walk into a new life to create a new world."

At the end of our self-mastery work, Michael asked us, "Are you ready now to integrate all of what you have learned and take necessary steps to trust yourself, regardless of your feelings? Are you ready to shift and change by honoring all of your feelings? Are you ready to give your greatness to the world? Are you ready to share your gifts—to share you—with the world?"

My response was, "Yes, I am Michael."

Chapter 10
The Seven Sacred Flames

One of the most loving gifts the Lemurians have given us is a way back home. The Lemurians cannot complete their own evolutionary mission until our two civilizations join as one. Thus, for eons they have been holding what they call flames or rays of energy and consciousness that basically contain the how-to instructions for us to ascend and meet them in the higher-frequency fifth dimension. Where they live is a parallel reality to ours, only energetically more refined than the one we're in. There are temples the world around honoring the teachings of these flames.

As we were beginning to plan the sacred journey to Mount Shasta, amazing teachings on the subject of the flames came to me via a book called *The Seven Sacred Flames* written by the late Aurelia Louise Jones (Mount Shasta Light Publishing 2007). The author had been the publisher of my friend Dianne Robbins' original book of channeled material from Lemuria. I immediately resonated with this book, and I knew I wanted to use it as a textbook for a course.

During the months of preparation for the trip, I co-founded a mystery school in Fort Lauderdale in partnership with my friend Jessie Keener, a gifted healer and nutritionist. The original mystery schools in ancient Egypt guided people through a series of initiations that led them to recognize their divine purpose. Our teachings were updated and contemporary, but truth is truth, so we named our program The Modern Day Mystery School. Its mission statement reads: We are a community of divine souls committed to offering love and support in a balance of giving and receiving. We seek to learn and teach spiritual truths in order to create master teachers while opening energetic vortices and facilitating ascension.

Having completed my New York City training in light ascension and relocated to Florida, I wanted to form a community of love and support around me that emphasized love of self and love of another. Our first course was about creating a loving relationship with one's self. The ascension process, so beautifully developed in Jones's book, was an evolutionary next step.

The Seven Sacred Flames explains that the Lemurians have been waiting hundreds of years for the right moment to release their information. I began to create a teaching guide and planned to hold the class immediately upon my return from Mount Shasta. It seemed perfect to teach the ascension process after having just been to the physical Lemurian home myself. I invited two other facilitators to join me in teaching the class, Jessie Keener, the co-founder of the school, and another, so we could create a sacred triad of energy.

Since the flames book is esoteric and contains minute details about the fifth dimension, I was concerned that it would be overwhelming for the average metaphysical student. Adama urged me to go full steam ahead and not worry about the outcomes; those who were supposed to receive the information would show up. The Lemurians had been waiting hundreds of years for the right moment to reveal their wisdom and the time was right. Indeed, the book was the most comprehensive how-to guide to ascension I've ever seen. It presents new ideas and concepts that would be challenging for us all. Our belief systems were going to be rocked.

My intention to teach this material became such a major focus of my life that I wanted to have the classes set up prior to leaving for Mount Shasta. It was going to be an eight-week commitment and cost more than other classes I'd put together. Would people be willing to commit a major part of their summer vacation to such an esoteric course and pay more for it than they were accustomed? Within two weeks we had bookings to fill our classroom to capacity. Adama was right: When the student is ready, the teacher will appear. They were ready.

The purpose of the manual I developed was to allow our students to connect with the seven flames and the ascended master associated with each, the goal being to energetically attune to the vibration of the flames and ascended masters in order to achieve self-mastery and join Mother Earth within the planetary ascension process. Everyone is born under the primary influence of one of the Seven Sacred Flames. The work of connecting with the flames does not have to be done in a particular order. But each is necessary for humankind as a collective to ascend. I did not know it for certain, but because of seeing the temples of the flames in my etheric visits to Telos, I suspected that the ascended masters would participate in our rituals on Mount Shasta.

The ascended masters are fifth-dimensional beings who were once human and walked the Earth, so they know what it is like to be human—what it means to us and how it feels. You may not have heard their true names before, but you may recognize their names from some of their human incarnations, as they were remarkable human beings. Going flame by flame they are:

Master El Morya is the spiritual leader of the first flame, which is the blue flame of the will of God. On earth, he lived as: the Hebrew patriarch Abraham, King Arthur, Thomas

Beckett, and Sir Thomas Moore. The relevance of this flame is that it teaches us to surrender our will. Surrender is essential for connection to the source energy of the Creator.

Master Lord Lanto is the leader of the second flame, which is the yellow flame of illumination and wisdom. On earth, he lived as the Chinese emperor Duke of Chou, founder of the Confucian tradition; and he was a ruler of China in several other lifetimes. This flame teaches us to strive for understanding.

Master Paul, the Venetian, is the leader of the third flame, which is the pink flame of cosmic love. On earth, he lived as: head of cultural affairs, in Atlantis; after the fall of Atlantis he went to Peru to establish the Inca civilization; in Egypt, he oversaw the construction of the pyramids; and his final human life was as Paolo Veronese, an Italian Renaissance painter. Love really is all there is. This energetic vibration underlies every dimension of our existence.

Master Lord Serapis Bey is the guardian of the fourth flame, the white flame of purification. On earth, he lived as: the high priest of the Ascension Temple in Atlantis; Egyptian pharaoh Amenhotep III, who had the Temple of Luxor built; and Leonidas, King of Sparta. Purification is a vibration that helps us shift from density and matter to sheer energy.

Master Hilarion is the leader of the fifth flame, the green flame of healing and manifestation. On earth, he lived as: high priest of the Temple of Truth in Atlantis; the Apostle Paul; and Saint Hilarion, the founder of monasticism in Palestine. This flame is the essence of healing. Healing of our emotional wounds enables us to manifest higher frequencies.

The sixth flame, the purple and gold flame of resurrection, is led by a couple, Lord Sananda and Lady Nada. Sananda lived on earth as King David of the Torah/Old Testament; Joseph of Egypt, son of Jacob; Joshua, who led the Israelites into the Promised Land; and Jesus (aka Yeshua). Lady Nada lived on earth as a priestess of the Temple of Love in Atlantis; a priestess in the Temple of Isis in Egypt; and as Mary Magdalene, wife of Jesus and mother of their children. In order to ascend, we need to resurrect our divine essence. This flame guides us.

Master Saint Germain leads the seventh flame, the violet flame of transmutation. On earth, he lived as: the prophet Samuel; Joseph, the father of Jesus and husband of Mary; Saint Alban, a martyr in Britain; Merlin, who lived in the court of King Arthur; Roger Bacon; Christopher Columbus; Sir Francis Bacon, the illegitimate son of Queen Elizabeth; and Count St. Germain. Along with the fourth flame, this one helps us in transmuting our density into higher-frequency energy.

Since the balancing of male and female energy is a necessity for ascension, there appears to be a contradiction in the list of names of the ascended masters who are keepers of the Seven Sacred Flames. With one exception, the names on this list are male. I have learned, however, that in the frequency within which they exist, their beingness is in complete balance and equality with feminine energy. Each male ascended master works in concert with a feminine twin flame counterpart and none could do his work without being balanced by the energy of a female ascended master. A good example is the relationship of Lord Sananda to Lady Nada. He cannot do his work without her. Likewise, St. Germain works in concert with Lady Portia.

Similarly the male archangels all work in concert with feminine archangels; Archangel Michael with Archangel Faith; Gabriel with Hope; Raphael with Mother Mary, and Uriel with Aurora. Mother Earth, Gaia, our home and the body we live upon, holds feminine energy, and therefore three female ascended masters govern the healing activities of the

Earth: Mother Mary, Mary Magdalene, and Meta, who is the Goddess of Compassion. And they are connected to their masculine twin flames mentioned here.

It is important to remember that sexual gender, as we know it, is not the same in higher frequencies; there are simply balanced energetic forces of feminine and masculine. The advanced civilizations have learned only too well the lessons of an imbalance of male and female energy!

Even the Lemurian leaders work in concert with female twin flames. Adama, for instance, works in concert with another Lemurian named Celestia. So it is only the human imagination really that cannot comprehend the balance of male and female energy in the fifth dimension.

Working with the Seven Sacred Flames of Lemuria on a daily basis is an easy way to balance the significance of their energy in your life. All seven of the flames fill the planet every day, but on different days of the week a different flame becomes dominant. According to Adama, for ascension to take place, eventually all seven flames will need to be thoroughly understood and held in balance permanently. They are keys of consciousness and instructions. Daily work with the flames is done in Lemuria. As Adama explained, "Ascension's progress is assured by everyday use of these flames." He also advised, "These energies are here to assist you, and all are important. None should be ignored, as they will work in unison to restore humanity to fifth-dimensional reality. If you work with them they will work with you."

Ascension Chair Ceremony

At the Modern Day Mystery School, we decided to hold a special ritual we learned of, which was developed by the ascended master St. Germain, the keeper of the seventh, violet flame of transmutation, whose main qualities, insights, and actions are related to freedom, transformation, diplomacy, ceremony, and the science of alchemy. Called an ascension chair ceremony, this ritual assists in raising the vibration of those who have declared themselves to be candidates for ascension. Our understanding was that the ritual would bring in the frequency of the pure white light of the ascension flame, and it would raise our individual vibrations gradually and gently.

We sent out invitations to our students and so had a group of about twenty people show up, which was very exciting. Not only were we hoping to affect and help the people participating in the group, we wanted to create a web of light that would touch the entire planet. To create a positive ambiance, we cleared the room energetically, lit candles, set out flowers, put on soft music, and placed chairs in a circle around a designated ascension chair. It was agreed that I would serve as the ritual facilitator for the event that evening.

After everyone had arrived, we gathered in the circle and opened our hearts. Then we took turns coming forward one by one to sit in the center of the circle, where we declared out loud, before our friends and before God, our desire to participate in ascension, the union of our human selves with our eternal spiritual beings. We stated our goals for our lives, and declared our willingness to do whatever it took to make them happen. While seated in the ascension chair, people held a special crystal in their hand that we provided them, and made the most honorable prayer that their hearts dictated or inspired them to utter in the moment. Each participant sat on the chair for three to five minutes.

It was an incredibly moving and surprisingly powerful event. As each candidate formulated an intention and a prayer, St. Germain flooded the individual's energy field with the level of the ascension frequency appropriate for that person at the moment. There was a natural flow among the group and all of us took our turn in no specific order. Everyone felt something, even those among us who were uncertain that they would be able to sense the energy. When finished, the candidates gave a sign of completion with the eyes to me and a designated person rang a set of Tibetan bells once, after which the group chanted the sound *aum* three times to assist in anchoring the energy in which they had been bathed while seated in the chair.

Adama has explained to me that repeated practice of this ritual following ceremonies would build the momentum of ascension. Apparently, each time this sacred ceremony is performed for someone the energies impacting that person double in intensity and beauty. As we evolve in our consciousness, the purifying effect of the ascension flame occurs in greater measure.

I went last and to me it felt like a re-affirmation of my purpose to be a messenger/light worker/way shower of Lemurian and other higher-frequency messages and teachings to further assist myself and others into the intention of ascension. As tears expressed my truth, I was incredibly moved by the experience.

When we were finished, sparkling apple juice was poured into small cups which we passed around to the group. I made a short invocation asking that the liquid we held in our right hands would be infused with the frequency of golden light. We paused for a moment to allow the ascended masters to transform the liquid in each of our cups to the frequency that was most appropriate for each person. Then I gave a signal, and we all slowly drank the liquid that had now become a sacred alchemical elixir. We finished by expressing our deep gratitude for the gift and rich blessings that were bestowed upon us.

Whenever people come together in a group and in community it reinforces our intentions, and thus the work we do in ceremonies has a powerful impact on everyone's life. It was my hope that my companions on the journey to Mount Shasta might be willing to host a similar ascension chair ceremony for the friends we met while we were there. It was a palpable reminder to me of how much I wanted to contribute to humanity, and the love and peace that are our birthright. That it affected our participants so deeply felt like confirmation that ascension was real.

Chapter 11
Specific Instructions for the Journey

As the five of us were completing the required self-mastery work and the date of our arrival upon the mountain was nearing, we had to deal with tangible matters. I called my Lemurian link, Dianne Robbins, brought her up to date on our activities and sacred intentions for the journey, and asked for her assistance locally. I explained to her that we needed to rent a five-bedroom house near the mountain and to hire a mountain guide who would not be freaked out by what we would be doing. At the time, I didn't realize that it would take a great deal to freak out the people in her town. Dianne connected me with Heart of Shasta Retreat Vacation Rentals. In a nurturing voice, Jacqueline said she had the perfect house with a mountain view that would only cost us a couple of hundred dollars each for the week. What a deal!

The next important item on the list was a mountain guide. Mount Shasta is a huge mountain and we needed someone who knew the mountain well and could organically incorporate into our five-some. I was given the name of a company called Shasta Vortex Adventures. How perfect was that? We were going to be visiting vortices on the mountain as part of our adventure, and here was a guide who had named her company what we would be doing. Within moments after speaking with the guide, Ashalyn, I knew she was totally plugged into the Lemurian energy. She did not sound surprised for one moment when I described our mission. After she agreed to take us on, we began to include Ashalyn in our conversations with Michael so she could understand firsthand what was going on and participate in the trip.

Our tour wasn't going to be your basic mountain tour and Ashalyn wasn't your basic guide. I definitely felt that Dianne knew exactly what she was doing connecting us with Ashalyn. It seemed we had another Lemurian in our mix. It was also wonderful to have a woman in our mix.

We booked our flights from our various departure cities and made a checklist of things we thought we would need to have on a very elevated, snowy volcanic mountain. We were all pretty much city boys. Myself, I had lived in Manhattan for forty years and lost any of the country ways I'd had in childhood. None of us understood how physically challenging, and how emotionally and mentally challenging, the journey would be. We would be in heavy weather gear and boots, tromping around in the snow at high altitude. This was going to make men out of us boys. (I can remember the military promising that also. But this was an entirely different type of "duty.")

Ignorance was definitely bliss in our case, looking back. What you don't know won't prevent you from doing it. Sort of sounds like a description of youth, doesn't it? From the beginning Ashalyn instinctively knew that the purpose of this journey went beyond other mountain tours. Even so, there would be times on the mountain when she had no idea where she was even though she knew the mountain well. Never mind the spiritual mumbo jumbo. This was not going to be jaunt.

Michael knew it was time to be more specific as to exactly what we would be doing on the mountain and why. In a group call, he began laying out the mechanics of the journey...

Michael's Message

Michael explained: "You now are continuing your journey in the ascension process—raising your frequency—moving into your heart space, and moving through a crucial period as you open to the depth of your heart to begin the final aspects of the voyage to begin to live your life's purpose and your soul's divine plan." As he continued, we learned this trip was not just going to be about meeting Lemurians. It was also about doing work with the angels, and most importantly, with ourselves! "The five of you are approaching an intersection. Some are standing at this intersection, some are approaching it, and some are wondering where it is. Some of you are ready to connect with your soul's divine plan. But none of you has fully connected with your divine plan because you are still moving through the final phases of knowing and living your purpose."

Hearing this, I thought for sure my soul's plan was teaching and entering fifth-dimensional reality.

Michael went on: "In these final phases of preparation for your journey, you are releasing old, karmic attachments outside of you in your third dimension, as well as to one another. These are the old karmic attachments that remain in relationships and aspects of the relationships each of you has. And this is why you have chosen to venture on this specific journey. It is time to sort out those old karmic aspects in all your relationships and with one another."

I was beginning to gain a deeper understanding why the five of us were doing this together as proxies. Although it was for humanity, it was also for us and our healing.

"In order to now clear these old karmic aspects in your relationships with one another it is important to clear and see clearly the relationship you are having with yourselves so you can determine the relationships you will be entering into outside of you on the pathway as you walk through the doorway and close the door behind you and connect with your soul's divine plan and begin building a new soul family."

My thought was, "I think I just heard the door slam!"

Michael continued: "This will be the soul family you will reside in most likely the remainder of your human incarnation. It is very important that you continue to look at the relationship you are having with yourself and continue the process of entrainment, raising your frequency, in the month before you leave. This is a period of processing and integrating all that you have learned up to this point. Also continue releasing what no longer supports your highest good, as well as releasing those in your life who no longer support your highest good.

"You are refining and defining the relationship you are having with yourself so you can embark on the physical journey to the vortex you will be visiting on Mount Shasta and continue, then complete this journey. Your journey to the vortex of Mount Shasta will be a completion of the entrainment period. You will be doing several rituals there. On the mountain you shall be performing three rituals with two parts each, creating a six-pointed star. The entrainment period will end with your third and final ritual as you move to the vortices of renewal and rebirth.

"When you complete the third and final ritual you will know your purpose. Some will know it more acutely than others. Some will only get a glimpse of it. But at that time you will all know in some way, shape, or form and to varying degrees what your purpose is on this earthly plane. You will also know about the relationships you are having with each other. At the end of the third ritual the relationship you will be having with each other as you move forward in the third dimension will be defined. You will know the true meaning, value, and purpose of your group. Your roles on this journey and in your group will be refined and defined for you."

Well, I knew my role was to get us to the mountain (not knowing what a process *that* would be) and I knew this didn't mean just getting on a plane and showing up, but much more.

Michael continued: "Where the group is headed on its new pathway entirely depends on where you are headed on your pathway. And this will be based upon you discovering your purpose and knowing who you are, including your talents and gifts. All this will culminate at the end of your third ritual.

"You will be meeting many on your journey. In some cases, these people will be members of your new soul family. You will not always be together on and off the mountain. When you are off on your own individual journeys, you will find those who resonate and vibrate at the same frequency that you do. Those you meet will be both third-dimensional and fifth-dimensional beings. Sometimes you will form groups and navigate to other frequency areas.

"Each of you will be revealed to the world on and off the mountain. Simply by being who you are, your talents and gifts will be revealed to others. You will be attracted to others as others will be attracted to you by simply being who you are. You will be offering your talents and gifts to others, and you will find locations on and off the mountain to offer them."

Michael concluded his briefing of us by saying, "This is a crucial journey, important because you will be refining and defining yourself, your talents and gifts, and your purpose for the life to come after the journey ends."

So if meeting an unknown fifth-dimensional civilization within Inner Earth was not enough, this journey was also to be a recreation of me and my companions.

The Outline for Our Journey

The last few weeks of Michael's instructions for the journey were spent in describing specific rituals we were to perform on the mountain. There were many, many details about things to be done at precise moments, while holding special crystals, at locations that either had to be found or created. If you are not familiar with spiritual rituals, I do not wish to overwhelm you with these details, but I wish for you to know what we experienced and why, and later what it felt like. So to begin I shall briefly outline what was required of us and why. In later chapters on the time we were actually on the mountain, I shall go into the fifth-dimensional experience of the rituals.

In my conversations with Adama during this period, he reminded me, "Your minds right now still demand rituals and rules and proof that is irrefutable before you can enter a journey like this one. Hopefully, these rituals can bring you back to the frequency of faith and trust, and not doubt and denial. Isn't that why you are being given this journey now? Ascension is nothing more than awakening to the truth of your divine self. The mind has limitless questions and now you shall use your hearts to answer them. The answers you seek lie inside you. The only spiritual practice you need is to awaken to this truth. True mastery is the understanding of how to use that which is within you, as well as outside you. True mastery is in knowing in the moment what is appropriate for that moment."

These were the instructions we received.

The Starting Point

Before the rest of us arrived in Mount Shasta, our mountain guide, Ashalyn, had to do the first task for our trip, which was to locate a specific main energetic marker. This would be the beginning point of the mountain journey. Michael gave her specific elevation points and described angles of the sun to help her. She was given no further information and had to use her intuition to find it. Angels don't always make things easy. Much to our delight, she came back to us rather quickly with email photos of a very large boulder that she said was our main marker and beginning point. "There was a large, dead tree pointing right to the rock," Ashalyn wrote, "and I knew this was our marker." Michael confirmed this spot in our next conference call.

Opening the Lemurian Gateway

The next thing we would need to do was create an energetic connection with the Lemurian subculture. One of us would serve as a "gatekeeper," Michael told us. The others would stand around him in a circle. Once the gateway was opened, a fifth-dimensional connection would be established between the Lemurians below, us, and the archangelic realms. Michael explained that we would be building, creating, and encoding an energetic connection, a funnel of energy "that will remain after you leave this mountain. This will serve as the main entry point for those who will be coming to visit Lemuria." A citrine crystal would be used by the gatekeeper to open the gateway.

I received a channeled message from Adama to bring five citrine crystals. David and George both felt they had a large citrine crystal that would be perfect for the gatekeeper. Already, a small opposition ensued in our group. Who had the right crystal?

Michael reiterated his point, "This ritual is being performed at a precise moment in time so that all of the energies—your individual energies, the energies of the Lemurian subculture that will be moving up from Mother Earth, and other specific fifth-dimensional energies will converge in that moment and allow the gateway to be opened and perpetually remain open."

For weeks we had been saying the same mantra three times every night. We now learned that this mantra would be used on the mountain to keep us connected to the main marker so we could fully encode our energy there. It would also sweep and clear the area of any unwanted energy.

Creating Six Outer Vortices

Moving outwards from the main marker, following the opening of the Lemurian gateway, we would be finding and activating six additional vortices where we would perform rituals. "When these vortices are activated, it will be at a very precise moment in time that will never happen again. So it is incumbent upon each of you to embrace your responsibility in doing this. At the end of your journey, you will have a newfound responsibility. As a group you are beginning to assume the responsibility of being a proxy for Mother Earth, your third-dimensional realm. It is why you have chosen and been chosen for this journey," Michael reminded us.

"You will be connecting these six specific points during three rituals (two vortices would be activated per ritual), and serving as a proxy for male and female energy, the energy of giving and receiving. After the completion of the third ritual, you will have created a three-dimensional Star of David or merkabah, and encoded these same energies in this entire area." Michael further explained, "You have each been chosen to perform these tasks, for it is about giving your talents and gifts to the world and receiving in kind.

Michael summarized, "Energetically, in your soul's divine plan you have been chosen to perform three universal tasks. First, you will be creating a Star of David to establish for eternity a balance of the male and female energies in this specific area. Second, you will be creating a vortex by encoding ley lines, or energy networks, and your own energies into this vortex. Third, you will be precisely holding the key at a specific time to open the Lemurian gateway.

"You have been chosen to perform your task in order for humankind to enjoy the fruits of your labor. Based upon your soul's divine plan you will be performing specific tasks throughout these rituals. Your main vortex will be the center point, the gateway to the Lemurian subculture. The six vortices outside of this will hold in place the energies moving from the Lemurian subculture outwards through the gateway and the fifth-dimensional energies moving into it. You, both as a group and individually, will be creating these six outer vortices by encoding your own energies into those areas. Later, others will visit these six vortices where they will be empowered to define and know their purpose," Michael detailed.

Giving advice for our bodies, Michael explained, "Because of your role in the divine plan, it is most important that the purity of your physical body remain intact from now until you complete the journey. It is your responsibility for yourself, the group, and the good of the whole. It is important to heed this caution, as what you ingest in your physical body can lower its resonance and vibration. Your frequency is determined by what you ingest, so ingest high-vibrational foods." Michael was putting us on the same diet as the Lemurians—a diet of live fruits and vegetables—so our frequencies would better match theirs to ensure our connection.

Michael also reminded us, "You have been chosen and you yourselves have chosen to take responsibility to create what has never been created before. You are opening the doorway to the Lemurian gateway so fifth-dimensional energies can connect with your Mother Earth based upon the energies of Lemuria. It is most important work and it is your choice to do it. We ask you, what could be more important? What else could be your priority at this time, as you are now a proxy for humankind and your universe? It is most important to see the responsibility you have to yourself, your brethren, and most importantly for those who will come for lifetimes to come."

The Exact Rituals

Remember, the instructions for the rituals came from Michael over a several-week period. This outline is an attempt to give you a rough idea of the three rituals that would be performed. It in no way reflects a complete description of events, nor the depth of the subsequent experience.

Michael told us, "Each entire ritual must be a stream-lined movement without interruption. Keep in mind that during each ritual you will be encoding energies. The rituals are to begin precisely at noon. They will end when your sun is at a 45-degree angle to your earthly plane, approximately at six o'clock in the evening. You will know intuitively when the ritual ends." And he exalted, "Within that time period you will be encoding energies and performing your service to the universe, as well as to yourself personally and to the group."

Here are some details about the rituals we would be performing.

Ritual 1: The purpose of this ritual was to open the Lemurian gateway. We would gather to connect all our individual energies and plug them into the main marker that Ashalyn had found. The crystals we would use were clear quartz and amethyst.

Following the ritual, we would connect our energy and activate two vortices: the vortex of intention and the vortex of the crystalline children, those who are born knowing why and how to effect necessary changes on earth. At the vortex of intention we would make two lists. The first list would declare five aspects of our lives that we wanted to release. It would be burned after we spoke a mantra: *"I now release these old aspects to Mother Earth. I proclaim acceptance, compassion, and my love for me. I now release these in acceptance, compassion, and love for me."* A second list would declare who we are and why we are here, the purpose we perceived ourselves to have in this lifetime. It would be put in a container. The ashes and container would be buried in different locations upon the mountain.

At the vortex of the crystalline children we would bring forth our inner children—the wounded child, the magic child, and the wonder child—to receive the healing and love these aspects of our energetic matrices needed and also to receive messages from them.

Ritual 2: This ritual would last for six hours, a period during which we would remain in silence. Its purpose would be to connect to the fifth dimension, so we could begin to hear, see, feel, and touch messages. It would begin with a meditation to let go of any third-dimensional attachments and move into the depth and breadth of Mother Earth and the gateway into the Lemurian subculture. The crystals to be used were clear quartz and smoky quartz. Smoky quartz is a grounding crystal that would aid us in entering into the Lemurian subculture.

Following the commencement of six hours of silence, we would connect with and activate two vortices: the vortex of the world and the vortex of the people. At the vortex of the world we would be writing, drawing, painting, or doing anything else that came to us to do. We were instructed to notice our urges. At the vortex of the heart, our hearts would open. We would connect to ourselves and express ourselves in a way we never had imagined. Each of us would be connected to the people, a person, a voice, or the energy of the Lemurian sub-culture.

Ritual 3: The purpose of our final ritual would be to examine what came to us, what we had learned, and also garnered energetically, during the first two rituals and then to write down five major aspects of it, as well as to describe new things we had learned about ourselves on our journey. Our pages would be buried later in the day. The crystals used for this ritual were clear quartz and tourmaline, the latter of which would connect us with our intuition and higher selves.

Following the ritual, we would create two additional vortices: the vortex of renewal and the vortex of rebirth. These would be created first together and then recreated individually. At the vortex of renewal we would renew our connection with our multi-dimensionality. Standing in a circle at the vortex, we would first take turns reading the lists we created during the ritual and then recite a mantra together: *"I am now clear. I am now open. I am now available. I am now here. I am now present in the very moment. I open my heart. I open the depth of my soul to progressively, honestly, and with the greatest intention walk the pathway being me. Together say, 'So be it.'"* Following that, we would put our pages in a container and bury them.

At the vortex of rebirth we would shift to a higher resonance within ourselves that was based upon our soul's divine plan. Then we would be able to go back into the world in community, harmony, and equality with ourselves, knowing why we are here. We would be ready to make decisions about our path and our purpose, so we would create new intentions. These we would write in our journals. Standing in a circle, we would then recite our new intentions aloud.

With these instructions in hand, apparently all else we needed do was to travel to Mount Shasta.

Parting Words from Adama

Before we began our spiritual journey to Mount Shasta, Adama also had a few things to say. He wanted us to know that the physical bodies of the Lemurians in the fifth dimension are being offered as a blueprint for us to consider when we shift to their frequency. He said we are currently functioning at a fraction of our DNA's total capacity. The Lemurians are functioning at a 100 percent level; we are at about 10 percent. The reduction in functioning from the capacity of our original DNA took place over thousands of years. As humanity abused its divine gifts, the decline in capacity continued. The destruction of Lemuria and Atlantis were a point of great diminishment. As a result of misuse of our powers, humans were slowly, but surely losing our direct connection with the universe and the Creator. This was all part of our freedom of will and how we were choosing to learn. No one had the right to stand in the way of our choice.

Nonetheless, the immortal god aspect of us never died within our DNA, even though it was greatly diminished for a long time. Needless to say, our journey back to wholeness has been a painful and long one. There were many attempts to assist us throughout our history, but they all failed. We would not listen or killed the messengers. But now there is a light at the end of the tunnel. A quantum shift in humankind has taken place, and through our free will, once again we are being given the opportunity to return to our divine wholeness: ascension. The promise of the ascension process, of entering a higher frequency of life, is to regain everything that was lost.

The long, dark periods we've experienced throughout recorded history were merely the way we chose to learn. We went as far from truth as we could go. Now, upon our return to the truth of who we are we shall become the most enlightened beings in the universe and never forget again. Humans will be in great demand as master teachers, for no one has ever accomplished what we have done, which is to go as far from the light as possible and return home to our Source.

It was amazing to me when I thought of how we had all signed up for this assignment on a soul level and were now ready to return home. The five of us would be proxies for our people!

Adama wanted us to know without a shred of doubt that the Lemurians are ready to assist humans in our "homecoming," but also that we have to choose through our hearts—through our freedom of will we have to choose love. For love is the travel ticket to immortality. When we ascend, we get to take our healed physical bodies with us, never to die again. Our bodies will be transformed and become immortal and without limit, just like the bodies of the Lemurians.

What will happen to the third dimension after humans choose to leave it? Adama explained that all dimensions exist simultaneously. The third dimension will still exist for those who choose to stay here. Once in a higher frequency, you can change frequencies at will. You can have lunch in the third dimension, and then return to the fifth dimension for dinner. But he warned, while Earth is shifting into a higher frequency, the third dimension isn't going to be a very nice place to be. Earth needs to heal and restore her balance after suffering human abuse. Preservation and restoration must take place in the third dimension or the planet will not be able to sustain life on her body in the way to which we are accustomed.

Many humans are now being called to act on behalf of the planet, even though many of those responsible for harming Earth are continuing their assault. Therefore, the planet's natural means of cleansing herself will intensify. Consider these events a kind of a healing crisis, an essential step in planetary purification. Mother Earth requires that we show compassion and support for her renewal, even though it may cause us massive inconveniences.

Humanity is waking up to a higher awareness of oneness with Mother Earth. We are becoming aware that her resources, which we have taken for granted for so long, have caused great depletion upon and within the planet's body. We have not recognized that the trees are her lungs that we cut down freely, the crystals/minerals/gems are her arteries in an energy system of which we have no knowledge, and the oil that we take in unlimited supply is her blood. If our bodies were treated the way we treat the Earth, we would already be dead.

When the Lemurian continent sank and 350 million Lemurians died overnight, the Creator elevated their continent from the third dimension to the fourth (the dimension we go to when we are asleep and when we die). Later, as the Lemurian civilization evolved back into higher consciousness, they were again elevated to the frequency of the fifth dimension. By saving the Lemurians, the Creator was demonstrating the contribution they would be making to our planet; if they were not going to contribute they would have been destroyed completely. Only the third-dimensional, low frequency part of Lemuria sank (the part that co-exists with us now).

Lemuria was elevated from the third, to the fourth, to the fifth frequency, but they also already existed in all those dimensions simultaneously. In those days you could move from one frequency to another at will. There was no veil of non-awareness between the dimensions like the one we humans live with right now. The veil between us and those who reside in higher dimensions was created by the misuse of our divine gifts, ultimate power corrupted. Now we know these misuses are giving us the greatest wisdom we could ask for: immortal consciousness that is teaching the entire universe what it is to go as far from the light as possible, and return, to never leave it again. You can call it learning the hard way. But maybe that's what it takes for us.

What was elevated from Lemuria when they went from fourth to fifth dimensions was an energetic blueprint of their civilization that had remained in service to the light: temples, ascended masters, and a small portion of the population. Only the highest level of consciousness was saved. There is no reason to believe that the huge continent of Lemuria will ever reappear in the Pacific Ocean. However, it is possible that we will be coming together in the higher level of consciousness through the Lemurians' extraordinary fifth-dimensional Inner Earth civilization.

There are living, crystal libraries in Lemuria that contain the real history of our planet, galaxy, and universe. Humankind knows little of the true history and united mission of our two civilizations. But Adama felt it was important to reiterate that the Lemurian mission cannot be completed until our two worlds unite as one civilization. They simply cannot ascend in the sixth dimension until we ascend to the fifth, for on a truthful, underlying level we are one.

Part Two
Our Sacred Ascension Journey

Chapter 12
Day 1, Arrival in Mount Shasta

Having received all the instructions from Adama and Archangel Michael that we were going to, it was time to go to the Lemurians' home, Mount Shasta.

Since there are no direct flights from Fort Lauderdale to San Francisco, I briefly stopped in New York on Friday to check on the old homestead. Then I traveled west with Joel and David on an early flight the next morning. Jeff and George had flown a day before us. At San Francisco International Airport, we made a direct connection with a fuel-fumed small plane that took us on a short hop to Redding. After landing, we met the others, picked up a rental car, and the five of us together drove the hour north to Mount Shasta. It wasn't long before we began to see the mountain, which is huge. Peaking at 14,162 feet, it's the second highest volcano in the United States and visible from miles away. Thankfully, we were not going all the way to the snow cap. We would gladly leave that honor for the spaceships that reportedly come and go behind hidden clouds.

When we pulled in front of our "Donna Reed-style" five-bedroom cottage on Alma (meaning "soul" in Spanish) Street, it was just as my newfound friend Dianne Robbins had promised it would be. Placing my suitcase on the sidewalk beside me, I could not go inside the house right away because I was mesmerized by the magnificence of the mountain looming above us. I stood in the middle of the road to get a full view of the breathtaking spectacle. It was a bright sunny day and the top of the mountain glowed with snow. It looked like a beacon to the cosmos. My heart began to pound in my chest and tears began to flow. I was home.

My colleague Jeff came toward me and put an arm around my shoulder, saying, "You really feel it don't you?" Never before had I felt such a pull from a piece of nature. It was more than a mountain that I was connecting with; it was my Lemurian brothers' and sisters' eternal love. A wave of gratitude came over me for all they had done for our kind for so many thousands of years. Now I would be a part of them further revealing themselves to the world.

For an instant, the filmmaker in me came to life. Where was George Lucas now, I wondered? I checked myself. Although I suspected our adventure might make an excellent film, perhaps this was one story I was supposed to live exclusively for myself. The film could come later...

Finally I was able to release my gaze from the energetic pull of the mountain and step into our charming cottage home. The five of us scrambled in competition for the bedrooms we wanted, some of us exchanging our rooms, others keeping the ones we first conquered. My bedroom window had a full view of Mount Shasta, the window panes forming a cross framing the mountain. "This trip is about awakening the Christ consciousness," I observed inwardly, smiling to myself.

The five of us were together for the first time in a long time. For months, I'd mostly been connecting with the others via speaker phone from my home in Florida. There wasn't a natural bond among us as a group; it was our mission that had brought us together. At times we had petty disagreements that were irritating. It is clear to me that we were serving as mirrors for one another, even as we were serving as proxies for humanity. We were being forced to see ourselves in the others—or not. Learning to accept one another's differences was part of our challenge.

Each of us had a main gift and a main challenge. George had prepared a comprehensive itinerary—a bible, really—for the entire trip, which was wonderful. Organization was his gift, as well as, in my opinion, his mechanism for controlling the environment. David brought his open heart and his attachments. Joel brought his wisdom and his separation. Jeff brought his channeling and his self-doubt. For my part, I felt I had it all. I certainly had brought us together in Mount Shasta so I could learn to see myself, my control, my attachments, my separation, and my doubt. How I felt about them was how I felt about myself. All the things I ever had judged and shamed in others, and was judging and shaming in them, I had judged and shamed in myself. There were things I had not yet fully and compassionately accepted in myself that I needed to forgive in me and others.

I have a confession to make. As I began writing this book, I wished to reveal Lemuria to you, but I also needed to revisit the journey to review that which I still need to learn in order to enter into a complete union with fifth-dimensional reality. Hopefully, this book will show the way and be a reminder for me and you to hold true to it. May the beautiful Mount Shasta be a beacon of light preparing us to join in oneness. I know we have a long way to go, nonetheless I also know that all we need, all we have ever needed, lies within us. The first step is to become aware of it.

Having brought you to the mountain with me, please understand that my purpose is not to show you how well I can or cannot connect with Lemurians. Rather it is to show you the ways I need to grow and expand that will allow me and others to hold a permanent place in an eternal, heartfelt frequency.

Hopefully, showing you the difficulties and frustrations I've experienced in reaching the necessary level to connect with the Lemurians demonstrates that others can attain the same. I discovered that I must be willing to weed my garden before I can fertilize it. That was the process that Michael put me and my four companions through before, during, and (speaking for myself) after visiting Mount Shasta: weeding our gardens, the work of self-mastery.

First on our agenda was to stockpile the house with food. At the store, we did our best to buy high-vibrational food: organic produce, whole grains, and preservative-free, fresh juices.

Then we went to meet our mountain guide, Ashalyn, in person so we could center ourselves in our mutual purpose and ground our energy. We were anxious to meet the "sixth point" on our Star of David. It is unusual for five guys to do spiritual work; usually sacred trips are populated by a majority of women. Since we were all men, it was necessary to have a woman join us.

On the phone, Ashalyn's voice had sounded like an earth-fairy's, so I envisioned her as an etheric creature. Though there was, indeed, a youthful quality and lightness about her, her presence was more mature and grounded than her voice. It would soon be revealed how much we needed Ashalyn's maturity and gifts to fulfill our purpose. She and I both had distant memories of time spent together in a past life in Lemuria, so meeting her felt familiar to me. The other guys also bonded with Ashalyn right away. Probably all of us were together in Lemuria long ago. While at her office, we did a ceremony to connect with the energy of Mount Shasta. We had our team and we were ready. The next day would be our first day on the mountain.

After the group met Ashalyn, I personally needed and wanted to go and meet Dianne Robbins. Dianne would not be joining us in our mountain rituals, but in my heart I felt the trip was largely happening because of her influence. I was grateful for her original transmissions from the Lemurians as recorded in her books, for connecting me with our guide, Ashalyn, and for helping us to find the house we rented. The foundation of our journey was Dianne. Surely, our mission was linked to, and would be a continuation of her work. Jeff and Joel agreed to join me when I phoned to ask her to an early dinner on our first night in town.

Dianne and I had spoken several times on the phone and exchanged numerous emails during the period of preparation for the journey. She had welcomed my connection with Adama and immediately saw us as members of a soul family. Accepting the invitation, she agreed to meet us at the house, which was the place she resided when she moved to the area a few years earlier.

When Dianne drove up, I jumped into the front seat of her car through the passenger-side door and hugged her like a long lost sister. I drove with her while Joel and Jeff followed behind in the rental car, as she led us to her favorite Japanese restaurant. Appearing to be a delicate, other-worldly flower, she stood most of the time during dinner, without explaining why. But any perception of her that initially seemed strange melted away as she opened her heart and told us her story of moving to Mount Shasta to be near the Lemurians and complete her work.

We told her the details of the rituals we planned to do on the mountain and why we were doing them. She understood it as part of a natural progression of the Lemurian civilization being revealed to humanity. She wasn't the least bit resentful that the Lemurians had not picked her to open the gateway or that strangers had come into town to establish this important opening. It was as if she had been foretold of the entire up-coming series of events. We agreed that what we were doing there would not be discussed with others while we were in the process of doing it. Our purpose was sacred, something that would be done in privacy and reported only later.

During our preparation for the trip, Michael had re-minded us that the process of ascension happening on the planet at this time is a natural part of human evolution. "The fifth dimension is not a place you shall be going, rather it is a state of being that you will attain. Humanity will gradually establish the fifth dimension in your present realm." Every-one alive is now being given a choice to ascend or remain as they are. It is our human birthright to ascend sooner...or later. What appeared new was the possibility of experiencing ascen-sion in a physical body. "Yes," Adama had confirmed. "This is what is special about what you are being offered now."

After enjoying a lovely Japanese meal in an authentic setting, we kissed Dianne goodnight, knowing we'd see her at the full moon ceremony we planned to hold at the house a few nights later. We guessed we would run into her during the rest periods between our mountain rituals. Mount Shasta is a small, enchanted village; those who are supposed to run into one another do. We drove home, exhausted from our long day of travel and the change of time zones.

Back in our cozy mountain home, our group of five men gathered together. We very much wanted to check in with Michael and any other frequency of consciousness that had something to say to us about our impending journey. Jeff went into a trance and channeled brief messages from Jeshua (the energy of Christ consciousness) and Michael. Then, a brief welcome message came through from the Lemurians. Here are highlights from those messages.

Jeshua: "The Christ light now shines down upon you to envelop and protect you. Lord Jeshua comes down, leads, and opens a pathway to your heart."

Michael: "You are now ready to commence your new journey, which you will be taking for the rest of your lives. You are moving to open the Lemurian subculture gateway, joining it with fifth-dimensional energies from above and from within your heart. The specific portal is ready to be opened by the one you call the 'gatekeeper' and by you all. This will begin your first ritual.

"It is time to connect with the depth of your intuition. It is time to create a brand-new life that begins with the joining of your energies. Are you ready for the full encoding of who you are and your talents and gifts? Do you know that you are greater than you think you are? You may be wondering what is going on here. It is time to release thinking about the outcome, time to move into the natural state of beingness, which is joy. Are you excited about opening the gateway to your new life or are you in judgment of yourself, afraid of not being good enough yet? Are you still trying to fix yourself?

"We ask you now to say this mantra individually: *I now joyfully move through the journey, with excitation for life, to discover what I shall discover.* The journey now is the life to assist the light workers to create a new world of community, equality, harmony, and balance. Are you in equality and harmony with yourself? It is time to live your purpose in this lifetime. You will know your purpose at your last ritual. It is time to begin your service to humankind, if you so choose."

The Lemurians: "From within Mother Earth, we are here to welcome you as representatives of the Lemurian subculture. We open our hearts to welcome you and join you on your journey."

Michael had set all of the rituals we would be doing to commence at noon and end when the sun was at a 45-degree angle in the sky, at approximately 6 p.m. Every move we were supposed to make seemed to revolve around sacred geometrics, a subject I do not fully comprehend. Rather than getting hung up on such details, I committed myself to remembering that our journey was a sacred way for me to resolve false beliefs I held about myself and, thus, others.

"Hey!" I thought, "Haven't we created this journey to activate a new level of healing? My fellow proxies are just being who they are. No matter what irritations might exist among us, I know these guys are not here with the intention to annoy or harm me. I will pay attention to the mirrors being presented. If I feel challenged, I can choose to accept my mirrors—knowing they are revealing who I am and my feelings about myself to me—and I can be compassionate. I can choose another feeling. My responsibility is to heal myself and raise my vibration into oneness so I may eventually join my Lemurian brothers and sisters."

I said goodnight to the mountain through my bedroom window. I couldn't help being excited about being on her surface tomorrow though I was trying not to have any expectations. Climbing into bed that first night in Mount Shasta, I asked myself, "Can I allow myself to experience this journey without expecting to ascend into fifth-dimensional reality? Can I let everything unfold without knowing how it will happen? Can I release trying to control it?"

ॐ

As I drifted off to sleep, I chanted to myself and handed over any doubts or expectations that remained to the Lemurians, who I knew I would join while asleep.

Chapter 13
Day 2, Ritual 1

I woke up with the mountain waiting for me outside my bedroom window. In my head, I heard, "All your lifetimes are attached to *this one*. Trust is the core energy of the heart. Your heart trusts and knows. Its energy keeps you alive, keeps you a player upon the planet. Now, come and play with us." It was the mountain herself speaking to me.

Four of the five of us had a high-vibrational breakfast of fresh fruit and whole-grain cereal. George made a different choice: bacon and eggs. A little judgmental voice in me made a mental note of his choice—another judgment to heal! It was becoming clear to me that George and I had a karmic divide, meaning we were resolving different issues in our lives. Through seeing our differences surface repeatedly throughout the trip, I began to view him as one of my teachers.

After breakfast, since we didn't need to meet Ashalyn, our guide, at the mountain until 10 a.m., we had time to look around the village. It was a bright, sunny day, the only such day there would be until our rituals were completed. The village of Mount Shasta had had a long winter, so the area was still experiencing the phenomena of early spring. There were a multitude of colored flowers everywhere. The redbuds and the dogwoods were abloom. Tulips and little blue and purple flowers were popping out of the ground at our feet. It was like a magic fairly land. No, it *was* a magic fairy land. "You could see fairies here," I reminded myself. Right away I sensed that we were in a higher frequency place than elsewhere—and it wasn't just due to the elevation. No matter where we looked, Mount Shasta stood watch over us, ever present.

Ours wasn't your basic rental cottage. The house was maintained by a spiritual community dedicated to serving those who came to the area on sacred journeys. It had a stone labyrinth in the garden. A sign over the kitchen sink read: "This is the purest mountain water in the world, so drink to your heart's delight." This was no joke. The water had so much *prana,* or life force, that I almost didn't need to eat when I drank it. Its properties reminded me of the water in Telos.

The early 1960s rock musical *Hair* was a motivational force behind my move to New York as a young man. The music, words, look of the cast, and the freedom that the show depicted reflected my aspirations, which were not entirely manifested when I went directly to Madison Avenue. On the outside, I had been a clean-cut ad man. On the inside, it was as if I had wild hair. Being in the village of Mount Shasta was like going through an instant time warp to the era of my twenties because the people walking the streets had the look of the hippy movement. But they gave off a different vibe than I remembered. Among the long, flowing clothes and hair I saw, there were crystal clear eyes that connected with my soul. Yes, we passed the occasional tourist and out-of-towner, like us, but many of the residents looked and also felt like the modern-day Lemurians.

The streets were lined with flowering plants and trees, and volcanic mountain peaks framed the sky. Between the living water and air, you didn't need much food in this town. It sure would be an inexpensive place to live! And I heard the rents weren't bad either. This was a paradise on earth, right at the base of the Lemurian home site. It was obvious that the community reflected the life beneath Mount Shasta. All the permanent residents had chosen to be there "on purpose."

Later, I learned that over a third of the children in the community are Lemurians who have incarnated as human beings. The Inner Earth Lemurians are allowing some of their children to come to the surface as a test market and teaching.

The storefronts along the main streets were mostly dedicated to promoting spiritual wisdom and selling crystals. The people in the stores and streets all felt so loving and welcoming. The town felt like home.

The main hang out/meeting place was Berryvale Grocery and Café, a large natural food store and restaurant. When I asked Dianne how she got herself settled when she first arrived, she said, "I just put on my 'Telos, Lemuria' tee-shirt, hung out in Berryvale, and I had a community of friends in short order." All the food in the place was high-energy fare: fresh-baked breads, live juices, and raw foods. There was also an array of homeopathic remedies and "fifth dimension" fashions, clothing that was free-flowing and used nature colors and designs. Yes, I definitely felt like I was back in Greenwich Village in 1968, only this time I had a different mission and much greater awareness.

"Now take and own this journey, and know you are of this energy. You can know your Lemurian-hood here, for we have done it all before you. We are the same, we are one," Adama echoed my own sentiments in my ear.

Before we met Ashalyn and went to the mountain for the first time, I wanted to go to the headwaters of the Sacramento River. Out of a small opening in a rock face, incredibly pure water flows (a small, yet powerful source) that forms the beginning of this mighty river. Joel and I had been to this site on our trip to Mount Shasta ten years earlier, and I knew the place was sacred. Local people came daily to collect water for drinking and I wanted to do the same. Some used it to water their gardens and their jars of growing bean sprouts. Some people even came from hundreds of miles a way to bottle it and take it home. Jeff, Joel, and I went to the waters.

"Kneel down and touch the water," I said to Jeff. "Feel its energy." He did. "Now cup your hands and drink it," I commanded.

"Wow, I never tasted or felt water like that!" Jeff exclaimed. In my head, I could hear Adama reminding me that their water in Lemuria was like this, and adding that the water on the planet's surface was once this pure and could be again. We filled our containers from the sacred pool at our feet and then headed to the sporting goods store to rent cold weather mountain gear.

Even though the sun was out, Ashalyn warned us how the weather can shift in an instant up on the mountain. It was best that we rent heavy-duty weather gear for our visit: outfits, including overalls, hats, and boots, which could be worn over other clothing to produce layers for warmth and dryness. We had a collective laugh looking at ourselves in the mirror in the store. I don't know if we looked more like a motorcycle gang or the Beverly Hillbillies gone wrong, but there was no doubt we would be warm and dry if snow or rain came.

We arrived at the office of Ashalyn's company, Shasta Vortex Adventure Tours, which is located at the edge of the village, as close to the base of the mountain as you could possibly get. She shared albums of photos of groups from all over the world that she had taken up on the mountain. Some of the photographs had "spiritual orbs" in them, images of spiritual beings her camera had picked up over the years, looking like patches of light. In addition to the Lemurians, it appeared that the mountain was alive with many high-frequency beings, such as fairies and other elementals.

"Have no expectations," I told myself. "This trip is about self-mastery and awakening, not seeing unicorns and dragons." Adama had once explained to me that unicorns and dragons do exist on the mountain in the frequency of the fifth dimension. Apparently many animals that used to live on the surface and are now considered extinct have actually ascended to live in peace and harmony, unseen by humans.

The six of us (Joel, Jeff, David, George, Ashalyn, and me) divided into two four-wheel drive vehicles and then headed up the mountain. Michael had told us that our first ritual, the purpose of which was to activate the main marker to the Lemurian gateway, would need to be done at an elevation of 4,500 feet. Ashalyn was instructed by Michael to find this marker before we arrived.

Still on hard pavement and heading upward, Ashalyn pulled off the side of the road for a moment. "See that parcel of land over there?" she asked. "That is going to be my Lemurian spiritual center some day. It will be a retreat for those who wish to stay on the mountain in order to be in the constant frequency of all that is here. People from all over the world will be coming to Mount Shasta and they'll need this." Back at home, Adama had alerted us that we were beginning our journey just before a major influx of people came. "This is to become one of the most powerful vortices on the planet to assist in the ascension process," he explained. A vortex is a spiral pattern of energy.

Shifting into a higher frequency of consciousness, I could see an etheric, magnificent Lemurian city in the distant meadows on the mountain, its crystalline temples and homes shimmering in the sunlight. Ashalyn's Lemurian city already existed in another dimension. Now her intentions would bring it into reality in the third dimension. It was her mission, her purpose to do so. We drove on...

As we continued our ascent of the mountain, I enjoyed looking at the ancient evergreen trees along the way, towering above us like great sentinels guarding the mountain. Once in awhile, we could see evidence of loggers. "Do they allow cutting of the trees here?" Joel, who had studied forest science in college, asked.

"Yes," Ashalyn replied. "We are fighting to stop it, but there are powerful forces keeping the loggers in place." One of the magnificent trees marked our turnoff onto a rough dirt road. We bumped along for some time, until Ashalyn said, "We'll park here and walk the rest of the way."

We were high on the altitude and the panorama around us. After donning our backpacks over our heavy weather gear, we felt like pack mules on a mission of mercy to save ourselves and the world. I kept telling myself, "Breathe deeply and stay in the moment." Sometimes it felt overwhelming not to truly understand all of the reasons why we were there. The phrase "proxies for humankind" kept swirling in my head. What *exactly* did that mean? I still felt a little weak from my healing crisis before leaving home, but I was eager for the adventure to begin.

Ashalyn was familiar with the terrain since she had hiked it to find the main marker. So, carrying the dousing rods in hand that we would need to verify the Lemurian gateway and any vortices we would create in the future, she took the lead. The rest of us fell in line behind her.

Across steep, narrow, rocky paths we hiked, doing our best to maintain our footing and balance in order to avoid falling into the ravine below. Up, down, up, down, the path crawled. Then we came to a large crop of huge boulders that seemed to be an entrance to something. "Stop and acknowledge the rocks," Ashalyn ordered. "Let us ask permission to go forward." We knew then that the path directly ahead would lead us to the main marker. We stopped, caught our breath, and held onto the rocks (as if to absorb some of their strength), silently asking permission to go forward. Then we hiked another mile through a fairly level and straight "road."

Ultimately, Ashalyn pulled out our set of dousing rods, which she held in both hands. From an initial crossed position, the copper rods quickly swung forward. "This is the energetic border of the main marker," she said. We had been instructed by Michael that we needed to be at the marker by 11:30 a.m. in order to activate it. The Lemurian gateway was to be opened precisely at noon. We drew a line across the dirt path to mark the point of this energetic zone. Onward we marched, like foreign legionnaires, not going into battle, but into a place of truth.

After another thirty minutes or so, our mountain matriarch pointed toward a rock on our right. "That's the main marker." We could see an old, dead tree pointing at it that helped her find it originally. It was like God's finger instructing, "There!" As large as the rock was, it appeared only to be revealing a portion of its mass. Looking like a piece of an ancient escarpment, we felt that the remainder of this main marker was connected all the way down to Earth's core. "Here is just enough for you to work with," Mother Earth seemed to be saying. The rock looked familiar since Ashalyn had sent pictures of it to us before the trip.

With little time to spare, we dropped our backpacks and, as instructed by Michael, put our crystals (clear and citrine) on top of the marker. At exactly 11:30 a.m., the six of us gathered in a circle around the main marker to open an energy vortex. We surrounded the marker with our group energy and set an intention for the rituals to come. As a group, we would now always check in with the main marker before proceeding with any further ritual acts, including the creation of vortices. We agreed never to influence it with our individual energy.

Ritual 1, Opening the Lemurian Gateway

As we were leaving the main marker to prepare for activation of the Lemurian gateway, I heard Adama say, "Change the energies of judgment, expectation, guilt, and shame. These lower vibrations keep you in the third dimension and prevent the fifth dimension from being available to you. There are no feelings in the fifth dimension that support judgment. When you catch yourself judging yourself or others, turn it over to a higher realm."

Michael's instructions for every ritual we would be doing on the mountain had been channeled for us by Jeff prior to the trip. Before almost every ritual, however, Michael came in with an additional message. For the sake of spiritual posterity and so you may experience the feeling of the actual rituals, I plan to use as much of the transcription of his recorded words as possible. During the rituals, tasks often were assigned to us to complete as individuals. I shall share my portion of these with you again, so in reading you may have something akin to the actual experience of the guided journey and actually take the journey yourself!

Adama offered some good advice about the journey and about reaching fifth-dimensional reality when he said, "Throw away all your expectations about how things should be and what you should have; simply throw it away. Then, with joy and gratitude, start creating and living your life in the present moment, open yourself wide to receive the desires of your heart, with no expectations about how it will come out. Just allow and be open to the surprise."

Our setting was the most pristine, magical mountain forest you could imagine on a sunny, bright-blue sky day. There were snowcapped mountain peaks all around us, trees so ancient that they have seen the coming and going of the follies of humankind, and a silence that had a sacred presence.

Into this came the six of us who had both chosen and been chosen to participate in one of the most important happenings that ever would take place for our race on the planet. That this event may only ever be recorded here and that many people will never know about it, understand it, or believe in it makes its meaning and outcome no less significant.

Fortunately, Jeffry was generously willing to go into trance and channel for us before and during the adventure. Through him, the rest of us were guided to do our service. Here are Michael's exact instructions, as he gave them to us at noon, just prior to opening the Lemurian gateway:

"You are now ready to open the Lemurian gateway, which lies at the center of the time-space continuum of your Mother Earth. You are now ready to connect deeply with your heart space, Mother Earth, and the Lemurian energies. You are ready to open the vortex!

"You are ready to choose your gatekeeper in order to open the depth and breadth of the Lemurian gateway. You have found that vortex; you are in the midst of that vortex. The gatekeeper will find the doorway, the entrance way, the gateway.

"You have your large mushroom-shaped citrine crystal in your right hand. It represents the Christ consciousness, the Jeshua consciousness, the All-mighty consciousness that comes to you, streaming down upon your heart.

"We ask you to now move into silence.

"Choose now the gatekeeper."

Immediately, David said, "George," and the rest of us agreed. It did seem right.

Honestly, I was a tad puzzled. George was dressed in a long, saffron-colored ceremonial robe, like a Tibetan monk would wear, and it seemed to me that he had dressed for the role. Ever since we had learned in one of our planning sessions with Michael that there would be a gatekeeper, it appeared he had intended to be the gatekeeper. He had sent me an email to this effect a week or so earlier when I mentioned five citrine crystals that Adama had asked me to bring along. In that email, he told me he thought I was trying to control the journey by suggesting myself as the gatekeeper. Maybe I was. At the time I mentioned the five crystals, I had thought I was simply repeating a message from Adama. In retrospect, I am not sure.

It was true that since the trip had been initiated by me, in my heart I had hoped I would be chosen to be the gatekeeper to my beloved Lemurians. But I also knew I must surrender and allow the event to unfold with neutrality. The trip was not about me or for me exclusively, but for the healing and transformation of all humanity. In the moment after George was chosen, I paused and caught my breath. My hint of disappointment dissolved.

Then, Michael unexpectedly announced, "The gatekeeper will be accompanied by an overseer, the overseer of the Lemurian subculture, the ultimate overseer in your five-some who will accompany the gatekeeper and guide the gatekeeper to open the gate."

My heart started pounding. "*This* must be me," I thought.

"You see," Michael continued, "the gatekeeper is a conduit for the overseer's energy. The overseer is the connector who will guide the gatekeeper to the specific area of the Lemurian vortex. The gatekeeper will hold the key and will point the key in the direction as guided by the overseer."

Taking a moment to address us on a personal level, Michael said, "You have arrived. You have arrived at your mission. You have arrived at the precipice of world service. Each of you is present and available, open, honest, truthful, and moving into the depth and breadth of your heart space to initiate this journey. At the end of your third and final ritual, you will know your purpose in this mission and your purpose in this lifetime.

Then he continued with his explanation of the task at hand. "The overseer will now guide the gatekeeper and they will move in tandem to the chosen location. In his right hand, the gatekeeper will simply hold the large citrine crystal, and he will recite the mantra you were given. The gatekeeper will hold the specific energy, as the Lemurian energy comes out beneath Mother Earth. The overseer and the gatekeeper in tandem are the proxies for humankind in this ritual.

"It is very important for you to understand that you are all gatekeepers. You will be forming six other vortices connected to this central one (the Lemurian gateway) and each of you will be the individual gatekeeper of one of those vortices."

Then he asked, "Will the one most deeply connected to Lemurian energy come forth now?"

Knowing this was me, I stepped forward without hesitation. I had never felt such joy and love in my life. Tears were streaming down my face.

"We ask you to move within," Michael said. "Each hold your energetic space for this most wonderful and glorious soul *to go home* at this time."

These were the words I had been waiting for; my heart had hungered for this moment. I felt myself joining my Lemurian brothers and sisters. They were surrounding me and I was finally one with them again. When I was working at Industrial Light & Magic, the studio that invented the special visual effect called morphing that allows one image to merge into another, never had I imagined what morphing might feel like. But that was what was happening to me in that moment: I was morphing, becoming one with my true home: fifth-dimensional consciousness.

"Travel home, dear one. Travel home," Michael encouraged. "Allow yourself the freedom to connect with your brothers and sisters. Connect to the past lifetimes you experienced in the most luxurious of places." I remembered being a priest in a handsome temple. "You also saw the destruction of Lemuria in this lifetime you are seeing." I recalled how I stayed behind and comforted my people as the waters came over us during that catastrophic annihilation.

When Michael said, "Now you are ready to go home," the strongest yearning I have ever felt came over me. In that instant, I knew that at some date in the future I would be able to return to Telos *in this body* through doing the self-mastery and ascension work to which I am committed.

Michael went on, speaking to me alone. "Now you are ready to guide your brethren on a journey home. You are now ready to guide the gatekeeper." To the rest of group, he said, "The gatekeeper will be the conduit for the energy of the overseer. Go home, dear ones, go home."

I walked around for some time, opening my heart in order to allow "my people," the Lemurians, to direct me to their energetic doorway in the midst of the mighty Mount Shasta, our homeland. Finally I was drawn to a clearing in a meadow. A small, proud evergreen tree stood in this clearing, quite alone among others that were giants. I recognized it as the gateway to Lemuria. I had not known the true purpose of the five small citrine crystals that Adama asked me to bring until that moment. I had thought we were only going to use a single, large citrine at the gateway opening, but now I understood that the ones I was asked to bring also had a purpose: They were for the five of us to hold and use while George was doing his work as gatekeeper.

Seemingly out of nowhere, I looked overhead and saw military jets and helicopters flying above us. They were dark in color. "The 'dark side' at work," I thought, jumping to a conclusion that they were watching us. Maybe there was too much *Star Wars* at work in my head, but it felt as if someone had warned them of what we were about to do. In any case, I got distracted. When their sound passed, I regained my focus. I knew we were protected from outside interference.

"When the overseer points the gatekeeper in the specific area and entrains the Lemurian energies to the gatekeeper," Michael instructed, "the overseer will step back and become part of the additional souls forming a circle around the gatekeeper. The gatekeeper will then, at high noon, recite the mantra. Precisely as the gatekeeper is reciting the mantra, the five other souls with the five mini-citrine crystals that the overseer gave you in your right hands will point them towards the sky in order to usher in the energy of the fifth dimension. As he recites the mantra, the gatekeeper will then point the golden key, the large citrine, to the overseer's point.

"At this moment, the overseer will be connecting energetically to the most important lifetime he spent in the Lemurian subculture and to important lifetimes to come connected to the specific Lemurian energy of this vortex. He is now merging within it. He, the overseer, will share private words with the gatekeeper; these are not for others to hear."

These words, when I spoke them, were about the continued work George and I could do together to bring forward the truth of Lemuria.

"Once the final word of the mantra is spoken, you'll all lower your arms with the small citrines pointing to the sky, stand for ten seconds, and allow the energies to fully come into your third dimension. The only souls having to do with the Lemurian energies are the overseer and the gatekeeper. You others are to focus on the fifth-dimensional energies above, as you raise your right hands with the small citrines to the sky."

Then we followed Michael's instructions. Here is the mantra we spoke as we performed the ritual: *We now clear this area of all low-vibration energies that no longer can support the highest good of the connection to the Lemurian subculture, in order to open the gateway for those who are ready to live their purpose in this third-dimensional realm, for those who are ready to connect with the energies, messages, vibrations, and resonance of the Lemurian subculture that will assist and guide the light workers on their paths to create the new world of community, harmony, and equality.*

"The gatekeeper points the large citrine crystal down to the ground, then passes the crystal to the guide, the overseer, and around to the others. At noon, after the last word of the mantra has been spoken, the gateway is opened for all eternity. The Lemurians below and the beings in the fifth dimension above are joined. Mother Earth's ascension process has begun for all those within and upon her body. Things will never be the same."

If you pay attention, you can already see the changes Michael mentioned coming into place. *We and the world will fully come to know what this event truly means in our near future.* We were merely chosen as proxies for humankind for this one purpose of opening the vortices on Mount Shasta; we are no wiser or better than others.

In conclusion, Michael asserted, "Your journey is in full force. The gateway is open. We now take our leave and leave you be in all that you have done." With that, Jeffry came out of trance, blinking his eyes. We welcomed him back and thanked him.

The Vortex of Intention

After opening the Lemurian gateway, we paused to have the lunch we were carrying in our backpacks and to ground ourselves. It was difficult to comprehend everything about what had just taken place. This much we knew: There had been a joining of inner and outer higher energies that would allow the inhabitants of our planet a pathway to move forward in our evolution into the fifth dimension. It was a unique event for which we had been chosen to represent humankind. And now for a tuna sandwich...that brought me back down to Earth quickly.

Part of our day's purpose was to connect our individual energy with the main marker. Another purpose was to open the Lemurian gateway. These two things accomplished, it was time to locate and create the vortex of intention and the vortex of the crystalline children. Overall during our trip, we would be establishing a six-pointed star (a Star of David), formed by six vortices that were equidistant from the main marker and each other. Two points (vortices) would be opened during each of our three rituals. By adding a third dimension to this six-pointed star, rather than viewing it two-dimensionally as lines drawn on a flat surface, it becomes a *merkabah,* an energetic vehicle that can assist us in moving ourselves and the planet into ascension.

The vortices we were looking for could be anywhere on the mountain. We would have to use both our intuition and the dousing rods we had brought along to assist us in finding their exact locations. Throughout the week, we would take turns finding the specific vortices, even though some of us appeared more facile at identification than others.

Off we marched into we-knew-not-where to find and create our vortex of intention. We were like blood hounds on a scent that only a discerning nose could find. Ultimately we would hike for many miles, usually in virgin forest in our mountainous landscape, sometimes on footpaths. In the silence and smells of the forest floor, we had the feeling no human had ever been there—or certainly, not recently. The footing was often challenging, filled with rocks and thick vegetation, and so was breathing the thin atmosphere of the high-altitude terrain. We were a hardy band of pilgrims on a mission fueled by inner- and outer-Earth energies. It was not a journey for the weak-of-body. This was definitely a mental, emotional, spiritual, and *physical* experience. I allowed the others to take the lead, as I was pacing myself to conserve my energy.

We had two vortices to locate on this day. This set us up with a pattern that lasted during the entire trip. When we did find a vortex—usually after several failed attempts—we would immediately celebrate by building an altar of pine cones, rocks, branches, ferns, leaves, and whatever else we could muster from Mother Earth right on the spot. Mother was most generous with the items she made available to us for the construction of our many grand creations. After building the altar, we would do a ceremony together to connect with the energy.

Throughout our ceremonies, our purpose would always be to combine our individual energy and the now-open energy of the Lemurian subculture with each new vortex we were establishing. The most important part of the mountain journey came to be the inner journey that each of us was experiencing as proxies. The healing and raising of our individual vibrations was what would connect us to the fifth dimension. We had to do the work—and so do you, dear reader.

Each vortex-opening ceremony had a different crystal assigned to it. For the first ceremony, it was *amethyst*. We had been instructed to hold an amethyst, a crystal designating the heart space, in our left hand. Through this specific ceremony, we would be forming aspects of ourselves based in Lemurian subculture that would allow masculine and feminine energy to unite within our heart space. The balance of these two energies is essential in the fifth dimension.

Before the trip, Jeff had channeled Michael for us, who explained, "You will unite within the vortex of intention and then branch out as you would imagine a tree would branch out after rooting into the soil of Mother Earth. Those roots, in this case, will branch into six equidistant vortices. Each vortex will represent an aspect of you that needs to be expressed to the world.

"During the first ceremony, we shall ask each of you to make two lists. You're going to write these down. The first list represents five aspects of you that you need to release: your old unhealed habits, patterns of attachment, and rituals to avoid your feelings. The second list will be a declaration of five aspects of why you are here—meaning, your purpose in life."

We had taken paper and pens out of our notebooks at lunchtime. When it came time to write the first list, we all whipped out our notebooks and began scribbling furiously. I wrote: "I wish to release shame of myself and others, judgment of myself and others, learning through physical illness, control, and non-acceptance." Once we had read our lists aloud to each other, Michael had instructed us to put all the aspects we were looking to release into a burning bowl and, after saying a mantra, bury them on the mountain.

Collectively, we said: *"I now release these old aspects to Mother Earth. I proclaim acceptance, compassion, and my love for me. I now release these in acceptance, compassion, and love for me."*

The second list we each made also would be shared aloud before it was put in a sacred container (David had brought some lovely biodegradable ones) and buried in another location. The list was to declare five aspects of who we are and five aspects of why we are here on earth.

For my "Who am I?" list, I wrote: "I am an eternal, spiritual being having a human experience; a healer of self, assisting others to heal; a teacher; a messenger of higher frequencies; and a Lemurian."

For my "Why am I here?" list, I wrote: "I am here to learn to love myself and others, to assist in the ascension process, to bring truth (long hidden) into the world, to reconnect with Lemuria, and to be one with all there is."

As each vortex was activated, we would be standing in a circle at arms' length from one another, meditating and sharing around the natural altar we had built together. The altars would come together almost like magic, one more beautiful and larger than the previous one. Once we would locate a vortex, which took us up to a couple of hours and involved many miles of hiking, the altars were an expression of our joy at finding the vortex. The dousing rods helped us confirm the locations, when we were in doubt. The copper rods were exact in pointing the way to our true vortex. At each vortex, one of us always knew when it was time to leave and another of us where the next vortex was. The day became about allowing the heart to lead the way.

The Vortex of the Crystalline Children

Feeling very excited to find the next vortex, we fanned out to see if we could get intuitive hits about where the next vortex would be. Ashalyn insisted we remain within eyeshot of one another so no one would get lost on the mountain. We agreed (also because even though we were having individual experiences, and fulfilling our divine soul missions, we were also keenly aware that we were working as a collective "we" for humanity).

It was much harder to find this vortex than the first one. It took us a couple of hours. Every so often, someone would sense energy and call out to us, "I think I found it." Then we would regroup to see if we could confirm the accuracy of this impression. Ashalyn was our designated douser who would confirm any suspected finding with her rods. In this case, we had many false discoveries. Each time it required us to surrender to not-knowing to allow the possibility of the next step to arise. It was all about knowing to trust our intuition. Finally, David found it and there was a clear knowing from the rest of us that this was the right location.

This vortex was to be known as the vortex of the crystalline children. Crystalline children are children being born now who are connected in their genetic code, their DNA, to the crystalline grid at the center of the planet and possess the wisdom to assist humanity in our ascension process. By doing our work with this vortex, we would facilitate the rest of humanity having access to the same wisdom. As the last ceremony of the day, we would remain at this vortex until the sun was at a 45-degree angle in the sky, approximately 6 p.m.

Once again, we individually and collectively connected with the vortex. Then we gathered our energies and went into a deep meditative state, this time bringing forward our wounded little child, our wonder child, and our magic child, three children within each of us that appeared to us as we stood at the vortex of the crystalline children. Our purpose was to heal that which needed to be healed within ourselves in order for that healing to reflect and mirror out into humanity.

In the healing arts, integrating these energetic inner children is an important aspect of healing. The wounded child is the part of one's self that was wounded in childhood and affects the course of one's adulthood. The wonder child is the part of one's self that through the imagination knows all things are possible. The magic child knows exactly how to manifest and how to achieve them those possibilities. We are born with wonder and magic, and only through our wounding do we lose contact with them. All people have these energetic children within them.

The portion of the western United States that we were hiking through was once part of the land mass of Lemuria, a huge continent much larger than North America. West of us, it had sunk into the ocean. We were mindful that it was a part of our divine soul plan to perform our rituals as a universal task: to create the Star of David for eternity, thus balancing the male and female energy in this sacred area and creating vortices encoded with the energy from below and above as well as our own, and holding the key at this specific time to open the Lemurian gateway.

My magic child came to me at this vortex and reminded, "It is not about wanting to move into a fifth-dimensional frequency because you expect it to take away the third dimension. It's about moving into the fifth dimension because it's who you are, your truth, and your next step."

My wonder child continued, "It is a vibration, a new way of being to live in the fifth dimension. The mind complicates and prevents it. True spirituality comes from the heart of the wonder child. It's that simple. You are feeding the mind at the expense of your heart. Your heart knows all already."

My wounded child then asked me to compassionately accept my wounds in order that I might forgive myself and those who had wounded me. He told me that the wounds were merely a way to learn and grow, "Your wounds are the source of life, just as life springs from the death of your wounded self."

Then, in unison, all three children chanted, "Ascension does not end in the fifth dimension. It's the beginning of a wondrous and eternal journey. You'll ascend from one level to another forever. This is your birthright." As the sun approached 45 degrees, I saw the three of them walking away from me through the forest hand and hand.

Everyone in the group intuitively knew when the day was done.

Day's End

We had completed our first day's ritual upon Mount Shasta and so we began our hike back to our vehicles. The exhilaration of the day prevented the six of us from feeling exhaustion. We had a long way to go, on the way passing the Lemurian gateway and our main marker. These would become familiar landmarks in the days ahead. Now it was time to return to the third dimension. Interestingly, the contrasts in the group on and off the mountain would be revealing.

After reaching our vehicles, we were still fairly energized from the day's activities, so as a group of one mind and spirit we decided to drive further up the mountain (matching our mood), rather than downward and home. Michael had designated that the main marker be at the elevation of exactly 4,500 feet, about a third of the way to the peak. So we decided we would drive as far as the snow line would allow. The winter had been long, so there was still much snow just a few feet from where we had been. We made it to about 7,000 feet in altitude and the snow banks were ten-feet high. The views on the ascent were breathtaking. We could see valleys and other volcanic peaks all around us. The air was crisp and pure. It was at this point, a few years earlier, that several groups of travelers had encountered people from Inner Earth telling them all about their civilization beneath the mountain.

Jeff, who is a professional photographer, pulled out his camera and began shooting the mountain panoramas. As we drove back, every half mile or so down the road another vista invited us, "Stop and enjoy me." So we did. We filled our lungs with the high-altitude air. Having been in flat Florida for several months, I found looking at mountain views refreshing.

We rode in silence and awe of the day, until Ashalyn finally broke the quiet by saying, "I have had many amazing days on this mountain, but I have never experienced anything like this before." It was clear that she had become an integral part of our six-pointed star.

Chapter 14
The Second Night on the Mountain

As we continued our descent and the sun was dropping over the mountain ridges, we paused once again at the proposed site of Ashalyn's Lemurian City. When I moved my mind out of the way and opened my heart, there before me stood the city's crystal formations, reflecting the surrendering sunlight in golden and purple hues. "Soon our two civilizations will join," I heard Adama whisper. "The tasks you performed today will assist us in knowing one another and being one again." I wanted to share what I was seeing and hearing, but as inspiring as it was to me, I didn't share. I felt shy about sharing Adama's messages with the others. George and David only seemed to honor Michael's messages and not those from Adama that were coming through me.

Looking back, I know now I could have stood in my truth and power more during the trip. But I wanted to avoid conflict. After all, the trip was about the inner journey and service to our race; it did not matter what any of the others thought or felt. That's why we were perfect proxies. Each of us represented a different aspect of humanity. That included holding different attitudes. Even though I felt frustrated and sad at times, I knew and accepted this truth.

What the six of us had just been through on the mountain was profound, even considering the spiritual paths that had led us here. All of us had participated in sacred journeys around the world. This trip was my fifth such adventure. It was David's fourteenth. But, as extraordinary as those trips were, none involved the combination of self-mastery and inner- and outer-Earth connections this one did. We were taking advantage of a special, limited portal of opportunity for our planet that was like no other. The journeys I had been on in the past to places like Stonehenge, Sedona, Egypt, and Brazil, seemed to be about what was "out there" rather than the "here and now." Maybe those earlier journeys were leading to this one? It really did not seem plausible to me that we could have chosen to take this one if we had not done the others. The situation was a perfect setup. As Michael and Adama would say, "It is always perfect, dear ones in the third dimension, for what you need to learn."

Even though there was a mutual desire to separate and absorb the day's events, it seemed organic for us to be together for dinner. Ashalyn selected one of her favorite haunts for our meal. It was nice to strip off the cold weather gear and to have a chair and table to sit at, along with some food options that did not come out of a backpack. At dinner, how different our personalities were was evident. Our third-dimensional dissimilarity, which had become similarity during our fifth-dimensional mountain experiences, had re-emerged.

George immediately ordered a Lemurian Beer (a draft produced by a local brewery), and proceeded to get a buzz. Even though Michael had suggested we stick to high-vibrational food for the duration of the trip, he did not mean "get high," which lowers one's vibration. George's personality promptly shifted from a fifth- to a third-dimensional frequency. David was consistent in bringing the conversation back to how the day had affected him, seeming not to realize that everyone had been similarly affected. Joel seemed relaxed, but annoyed with George and David. Jeff sat at the table, observing everyone's behavior closely. For my part, I knew that I had to stay neutral. Ashalyn seemed thrilled to be a part of our adventure, but confused at the contrast between our behavior on and off the mountain. The separation between us when we weren't doing sacred service would last for the entire journey. Even so, we were all there to do the tasks in spite of our third-dimensional frequency.

As we enjoyed our meal and reflected on the day and one another, fatigue began to hit me. Since my body was still on East Coast time and this was not your basic workday, my energy drifted into the loving frequency of Lemuria where my fatigue abated.

"It is now time for you to make the differentiation between your true identity and the illusion of the third dimension. It must come through your heart, child of the awakened heart, not your mind," Adama reminded me. "Ask in every moment of the now is this a third-dimensional vibration or a fifth-dimensional vibration? If it is third-dimensional vibration, turn it over to a higher realm and ask, 'What am I to learn from it?' Let higher realms purify the energy for you."

"Your job is simply to trust and to love your healing without expected results, surrendering to the unknown," Adama added.

"It is time now to learn that you can embody your divinity. Experience divine union with yourself first, and then with the other proxies," Adama continued.

My consciousness popped back to the dinner table. It was time to pay the check and leave. I suddenly felt overwhelming love for myself and my companions. Even though that could possibly shift at any moment, maybe it would not go as far into the third dimension the next time. Jeff said, "I know everyone is tired, but I feel Michael has something to say before we all go to bed. Let's gather at our Alma Street house and hear his goodnight words."

In the sanctuary of our home away from home, the six members of our star huddled together to hear words from the archangelic realm of Michael, as channeled by Jeff Fasano, following our first ritual and day at the Lemurian home. *Note: For the purpose of spiritual history and those wishing to experience the complete journey, Michael's complete exact words are shared here.*

Michael: You have now completed your first ritual and opened the Lemurian gateway or portal. The fifth-dimensional energies are combining with the energies from the Lemurian subculture. In many ways, you have completed your first task on this journey, as you have implanted the first two outer vortices. Energetically, you are now beginning to go into your second ritual—and then to implant the additional outer vortex, leading and moving toward your final ritual. These rituals have been designed to release old patterns, rituals, karma, and old aspects of old lifetimes.

Does anyone of you have questions?

Joel: Can you further explain what was meant by the Lemurian energy coming up and the fifth-dimensional energy coming down?

Michael: Balancing of the masculine and feminine energies. It's as simple as that. The Lemurian gateway is a portal in Mother Earth for balanced feminine energy. The gatekeeper and overseer performed the task of opening the fifth-dimensional energy of the Lemurian subculture coming from below. Others of you, holding the citrine crystals pointing to the sky, were proxies for the fifth-dimensional energy coming from above. These proxies for humankind ushered in a specific fifth-dimensional masculine energy that is assertive in nature to combine with the compassionate feminine energy moving up through Lemuria.

The basis for your journey is about giving and receiving in balance, about balancing the male and female energies in your human earthly plane. This is the importance of the fifth-dimensional energies. As you move along in your rituals and journey, you will see to a greater extent the importance for you of bringing in the specific fifth-dimensional energies that moved through you.

Joel: Can you be more specific about fifth-dimensional energies?

Michael: In the depth and breadth of your heart space, is a frequency unique to you and unto you. That frequency resonates in a specific fifth-dimensional realm. Each of you resonates at a specific frequency through the depth and breadth of your heart space. This frequency in your heart space has a matching frequency in the fifth-dimensional realm whether you are aware of this or not. This is the frequency that connected with your heart space through the citrine crystal. Above and below have joined.

What you have done is connected with a specific frequency in the fifth-dimensional realm to bring in that frequency and combine it with the Lemurian energies, to hold the flow in place. You'll now be building and creating outer vortices that will keep this flow in place at all times.

Whether you are conscious of it or not, the energy that you connected with in the fifth dimension is the energy that resonates and vibrates in your own heart space.

George: Sometimes we were sure about finding a vortex. Other times, we were confused. Can you give us any clarity on this?

Michael: It is an individual, specific situation, based upon your soul fragments' divine plan and based upon the situation. That's why we ask you to move into your heart space to connect with your intuition. Each specific situation will be different in your entire life. In this specific situation, locating the first outer vortex seemed easier to you than locating the second outer vortex. But when you came finally upon the second vortex, it was also natural, easy, and free. You all resonated with that vortex.

Everything in life on your earthy plane is not the same. You will have different experiences in different situations. So you had a different experience in a different situation. You had a different experience locating the first vortex from the experience of unlocking the Lemurian gateway. Each experience in life is different. It all depends upon how you respond to it.

George: The vortices are supposed to be equidistant. Are we actually creating an equidistant merkabah?

Michael: By in large you are. What you are forming is an encasement to hold the flow of fifth-dimensional and Lemurian energies in place. That is why it is most important to be in your heart space, not in your mind. There is a difference.

During the day, some of you vacillated between your mental body and your heart space. Some remained in your heart space. Some remained in your mental body. What can assist, support, and guide you in the next ritual is to determine, as an individual, where you were during the first ritual. Were you in your mind? Were you trying to control the outcome based upon what you thought it should be, could be, and would be? Or, were you in the depth and breadth of your heart space so as to allow it to be?

The most important thing for each and every one of you to remember is that this process is part of your soul's divine plan. Does it make sense? What was transpiring while you were looking for the vortex that each and every one of you can now see? Where did you think it should be, as opposed to where it actually was when you trusted your intuition and followed in your soul's divine plan from the depth and breadth of your heart space?

George: Some vortices seem to be similar in nature or configuration. Is this a reference point for us?

Michael: Allow it to unfold. In the divine plan, what you did was perfect. It is what it is, when it will be, as it is already. It is most important that you have been chosen, as you have now chosen to perform these tasks on your earthy plane. These tasks are based upon you allowing yourselves to remain in your heart space, in your intuition, to allow it to unfold perfectly. For these areas already exist; you are just finding them to implant your energy in them. They are there. It's up to you to release the mental body, to let go of trying to figure out what it should be, could be, might be, or is supposed to be. Allow it to be as it is.

What we suggest for support and guidance in your next ritual is to move into the depth and breadth of your heart space and remain conscious. When you begin to think about what the vortex is supposed to be, what it might look like, what it could or should be, let go. If you think, "The last one looked like this. Maybe the rest of them should look like this," let go.

These areas, these vortex locations already exist. This journey is about releasing the use of the five physical senses as your reference point in the third-dimensional realm. Move into your heart space and simply ask, "Does it resonate or doesn't it?" It is simply time, if you so choose, with acceptance and compassion, to realize consciousness. When you are in your mind, trying to control the outcome, allow yourself simply to follow your heart space.

Ashalyn: Do you have any further instructions for the next ritual?

Michael: Not necessarily. The instructions were laid out for each and every one of you. The most important thing is to review, through the eyes of acceptance and compassion, if you so choose, where you might have moved into your mental body and into an aspect of control. Be aware of wanting to figure things out. You are human beings. You are not perfect. But you are perfect at being perfectly where you are. Allow yourself the freedom to feel during this extraordinary time for each of you.

৯৯

Michael's review of our first day on the mountain was helpful, but I felt it was time to release myself into the fourth dimension of sleep. The moon was approaching fullness as I gazed out of my bedroom window to the mountain. Her snow-covered peaks were gleaming in the moonlight. I could just about figure out our position on the mountain, as I tried to remember the wonderful words and tasks for humankind that had been accomplished during the day and thought of all the amazing things that were taking place underneath the mountain's peaks...

Asleep, I could now easily go home.

Chapter 15
Day 3, Free Day

Michael had set up our schedule so we would have a day free between rituals. This gave us time to assimilate the energy and lessons of the rituals and the creation of the different vortices. Our third day in Mount Shasta was such a free day. It gave us the opportunity to rest from the physical, mental, and emotional challenges we'd just endured. Everyone in the group was fairly fit, but high-altitude hiking over rugged mountain terrain and the intensity of the type of spiritual work involved in opening the vortices had pushed most of us to our limits. We didn't say so at the time, but it did. Fortunately, we were able to gain much-needed energy from the pure water and air and high-vibrational food of the region. We seriously needed energy, since the weather was still very much that of early Northern California spring off of the mountain, and that of winter on the mountain. The weather would become even more of a challenge as time went on.

Ours was a two-bathroom house for five people—five men!—so we very much became like a family in our bathroom habits and while having meals together, meaning it was an intimate physical environment. George established himself in the kitchen and several times cooked meals for the rest of us as an offering from his heart. Sometimes we ate out. In either case, we always took our evening meals together knowing that Michael would be speaking to us afterwards.

The first order of our free day was to return the rental weather gear from the day before and then explore the aspects of the village and surrounding area that resonated with us.

Michael had suggested we spend the day by ourselves having individual journeys going or doing whatever we wanted. As we were in one of the most awesome natural areas in America there were lots of options to choose from, including making visits to Black Butte, Everitt Vista Point, Panther Meadows, Lake Siskiyou, Castle Crags, McCloud Falls, Fairy Falls, Glass Mountain, Stewart Mineral Springs, and Pluto's Cave. The names alone made me want to see them.

We would get to know the rental people in the weather gear store fairly well. For each day on the mountain we came in. I'm sure we didn't resemble usual mountain climbers or tourists. As we were being suited up each day, it turned into a mountain gear fashion show. We were achieving wardrobe looks never achieved before from mix-and-not-so-matched overalls, hats, gloves, and hiking boots. You could have mistaken us for Big Foot on the mountain in some of this gear!

After returning the gear, what I wanted to do was just to experience the village and the people before adventuring further out. There was no better place to start than to return to the headwaters of the Sacramento River to bottle the day's drinking water. There was definitely something mystical about the place where pure water gushes endlessly from a mossy rock face. It had sacredness, with peaceful walks along the creek and footpaths, which meandered across small bridges and through hedges of horsetail fern and fragrant willow. It felt like the closest thing we have to Lemuria in the third dimension. One of the most fascinating parts of being there was watching the people who came to drink and take the water home. Bending over to collect my water, I was likely to turn around and face someone who looked like Christ or Mother Mary. There was such gentle, clear beauty in their presence that I knew some of them were Lemurians. We would see others like them throughout the village.

It was wise to begin any stroll through town at the local meeting place, the health food store. Even though we had just had breakfast, the fresh-baked goods and fresh juices were too tempting to pass up. As we were noshing, Jeff, Joel, and I decided to be the Three Musketeers for the day, while George and David decided to go off on a mutual journey. Our five-some usually broke down that way. David and George had a natural connection and Jeff, Joel, and I gravitated toward one another. Life experience has a way of putting certain people together.

As soon as we had settled at our table with our good-ies, Dianne Robbins walked in. She knew we'd had one day on the mountain and smiled, kissed us, and then disappeared. The dining area was filled with people who looked like they were from another time period and/or realm. The place had a beingness of its own, as if it was built on a vortex of energy. Michael had told us the region was filled with vortices, and we were discovering ours on the mountain. This place was a meeting-vortex, a place for like-spirited and like-minded peo-ple to gather and move out into the world with their purpose. It felt so good just to hang out there.

The storefronts along the two (and only) main streets of town were filled with metaphysical libraries, bookstores, tea-reading parlors, and crystal shops, all of which seemed to be geared toward the Lemurian presence around them. The shops were filled with photographs of ascended masters teaching ascension and every possible book on the subject. I checked in with the store that carried the textbook from which I was going to teach at my Modern Day Mystery School upon returning home. It felt fulfilling to be in the presence of awareness and harmony.

I wanted to purchase Lemurian crystals for friends back home. Both Dianne and Ashalyn recommended the shop

Sacred Seed Crystals. Now, mind you, the town was filled with millions of dollars' worth of the world's finest crystals. It even has an international crystal hospital for valuable ones that need a recharge and/or rest. I had bought a few crystals in my day and David had helped me gather the ones I needed for this journey in New York. But the Mount Shastans had a whole other way of crystal selling and buying than we were used to. You weren't just buying rocks in this town; you were purchasing important tools to receive and send energy.

As we walked into the shop, another man with a Christ-like face and beingness greeted us. Miguel. Compared to the quantity and quality of crystals in some of the shops, there wasn't an overwhelming amount of crystal in the place. We surmised that Miguel had handpicked each one of these crystals for some yet-to-be-known reason. When Miguel looked into your eyes, you felt he saw into your soul and you saw into his. He wasn't there to sell crystals to tourists, he was there to make sure you and the right crystal became companions. The price of crystals had recently gone up in the world market, but I could see that Miguel's prices were fair.

When I told Miguel I wanted a Lemurian seed crystal for my friends and me, right away he began to ask detailed questions about each person. It was as if he was going into their light bodies energetically and determining what they needed. He gave an accurate reading of each individual for whom I was buying and then programmed a crystal for them. He appeared not to be aware of the time and focused his attention entirely on my needs. He even prepared a detailed, written explanation of each crystal. "Please come back in a day or so and my wife will have put these in a setting so they can be worn," Miguel softly concluded. It was good to know we would have a reason to return to this special place later on in our journey. I left the shop knowing I had been in the presence of a higher frequency. I believe Miguel is a Lemurian or, like me, is someone intimately connected to Lemurian energy.

Due to the healing crisis I experienced prior to the journey, I was having some residual aches and pains. Ashalyn recommended Dr. Alan Cooper, an intuitive chiropractor located near the health food store. I called him on my cell phone and his soothing voice said, "Come over right away." Walking down the old sidewalks to his office felt a little like being in *The Twilight Zone*. I knew I was in another reality. The good doctor lived and practiced alternative healing in an ancient Victorian house that he and his wife and their ten children had restored. He was dressed like the house, in a nineteenth-century style jacket, shirt, and trousers, completed by a goatee. Being a healing arts therapist myself, I quickly explained my problem, knowing he had already zoned into it without me telling him. Dr. Cooper asked me to lie down on his adjustment table. He put his hands on my head and neck and began a Buddhist chant. He said, "This has to do with the death of your twin brother," and then, before I knew it, he had adjusted my neck and spine in a spiral column of corrections that sounded like machine gun fire spinning down my spine.

"Wow, I never had a correction like that," I panted.

"You'll be fine now," he said.

"What do I owe you?" I asked.

"Whatever you feel it is worth to you," he replied.

I paid him my professional rate and marched down the front stairs singing, "Everything's coming up roses." Now I was ready for my journey with my two cohorts.

We had seen many photos of Mount Shasta reflected in a certain lake. Being a professional photographer, Jeff wanted to capture his version of the mountain from this lake. A short drive through the village and over a dam and we reached Lake Siskiyou, the name of which echoes the ancient Lemurian language. If you listen carefully there, you can still hear it being spoken through the wind and other elementals. The water of the lake was sapphire blue and the shore line was rimmed with volcanic mountains. Of these, the largest and most majestic was Mount Shasta. Reflected in the lake was her twin, making this monumental mountain look even larger.

We decided to pause and meditate along the shoreline, sitting in a row on a long-dead tree trunk that long ago had yielded itself to becoming a resting place for other beings. As I shifted frequencies, I heard the lake say, "Become this, become the love that created this that you are. Embrace the 5D vibration that creates the new you and let go of the old. Only through this new, higher vibration can you see and be the force that creates. Former knowledge will not serve you much in this new vibration for it is the fifth-dimensional frequency that you feel here."

A twin is one soul that divides. My fraternal twin brother was my polar opposite and died at twenty-nine years of age in a motorcycle accident. When Dr. Cooper adjusted my neck, I felt I was reconnected with my twin in fifth-dimensional reality. In metaphysics, the neck has to do with the support of your creations. Now, from receiving this message, I knew I would be fully supported and joined with my other half for the duration of this journey.

As I continued to meditate, Jeff began shooting rapidly, as only a professional does. He was playing with his creative energy. He knew he wanted to capture the mountain in the lake and that he must also step out of his own way to simply allow the photo to come forward. He was waiting with joy and gratitude for surprises that would show up in his digital lens. I heard Adama say, "We love surprises in the fifth dimension." What Jeff paid passionate attention to, and intended was manifested in his camera. The shots were simply glorious.

Incidentally, one of these is on the cover of this book. He captured the Lemurian home in the third dimension.

We drove back through the village, stopping for an energetic boost at the health food vortex. Then we continued to stroll, endlessly getting lost in various mystical shops peppered throughout the two main streets. This was indeed a paradise on Earth, a reflection of Lemuria. We discussed how we had the feeling that everyone was there by conscious choice. How could I have not discovered it my first time in Mount Shasta, I wondered? "It's all about being ready," I said to myself.

On our way back to the house, we decided to drive toward another peak whose appearance was an extreme contrast to Mount Shasta, which also was usually seen in the distant landscape. Like the shadow side of Mount Shasta, being an almost entirely black "plug dome" volcano that rarely had snow upon it, it was appropriately called Black Butte. It was as if it could not accept the purity of the white. Some say it was caused by past eruptions from Mount Shasta, rejecting negative forces from inside her. It reminded me of the mountain in the 1977 film *Close Encounters of the Third Kind*.

From the car, the three of us sensed that it had a very dark nature to it, which reminded us of the importance of balancing all the energies in nature. Black Butte punctuated the skyline with an otherworldly look and feeling that was intriguing. But we decided the only mountain we would climb upon this journey would be Mount Shasta, and began our short drive home.

When we got to the house, George and David were back from their journey to Pluto's Cave. True to the sound of its name, they found the place did not share the energy of Mount Shasta. It was covered in bat guano. "Well, even the bats need a home," I remarked, laughing. "I guess this is one thing I can cross off my list of things to see while we're here." Since our bodies were still three hours ahead, we all decided to rest a little before having another early dinner.

Ashalyn had suggested that we go to dinner with her at another of her favorite hangouts, a roadside inn type of restaurant. Sitting there, waiting for our dinners to arrive, we became aware that our energies were shifting and we were very sensitive to the frequencies of the others in the room. Since Michael had promised us another message before the ritual the next day at noon, we opted to eat quickly and return to the solitude of our home so we could hear what he had to say.

We were becoming aware of the contrast between third- and fifth-dimensional energy in others. This begged the question: Could we become aware of it in ourselves?

After our free day of exploration, that night Michael shared these exact words.

Michael's Message

Now that you are beginning to move into the depth and breadth of your heart space, we ask you: Is your purpose coming to you? What is in your own heart space? Is your purpose coming to you? Is your purpose in the third-dimensional realm coming to you at this time? Are you getting a glimpse of your purpose?

Do you know your purpose? Do you know why you are here? Do you know what your talents and gifts are? Do you know who you are?

What we ask you to do in this second ritual is to reflect. Move into meditation from time to time throughout the six hours of silence and ask yourself: Is my purpose being revealed to me? What is my purpose? Am I getting a sense of myself? Do I know who I am? Do I know what my talents and gifts are? Am I using my talents and gifts in giving them to the world in service to the world?

We are asking you to add these reflections to your second ritual, to look at all this. We also ask you to find out and begin to formulate with your second ritual, in silence, your definition of the new group order of Children of the Awakened Heart. What is the group to you? What is your role within the group? Is the group something that you would need to be a part of, like to be a part of. If so, what is your role? What is your vision of the new group order?

As we said to you, as you move toward the end of your third ritual you will culminate and begin to formulate if, in fact, you have a meaning, value, and purpose for this group. You see you're coming to that time-space continuum in your third-dimensional realm where you are to begin to clear the old karma between the individuals in your five-some. Wondering what this is about? Are you wondering what this group is about? Are you wondering why you are here? Are you wondering what your talents and gifts are? Are you wondering what your purpose is?

You see, this is the focus. The focus is not the drama and the glamour of what you are receiving, or what is happening to you, or the way it happens to you. The focus, as we have said all along, is...at the end of this journey, you'll know your purpose! Some will know it acutely. Some will understand it in their mental body. Some will just get a glimpse of it.

You see it is now about dropping, leaving behind, releasing, letting go of the drama and glamour of why, when, how, and what you're doing in this journey. It is now time, as you move into your second ritual, to contemplate all of this in silence. For you are moving along a pathway that will define your purpose for the new life you'll be creating for yourself. By adding this to the second ritual, do each and every one of you see a glimmer of what that new life will be for you?

Throughout the entire ritual, we ask you to consider: What is my purpose? Am I seeing my purpose? Am I moving into the depth and breadth of my heart space and focusing on the future of my life? What am I giving to the world? Am I still in the drama, the glamour, the wounding, and the mask? Am I speaking my truth? Am I living my truth? Am I being my truth?

Beginning with this second ritual, you are now at a turning point in many ways. You are moving to a place where it is as if you're looking toward the end of a highway and seeing your purpose. For some, this highway will be five miles long. That highway for others will be 105-miles long, and for yet others, possibly it is 900-miles long.

What is your purpose? It is time now to ask this question as you move through this ritual—this complete ritual—in silence, as you'll be moving into the depth and breadth not only of your heart space but also of the depth and breadth of your soul. What you'll be doing is connecting, first and foremost, to the depth and breadth of you and looking at your old habits, patterns, and rituals without the use of verbal communication, without having to tell everyone about you.

Look at your urges. Is there an urge to tell everyone about what you are experiencing and the drama and glamour of it? Are you doing that? Do you have the urge to speak about yourself constantly? What is your urge? When feelings come up, do you feel them or do you have the urge to run over to someone and deflect your feelings by utilizing your voice? Do you speak in order to resist and avoid feeling your feelings? We are giving you examples of what you may encounter on this journey.

We also ask you to release any expectations of what you might, what you could, and what you should do, find, be, or think. **Release expectations.** Allow what comes to you to come to you. Allow connection to the Lemurian subculture. For many of you, for some of you, for a few of you, you'll be connecting to a special Lemurian guide who will guide you throughout this journey, taking you to places that you never thought, in your mental body, you would go. You just may connect to a fifth-dimensional guide. Some of you will be amazed. Allow yourself to expound on the information given you.

Do you see the reason why this is the turning point? It is because you will now be able to focus on all of this without having to tell anyone everything.

It is also most important that you focus on the meaning, value, and purpose for you of the new group order of your group.

Does anyone have a question?

George: Would crying and laughter be considered breaking the silence of the ritual?

Michael: Discernment is always appropriate. It is time to move into a place of discernment about when you're making the moment about you or calling attention to yourself for some reason. Are you calling attention to yourself to make yourself seem special? Or are you using a tool simply to move energy, to allow yourself to self-process in the moment? It is important to see how you have used words to call attention to yourself. Discernment is a tool. Utilizing your tools is important not only for this lifetime, but for the rest of your lifetimes.

George: If we end the ritual before six, do we need to stay in silence until six o'clock?

Michael: You'll know intuitively when you feel complete. Then you won't be ending for a narcissistic reason; you'll end because you feel this feeling.

Remember, you are performing a task at each outer vortex. You are combining your energy, the energy of the Lemurian subculture, and the energy of the fifth dimension to create a vortex. It is most important that you remember that not only are you there personally and individually to receive what you are there to receive, you are also there to give what you are there to give.

Collectively, you are on a mission to complete a task based upon your souls' divine plan. This is based upon your agreement, as you have both been chosen and chosen this mission. You're on a mission to create six outer vortices that hold the flow of energy from the Lemurian subculture and the fifth-dimensional realms. We ask you to remember this.

George: Does the specific configurations of the vortices matter?

Michael: Whatever it will be, it will be. When you leave the main vortex, the soul who feels the need to move on, who feels things are complete, will simply move on. An important part of your task is to trust your intuition.

It is important to remember that you are performing a task based upon your soul's divine plan. That task is to create outer vortices wherever you are led to do so. In the soul's divine plan, you will create the precise vortex you are supposed to create in a precise moment in time, regardless of whether it meets someone else's expectations of it.

As we have said to you: This is a precise journey. Every ritual is precise and will be in the divine plan of the ritual of the journey. Where you are called to be is perfect and precise based upon the divine soul plan of this mission.

Joel: Does it matter if we are following the exact formation of a six-pointed star?

Michael: That is not necessary. Pay attention where the "me" overtakes the "we" in any creation. You are on your own individual journey. But your intention for each of you is to begin to form a new soul family within the new family. You'll always be on an individual journey. But is your focus on your individual journey constantly, so that you forget that it is also about the new soul family's journey? Do you understand that you are a part—an integral, unique, perfect part—of the new soul family, joining in unison with those who have the same or a similar purpose? Those who resonate and vibrate as you do, with a similar mission as yours, are choosing to contribute to the mission with the focus on the new soul family.

Is your focus on world service? Or is it on what you'll get from the world, or get from the rituals? Is your focus on the "we"? Your focus should be balanced equally at all times if, in fact, you are discovering your purpose.

Joel: Do we need to conform to an exact six-pointed star?

Michael: Go with what you feel in your heart space, as opposed to feeling yourself through self-imposed limitations in the head. When you move into your heart space, do you feel any self-conditioned limitations? No. Allow for the joy of discovery and you'll allow for the joy of living life. Allow for the joy, the excitation of the magical inner child you connected with in your first ritual. You'll also find where you are still trying to control everything outside of yourself based upon the feelings that you are continually looking to avoid because you are, naturally, never in control of anything.

The reason why you move from your heart space to your mental body is to try to figure it out, to try to put down rules, regulations, and the way it should, could, might be. Deepseated and deep-rooted feelings come up when you move into your heart space and release trying to control it all.

On your second ritual, can you contemplate breaking free of the wounded child? What we ask you to do in the second ritual is to picture yourself breaking free. This is an important turning point on your journey where you are breaking free. When you do, look at your urges and feelings. Where is your focus on "me, what I'm to receive, what I am to get, and how I am going to change"? Is there an equal focus on the "we," the tasks, the mission?

Also, have you found your purpose? Do you see your purpose? Do you care about your purpose? Is your purpose important to you? Or is it important to you to allow yourself to stay in lack and limitation, and to struggle to survive life? Do you see a bigger picture for your life?

You'll be writing this down in your third ritual journal.

Begin now to see this as well, for in silence you'll have an inordinate amount of free time to begin to focus on what is important for you and important for the new group order.

જ્જ

With Michael's words swirling in my body and soul, I went to my bedroom window once again to kiss Mother Mountain goodnight. Tomorrow would be another adventure upon her body.

Chapter 16
Day 4, Ritual 2

Since my body clock was three hours ahead, during the entire trip I would wake up early in the morning. This allowed me private time and privacy in the aptly named Lavender Bathroom, complete with lavender wall, lavatory, tub, and toilet. The bathroom spray was even lavender scented. The hands of mountain fairies were definitely at work in this bathroom. My open-eyed morning meditations allowed me direct contact with Mount Shasta through my bedroom window, as the sunlight also awoke her to a new day in the third dimension. I was very aware that while I was sleeping I had been visiting the Lemurians in my light body in their dimension. There would be reviews of past rituals and tasks, and preparatory discussions for the ones to come. Adama and the Council of Twelve very generously gave me their attention and intention.

About the time I would be finishing my breakfast, the others in the house would begin to stir. I loved the solitude before they awoke. Right outside the kitchen window there was a gigantic primordial tree, its branches covered in green moss, which looked like something out of *Harry Potter*. It could have been there when Lemuria was still on the surface, it looked that old. She would welcome me each morning. Just me, the tree, the mountain, and Lemuria communing; a dream come true. And since this journey wasn't intended for me alone, my thoughts also were often intently focused on the "we" of humanity to which I felt our actions were in service.

On the fourth day in Mount Shasta, when I got up, it was raining, which meant it was probably snowing on the mountain. We would have rain, snow, and hail as we opened two more vortices and conducted our second ritual. In fact, we would have rain, snow, and hail for the rest of our stay. Another task we therefore faced was not to allow the weather to affect our mood adversely or interfere with our ability to perform our mission.

We made a stop at the weather gear shop to rent outfits for the day. The five of us were good sports about surrendering to the weather and our gear. We had to stay warm and dry or we simply would not be able to stay on the mountain as long as necessary. Ashalyn knew exactly what we needed to wear. The folks at the sporting goods store, anticipating these needs, had most things laid out for us and had prepared the billing so they could speed us on our way.

The mountain, covered in mist and clouds, took on an extra-mystical feeling as we ascended her body once again. Today we would perform our second ritual and identify two more vortices under harsher conditions, but it didn't seem to matter to us. We were ready for the commitment. Every one of us was in bright spirits, which was excellent since our sunlight would have to come from within, like the Lemurian sun lights their region at the center of the planet. Of course, we also had many higher sources to call upon to give us a boost if and when they were needed.

In my mind, I could hear Adama say, "The more you can turn problems over to other realms and seek support, the sooner you can enter the fifth dimension."

"This just might be the day we do that a lot," I thought in response. And I determined that I would do my best to stay out of judgment of what the third dimension had brought us.

Earlier Michael had explained, "This ritual will be connecting the Lemurians not so much to those in the third realm, but to fifth-realm energy. This will be a ritual where you will begin to hear the messages, see the messages, and feel and touch the messages."

"And it will be done in six hours of silence!" I thought. Actually, that was the part I liked best. No words. "But have no expectations," I kept reminding myself.

We made the turn onto the dirt and rock road leading us to where we would park and hike from. We passed our "entrance boulders" and asked permission to go forward. "I wonder if they ever say no," I mused. Even if they did, as we were on a mission for humankind, of course we got the go-ahead again. The line we had drawn in the dirt pathway marking the beginning of the main marker's energetic field was still there in spite of the foul weather. The moisture in the air was shifting from rain to snow with occasional small pellets of hail.

There was our main marker rock and, not too far from it, the opening of the Lemurian gateway. The main marker was always our starting point for our rituals. On this day, we would be using *smoky quartz crystal,* a grounding crystal, as it would allow us to enter the Lemurian subculture. I'd been playing with crystals all my life. Who knew they had these powers? (Now *I* did.) After our ritual at the gateway, we would subsequently be working with the energy of two vortices: the *vortex of the world* and the *vortex of the people.*

"The vortex of the world represents the all-encompassing world where multi-dimensional reality combines with third-dimensional reality along with the Lemurian subculture," Michael had reminded us the night before. The vortex of the people is where your heart will open and you will connect and express yourselves in ways you have never before imagined. Each of you will be connected to the people, a person, a voice, and energy of the Lemurian subculture."

We were carrying journals with us in our backpacks in order to record the information that came to us throughout the day. Minutes before we did the second ritual on the mountain, Jeffry slipped into a trance state and Michael gave us the following message.

Michael's Message

You are now ready to begin your second ritual, the midpoint of your three rituals, the "turning point," as we said to you last night. You are at a place where you are looking to balance, searching to balance, and, in some cases, yearning to balance the "me" and the "we."

It is most important that you now, at this moment, connect with your main vortex. Move into your hearts and focus on the Lemurian gateway and energy. Focus on the vortex. To commence your second ritual, we will ask you to stand in a circle around the main marker, two-feet away and only an arm's distance apart from one another. Then you will do a meditation. To begin it, we will ask you to join hands and move into the depth and breadth of your heart space.

Place your smoky quartz crystal in front of you, signifying your oneness with Mother Earth. This is a grounding mechanism so you can remain entrenched with Mother Earth—for you are now being shown the people of the world. And not only the people in physical human form, but also all of the people who inhabit all the worlds you will be visiting during the day.

It is time you begin to congregate in your heart space. You are moving from the "me" into the "we" of oneness for all at your vortex of the world and at the vortex of the people. It is oneness because you are not singular. You have individuated from the parental unit of your mom and dad. You are now individuals, yet you are not singular. Singularity implies isolation and separation. Be aware of your fight for separation and isolation. Keep it in mind on this journey.

Be with yourself. Heaven now opens the gate to each and every one of you to connect with the fifth-dimensional energy. It is time to see where you still continually make life about you. Demonstrate that life is about you. Be aware that life isn't just about you. See where the shame and judgment of you and others comes up. In fact, if shame and judgment come up, this might be an implication of truth in the depth and breadth of your heart space. Become conscious. Yet, be aware of the "we" of the new group you are in. You can see you are a part of a group, yet you are individuals within the group.

We take our leave at this most important time, as we leave you be to discover and move through the joyousness. Now declare this a journey of joy—the joy of discovery, the joy of oneness, the joy of individuality, and the joy of togetherness.

Ritual 2, Balancing the "Me" and the "We"

At the main marker, at the designated hour of noon, we followed Michael's instructions. As a group, we encircled the main marker and laid our crystals before us to ground our energy. Then we joined hands, closed our eyes, and began the specific, individual meditation that allowed us to let go of any attachments we felt to our existence in the outer, third-dimensional realm and to move into the depth and breadth of Mother Earth through the gateway connecting us with the Lemurian subculture. We stood together in silence for close to ten minutes, holding hands, but each having a very private experience. Within that span, I was aware of my breath rising and falling in my body, steady and even, and the cool wetness of the snow touching my face and eyelashes. I also felt intimately joined in communion with the mountain and divine beings. It was exhilarating.

At the end of the meditation, we opened our eyes and connected with each other. One by one, I looked directly into the eyes of my companions and exchanged love with them. So much love was alive in us. Then, we took turns simply stating where we were and what we were feeling in the moment. I shared that I was fully present and feeling unconditional love for all that there is. After each of us had spoken, the silence began. It would continue for the next six hours.

We knew one of us would lead us to the vortex of the world.

The Vortex of the World

Since I had been chosen to be the overseer of the Lemurian gateway two days earlier, I very much wished for the others to use their intuition to find the remaining vortices. Jeff, George, and David had an uncanny ability to find these spirals of energy, which I enjoyed watching them put into action. Ashalyn had her dousing rods for confirmation. I also loved watching Joel surrender to his intuition, knowing that in the past he had not always trusted it. He was a forest ranger at heart and his relationship with the trees was also beautiful to observe. Up on the mountain, he frequently hugged and held the trees like they were his children.

It was raining and snowing fairly consistently as we marched off on our mission to find the first vortex of the day. Some went off alone, others in pairs. I pretty much followed whomever I felt had a good sense of where the world vortex might be. In part, I was conserving my energy so that I would have the necessary stamina to make it through the day. My healing crisis had left me with lingering subtle after-effects, but I felt I was doing well at keeping up. Our mutual instinct was always to enter into what appeared to be virgin forest, where there were neither trails, nor paths. We were stepping over five hundred-year old fallen trees and vegetation that had never experienced human footsteps. The earth under our feet was as unsure as we were as to where exactly we were going. Deeper and deeper into the forest we trailed, leading to where we knew not. It was thrilling to surrender to not knowing anything about where you were or where you were going. There was an inner being, coupled with an outer one directing you step by step.

Onward we went for miles. In silence, one of us would signal the possible vortex with hand gestures. The rest of us would then gather around to see if we could confirm it. There were many failures. And we pushed on, deeper into the forest floor. Then, we came to a circle of trees with a clearing in the center, the trees so tall we could not see their tops. Like a family of brothers and sisters and a mom and dad, they almost looked old enough to have been there when Lemuria still existed in our frequency. Ashalyn pulled out her dousing rods. They swung straight around to the center of the tree circle where there was a beam of sunlight. Eureka, this was it! We had found the vortex of the world. Every one nodded their heads in approval.

We scurried around to gather materials to build an altar for our newly found vortex. Pine cones, some almost three-feet long; exotic bright green ferns that looked like fairy hair; rocks that had been pushed out of bowels of the volcano long ago; delicate pieces of evergreen; twisted, fallen branches: These were our building materials. The only thing you could hear was our panting to catch our breath in the thin mountain air. As if by magic, we all stopped at once, knowing the altar was complete. We joined hands and went into meditation. It was sheer bliss.

This was the vortex where we would connect with whatever energies we needed to connect with individually, writing as we would go along, recording what we were feeling, processing our urges to describe all we saw to the others and couldn't.

We separated and found sheltered places to rest our bodies as we opened our hearts to connect with different energies.

I closed my eyes and took a deep breath, and it all began...

"Greetings, beloved child of the awakened heart, I am a blue-green dragon from Lemuria. I am from the same blue ray as your beloved Archangel Michael. We both love Lemuria very much. You have thought about me a lot ever since you learned I exist. My species left Earth many thousands of years ago because we were hunted and killed. We are immortal, intelligent, powerful beings and much of humankind resented us and wished to capture us for their own purposes, or to kill us due to their fear of us. Knowledge of us has only survived in the third dimension through mythology. Some of us have come back to Earth to be in fifth-dimensional reality in Lemuria. We live on this mountain in that frequency. Your higher self is able to see me and you draw me in at this time. I am a light being that cannot be seen by most in your frequency, as with the Lemurians.

"Many species opted to move into fifth-dimensional frequency when things became too difficult on Earth. You call many of them extinct, but they have merely changed frequencies. Many of your drawings of what we look like are fairly accurate. My body is about thirty-five-feet long and my wingspan is eighty feet. When Lemuria was on the surface, we were in service to life for eons. In spite of our great size, none feared us for they knew the great work we did.

"I am telepathic and can read your thoughts. I have made my home rather high on the south side of the mountain you stand upon now in your sacred mission. As long as I stay invisible, life remains safe and harmonious for me.

"Please know, dear one, that very few beings on your earth plane now could achieve the intelligence, the love, and the strength of dragons. The truth of our existence teaches that compassion and high purpose can come in diverse physical forms. Dragons are tremendous lovers of freedom and we achieved high spiritual mastery long ago. And we are not interested in the enslavement of ourselves or the killing of us by less evolved humans.

"Most dragons left Earth due to our treatment by those who feared or resented our gifts. Dragons were the masters of the elementals and it was falsely believed that we possessed magic that others could transfer to themselves. After eons of mutual love and support, humans and dragons became in opposition to one another. We lost our trust of people and began to hide in obscure places until eventually most of us had to leave all together, shifting into a realm of another frequency. The reason we are contacting you now is that we are on a similar mission to assist the planet and humanity to regain equality, harmony, and balance. Without this, Earth cannot shift into a higher dimension, as it is destined to do. Right now, we are in the fifth dimension, like the Lemurians, ready to be seen when you are ready to receive us.

"You are in a place on the mountain where I often play. That is why I come to you. You are connecting with me through meditation. There are also places inside the mountain designed to receive light beings like us. When some of us dragons first met the Lemurians, they invited us inside. So now you know, not all beings of light have human form. We come in all shapes, sizes, and forms. Through the tasks you perform here, our service to the planet and humankind will manifest in a more elevated way through communities of equality, harmony, and balance. I leave you now with these thoughts and wish you an enlightened journey upon our mountain."

As I nestled under an evergreen branch to protect myself from the falling hail and snow, I next went deeper into meditation and connected with the Lemurian Council of Twelve and Adama. With them was the ascended master, St. Germain, who wished to acknowledge my connection to the Seven Sacred Flames being kept alive in the temples of Telos.

"Greetings, beloved proxy for humankind. I am St. Germain, the guardian of the violet flame. This flame began the ascension energies for Mother Earth. Please know that the Lemurians have kept this flame and others alive since they went underneath the earth, even as the people on the surface continued to kill one another for centuries more. If it had not been for the Lemurians and the other races that live beneath Mount Shasta, the ascension flame and the other six flames would have died and humankind would not have a way back home.

"The opportunity for ascension has never been so easy or available to humankind as it is now. Lemurians did not have it as easy. Their vigil has made it possible for you in a way that was not possible for them. The Great Pyramid in Egypt held the ascension flame for eons, but it is mainly in Lemuria now. This is the goal you on the surface have been seeking to attain lifetime after lifetime. Please know I support your victory into ascension with deep love from Mount Shasta and Lemuria."

In silence and solitude, I decided that it was time to take a lunch break and ground myself. My outer garments were soaked through, but my heart was soaring. Although I had an urge to share with my follow proxies what I was experiencing, I knew this was not possible because of our mutual pact to maintain silence until the day's activities had been completed. To contain the energy made it even more powerful. A peanut butter and jelly sandwich and water brought me back fully into the third dimension.

After eating, I pushed myself against the trunk of a massive spruce and fell into a deep sleep. The tree that I was leaning against began to speak:

"Welcome to our forest home, dear one. We trees are living, conscious beings just like you. We have been the guardians and protectors of Mother Earth every since we came here. Through the vast network of our root system within the interior of the Earth we are able to communicate about everything going on in your world. This is a critical time for you and your planet. Our mother, the Earth, has reached critical mass in the abuse your kind have inflicted upon her body and all things within and upon it. When will you remember that all life is interconnected and sacred since it all comes from the same source?

"The Lemurians had to learn this the hard way. Are you? Our intention as trees was never to be your fuel, paper, and building material. We are here to protect this planet and to supply it with the air necessary so that you can breathe.

"Many of you are waking up before it is too late. Some of our forest fires are a way for us to leave this world before you destroy us. Soon, through your thoughts, you will discover ways to create everything you need without killing us and others. A new world order awaits you..."

Drifting gradually back into consciousness, I looked around me. My fellow proxies and I were positioned in an exact six-pointed star about twenty feet from the center of our vortex and altar. I felt an unconditional love for each of them. There we all were, in the snow and hail, wet to the undergarments, doing our best for ourselves and humankind. One by one, I walked over and hugged and kissed each of them. I felt their loved returned. Joel didn't seem to have brought enough to eat, so I pulled some of my food out of my backpack and shared it with him. I felt such great gratitude for all the gifts that had come into us and the intention of sharing them with the world that I pulled out my very wet journal and tried to write on wet pages. It didn't go very well. I smeared a few words on paper. At that moment, I committed to write down as much of it as I could remember as soon as I got home.

A voice told me, "Get up and walk around." Through the thick brush, I saw that Ashalyn had moved and was sitting high upon what seemed like a cliff's edge. As I looked for a way to get to her through the thick forest vegetation, I pushed myself through what appeared to be an animal's narrow trail. When our eyes met, she silently signaled me onward. It was worth the effort. When I got to where she was perched upon a cliff face, below us was the most magnificent valley. My initial urge was to go and get the others so they could also share in this beauty, but I allowed myself to find my own roost and simply take it all in.

As I was mesmerized and surprised at the beauty beneath me I heard:

"Dear proxy for humankind, what you see before you is the result of a crystal grid that is now growing again upon the surface of Earth. We are members of what has been called the culture of the crystal energy workforce. In fifth-dimensional consciousness, we are holding the ability for Mother Earth and humankind to shift into the completeness of your crystalline structures. This is part of your planet's ascension process and the task that you are performing assists us. Through the union of masculine and feminine energies and the balance of elementals we grow. The work that you are doing is also assisting in the balancing of two crucial energies, the male and the female. Their current imbalance is creating much of the duality and separation in your world.

"The same thing that is happening within we crystalline people is happening with the human DNA. You are adding the structure needed to move into the higher frequency of the fifth dimension (where your beloved Lemurians live) to your makeup. The time has come for you on the surface to awaken and merge masculine and feminine energy. There are many vortices on this planet. Mount Shasta is one that has blended the male and female as a prototype of what is to come. Soon the rest of humankind will follow. There's nowhere else to go. Those who do not wish to balance the two energies will simply live elsewhere.

"Like many other light workers, we have our control center within Mount Shasta and work intimately with the Lemurians. As you know, crystals are the foundation of Lemurian life. Crystals are the source of their energy, their building and storage material. It will be yours also one day soon. All advanced civilizations rely upon crystals and electromagnetic force fields as the basis of their culture. Your 'crystalline children' who are being born now already contain the new structures and fully know of an existence beyond separation and war. You also came here at this time to add structure to increase your consciousness and open your heart space. That's why there are more of you on the planet now than at any other time. It is an essential part of your divine soul plans to become part of the ascension process.

"We of the crystal culture intend to hold the openings for you to ascend. It is our mission to support you with all the alternatives and possibilities of ascension that are available. The tasks you are performing upon the mountain are very important and will support the changes that must take place during the planet's physical advancement. While these may be disturbing to many people, they are necessary for the survival of the planet herself. They are necessary to clear and cleanse her of your abuse. We are here with you and the planet to maintain and sustain your uppermost capability in the physical dimension.

"In the fifth-dimensional frequency at the core of this planet, which some call the central sun, is a grand crystal. This crystal transmits the frequency to the planet that she needs in order to advance. We know we are only one of many expressions of love and light that glow from the heart of Mother Earth. You have much to discover about that which lies within the interior of your planet. The work you are doing now assists the planet in making her shift. We honor your efforts, we crystal people."

At the vortex of the world, I could feel my connection to the entire living planet. Everything was alive, connected, and had consciousness. How could we have not known or felt this before?

My fellow proxies' body language was saying it was time to move on. We had been in one place for several hours in fairly foul weather and moving our bodies to get warm seemed like a good idea. I felt I'd had a fulfilling multi-dimensional experience.

As we gathered together around our altar one last time, knowing I would probably never see this place again, I became very emotional. "Will anyone else ever see this altar or know what we have done here? And does it matter?" I wondered.

The Vortex of the People

We had descended deeper into the forest floor than I had realized on the way down. Going back to the Lemurian gateway would involve a relatively steep climb carrying a significantly-sized backpack and wearing now-heavy, wet weather gear.

After about an hour of uphill hiking, I began to feel strange. Despite my serious healing crisis before the journey, it hadn't seemed to affect me much thus far. Now, all of a sudden, my heart began to race and my breathing became labored. My body seemed to freeze in position. I leaned back into a rock face and thought, "Is this it?" I'd had a vision before leaving home that I would not be physically coming back from this journey. That vision had been so strong that I had even settled my affairs with my spouse. I could see my other proxies far above and ahead of me. They seem to take no notice of my situation.

As I began to surrender to what I believed was my transition (and hopefully into the fifth dimension), I heard Adama's voice say, "It feels like physical death, dear one, but you are not going to die. We are re-encoding your DNA. What you are feeling is the death of the old. It will only take a few minutes." Sure enough, I was able to catch my breath in a few moments and hike the rest of the way up the incline. As we all gathered to check in with each other on flat ground, they let me know that they could see I'd had some problems below. Since we were still maintaining silence, I wrote them a note: "Guys, I sure hope the next vortex is a gentler hike. You almost lost me on this last one."

It was time to plug into our intuition, get out the dousing rods, and locate the next vortex. But before we left our position, Jeffry went into trance and channeled Michael for us. "This next vortex is the vortex where your heart will open and you will connect and express yourself in ways you have never imagined before. Each of you will be connected to the people, a person, a voice, or a specific energy of the Lemurian subculture," we were reminded.

We would be going back to the main marker to regroup and then move out again into this new vortex. I could tell that even as an experienced mountain guide, Ashalyn was in parts of the mountain she had never experienced. We all relied on our intuition to find our way back to the main marker. It was not a short hike. If not knowing where you are most of the time is the definition of "adventure," we were having one, yet I can't remember ever being frightened or fearing that we were lost. The presence of the Lemurian guides was always around us, thus I felt quite safe.

The weather would go from bad to worse—from rain to snow to hail to rain—for the remainder of the day, but even so, we marched onwards in pursuit of our divine mission. For a bunch of cities boys, I would give us excellent marks. Please know I do not recommend such an adventure journey for anyone with serious physical limitations. Staying hydrated was important and I am sure the power within the local water was essential to sustaining our high energy level.

The usual suspects for finding a vortex were Jeff and Ashalyn. David and George also had a natural bent for it. Joel was developing fast. But I was stuck in neutral. Michael had told us that the vortices we were looking for existed already and we just had to find them. But, as usual, the process of finding this vortex was more difficult than I had imagined. It was a big mountain with many miles of landscape to cover and we had to be careful that the mental body did not take over and look for the convenient route or location. Our search parameters always began with the idea of a six-pointed star configuration centered on the main marker, even though Michael had told us that when our intuition said yes the spot we identified would be perfect. But no one in the group was looking for the easy way out. We forged the tough terrain, even when our bodies said no.

After hiking through Jurassic-looking forest for a couple of hours, again we came to a family of huge trees that seemed to be saying this was it. These trees had never been cut and were hundreds, maybe thousands of years old. Although none was old enough to have been present when Lemuria was on the surface 12,000 years ago, there seemed to be a connection between the tree circles and our vortices. We believed these brother and sister trees had encircled the vortex to protect it, and sure enough, the dousing rods confirmed this intuition. We had found the vortex of the people!

Like clockwork, we all went out into the woods around the vortex to find the building materials for our altar. With every vortex, the altars seemed to be growing in size and beauty. Though we used the same basic organic building materials, no two altars looked the same. All were built very quickly and appeared to be connecting the lower energy and upper energy. There would be heavy rocks connecting us to the lower and reaching tree branches connecting us to the upper. When we finally gathered in meditation around the altar, I felt a deep connection to the heart and emotions. I could feel the gratitude of the Lemurian subculture emanating from below my feet and the gratitude of the ascended beings through my crown chakra. In both cases, it was palpable. We settled in and ate a snack in silence and resumed our connections with each other, ourselves, our spiritual guides, and the Lemurians...there were many options.

As we individually began meandering around the vortex and meditating, I realized how much words tend to get in the way of my emotions. Here I was spending an entire day not talking and yet I was perfectly aware of how I felt about the others without telling them. I was perfectly attuned to my own emotions. I had been on silent retreats in the past, but being in this setting, on this mission, made silence seem more profound. The largest feeling in my being was gratitude that so much wisdom and truth was coming to me and others in our current lifetime. It was humbling when I thought about the magnificence of ascension and our part within it.

The first connection I made at the vortex of the people was with me. The thought that I had chosen and had been chosen to take part in this journey, that the idea for it came through me, was humbling. I was moved that I had so connected with the Lemurians (and they me) that I would travel to their physical home, Mount Shasta, and I knew that I would dedicate the rest of my life to the teaching the truth of their existence and the Seven Sacred Flames.

While it might seem unusual to some, the realization and everything I was doing seemed very natural to me. Everything in my past seemed to have been preparation for the moment of me sitting in rain, snow, and hail in an ancient forest on a volcano talking to the members of different amazing, unseen civilizations. It didn't matter to me if people believed me or not. That wasn't important. What did seem important were the messages and lessons sent by loving beings to help us. Be careful what you ask for! As a little boy, I always wanted to know the mysteries of life and the universe. Much of what I was told back then I didn't believe. And I didn't care if I fit in or not. That was not the card I picked to play in this life. I know that in past lives I had been destroyed for telling truths that were not the accepted truths of the day. Now I would live in a moment when the world was ready to accept a new truth because it was evolutionarily needed.

I looked around me and took in the presence of my beloved proxies, all at whatever stage they needed to be on their individual paths of development. Where was I not compassionately accepting them just as they were? Were we going to be able to get out of our way as a group and continue our mission after this journey, or was this journey the ending of the beginning for all of us? In my heart, I knew the answer:

The relationships among us would change. Right then, however, I was in the moment with the vortex, loving all aspects of the experience. My urge was to share my discoveries with the world, but expressing them would just have to wait.

The most significant connection I would make at this vortex was with Adama, my personal spiritual guide. When he spoke to me, his intention was to speak to all of humankind.

"Welcome, beloved proxies, to our spiritual and physical home. Even though your Michael has advised you not to expect, you have been waiting with much expectation for this journey, haven't you? And we have been waiting with expectation for you, for only through your ascension and advancement can we advance, since we are one. We cannot interfere with your freedom of choice and your will; nonetheless we continue to bring wisdom into your world that can make it easier for you. We have been doing this for millennia, but few have listened. Maybe now that it is essential for you to listen to higher truth, you will do so. That is our intention.

"So the big question is this: Do you want to move into a higher vibration and the world that has been shown to you or do you wish to stay where you are? You can stay. You just won't be able to do it here, for the planet herself has shifted vibration and all those upon her body who would stay must do so also. It will be much easier to choose to shift to a higher frequency than to stay where you are. There is going to be much change upon the surface of this planet in order to affect the necessary shift into a higher vibration. This is the way the planet will cleanse and clear herself.

"Let's go through a few teachings we have learned that may help you now, if you choose to shift your vibration. Can you give up all the thoughts, words, actions, and needs that keep you in the third dimension? In the fifth dimension we have learned that there is nothing you need or have to do. Everything is always a choice. Can you choose to change the thoughts, actions, and needs that have created the world you have now? Moving from the third dimension to the fifth dimension requires willingness to leap into the unknown, to surrender to not-knowing. Surrendering allows for all possibilities and probabilities to exist.

"Can you be open to possibility as a new way of seeing, perceiving, doing, and being? Put the state of beingness before doingness. Are you ready to live in the now moment (since that's all there is) without expectations of particular outcomes. We expected you on the mountain, but we have no expectation of the outcome of your visit. Holding on to what you have known (which is not always the truth) will keep you in the third dimension. Can you see yourself as good enough, worthy enough to be open and have the equality, harmony, and balance of the fifth dimension?

"What is needed is for you to integrate and apply the teachings that we and Michael have given you, rather than for you to move on to learn other truths without applying these. We call that 'metaphysical masturbation.' The heart already knows all you need to ascend; the mind and body just need time to integrate this wisdom. It's simple to shift; just love yourself enough to come all the way home now. And if you don't know how, turn the matter over to the energy of higher realms that can transmute what prevents you. Almost everything you have learned in the third dimension won't serve you well in the higher vibration of the fifth dimension.

"Here's the formula. Become the love that you are + embrace the higher vibration all the way + let go of the old = ascension = fifth-dimensional reality = coming home.

"Are you willing to release everything you know, that which you have learned in the past, which no longer serves your highest good? Are you willing to trust yourself and step into the unknown, where everything you have ever dreamed of is waiting for you? We await you."

Prior to our second ritual, Michael had said that we would be balancing our individual energy, the "me," with the energy of the collective, the "we," and that we would be given the opportunity to consider our role going forward. Thus it came as no surprise when Adama continued, addressing my spiritual path in the immediate future. "Beloved proxy, at this time we would like to invite you into one of our sacred flame temples in Telos. We know you will begin teaching others about the seven flames upon your return from this journey. At this time, we would like to summon you into a temple in order to assist you in equalizing and harmonizing any imbalances that are currently present in your mental, emotional, and physical body.

"We turn you over to the healing hands of Master Hilarion, who oversees the flame of healing and manifestation, also known as the fifth ray, which is your soul flame and the reason why you resonate with the number five. The temple you will now journey to is the Great Jade Temple. Close your eyes, take several deep breaths, and travel there with us in your light body...Imagine a wondrous temple built mostly of the highest grade of jade. This temple is designated for cleansing and recharging. Galactic beings from all over come to this well-known temple.

"Master Hilarion is supported by Archangel Raphael, known as the physician, and Mother Mary. As Michael has taught you, it is now essential to connect with your heart space. Your heart will be your transport to this healing temple beneath Mount Shasta. Your guides are all familiar with this temple and they know how to get you there. Take a few more deep breaths and relax, knowing you are worthy to receive all you are about to receive."

Master Hilarion now spoke: "You are now standing at the entrance of this glorious temple. It is a four-sided pyramid made of jade (it looks similar to the Great Pyramid in which you were initiated in Egypt). The high priest welcomes you. Fountains of golden green healing lights are everywhere. Feel this light go through your mental, emotional, and physical bodies. Keep breathing deeply so you can take as much of this healing energy back with you as possible. The entire temple feels sacred and magical with beautiful flowers and plants everywhere.

"Inside the temple, your personal guide takes you to the flame of healing, which has been burning for millions of years for Lemurians and you on the surface of the Earth. This flame has the ability to enter your soul. It is fed by your love, the Holy Spirit, and the angelic realms. You are asked to sit in a chair of pure jade and to state what it is you need most to heal? What changes in your thoughts, actions, and feelings are you willing to make to manifest the desired healing? Pause and take a moment to review these needs. While you are meditating, you are receiving love and support from your guides, which is going into your heart and soul.

"Now spend a moment with your guides, your higher self, and the energy of the healing you desire. Breathe in as much of the healing energy as you can. You'll bring this back with you into your physical body. Keep breathing. Take all the time you need. Know this is the most sacred healing vibration located on this planet.

"When you are complete, stand up and your guide will show you the rest of the temple. Look and feel the beautiful healing energies around you. Feel free to hand over any unresolved issues to your guide for further healing. Breathe deeply again and return to your vortex of the people. Know that this temple is only as far away as your intention to be here.

"Love, light, and ascension, Master Hilarion..." he said as I returned to my body resting where I had left it in the third dimension.

The End of the Day

My urge was to jump up and tell everyone in the group about the wonderful temple I had visited, but I knew I couldn't. The healing temple reminded me of the importance of staying centered in my heart space. I was feeling thankful for the guidance of the fifth-dimensional energies and beings with which I had connected throughout the day.

As I looked up, the sun appeared to be approaching 45 degrees in the sky. I checked out the others' body language and they, too, appeared complete in their vortex tasks. In continued silence, we gracefully signaled one another to prepare to leave. What I was discovering was that we spent enough time at each vortex that they would begin to feel like home, so leaving was not as easy as just walking away. To say our good-byes, we gathered hand and hand in a circle around our vortex and altar. You could tell in everyone's eyes that it had been a soulful experience. Perhaps the biggest lesson for me was awareness of how much words can get in the way.

After a few moments, we began our long hike back toward the main marker and, from there, to our four-wheel drive vehicles. On this particular march, I mused that Joel was amazing. The oldest in the group by far, the younger ones were trailing him. Through the entangled, virgin forest floor we hiked, like six dwarfs pulled out of a fairy tale. This vortex was nowhere near the others or the main marker, so it was only after a couple of hours that we approached the main marker again. Although I had felt certain I would be tired after my "near-death experience" earlier in the day, in fact I was feeling energized. As I looked back over my shoulder, I saw that I was several yards ahead of everyone else. Something must have been done to my DNA!

We had been wetted the entire day by every form of moisture that can fall from an Earth sky. As we finally broke our silence and took off a layer of wet weather gear, we vocally celebrated how much we enjoyed the comfort of climbing into a dry vehicle. Even when we could talk, no one felt much like saying much right away. This day had been quite an experience for all of us. We were anxious to clean up, eat a hot meal, and hear what Michael had to say that night. But the drive into town was fairly quiet.

As we descended the mountain, I realized that never before had I developed such an intimate relationship with a piece of geography. Mount Shasta was no longer just a volcano, a mountain, to me. It had become a living being that I grew to love. It housed my people. Funny how I could have come to this location the first time years earlier and not seen it as I did now...

Chapter 17
The Fourth Night in Mount Shasta

We entered a friendly restaurant and asked for a secluded table in the back. The six of us wanted to continue to be quiet and together. It was difficult to re-enter the third dimension, and seemed to be happening too quickly. We were exhilarated and exhausted. After the silence of the mountain, the environment felt a little too loud, dense, and stimulating for comfort.

Soon the patterns of wounded behavior among our group members began surfacing. George chose to drink beer, which helped him to shift fully back into the third dimension. David described breakthrough moments on the mountain when he had the recognition of how he had made past situations "be all about me," yet he couldn't resist continuing this behavior at the table. I sensed an intense inward pull for him to remain in a longstanding comfort zone, as he seemed to be processing everything we said through him. For his part, Joel seemed disappointed that he didn't have the same kind of multi-dimensional experiences he thought everyone else had. Rather than allowing himself to fully receive and celebrate what he *did* experience on the mountain he was caught up in his comparison.

Jeff was acutely observing the interactions among people at the table, marking the contrast between our time upon the mountain and our time off of it. He appeared confused.

Ashalyn held the space in balance and harmony with her wise, calm feminine presence, staying focused on the mission even though it was clear that she was somewhat mystified by the rest of our group's changed behavior. I kept fairly silent. I wasn't ready yet to share details about the connections I'd made to the dragon, the crystalline people, Adama, and Hilarion, or to talk about my "near-death" experience. I could see a reflection of myself in all five of my companions and I had a longing for harmony within our group. I was also keenly sensing the perfection in our being chosen as proxies for humanity. We each perfectly represented an aspect of the whole.

Our mission (the journey we had undertaken and were now halfway through) was part of a divine plan. Deep within my heart, I felt that this mission would not be complete when we left the mountain, even if as individuals we chose separation and isolated ourselves from one another afterwards, as it seemed that we almost inevitably would. On the mountain Michael had asked us to consider our future in this group or in new groups we might join, so the question coursed like an undercurrent of our collective energy. But no matter where we were individually right then, there was no doubt that our higher selves had chosen this journey and that everyone was taking it most seriously. My intuition told me that the golden key, the large citrine crystal we used in the first ritual to open the Lemurian Gateway, which would be planted on the mountain in a hiding place known only to us on our last day, would be used again in the future. No, the journey was not about us and I was sure it would not be over when we left the mountain.

We enjoyed our warm dinner in the restaurant's dry setting and then headed to the Alma Street house to hear Michael's recap of the day's event. It had been a most challenging weather day and we were fatigued, but in general we were in hardy spirits. Power to the proxies!

Michael's Message

You have now reached the midpoint on your journey, the midpoint moving toward the end of your journey as the forbearers of the group known as Children of the Awakened Heart. You're moving toward the end of the physical journey and you are now moving toward other endings—endings and beginnings. You are facing a new beginning with a new purpose, a new meaning, and a new value for your own lives.

You visited the vortex of the world and the vortex of the people today. For some, your purpose is being revealed. For some, you are getting a glimpse of it. For some, it is becoming more acutely refined and defined. And for some, new parameters are opening up, revelations for those who have realized their purpose on this earthly plane. Some of you realized today that your purpose is becoming broader. Some of you acutely realized—through your heart space—the reason why you are here. What has been added to your understanding is a broader scope of why you are here. You've realized that your purpose is not a finite aspect of who you are. For some, your purpose is about reaching the masses in a broader way and leaving behind the smallness of your purpose. In refining your purpose, some of you are being called to move out jointly in the world together with others who have also realized their connection with the same purpose. What is happening is that you've realized your world service to a greater degree.

World service means providing different kinds of service to the world. This, for each and every one of you, is quite individual. It takes on various levels of world service, which all depend upon your soul's divine plan. Where would you like to reach? Who would you like to reach? And what would you like to bring out into the world? What is now becoming acutely defined for you is something that you were seeing today on the mountain.

Some of you realized your purpose today. Some heard it. Some moved into the mental body and it lies there. What you are doing now is moving toward your endings, the endings of your old ways of life. You're winding down the old and moving toward your next level, which you will learn more about through the next ritual of renewal and rebirth.

In the renewal and rebirth ritual, you will realize what is ending in your life. What is that for you? We ask you in the final third ritual to be aware of endings and new beginnings. At the ritual today some of you have already realized your endings. So we come to you at this most important time to reveal to you that you need to be aware of the endings in your life. And we ask you, what now needs to come to an end in your life personally so that you can now fully begin a new life for yourself, forming, joining, and capturing your new soul family?

At the present time, you are moving into your new soul family. What is happening is that your "ley lines" have been injected into the Earth. These are now encoding your energy into the vortex. You are shifting energetically on this journey as we said to you that you would from your preparatory period until the commencement of the physical journey. In this shift, you are moving inward and raising the level of resonance and vibration within yourself. You are also releasing old patterns, habits, and rituals, and thoughts patterns, for that matter. Old ways of doing things, old ways that do not work based upon your purpose and your vision for your life, are being let go.

At the end of your third ritual, you will be writing down your vision and intentions for your new life. This will be a culmination of what you have learned and garnered up until that point in time. Before that can happen, endings must occur—finite, definitive endings, not only in your mental body. These must occur for no other reason other than that it resonates in your heart space to complete the karmic cycles, to complete the mission of whatever it is that comes to you to be completed. This process has already started for some of you. It will happen between now and the end of the journey for all of you.

You are now realizing what must come to an end. And realize this must be so, because for each and every one of you there are aspects of your life—old habits, patterns, and rituals in your life, and relationships in your life—that you know must come to an end in order for you now to move out into the world based upon your soul's divine plan and your purpose.

What you are connecting to, and ready to connect to is that divine soul plan. And within this divine plan are new relationships. Your new soul family will be based upon the relationship you're having with yourself.

As we asked you in your preparatory period before commencement of the physical journey: Have you looked at your relationship with yourself? What is that relationship? Do you love yourself? Do you honor and value yourself? For if you do, the relationships that you'll be having, creating, and choosing to move forward with will be ones where you are loved, honored, and valued; relationships that simply reflect the relationship you're having with you. If you're fully honoring, valuing, and loving of yourself, you'll see what needs to end.

Questions and Answers

David: I got in touch with narcissistic beingness today, letting go of some of the aspects of myself, and connecting with my purpose. There was a moment when I appeared to pull Ashalyn and Phillip into some type of Lemurian ritual. They were priests. It felt like an initiation of some kind. Can you help me understand what took place?

Michael: It's about feelings that came up for you that you have long avoided. Be with those feelings now. Release having to explain your experience. Have your experience, embody it, be it. You have revealed to yourself aspects of your beingness. There was a purpose to do this ritual in silence. What of your beingness was revealed to you? Did you find your urges? What did you find in your heart space as you remained in silence? Write down what was revealed to you about you for you. Keep that for yourself. You'll be revealing you to you. Release having to explain your experiences all the time.

George: I experienced a female guide taking me to the Lemurian subculture. I can't remember her name. Can you help me with this?

Michael: What transpired in that moment for you was that you were observing the Lemurian Council of Twelve. What were the messages that they were imparting to you? What did you feel? Did you feel knowingness in that moment that it is time to live your life in the bigger picture, to a far greater extent than you ever imagined. The Council of Twelve convenes for those asking for guidance, based upon looking for their purpose. The Council came to you with pertinent information. The final message is that it is now your choice.

How does it make you feel? It is now your choice. As you move toward ascension, you're on the final pathway where the world of form, as you know it now, will no longer exist on a personal level for each of you. Each of you knows what that is. The Council of Twelve reminds us of what that is. You now realize it is not so much a choice as a pertinent decision based upon the movement toward ascension, based upon walking through the doorway to the new life, and based upon the thought of that doorway closing and you not having walked through the doorway.

Joel: I didn't seem to experience the fifth-dimensional aspects of the day that others did. I felt I was communing with nature (wet). Did I miss something?

Michael: So your experience wasn't what you expected. How does that make you feel? You weren't able to access higher vibrations and were disappointed. What did you access? Before the next ritual, focus on what is. Refrain from explaining it to others. Write it down for yourself. When you fully feel that you have felt what *did* transpire, you can make the choice to share this information. Can you allow the experience to be wonderful for you? Can you give yourself this gift and receive this loving gift from you to you?

Ashalyn: Is the citrine crystal at the Lemurian gateway to be left on the mountain?

Michael: The citrine crystal remains in the vortex of Mount Shasta, held in a place that is sacred. The six of you can convene and decide where that should be. The Lemurian gateway was opened and connected to the fifth-dimensional energies above. That key is to unlock and possibly lock that gate. So it is most important that the key remain in the vortex of Mount Shasta. It will resonate for each of you where it should be stored. The key to that gateway must remain accessible to you forbearers. If, in fact, the position of that vortex, for some reason, moving forward in time, must be altered, shifted, or changed—which might happen—the key must remain accessible to each one of you.

David: Are there any messages for Jeff, our channel?

Michael: The channel is moving through a deep, introspective process based upon his life's purpose. There are many decisions and choices for this glorious soul. As he is connecting with various and new, most wonderful souls and new opportunities based upon his divine soul plan and his purpose in the third dimension, there are endings for him and brand-new beginnings.

As we take our leave, we ask that you write in your journal before your last ritual. Write down everything that has come to you on this journey. Be precise. And enjoy what you have received. What shift and changes have come to you? Between now and the next ritual look at endings: What is ending in your life? What no longer resonates for you? What relationships no longer resonate? As we've said to you many, many times, ask do your relationships support your highest good? What is your highest good? Are you loving and honoring yourself? Are you valuing you? Are you giving to yourself? For you see, the new life (as you walk through that new doorway) is a life that you'll be giving to you.

☙ ❧

We were all exhausted on many levels after what anyone would call an extraordinary day. We needed to be with ourselves and do our best to assimilate all we had received and were to give. Again, I went to my bedroom window and kissed my Lemurian home goodnight.

Chapter 18
Day 5, Free Day

We had our mutual rituals on the mountain. By the fifth day, I also had my private rituals off the mountain. Throughout all the years I worked in Northern California, I never adjusted to the time zone and that stayed true for me on this journey. Up before dawn, I received first crack at the bathroom. It was relaxing to be up before the others and leisurely prepare for the day. After I bathed and dressed, I'd meditate and send email from the old, but reliable computer in the living room to Jessie at the mystery school. Other than my spouse, James, she was the only other person in my life outside Mount Shasta who had any idea what we were doing. Since we would be teaching the wisdom of the Lemurians, she needed to be plugged into what was happening.

During the morning's meditation, Adama decided to make a house call.

"Good morning, beloved proxy and brother. The Council of Twelve and I greet you at the midway point in your visit upon our Mount Shasta home. We honor your presence and want you to know that your being here brings great joy throughout Lemuria. The preparatory work you did prior to your arrival, in addition to the tasks and rituals you are performing upon the mountain, is quickening your ascension process and raising your frequency.

"As you, the overseer of the Lemurian gateway, approach your last ritual, we know it has become clear to you that your purpose is intimately connected to our Lemurian mission: to assist all who resonate through their ascension. We know you will return home and begin teaching our most important lessons about the Seven Sacred Flames. This will create a new soul family around you. We also know that through your talents and gifts you will reveal to those on the surface that we exist, explain our purpose, and, through your world service, assist in joining our two civilizations. The more you become a spokesman of the Lemurian energies and the more often you embody them, the more you yourself attain our frequency.

"You will leave the golden key in a sacred place on the mountain. Mother Earth and we shall protect the citrine crystal until your return. There will be many shifts soon within your third dimension and we may need to enter the gateway again at a future time to alter it. We shall stay connected on this point. The last steps to ascension are often the most challenging and difficult, but all must go through the same initiations you are teaching. So we urge you and others to stay the course. The moment you feel yourself falter, you can choose to raise your vibration immediately by turning your doubt over to a higher realm and frequency: ours. Within the unknown of this journey lie limitless possibilities we wish for you and others. Now follow your heart into the unknown and into all the magic that will be revealed.

"Our hearts are filled with gratitude for you becoming another one of our messengers on the surface. Your numbers are growing. We caution you not to allow others to alter our words or intentions for their benefit. There are still forces attempting to prevent your ascension, but they cannot. It is your divine right and destiny to ascend.

"The frequency you seek and wish for is within you, nowhere else. Release your attachment to the third dimension and the truth of your divinity will arise. Within yourself is the only place you can seek true union with all. Once you attain that union, everything will be added unto you. You'll never need to look elsewhere. All you need to know is who you are and why you are here. Discern the difference between your vibration and those around you.

"Soon more of us will be coming to the surface to connect and communicate with those who resonate with our frequency. Their vibration will be high enough for you to see us. This is a most exciting time for you and us. Mother Earth has already chosen ascension, and only together can our two civilizations advance as well...moving into a world of equality, harmony, balance, and oneness.

"It does not matter what takes place from this moment forward in your external world. Release all attachments and be free! I am Adama, your Lemurian brother."

It usually takes me a moment or two to "come down" after I receive these messages. Happily, I had a few moments to settle into my body before needing to interact with anyone. The other inhabitants of our mountain sanctuary were beginning to wake up. Since it was our day off, George had offered to fix us a pancake and egg breakfast. Feeling as if we needed fuel to recover from the previous day's rituals, we all gathered around our round dining table and ate like third-dimensional pigs. It was great just to be together, to be guys, and to have few objectives. The day would be a free day to do whatever we wanted and to explore the area. The only pressing thing we had to do was to return the rental weather gear before 10 a.m.

When we returned the weather gear soiled from the rain, snow, and hail we had endured we got harsh looks from the check-in gal. Now we knew: Everything had to be returned clean. The next day's clothes would be returned that way. Jeff had hopes to connect socially with the attractive rental gal, but the soiled return seemed to put a damper on that possibility. Oh well, tomorrow's another day...

On my to-do list were 1) pick up water, 2) pick up the crystals I had bought, and 3) go out to McCloud Falls with Joel for a personal journey. George had decided to travel to Stewart Mineral Springs for his day off. David wanted a day alone, hanging out in town. And Jeff needed space and wanted to do some photography. We would all meet for an early dinner and message from Michael, with sleep soon after, in preparation for our final ritual that would take place on the following day.

We were planning to hold a full moon ceremony at the house after the third ritual and would be inviting people we had met along the way to join us. Knowing the next day was going to be a packed day, I was looking forward to the current day being rather relaxed.

Back to the Headwaters

Joel and I headed to the headwaters of the Sacramento River. Every time I went there I became very emotional. Being there on this occasion brought back vivid pictures and emotions of when James and I were in Lemuria in another lifetime together long ago. I knew we had stood at these same waters together back then. The place was sacred; this was holy water to-go—and people have taken advantage of it for eons. You could feel the powerful life force in the water when you touched or drank it. Grandmothers were there, anointing their grandchildren's heads with the water and teaching them about it, and there was a seemingly endless stream of people who looked like Lemurians to me, collecting water for the day. All I wanted to do was jump into the sacred pool naked, but I never got the chance. We drank our fill, filled our bottles for the day, and lovingly said goodbye.

Off to Maple Street

Miguel at Sacred Seed Crystals had said his wife would have the crystals I had bought for my friends ready. His wife was setting them in silver. So Joel and I went off to Maple Street next to pick them up. These crystals had been programmed for the individuals receiving them. Each delicate silver setting was unique; and no two crystals were the same either. Some people were to receive a Lemurian seed crystal that would connect them with the Divine Feminine energy and unify them with Ancient Lemuria while awakening their dormant DNA and working on the crown and soul star chakras. The soul star chakra is the etheric chakra located about a hand's width above the head that connects each of us to the original star system we came from. Earth was seeded by twelve original star systems. Others were to receive an apophyllite crystal, which would connect them with inner-dimensional awareness, lifting the veil between worlds and attuning them to higher realms, and working through the crown chakra and the third eye chakra. Some were to receive a stillbite crystal, which would clear their thinking, bring them inner peace, and amplify the dream state of the heart. Still others would receive dow (temple heart) crystals that had three seven-sided faces and three triangular faces, which are powerful heart activators, allowing quantum leaps in the transformation of consciousness and compassion. These would be the perfect gifts for the perfect people in my life.

There is a spiritual crystal science and Miguel was making sure that the stone matched the person who was to receive it. He had just become a father and had an inner glow about him. He knew his child was a crystalline child, someone able to assist in making the shifts on our planet necessary for ascension. It was wonderful to be in his presence again and to support his and his wife's work. We invited Miguel and his wife to our full moon ceremony.

You really could not go into town and not stop in at Berryvale. Sure enough, when we arrived there was Dianne Robbins having her fresh juice. We invited Dianne to the ceremony, too. This would be the first time she experienced a Michael channeling session and it would be our last ritual on the mountain, so I really wanted to be with her. She had shared so much with me. Seated in the café, I had my usual carrot juice with ginger and a tuna melt. That would tide me over for the time being. Every two hours my body needed to eat again in the high-vibrational world around Mount Shasta. I also bought some ginger dipped in dark chocolate, which would be perfect to carry in my backpack the next day. We probably could have sat there happily all day and not needed to leave. But I wanted to stroll the streets some more and then head out to McCloud Falls, which I had heard were magnificent.

As Joel and I were dodging in and out of all the fascinating metaphysical shops, we came across a mother sitting with her child on the ground in a side garden. The two of them were so bonded and looked absolutely beautiful. Jeff ran into us right then, carrying his camera, and he began taking photos. Before you knew it, we were in intimate conversation. The mom told us all about how her child had selected her to be his mother and what he planned to do by coming here. You had the feeling there were many conscious children like this one living in Mount Shasta. Adama and Michael had told us they were coming in greater numbers.

After saying goodbye and walking farther down the street, Joel and I stopped into a tea shop where we found George having his tea leaves read before he left for the mineral springs. We smiled and left him to enjoy his adventure. I don't think I had felt as peaceful in years as I did that morning. My heart connected to James, the man I would return home to in Florida. I was fantasizing that we would be moving there. We strolled a bit more with no destination in mind, stopping into one of the muffin shops for the best muffin I ever ate—a once in a lifetime treat. Before leaving town, I would stop back a couple of time to see if they had another muffin like that one, but they never did.

Finally, Joel and I decided we were ready to walk back to the house, pick up one of the cars, and head out to McCloud Falls.

McCloud Falls

The weather was constantly shifting from rain to sun in Mount Shasta, but where we were headed was another type of ecosystem entirely, one that promised to be dry. It was nice to get in the car without a task at hand, just to be free to enjoy each other and the scenery fully.

To reach these highly praised waterfalls you had to drive about fifteen miles outside of town. There are three levels to the falls: the lower, the middle, and the upper. The upper and lower falls are accessible by car, and you have to hike to the middle falls. We decided to visit them, going from high to low in sequence. I don't think I had any real expectations, but I was not prepared for what we experienced. The grandeur of the falls blew me away. Each had its own personality.

At the upper falls, the quiet river gathers itself into a massive stone chute, charging the waters with enormous energy before they spill into a pool far below. The middle falls, the most inaccessible, spreads a sheet of falling water over a lava cliff. The scene of the lower falls is more peaceful, a place to rest and meditate. We watched the dipper birds flying low and plunging in and out of the cascading water. Chipmunks were everywhere, sometimes being brave enough to come to your hand, other times darting far away from you. The scale of everything was like a miniature Grand Canyon. At the highest point you were looking down thousands of feet into roaming, white water, falling dramatically before you. The warmth from the sun had released the sweet smell of pine needles into the air. You just wanted to curl up in a ball and take a nap.

The hiking trails were challenging, but safe, and led to spectacular views in front and below you. I would describe the experience of visiting the falls as thrilling and a marvelous contrast to our time on Mount Shasta. Whereas Mount Shasta was quiet and mysterious, McCloud Falls was loud and had a feeling of danger to it. Joel and I spent as much time here as the day would allow. But we had to get back for dinner with the others and to hear what Michael had to say to us before our final ritual.

Dinner at Home and a Conversation with Michael

We invited Ashalyn over for a home-cooked meal. George made a delicious vegetarian pasta and salad. It felt good to attempt to be together as a soul family, but our natural resonance mostly existed in the fifth dimension. So often we did not connect as well off the mountain as we did on it due to our individual unhealed "stuff." I kept reminding myself that we were people, doing and being the best we knew how to do and be at the moment, and who happened to be on an important mission for humankind and ourselves. I wanted to complete the mission as lovingly as possible. The mission was what mattered.

I felt as if my life had been shifting in many ways lately and in some areas the trip was giving me closure. The following after-dinner message from Michael confirmed my feelings...

Michael's Message

You're now moving into a concept of change. The reason we tell you it is a "concept" of change is because some of you, if not all of you, are wondering what change actually is...as you were moving toward endings the last time we came to you.

Endings in your specific personal life involve the realization that the old habits, patterns, and rituals are no longer working for you. You are experiencing endings of old relationships and you are moving from endings to change, moving from endings to making choices, to change.

You are moving through the process of seeing these endings and seeing what you have learned on this most wondrous and glorious journey. As you move into your third ritual, it is important to look at the endings, to look at what has transpired. You're looking at the first list you made, a list of what you have released. Possibly changes have come to you during this journey or you're looking to make changes in your life. Looking at endings, what you'll be doing is writing down what you have learned and garnered, and possibly what you have released in order to make the changes in your life that need to be made...in order for you to support the purpose of this journey, and to support the purpose of your journey to and through your new life.

What changes need to be made in order for you to support yourself in your new life after this journey—your own life moving out into the world and possibly forming your new soul family? Some of you may already realize who that soul family is and who its members are, and who the members resonate with as individuals. Some of you might not know yet. But knowing who you resonate with based upon—once again—your relationship with yourself, consider this question: Has that relationship changed on this journey so far?

Did your relationship with yourself change as you moved through the first two rituals? We ask you that question. Has that relationship with yourself changed? Are you clearer, more defined, or more refined where this relationship is concerned? Can you look outside of yourself to see the relationships that are important for you to form, if they are not already formed?

What relationships are you in now that are based upon self-relationship, knowing that they bring you joy, knowing who supports your highest good, and knowing that is based upon your definition of supporting your own highest good? Are others doing that? With whom do you resonate? With whom do you no longer resonate? You see you are moving to a time of endings where you are now faced with the decision and choice to change the old. We've ask you many times, can you make a change? Will you make this change?

If change is an imperative in your life, then you will move to make that change. As you meander about during your third ritual, we ask you to look into the question "Will I move toward making change?"

What change are you looking to make in your life? Can you make the change once you identify the change? Will you take responsibility and make the change? Or are you looking for those outside of you to change, so you can feel comfortable or have them be who you'd like them to be? Looking at those old relationships, can you see in them what no longer resonates for you based upon the new relationship you are having with yourself? You're creating an equal balance of giving and receiving in this new relationship, based upon what you want in life, based upon why you are here, based upon knowing who you are, and based upon your talents and gifts.

At the end of your third ritual, you'll be writing about your future, about that which the new life will be and already is for you. We ask you to write this down in the present tense, as if you already are having that life. See that life. The end of your third ritual is a declaration of your life moving forward, the life you are already having, as it is, in the present tense.

Questions and Answers

George: When I went to the mineral baths today I could not meditate. Is there any significance in that?

Michael: Remember your mantra for the third ritual. *I am now present in the present moment.* Meditation can be escaping the moment, looking for your future. Most often it is important to remain in the moment and for whatever reason to remain conscious in the moment. Allowing yourself to receive your physical surroundings fully enables you to receive others.

Joel: You are speaking a great deal about endings and change. How does this relate to our group, Children of the Awakened Heart?

Michael: What happens next will be a joint agreement among the five forbearers. More importantly at this moment in time, as you prepare to enter your third ritual, are the endings of old habits, patterns, rituals, attachments, routines, and relationships. You are even ending old aspects of the relationship with yourself—looking into the mirror. This is how I used to treat myself. How do I want to treat myself moving forward? Do I love myself? Have I loved myself enough? Have I been giving to myself enough? What have I been doing to avoid full intimacy with another? What are the habits, patterns, and rituals that keep me at a distance from my brethren in the relationships I am in? What habits have I been using? Then you can make a choice to change a habit, to move into a new life based upon a new soul family.

As we said to you many times in the preparatory period leading to this journey, the old karmic patterns, relationships, and aspects of the relationship among the five of you will come to the fore. As you forbearers convene to look at the new group order, look at Children of the Awakened Heart as a separate group to define and refine as you so choose. To see, refine, and define your role in the new group order, consider the meaning, value, and purpose of the group for you. What is the new group order? Is it about coming together and sharing all of this? As individuals have you changed? Have you moved through aspects of endings with yourself, possibly knowing who you are?

This will all take place when you convene to look at your group as a separate group and to decide what your role will be. What are the meaning, value, and purpose of it for you? Are there meaning, value, and purpose for it? What is its definition for you?

Are you are ready to embark on the final task of the forbearers of Children of the Awakened Heart? The final task that you will perform is your third ritual. We now take our leave.

Sleep

When the idea of taking a journey to Mount Shasta originally came to me and I presented it to my collaborators, in my heart I knew it would be our final task together as a group as well as marking the beginning of exciting future work. I sensed that our time together on Mount Shasta would reveal to some of us that it was time to move further into world service, and that's what Michael had said in his message. Our trip was about being ready to do world service. The group Children of the Awakened Heart gave us a wonderful foundation for which my heart was filled with gratitude. We would not have become who we were now without it. But some of us were no longer children. None of us was better than any other. We were at different points on our paths to embracing our talents and gifts. In the end, after ascension, we would all be the same frequency.

We did a group hug, some knowing more than others that endings and new beginnings (change) were about to affect us all. But we had one more important final ritual and the creation of two vortices essential for humankind to perform the next day. This would complete our tasks on the mountain and set the stage for our growth and expansion as individuals outside our group.

చ్ళ

As I gazed out my bedroom window once again at this being called Mount Shasta, I was in awe of the perfection of all that was taking place. I felt my feelings (excitement, sadness, joy, anger, and peace) and handed them over to the higher Lemurians realms. I would join them in my light body throughout the night and one last time in the flesh the next afternoon.

Chapter 19
Day 6, Ritual 3

Day 6 dawned. It was to be our final day upon the mountain and there was a great deal of emotion and commitment around the prospect of our ritual, which would be our fivesome's final task for humankind in our capacity as the forbearers of Children of the Awakened Heart. In looking back, our preparation for the journey really had been a two-year process, with a repeated, extensive course of study in the preceding few months. And in many ways, all of our lives up to this point were a preparation for this journey. Whether we continued together afterwards did not matter. What mattered was that what we were doing was an important part of each of our divine soul plan, which would affect our planet and all those within and upon it forever.

I got up at my usual hour, fully aware how that which was to take place today would show me the blueprint for my life to come, as well as revealing a path for the planet. Michael and other higher beings had carefully orchestrated the blueprint over an extended period of time. Their way of teaching us could change our lives and the world, if we chose to let it. Retrospectively, I was still amazed at how Adama and Lemuria had come into my life and what was taking place on the journey, and yet everything we were being asked to do felt natural.

The members of our household were unusually resolute about our mission this morning when everyone finally got up. This was not only going to be the day of our last ritual, but we were also going to have a house full of guests that night for the full moon ceremony. Throughout the trip we had been asking the people we met to join us, giving veteran spiritualists and first-timers alike a chance to experience Archangel Michael "live" and "in person."

Day 6 also was Jeff's birthday. There was definitely synchronicity in it being the birthday of Archangel Michael's channel, the day of our final ritual, and the day of a full moon. There seemed to be sacred geometrics in the shape of a triangle being applied. The Lemurians love sacred geometrics and they would be evident in our final ritual.

For a change, the weather didn't look too bad. Nonetheless we knew we'd need to rent weather gear again. Our outfits were becoming more and more like costumes for a cosmic play; perhaps called *The Hardy Boys & Girl Ascend Mount Shasta.*

We went through our usual drill: eating a high-vibe breakfast, spending sacred moments at the headwaters for the purpose of hydration, making sure everyone had proper gear for the day, meeting Ashalyn at her office, and heading up the mountain...

Ritual 3, Connecting with the Ascended Masters

As we climbed up the mountain from the road where we parked our vehicles for the last time, I felt nostalgic. After this day I knew it would be some time before I was on these slopes again. I looked at everything intently for I wanted to remember as much as possible. We knew our way to the main marker quite well and arrived there faster than ever before. Once again we gathered in a circle around the marker at arm's length from one another to prepare for our meditation.

Jeff slipped into trance and Michael reminded us, "You will bring to this final ritual what has come to you, that which you have learned and garnered energetically from the first two rituals. You will bring the wonder child with you, as well. The movement to the outer two vortices will be done as a group, but when you reach them you will also do each ritual as an individual."

We would each hold a *tourmaline crystal* in our left hand the entire day to connect us to our intuitive nature so we might more easily connect with higher-frequency energy.

Michael also spoke these words. "You are now beginning to ascend. You are moving through the ascension process you've been in all along. You're ready to rebirth yourselves to the ascension process. What you are doing is rebirthing yourselves to connect with the ascended masters. You are now moving into the realm of your individual purpose on this journey, after the creation of the next two vortices: the *vortex of renewal* and the *vortex of rebirth*. After you leave the vortex of rebirth, you'll be connecting with a specific ascended master who will be revealed to you on your pathway, after you leave the vortex of Mount Shasta and return to wherever you have come from to join with your brethren. You are now ascending. You are moving into full ascension.

"Full ascension means connecting with your purpose. You have ascended within yourselves by looking at aspects of who you are; by finding out who you are and loving, honoring, and valuing yourself; by discovering your talents and gifts. What you are ready for now is to ascend fully into your purpose. You are now ready to walk the path alone. You are ready to walk the path as the master of the self. This will commence after your ritual of rebirth.

"You are being rebirthed to your ascended self, where the drama and glamour and the ego no longer matter. What matters is service to your world."

With that, Jeff came out of trance and rejoined us. Then, we did as Michael had instructed us. Prior to our meditation we were to write down five major aspects of what we had learned, released, or garnered while doing the first two rituals that pertained to something new that we had learned on this journey about ourselves. "For some there will be five items on this list and for some fifty; yet there must be at least five. Bring this list of what you have learned anew about you. Share these five aspects with your brethren," Michael had said.

We wrote in silence for several minutes. When everyone was ready, we read our lists aloud to one another. From my list, I shared that:

1. I had released the need to learn through physical and emotional illness, and the shame surrounding illness.

2. It was confirmed that Lemuria is indeed my home and I shall return there.

3. I learned that I do not have to be in control and surrendered to others being so, while setting my boundaries.

4. I garnered that a fragment of my divine soul plan is to be a messenger of multi-dimensional realms.

5. I garnered that I was fully within the ascension process.

After the six of us read our lists, we grounded our energy into Mother Earth and the Lemurian gateway, and we joined our energy with an open-eye meditation. We looked deeply into one another's souls. "Look at each other and around your surroundings because this is your last ritual and neither as a group, nor as individuals will you come back to this main vortex," Michael had revealed to us.

At the end of the ritual, we would know our purpose in world service. We would choose or not choose it. For myself, I knew that I would return home to teach and practice using the most comprehensive tools of ascension, the Seven Sacred Flames.

The Vortex of Renewal

In order to locate the fifth outer vortex, we hiked deeper into the wooded heart of Mount Shasta than ever before. Again we were in a prehistoric forest, untouched by the beings (human beings, that is) that are largely at war with themselves, and thus mirror that to others. As we hiked relentlessly, in full weather gear and backpack regalia, there was no mistaking us for Lemurians. Seeing me struggling to keep up, Ashalyn loaned me her hiking poles, which helped greatly going uphill over forest floor that would hopefully never know what "clear cut" means.

As usual, there were several false "alarms" regarding the site of the vortex. The dousing rods were invaluable in our confirmation of this vortex. Interesting, dousing rods are also known by some people as "divinity" rods, a name that was appropriate to the matter at hand. We were on a divine mission to discovering ourselves and our purposes, and this discovery would help us to connect to a higher frequency of consciousness. When it didn't seem as if we would ever find the vortex of renewal, another familiar circular pattern of mammoth trees appeared before us. Jeff, David, and George, our vortex hound dogs, were certain *this was it* and Ashalyn's rods agreed. Following confirmation, we settled down to build the largest altar to date to honor our fifth point on our six-pointed star. Again, we dashed about the forest looking like organic architects going totally green. When it was done, we were quite pleased with ourselves and our creation.

At the renewal vortex, we brought out our five-aspect lists created during the ritual at the main marker. We read them aloud for the second time. Then we joined hands in a circle and in unison recited the mantra: *"I am now clear. I am now open. I am now available. I am now here. I am now present in the very moment. I open my heart. I open the depth of my soul to now progressively, honestly, and with the greatest intention walk the pathway to being me."*

We concluded by affirming, *"So be it."*

We then placed our lists in a container David had brought, dug a hole near the vortex and buried our lists in it. After releasing our lists in this way, there was an extreme sense of renewal. Individually we began to meander about the area of the vortex and the adjacent forest, always attempting to stay in eyeshot of one another. At times we were seated up to one hundred yards apart, writing in our journals. It would have been easy to get lost. Even Ashalyn admitted that at most times she had no clear idea of where on the mountain we were. Intuition was our true guide.

In that period immediately following the vortex ceremony, I was aware that I felt a deeper sense of self, like a remembrance of myself, but really of the new me. It was a renewal (taking place in the rain) of my multi-dimensionality, of being able to pass between and bridge the third dimension and the fifth dimension at will. As Adama had explained, this is the way all advanced civilizations live; they choose the frequency that best suits them at the moment.

My wonder child and magical child were ready to play and I was about to indulge them when I looked up and saw Jeff signaling us to gather around him. He had a message coming in from Archangel Metatron, who works closely with the Christ consciousness.

Metatron's Message

Streams of light are lighting your pathway at this time. This is the Lord Metatron. We come to you at this most important time in which you are renewing the soul, the soul's path, the soul's destiny. What you've seen behind you is divine. What you see ahead is destiny. What is destiny for each and every one of you is complete. It's finite. It's what is in your heart. The streams of light will follow your path. The streams of light will light your path. See those streams of light that light your path. See those streams of light. See those streams of light that are lighting your pathway into your life's work, into your life's purpose, the streams of light that light your path.

We, Lord Metatron, come to you at this time. We grace your presence at this time and come to you and oversee the following aspect of your journey moving from the mind into the heart. We oversee the following on your pathway...Follow the light not only on this pathway, but for the duration of your human life on this planet.

Thank Mother Earth, for Mother Earth works in conjunction with us, the angelic realm of Metatron that comes to you to light your pathway. We come to you at this most important time asking you to move into your heart. Connect your heart with your mind and with Mother Earth. Connect your emotional body, your mental body, and your physical body with the earth below. Follow the path. Each and every one of you has a singular path. It is up to you to choose the path and to commit fully to the path. Commit to the path that is your divine purpose in your third-dimensional lifetime.

You've now seen the path. Follow the path, the light we lay down at your feet. What is your path? Do you know your path? Follow that path into your purpose in this lifetime. Why are you here? As Lord Michael teaches and brings messages to you, we are holding the light for you to follow.

Gratitude

At this vortex, I felt renewed knowing that I had gained a greater awareness of myself through participating in the rituals on our journey and experiencing the energy of the vortices on the mountain. I felt great gratitude that I had been able to release aspects of my life that no longer served me and bury them here. I had been able to declare who I am and why I am here. I was able to bring my wounded child out to play with my magical child, so he would know he was loved and could continue to heal. The mountain and I had become one. These truths about me would always be here at the mountain to give me strength. I was thankful that it was a part of my divine soul plan to connect with multi-dimensional realms and to be able to share those teachings with the world. As I meandered about the vortex for several hours, at moments drifting in and out of sleep when I was resting in the arms of Mother Earth, these were some of my thoughts and experiences.

The forest was filled with unseen beings that were there to be seen. Fairies flew across rays of sunlight and elemental beings like earth gnomes were pleased to show themselves when they thought I wasn't looking. This was a vortex within which to relax and enjoy the life around you.

My beloved Archangel Uriel is all about elemental life. They, the beings of the consciousness of Uriel, were the first fifth-dimensional energies to invite me to channel them. They taught me to release myself from myself so I could allow them to flow within, and through me. Uriel is connected to the forces within and upon the planet. Along with Archangels Gabriel, Raphael, and Michael, Archangel Uriel forms the mighty foursome that loves this planet very much. I am so blessed to be connected to them. Much of my metaphysical training comes directly from their higher realms.

At the vortex, my intuitive sense was that all of the ascended masters were about us. Many of them are unknown to the majority of humankind, yet they do such great work for us. I could sense the presence of El Morya, who teaches the will of God; Lord Lanto, who teaches illumination and wisdom; Paul the Venetian, who teaches cosmic love; Serapis Bey, who teaches hope and ascension; Hilarion, who teaches healing; Lord Sananda (aka Jesus/Jeshua) and Lady Nada (aka Mary Magdalene), who teach resurrection; and St. Germain, who teaches transmutation.

If this is the first time you have heard some of these names, it certainly won't be the last. As Michael has said, they are coming to us one by one, and they are very important to the ascension process of our world. They wait for you to know them, for they already know you.

As always, when the time came for us to leave the vortex all of us knew simultaneously that it was time to begin our next exploration.

The Vortex of Rebirth

It required our combined intuition to determine the location of the final outer vortex and point on our six-pointed star. The vortices we had been working for the past six days had existed far longer than our concept of time. They are powerful tools that were put into place to ensure the survival and ascension of Mother Earth. We had been chosen (and we also chose) for them to reveal themselves through our hearts so that we might serve humankind in its ascension process. Locating the vortex would be one of our final acts of unconditional love together as a group.

Going into the deepest recesses of our hearts to locate the final vortex, we seemed to come together as one heart beating as we moved forward toward the moment of our rebirth. We were in sync as to which direction to go. Mother Earth, our Mother, was guiding us, her children onward—not doing the task for us, but allowing the seeking and discovery to happen.

After the Lemurians felt that there had been an appropriate amount of effort put in, the vortex appeared in front of us. Like the others it was located within a pristine, virgin landscape so pure that we felt awkward walking upon it and potentially disturbing what had never been touched. But there was a divine purpose in the disturbance. We could feel the forest welcome us to do our sacred work, we who would have been intruders otherwise.

Having found the vortex, we scattered to gather fresh materials from the forest floor to build our final altar. This would be our grandest and most expansive vortex monument yet; more of every type of organic building material seemed to be available to us for this last point in our star than we had found elsewhere. When it was completed with only what the forest offered, a green, grey, brown, and gold sphere lay on the ground at our feet. Massive, it appeared to be able to rotate from its center. The altar was, in fact, a wheel, and the center of the vortex was its hub. There were also six spokes radiating out from the hub; one for each of us.

Earlier Michael had explained, "You will connect to a higher resonance of yourself. What will transpire here is that you will shift the resonance in the depth and breadth of your physical self. Based upon your soul's divine plan, your resonance will rise to a level where you will be able to move out into the world in community, harmony, and equality with yourself and you will know why you are here. At this moment, you will be ready to make a choice. You will make a decision regarding your path and your purpose. You will know and create new intentions."

One final time we formed a circle, joining hands around our altar. In this moment, we moved into silence and connected with either our inner child or our higher self. I chose to connect with my higher self. As soon as we did, Michael had said we would be ready to make choices about our paths and purposes. Mine were clear to me. We wrote these within our private journals. These were for us and not to be shared with anyone until we left Mount Shasta and arrived home. The rest of the time at the vortex was spent experiencing and knowing our intentions and purpose in the fullness of our being amongst the third- and fifth-dimensional frequencies.

I knew I had fully grown into being committed to world service and it was time to apply my known talents and gifts even more. I had done much professional and personal preparation to ready myself for this moment. I had been working on self-mastery for years, recognizing that it is an endless personal process for one's self and not something to be taken into the "we." I was currently applying my learning, which I also thought of as my receiving, into my private healing arts practice. I was sharing the messages from the Lemurians and other fifth-dimensional realms of existence that come directly through me (being a multi-dimensional being) and through others, as their teacher, by co-founding the Modern Day Mystery School. This was my form of giving. Seeing classrooms filled with those ready to know the truth thrills me. Watching their growth is even more exciting. I had already begun teaching what I needed to learn myself and I was committed to balancing giving and receiving in life, as well as balancing masculine energy and feminine energy (the core issues in our world) within and outside my life.

In addition, I knew my passion was awakening fragments of other people's divine soul plans, as I more fully embraced my own. During our trip, I had more fully been able to see my fellow proxies and others as wondrous mirrors of myself, eliminating judgment and shaming of them that formerly had been coming from my judgment and shame toward me. My heart was filled with gratitude for what is being revealed in this lifetime. I was thankful I chose to be on Earth with so many others during this unique time of opportunity. Ascension is the main purpose for our many lifetimes on this planet. I could see how a plant must feel to be able to take in eternal light and create renewable life from it every day. Being my purpose and my divine soul plan was what this trip was all about for me. I pledged I would go back home and share the truth I had discovered with whoever resonated with it. I would compassionately accept those who could not.

All of these ideas reflecting my higher self were present at the vortex of rebirth. I meandered in the forest as a multi-dimensional being mulling over my purpose and intentions until the sun hit the 45-degree mark in the sky. I understood on a deep level of my being that our final ritual had not been an ending; rather it had been a beginning, a renewing and re-birthing of my commitment for the journey to never end. I would be going further and further into the world of service.

I looked around the vortex and saw my fellow proxies doing as they would nearby and most likely having similar experiences to mine. My heart opened and I felt a great wave of love and compassion for each and every one of them. Jeff motioned us over, as he had a message coming through him. His body went into convulsions and sputtering noises came from his throat, like he was choking, as his body assimilated a much higher frequency than his own. This was normal for his channeling. If these frequencies ever came in full force, I felt sure his body would explode. David hooked up the digital recorder. The energy coming in did not feel like Michael.

Message from Jeshua, the Christ Consciousness

From high upon the mountain, we come to you at this wonderful and most important time, this time of rebirth. We are Lord Jeshua. We come to you at this time to make our presence known, as we shall join you more often through this most wonderful and glorious soul you call your channel. We come to you with a message for each of you.

It is most important that you hear us at this time, as we are now ready to usher you through your personal process, through your personal purpose. It is time for each of you to move out singularly, to move out solely, to move out alone with the message.

You will be moving from the hub, the home, moving from the birth canal, as you move out into the world with the message, as the messenger utilizing your gifts, talents, and the love from your hearts. It is now time to leave the mother's womb. You are being rebirthed as individuals, as adults. It is now time for you to move out into the world alone and singularly, and we are lighting the pathway for you through the most wonderful and glorious soul you call the channel. In this way, we shall come to you more often.

It is time to see your unity. It is time to move out from the unity of your group and to branch out as spokes on a wheel. As you see, the hub of that wheel is your center, your guiding point. It is the wheel you have built for yourselves. It is now time to move out singularly, as individuated souls, into your souls' plans. Now you've reached the intersection of the old life and the new life. As Lord Michael has said to you many times, you have reached this intersection. You all stand at the intersection as unique individuals. It is now time to make a decision. Will you connect with your soul's divine plan or, as you look back at the center, the hub, will you scurry back wondering if you are ready?

Are you ready? Are you ready one and all? As we come to you, Lord Jeshua, we shall come more often through this channel. This channel has chosen his pathway. He knows his pathway and has chosen to be the messenger for us, for Lord

Michael, and for many angels who will now join within his soul. Many frequencies in the depth of his soul are now connecting with many frequencies from the archangelic realms. He has chosen his purpose in this lifetime to move out and be the messenger of our messages and teachings.

However it is time, if you so choose, to engage in a decision-making process at the altar, as to how to move out singularly with your message and with your divine soul's gifts. With the divine soul gifts in hand to give to others, to now raise the resonance and vibration, as the Lord Michael has told you many times, you are to raise the resonance and vibration of your good Earth, the good Mother Earth that you're connected with on this journey.

All of you are now at a juncture. Picture the spokes on a wheel. Each of you is a spoke on this wheel. You each move our singularly in this lifetime, containing the hub you have built together. That hub is merely a home you visit from time to time. The hub now is your center. You move out from that hub, as spokes on the wheel. How depends upon your decisions. The decision you make now depends upon yourself, for no longer can you look back to Mother and Father to guide you.

It is time, as Lord Michael has told you, to move to your divine soul path, as a way shower. Move from being a follower. Who amongst you is still a follower? Who are you looking at—is it Mom and Dad—to guide you? Are you still looking for someone that you feel, think, or see as better than you to guide you? We are now here to support you and you are now here to take charge of your life.

Are you in charge of your life? Are you the soul of the planet, the soul proxy of the planet? Are you here? Do you hear your heart beating?

We are the Lord Jeshua. We come to you at this time to tell you that you have a very, very important decision to make.

What is that decision for you? Right now is the decision not for the world outside of you? Are you the follower? Do you continue to be the follower?

The door is now ready to close. Are you now ready to move forward on the pathway? The door is ready to close. Which side of the door are you on?

Placing the Golden Key

When I opened my eyes from Jeff's channeling, David was laying spread eagle on the forest floor with his eyes rolling into the back of his head. The energy of this message had literally knocked the dear proxy for a loop. The energy and the message were very powerful. It was my desire for the members of our group to go forward confidently to pursue the divine soul plans and purposes we had discovered and which Jeshua had affirmed for us. Would I accept whatever choices the others and I made, and not judge them?

For me, this message was the perfect ending/beginning to the journey. Jeshua had laid out the options for us, and I knew what I had chosen: to move out from the wheel's hub and take my "spoke" further out into the world.

We lingered at the last vortex as long as we could, but we did have guests coming for the full moon ceremony and we needed to prepare for it. Honestly, I did not resonate with the ceremony. I would have preferred to do an ascension chair ceremony. But it did ease leaving the mountain. Our mission was complete. The full moon ceremony, which George would be leading, was also a chance for me to surrender control. I did not even fully understand what it was about, but I felt neutral about doing it. I was looking forward to being with Dianne that evening. The journey had begun with her and I would now see her at its end.

Since we were deep in the forest, it took us quite some time to get back to the main marker near the Lemurian gateway. We only had one final task to perform. We had to place the citrine crystal, the golden key to the Lemurian gateway, in a hidden, sacred place. This place would be accessible to the six of us if we needed the key at any point in the future.

It was clearly difficult for David to leave the citrine crystal on the mountain. He had brought it from home, thinking he would bring it back charged with the energy of Mount Shasta, and he had already packed it in his suitcase ready for his flight the next day. Then he had learned from Michael that it must be left behind on the mountain. The five smaller citrine crystals I brought, which we had used in the first ritual, were already safely buried at the Lemurian gateway. After much searching, we found the perfect hidden altar for the bright orange stone on a rock face. Since David was attached to the crystal, we agreed that he should place it in its resting place.

As we hiked back to our parking spot, my nostalgia returned. If I came this way again, it very likely would be to alter the Lemurian gateway for an unknown divine purpose. The planet was going to go through major shifts as ascension continued and we would have much to accept in order to reduce our pain during the ascension process. This would enable necessary planetary shifts to occur. Acceptance eliminates resistance, and, as you surely know, what we resist persists. We stopped and said goodbye to the entrance boulders, then hiked further around the ravine, unloaded our gear, and piled into our third-dimensional vehicles. We would be in the village of Mount Shasta for a couple more days, but we would not return to the mountain. The mission of the forbearers of the Children of the Awakened Heart was complete.

Chapter 20
The Full Moon Gathering

Before taking our trip, Michael had suggested that an important part of our journey off of the mountain would be connecting with other people on their spiritual path. Throughout the week, as we made our way about the village, we had therefore been asking different people we met to join us on the evening of day 6 for a gathering of likeminded, like-spirited people. Finding such folks wasn't difficult in Mount Shasta. The entire village was full of metaphysicians and businesses that supported spiritual endeavors. The weekend ahead included the annual Wesak Festival, celebrating the Buddha's birthday. People were flocking into town from all over the planet and there would be a full moon to boot. Yes, Mount Shasta was a spiritual junky's paradise.

For the gathering, George had proposed doing a full moon ceremony. I wasn't sure what this had to do with the mission of our journey, which was ascension. But David and George were really into doing it and so I went along with them. The important thing to me was that our sacred tasks on the mountain had been completed. The group had decided it would be best not to discuss the mountain journey in much detail, so a moon moment just might do!

After a full day on the mountain, we didn't have a lot of time to prepare for guests. Jeff and Joel weren't resonating with the ceremony either, so they disengaged. I did my best to pitch in around the house. Jeff knew that his big contribution for the evening would be bringing in Michael for a message. This was probably the biggest attraction for most of our guests; they wanted to "meet" an archangel. For myself, I was looking forward to spending quality time with Dianne Robbins. It would feel good to have her present at the last day's ritual. While everyone else was mingling before the ceremony, I planned to share in detail with her what had taken place on the mountain. I felt that she, of all people, should be told since she was seminal to the creation of the journey. After engaging in a delirium of third-dimensional preparations for a couple of hours, David, George, and I finally got our work done. Before the first guest arrived, the house was aglow with candlelight, chairs had been arranged for group seating, and finger food had been set out. At the appointed hour, our house was swiftly filled with divine souls having a human experience.

George had created an altar in front of the fireplace in the living room. This would serve as his podium for the ceremony, which involved him reading material from a set of computer printouts. George is a brilliant and gifted healing arts therapist, but this ceremony was not the most synchronistic moment. Of course, what mattered most was his intention. People were reluctant to come up to the altar and drink out of the same cup. Attempting to be supportive, I went up to share the liquid from the cup George offered after only one other person had come forward. Soon the ceremony was over. Everyone, including George, was ready to move on with the evening.

Once Jeff saw that George had finished, he entered into a trance. Having just experienced such an astonishing day on the mountain, I was curious what Archangel Michael would have to say to this "virgin" gathering. I had experienced hundreds of Michael sessions over the years and was always delighted and amazed how he tailored his message for the members of each group...

Michael's Message

Welcome. You are beginning to find your pathway, all you people enjoying this wonderful evening. Meandering about at the beginning of your pathway, that new pathway into the realm of the unknown, you can now move out into the world with your talents and gifts and begin to give to the world. Each and every one of you is looking for the new beginning on the new pathway. You are being rebirthed and you are meandering about, looking to find that place, that specific place where you need to begin, where you need to build a foundation. Some of you have the foundation you seek. Some of you are not quite sure what the foundation is. You're beginning to look for the foundation.

Each and every one of you is curious about what your life holds for you as you go forward and toward your new life, for each and every one is looking to build a new life. Many of you are not quite sure what that new life has in store for you. Yet, the most important aspect of where you are is building a foundation so you can use it as a springboard toward a new life.

First, it's important that you realize who you are. It's important to go through a process of moving into the depth and breadth of your heart space to find out who you truly are. It's important to learn to love, honor, and value yourself in the deepest sense you could ever imagine. This means coming to love every aspect of yourself fully, even those which you shame and judge. You have been conditioned to shame and judge these aspects by Mom and Dad. You've been taught by Mom and Dad.

It is time now to fully move into the depth and breadth of your heart space to learn about you, to love you, to honor you, to value you—and to the greatest extent you have in your life. When you do this, you can look in the mirror and know in full who you are and what your talents and gifts are.

What are your talents and gifts? What are the things you simply love doing and giving to the world? What are they? Do you know what they are? All of you know there's something or many things that you do that you enjoy and can bring into the world. Now you can begin to look at all of these things with a new meaning, value, and purpose. You may know what your talents and gifts are, but you're not quite sure what meaning, value, and purpose they have.

It's time to embody you, to begin to know what your needs are. Begin to know that as you move out into the world, it's important to give to yourself. Give to yourself that which you say you want. Live the life that you say you want to live.

Are you living the life you say you want to live? It's an important question because you are all living the life that you have right now. Is this life you are leading the same life you say you want or are you just meandering about in your life getting by, struggling to survive your life? This is about giving to the world from the depth and breadth of your heart space so as to create the life you say you want to create. Are you creating the relationships you say you want? For others, getting to know you is about getting to know the relationship you're having with yourself.

What is the relationship you are having with yourself? Do you love yourself? Do you honor yourself? Do you value yourself? Are you using the relationship you are in now to get something? Are you using the relationship that you are in simply to resist moving out in the world as an individuated adult having the life you say you want? It is quite important that you move into the depth and breadth of your heart space to know who you are. Then you can move to a place of realizing, remembering, and rediscovering your talents and gifts.

You are all ready to change. Some change to a greater extent. Some are subtle changes, some drastic because you're all realizing that the old lives have lost their meaning, value, purpose. Some are asking, "What can I do? How can I live? Or more so, how can I give? What can I give in a third-dimensional world of upheaval? What are my talents and gifts to give and who am I?"

As you move through the process of discovering who you are, discovering and remembering your talents and gifts, you move to a place of peace to find your purpose in the third-dimensional realm. What is your purpose in this lifetime, the lifetime you chose to live, the lifetime in the human condition you choose to live? Moving forward is quite practical. It's practical in looking at your brethren, your fellow man and fellow woman around this room, wondering, "How can I give to make this world a better place to live?" since this is the lifetime you are living.

It's most important to ask yourself questions as you now look for this new life, as you stand at the doorway, at the precipice, at the intersection, at the crossroads to the new life. Do you honor, value, and love you? Do you even know what that is? Can you give to yourself the life you say you want? What is the life you are living now? Can you see your talents and gifts? Can you remember your talents and gifts? Can you discover your talents and gifts?

So we ask you simply, what brings you the greatest joy in your life? And what we ask you also to do now is to write down that which brings you the greatest joy in your life. Realizing that you are often looking for an outcome, how, when, where, and who will this come from? Can you simply be in a place of finding that which brings you the greatest amount of joy? Then, once you have identified that, ask: What talents and gifts do I possess that bring me the greatest amount of joy in my life? This will lead you to find out why you are here. Because the natural state of being is *being you,* can you be you? Are you fully being you?

Reveal who you are to the world. Reveal the depth of you and who you are. Are you revealing who you are, the essence of you, the depth and breadth of your heart space to the world? Are you revealing yourself to the world? If so, are you enjoying, valuing, and honoring the process of revealing yourself to the world by simply being you?

You see, moving into your heart space and revealing to the world the depth and essence of who you are is the greatest, most joyful process you can ever be in. To be that essence in the world is the greatest state. The greatest sense of joy comes when you allow yourself to release the layers of the mask you've created around your heart space.

Perhaps you created those layers to be someone else or perhaps so you could be who you thought another person would like you to be, so this person would love you.

You see, moving forward now is simply about being you. But first you must know the essence of you, know the depth of you, so you can walk into your new life simply radiating with the effervescent joy from your heart space: being you, and then, along with that, bringing forward your talents and gifts. What you love doing in the world is embodying your talents and gifts. There is joy in doing whatever it is you do, using whichever talents and gifts you utilize out in the world. What do you enjoy? What are these talents and gifts? What brings you joy? When you do all of this, you'll move organically on the pathway toward realizing your purpose.

You see the only way in which you can find your purpose in life is through embodying your divine soul plan in this lifetime. When you have fully honored, valued, and loved yourself and embodied the depth of you and your talents and gifts, you have activated your divine soul plan.

You see you are all moving to this precipice. So we ask you again, do you love you?

People's Responses

Hearing Michael's message was like taking a crash course in life! As I looked around the room to see people's responses and reactions I could tell that Michael's message had gone straight into their hearts. Their minds may have still been questioning what they heard, but their hearts knew this was a blueprint for a new life. Once again Michael had given the greatest gift he could have given this gathering: unconditional love and eternal wisdom.

The full moon gathering had joined the mountain rituals in being complete. However, our guests lingered, not wishing to leave the candlelight, the high-vibrational energy of Michael's words, and our intention to be with them. Knowing that the five of us would be in town for a couple more days, we were being invited to attend other activities. There would be plenty to do or not before we left. Right then, all I wanted to do was further absorb all that had taken place during the miraculous week. The idea of doing nothing felt great. I just wanted to be.

The next night, we were going to have a powwow on the future of Children of the Awakened Heart. I knew it was going to be an emotional meeting, and challenging. Things needed to be said that had never been spoken in total truth. Michael had asked us to define our individual roles in the group and the service we intended to give the world. It was time to move from the wheel's hub and take our singular spokes out into world service—or not. It was all about being ready.

I held my Lemurian sister, Dianne, in my arms as I kissed her goodnight. I knew she understood everything and there was no need for words between us. We felt each other's heart space and knew we were committed to Lemurian truth and teaching. We'd see each other and speak when we were supposed to. Her departure prompted the other remaining guests to leave.

In the solitude of my bedroom, I felt grateful for what we had accomplished on the mountain. We had done what we were chosen (and chose) to do, even without always understanding it all. I was very aware of the contrast between the fifth-dimensional energy on the mountain and the third-dimensional energy off the mountain that the five members of our team often experienced. "This only matters in matter," I said to myself. Our not always connecting had frustrated me at first, but then I came to know the wisdom and purpose within the contrast. Since we were indeed proxies for humankind, how could it be otherwise? Look at the world now; we had to reflect it. It was all a perfect reflection of the world's soul plan and each of ours.

ॐ

As I focused on the silhouette of Mount Shasta outside my window, I thanked her for bringing me here and all she had revealed. I connected with Adama and shared that I knew this was just the beginning of our work together. I asked him to take me into the heart of Lemuria while I slept. There I would be with all the loving beings of the archangelic and Lemurian realms that had made this journey possible. I was at blissful peace.

Chapter 21
Day 7, Saying Farewell

The Bible says something like this: "On the seventh day God ended his work and rested." On the seventh day of our trip to Mount Shasta, in my heart I also knew our work there was done. The remainder of my visit would be used to rest and reflect on the truth of what I had learned.

In the teachings on the Seven Sacred Flames, Friday is the day of the ascension flame, which is a dazzling white ray of light. I put on a bright white shirt and reflected on the importance of *this Friday*. In my morning meditation, I drew the ascension flame into the cellular memory of my physical body and into my emotional and mental bodies. I focused on clearing negativity, false beliefs, and poor patterns of thought that were hindering my self-mastery and ascension. I reminded myself that everything I experience is merely a teaching tool of love and that ascension is a union of my human self with my divine presence. Although I couldn't conceive of all the misuses of my divine presence I must have created and experienced in this life or past lives, I knew I wanted any karmic cycles to end now. Endings of old ways and beginnings of new ways were just some of the many great gifts of this journey that I received.

I really didn't feel like doing too much and mainly wanted to rest and reflect even though I knew that some of us would check out the Wesak Festival. Our group had been invited to a crystal bowl orchestra event. We also had scheduled a farewell dinner and forbearers meeting. David would be leaving in the morning on Saturday and the rest of us would depart on Sunday.

A Review of the Seven Sacred Flames

While still in my meditative state and feeling multi-dimensional, I reviewed the days of our week at Mount Shasta in light of the Seven Sacred Flames. How had our activities aligned with the seven flames of ascension?

Our travel and arrival day had been a Saturday. This is the day of the week on which the earth is penetrated by the violet flame of transmutation and freedom. Six days earlier, we certainly were about to be transmuted and set free, if we so chose. The violet flame brings the vibrations of change and freedom, and it assists in people clearing any issues standing in the way of their self-mastery. Knowing this correlation, I had purposefully worn a violet-colored shirt on the plane to California. We knew changes were coming for us and the world and we had felt sure that we could choose whatever was necessary to implement these changes and freedom.

The first ritual and the two ceremonies at the vortices of intention and of children had taken place on a Sunday, the day that the earth is penetrated with the yellow flame of the mind of God and wisdom/illumination. The yellow flame assists people in attaining higher consciousness, which is essential to ascension, for if one can join one's mind with the divine mind one can make better decisions and bring more positive conduct into your life. As we joined our minds in the ritual that opened up the Lemurian gateway and helped bridge that subculture, as Michael would say, with the energy of the fifth dimension, all things became possible. What a perfect day that had been for our work at the vortex near the main marker. I was beginning to see another level of the divine perfection in how this journey had been set up.

Our first free day and day to explore had been on a Monday, the day of penetration by the blue flame representing the will of God. Now I know why Monday is sometimes called "blue Monday." I previously thought it was because Monday is the beginning of the workweek. Now I saw that expression differently. The blue flame assists us in surrendering to divine will in every area of our lives. Surrender is one of the fastest ways to achieve self-mastery and spiritual mastery. I could not help making the connection between our activities on day 3 and the blue flame. All of us went out into nature that Monday and saw the will of God at work.

Ritual two, along with the ceremonies at the vortex of the people and the vortex of the world, had taken place on a Tuesday, which is the day associated with the rose-colored flame of divine love. Love is the glue that creates, transforms, heals, and harmonizes all things. This flame teaches us to love, and what we and the world need now is love. If we can simply love ourselves and one another, all separation can end and humanity shall move into fifth-dimensional reality. That had been our day of silence. Through our silence, I learned how words and actions prevent the exchange of love and create separation.

Our next day of free exploration had been on a Wednesday, the weekday related to the emerald green flame of divine healing and abundance. It didn't pass my notice that the members of our entire group were originally attracted to metaphysics because we were (and we still are) looking to heal something within ourselves. Many people in the healing arts suffer from a lack of abundance. This flame reminded us that we needed to balance our personal imbalances before we could help others. To focus on "what is" with gratitude is the fastest path to abundance. Focusing on that day, I was filled with an "attitude of gratitude" for all that is in my life (rather than what is not).

Our third and final ritual, which took place on day 6, came on a Thursday. On this day of the week, the earth is penetrated by the golden flame of resurrection, which assists us in bringing all of our divine talents and gifts out into the world. Anything dormant can be resurrected, if we so choose. This flame, along with the others, prepares us for ascension, moving into higher dimensions and frequencies of consciousness, the ultimate purpose of all our lifetimes. Due to the presence of the resurrection flame, our Thursday on the mountain energetically had been the ideal day to set out to find the vortices of rebirth and renewal.

Friday, as we have already discussed, is the day of the white flame of ascension.

Our last full day in Mount Shasta would be on a Saturday, returning us energetically to the violet flame of transmutation and freedom. Violet was the alpha and the omega of the journey. We could be changed and set free from our self-imposed limitations, if we so chose. True wisdom had been given to us from higher realms and we could choose to make choices and decision based upon the truths we had learned or not. Most of us would travel home on Sunday on the yellow flame of the mind of God.

As I meditated, I saw how perfectly the tasks accomplished during each day of our trip had related to the different sacred flames. Just like me and my fellow proxies, and you and I, the entire journey clearly had a divine plan of its own.

The Wesak Festival

The Wesak Festival is an annual celebration of Buddha's birth and enlightenment, which is marked by the first full moon in May. According to the people I encountered at the festival, it honors his energetic return to bless humankind through the renewed spiritual commitment of the Christ consciousness. In addition, it is said that Wesak is the time when the ascended master known as Christ gathers the entire spiritual hierarchy together in meditation to bless humanity. Archangel Michael has said that the ascended master known as the Buddha is an expression of the wisdom of God, an embodiment of light, and an indicator of divine purpose—and he works with the Seven Sacred Flames. The Buddhists consider Wesak the most powerful full moon of the year, an event with the capability of "pouring an elixir of healing over the entire planet."

When I found out about these details at the Wesak Festival, I thought, "Maybe this is the reason George wanted to have a full moon ceremony!" For certain, it was the reason that thousands had made a pilgrimage to Mount Shasta that particular weekend we were there. It was also the original reason our group had decided to stay over for an extra day after our final ritual was done.

Though it was wonderful to be in the energy of Wesak, after everything we had experienced on the mountain during the week it felt like a slightly disharmonious frequency to me. Among other things, much of the festival involved presenting and selling products and services related to the healing arts and spiritual growth. While I see the purpose and value in that, I simply could not resonate with that aspect of the festival right then even though on the inside I was honoring and having gratitude for the Buddha energy. What I really wanted was to get back to nature.

Jeff, Joel, and I ditched the festival and headed out to Castle Lake, an incredible natural wonder surrounded by mountains with rocky cliffs, which is located just outside

Mount Shasta near Lake Siskiyou, the body of water that Jeff and I had visited a few days earlier. If you begin hiking at Castle Lake, the trail actually takes you to another lake a little further along. Soon you reach the heart-shaped and aptly-named Heart Lake nestled in the cliffs high above.

With all the dialogues on being in the depth and breadth of the heart space that I have heard and participated in throughout recent years, it was wonderful to experience a perfect heart-shaped body of water in such an incredible natural setting. It seemed to be an earthly personification of Michael and Adama's teachings during our journey.

Jeff, Joel and I hung out by the lake, steeping ourselves in the refreshing energy of both the lake and the cliffs until it was time to head back into town to meet David and George for our farewell dinner. This would be followed by the crystal bowls concert and our Children of the Awakened Heart meeting.

The Last Supper

Since David was leaving a day earlier than the rest of us, we had decided to have our last group dinner on Friday night. This trip had been one of the most amazing experiences of my life and I've had a few big ones, including being initiated in the King's Chamber of the Great Pyramid on the Giza Plateau in Egypt by Syrian star masters who taught me the secrets of the universe. But I knew that what had happened on Mount Shasta had changed and would continue to change my life. My earlier spiritual journeys had been connecting with something/someone outside me. This current journey had been helping me to connect more fully with aspects of my higher self that lived in another dimension and inside the planet. Gathering for the last supper was really bringing home to me how highly personalized the journey was for me.

Everybody resonates with what he or she needs and is capable of experiencing in a given moment. There is no right or wrong about needs or subjective experience. I don't know if my fellow proxies had the same experience as me on the trip. That does not matter. They had received that which they came to Mount Shasta to receive. I knew this even as we were seated at the dinner table that night. I found myself feeling "individuated" from the others—almost separate, but not quite. It really isn't possible to feel entirely separated from people with whom you have just had this type experience. But the situation among us felt like we were a couple (even though there were six of us in the "marriage") who have had children together and are breaking up. I would have liked for there to have been more of an organic connection among all the members of our group. But that's not the purpose of proxies, is it? Each of us had been chosen and chose this trip for our own divinely soulful reasons.

We had a lovely last supper. There was sadness in my heart, but an even larger sense of joy. After dinner, Jeff, Joel, George, and I headed to the crystal bowls concert. David went home. Ashalyn went back to her house to rest up for another tour group coming in over the next day or two. Of course, we knew she would not be having another adventure like this one soon!

Singing Crystal Bowls Concert

The vibrations created by crystal bowls are awesome and we often use them at the wellness center where I am co-director of the mystery school. But the concert we were about to experience was unparalleled. We had been invited to attend by some of the people who had come to our full moon gathering. It was a private after-hours event at a mammoth crystal store. Sort of like going into a 1920's speakeasy, you knocked on the locked door and said you were there for the private concert and then they let you in. This crystal store was amazing; it had hundreds of thousands of crystals in it harvested from all over the world. It held a fortune in the crystal bowls, and included a hospital for recovering and sick crystals. We walked around this cavern of crystals, not believing the quantity or quality. The price of crystals has steadily increased over the years. This was a big business!

After touring the space for awhile, basking in the crystal displays, we were taken to another room for the concert. A rather grandmotherly lady with a glowing face greeted us with a baton in her hand, looking like a fairy godmother and orchestral conductor rolled into one. There were about fifty or sixty crystal bowls of all shapes, colors, and sizes in the front of the room. The guests were lying on the floor adjacent to the bowls. "I shall answer no questions," our conductor began. "You are here to experience something magical and wonderful just for you." I found a place on the floor to spread out my entire body. When it was time to commence, the conductor sat on the floor nearby and began playing the bowls by rubbing her felt baton against a single bowl, then two bowls, then three. The entire room began to vibrate. By the time she had added a fourth bowl to the mix, I had begun to vibrate. First my feet, then my legs, my torso, and finally my head were vibrating along with the crystals. I closed my eyes and surrendered to the sensation of the vibrations.

By now the conductor had many bowls vibrating at the same time. She knew exactly what she was orchestrating and its effect on us. As I allowed myself to shift into a higher frequency of being, I felt my body lift off the floor. I was experiencing a master crystal teacher connecting us to the Buddha Wesak energies. Now I knew what Wesak was! I fell into a deep sleep as my body settled back onto the floor. Over an hour went by, as the woman continued to weave frequencies with her huge array of bowls. Few will ever experience such an event. This was my dessert for the farewell dinner: to join with the harmonics of the highest frequencies.

Meeting of the Sometimes-Awakened Hearts

This was our last night of the five of us being together, as David was leaving in the morning. Michael had been encouraging us to define and refine our roles as forbearers within the Children of the Awakened Heart group and to articulate how our purpose, as individual souls, would be expressed in world service. So we had planned to have a meeting at the end of the trip to discuss our vision of the future. After the concert, the five of us met in the living room at the cottage.

For the past couple of years, the five of us had maintained a website dedicated to Michael's messages and inviting people to attend live gatherings in New York either at my apartment or at David's. During these gatherings, Michael would deliver a message for the group after which he would open the floor to questions. Over the past year, the five of us had not always been in agreement about the role we forbearers, as hosts, should play. Was it okay to use the gatherings to ask questions about our own personal process or should we be facilitators for the experience of others? Some wanted the direction of the group to shift. Some did not. So we thought it best to attempt to resolve where we all were in our thinking and expectations.

From the journey, it seemed clear to me that Archangel Michael and the beings of the higher realms were urging us to move out singularly in service to the world, using group meetings as a hub for our individual work, but not its central focus—not as "spokes" on the wheel of our collective. Co-founding the Modern Day Mystery School represented me following my new path, of this I was certain. It seemed important to me to continue healing myself, but not desirable to bring my unhealed aspects into the pursuit of my world service. That could be done privately.

Remembering the Five Agreements that Michael had given us as guidelines for our lives soon after we founded Children of the Awakened Heart, it was now time to see where everyone was in regard to the matter of his individual world service, if he looked at it without the "narcissistic me" in it. It was time to declare our intentions for what we each would bring into the world. Much of this information had been gleaned during the six hours of silence during the second ritual on balancing the "me" and the "we" and the third and fourth vortex ceremonies. Each of us had made profound discoveries during the six-hour period, which we had been processing on our own ever since. Now it was time to reveal what was relevant to one another.

First, Jeff announced that he no longer wished to bring in Michael for group or individual personal processing. He shared that he was ready to move his work out into the world through the publication of his first book, *Journey of the Awakened Heart,* which he had been working on during the period of preparation for the trip, as well as through giving lectures and workshops.

Joel said that he felt part of his purpose was to bring Michael's teachings to audiences of people who were like him. He had already created an eight-week life mastery course from the teachings of Michael, from which curriculum he had created an introductory workshop for my school in Florida. He was in the process of revising and refining this course, and would launch it in the fall. He is a journalist and intended to use these skills to continue his world service, as the host for our YouTube interviews with Michael on current events and by writing more books. Joel was already the author of *The Second Coming,* an amazing book of the teachings of Archangel Gabriel.

I shared how I had been applying the Michael and Gabriel teachings both in my private practice and through the Modern Day Mystery School. My world service would include returning home to continue teaching about the Seven Sacred Flames and the Lemurians. I explained that I intended to use my film production and writing skills to spread Lemurian teachings throughout the world.

When it came to developing a new vision of Children of the Awakened Heart, my recollection is that David and George were uncertain, and said they were happy with the way things had been. They made it clear that they were unwilling to embrace the majority's wishes. George, our treasurer, had been our can-do guy from the beginning. He is also a skilled Reiki master teacher and light ascension therapist. David is a gifted channel and healer in his own right. Both men stated that they wished to keep things within our group largely the same. But creation means growth and expansion through change, which is all there is. The status quo had reached its end.

Emotions ran high. But by the end of our meeting we had all spoken our truths, stated our needs, and set our boundaries without malice or the intention of harming one another. I went to bed knowing that my intention was to move forward beyond the doorway of which Michael and Jeshua had spoken—the doorway of world service leading to the new life of community, harmony, and equality—upon our return home from the trip. If others did not feel ready to move through that same door, then they would and could stay right where they were until they were ready.

It had been foretold that the gatekeeper would eventually move to Mount Shasta. While on our journey this prophecy was confirmed. George had the revelation that he wanted to move there. It gave all of us shivers when we heard him say so. The community seemed so suited to him. In my heart, I felt that doing so would help him to fully embrace himself as the mystic and master healer he is. David is already on a clear soul path in the acting community. In my heart there also was no doubt he would continue to bring his gifts and talents into his career. His compassion, wisdom, and discipline make him an extraordinary, soulful actor.

≈❧≈

Up in my bedroom, as I closed my eyes to join my Lemurian brothers and sisters within their frequency, with their Earth home rising outside my bedroom window, I knew with certainty that although our mutual mission was ending, our work with Michael's agreements would continue.

Part Three
Lemurian Wisdom

If you read about Lemurian wisdom only once for the sake of information or entertainment it can do little to enhance your overall preparation for ascension into higher frequencies of consciousness. And that would be okay, of course. But if you allow it to become your daily truth, the world of the Lemurians could become your reality. This I know and aspire to. Eventually we're all going to end up there. It's our divine destiny.

In this final section of the book, I am going to share more of the wisdom that the Lemurians have taught me. Some of this material comes from conversations with Adama that I channeled on behalf of the students at The Modern Day Mystery School, and some was specifically provided to me in answer to questions that came up as I wrote this book. It is an idiosyncratic mixture of commentary from Adama, questions and answers, and my own opinions. The purpose and intent is to offer some guidance on a lifestyle conducive to ascension.

Adama has said on numerous occasions, "Our confinement in the center of the planet away from humanity has served an evolutionary purpose, enabling us to strive for, and reach heights of accomplishment that we could have never achieved on the surface. We have been free to evolve into spiritual warriors of light. But someday soon we shall join one another."

Boy, I am ready now. How about you? I've always known in my heart that we were beings of light. And while I was not willing to fight wars on the surface of the Earth through the American military, I am willing to be a loving spiritual warrior of light. By being the light, we no longer need to fight. That's an important message.

Chapter 22
As Above, So Below

"As above, so below," I remember hearing this all my life. Now this ancient adage is finally coming to life for me. Before the Lemurian adventure in Mount Shasta took place I never imagined that there were forces below us, as well as the ones above, supporting our highest good. This cosmic sandwich we're in is allowing us to evolve into our essence as light beings.

Did you ever wonder why there are so many people on Earth now? I don't think it's because of the standard of health care we've achieved. All of us are part of an experience/experiment. We are here to experience the coming together of two great forces of light. Nothing can be forced on us because we have our free will. As for me, I choose a big bite of the cosmic sandwich.

Adama: We are grateful for being part of this wondrous experience/experiment. The purpose of life is to learn to love. Earth is a great "lover-versity," where we are all being schooled in life's evolutionary process. At some eventual point, we shall all come together in love, in oneness. There's nowhere else to be/go, for we are all one.

Phillip: Adama, while we are talking about light, would you please explain to us how you achieve light within the Earth?

Adama: We use light's energy (we are nothing except for energy), to create and develop our entire underground world. We use light to travel in our astral bodies and to light up our underground passageways with our crystal-light energy technology. We are connected to all star systems in our galaxy via our amino acid computer networks. These are similar to your Worldwide Web, but more advanced. These systems have allowed us to gather enough light (energy) to create the central sun that lights our skies and powers our world, just like yours.

Light is the great force of the Creator, and it is our attunement with the Creator that generates all the light force we need. Much of our technology will be revealed to humankind on the surface soon. Remember, we also have the ability through telepathic thought to create our reality. While your thoughts are also creating your reality, yours are more limited due to your lower frequency. Once you raise your frequency to where ours is there are no limits.

Our light is no brighter than your light. It's just that our hearts are open wider to the Source of all creation. And we are conscious of Source more often than you. So it is our consciousness of where light comes from that creates the difference in our lives. More and more of you on the surface are awakening to the light, which will allow the two great civilizations to merge soon. At that time all of our advanced technology will be yours—meaning, when you are ready to apply it towards peaceful means. It is this spiritual evolution that is causing some confusion and chaos on the Earth's surface. What you resist persists. Those who are not prepared to evolve are resisting the new energy coming in, and when light is resisted the opposite of love and light exists.

In truth, we are brothers and sisters sharing the same genetic makeup. Both of us have lived on the surface at one time. Since we are connected through our genetic coding and living on the same planet, it's only natural that you on the surface would be curious about us. Many of you are learning of us for the first time, but we have known about you for a very long time. And we do know all about you. So let's see if we can tell you a little more about us.

You already know we are taller and sturdier. We also can stay in physical format as long as we choose and move back into a higher dimension whenever we are ready. We can even shift how we look at will, and can become visible and invisible. If you feel envious, remember that your race is headed in this direction also. Being in a dense, low-vibration format is not the structure of choice for higher beings. When we resurface, we shall reveal all you need to know to achieve everything we have achieved. We have kept this wisdom safe for eons for both of us.

The fact that we know what is destined to be is the result of a contract we made prior to incarnating on this planet. Yes, your race and ours come from somewhere else. We are all ETs. The ETs are us! (And we're not the only ones). Our contract is called the "so below, as above" contract. Many of you are aware of this notion and do not find it unusual. For others, it's a nice surprise. Right now incredible ascension energies are coming to you from below and above, on and in the Earth to assist in the ascension process. It is time for us Lemurians to appear and to be reconnected with you, and for you to be reconnected with the entire universe.

More Details about the Lemurian Lifestyle

Living a long time, without aging, has allowed the Lemurians to become wise and apply that wisdom within their civilization. They have learned wars don't work and that equality for all is a must. Adama says, "You simply cannot advance without conscious immortality. Your bodies are designed to live forever. It is your thoughts and emotions that prevent this from happening. And now many of you are becoming aware of the relationship between your thoughts and emotions and your bodies. The fountain of youth is real and it's located in your mind and emotions. I am a very old man by your measurements and yet I maintain a youthful appearance. You'll be pleased when you remember how effortless it is to maintain a similarly vital countenance."

Much of my healing arts practice utilizes these truths. In Western medicine we are largely treating symptoms, not cause and effect. Ancient truths are resurfacing because, quite frankly, there hasn't been a lot of healing in the practice of most of our medicine. We know how to turn a disease into a money-making maintenance system. Thus, we are surviving with diseases such as cancer, diabetes, and HIV. But there isn't a lot of curing going on.

Adama often reminds me of our freedom of choice and will, and that no one is allowed to interfere with it. For this reason, the Lemurians cannot interfere with our modern medicine, our stressful lifestyles, and our poor eating habits. My country-people, the Americans, are some of the fattest people in the world. We came here to experience this freedom of choice and will, and by gosh we have! But the Lemurians can make suggestions. Are we ready to listen? Let's contrast some of things Lemurians do with what we do...

You've probably figured out there is no health insurance in Lemuria because they don't need it. There are no hospitals, no doctors, and no nursing homes. Disease does not exist. The civilization stays connected to universal laws and divine principles in all they think, feel, and create. They know their bodies are meant to live for thousands of years without aging or death. Since this is what everyone experiences, it's completely normal and doesn't take much effort.

By contrast, look at all the effort and expense we put into trying to be here a few decades. Live, high-vibrational, pure, organic food is vital to the Lemurians well-being and ours. Contrast this to the processed, dead, non-vital foodstuffs we often eat. There are more artificial toxins in our food supply than in anything real anymore. That fact is that our food is often stale and dead, and there is little or no life force in most of what we eat. And we wonder why we get ill?

Many of us know these facts, but it's helpful to be reminded at times. What we eat is critical to sustaining a healthy, vital body, and achieving the Lemurian reality of immortality. Our brothers and sisters below suggest that we start paying more attention to what we put in our bodies. So let's read labels, avoid synthetic food. If you cannot pronounce it, don't eat it.

The Lemurians have been watching and monitoring us for thousands of years. Did you ever have the feeling someone was watching you? Well, they were, right under your feet. Watching us with loving and supporting eyes, waiting for the day we would join together and create a world beyond our imagination on the surface. A world many have given up on.

We have all heard the body called a temple, but our science is only beginning to understand what's housed in that temple and how amazing our bodies are. We still actually know little about it, even though we have learned a lot in the last two hundred years. All most have studied are the physical components of the body, yet some of the most astonishing aspects of the body are unseen/energetic. And natural science does not even recognize that these exist. Most of them would not acknowledge this book and the information in it. So if you have gotten this far in your reading, thank yourself for being willing to know the truth no matter what container it comes in.

We do not need universal healthcare. What we need is a deep awakening and gratitude for our physical bodies, and to start properly caring for them. It's understandable that our bodies begin to age a few years after puberty. By the time we hit middle age, the maintenance of health problems becomes the focus of most of our lives. How many of us even make it to a hundred years of age, let alone ten thousand years, like our Lemurian friends? It's fair to conclude that most of our diseases are the result of our lack of consciousness about the way we live.

"Oh, I'm going to die anyway, why take care of myself?" How many times have we heard statements like this one from those who are not caring about themselves? Suppose we changed our thinking into, "I'm going to be taking this body into an immortal state of being"? What would this do for us? This is what the Lemurians are attempting to teach us.

Already we are seeing new awareness regarding what we eat, exercising more often, bringing joy into our lives, finding ways (meditation, yoga, deep breathing) to reduce negative mental and emotional elements in our lives—the very negatives that make us ill, age us, and ultimately, kill us. Adama reminds us, "True healing can only originate from internal awareness. Anything outside the self is secondary and can only work if they support your internal awareness."

"Know thyself" is one of the wisest things ever said, followed by "Heal thyself."

Relationships, Marriage, and Sexuality in Lemuria

In my five years of healing arts training in New York, my colleagues and I were taught that the erotic sexual love life force is one of the most powerful forms of energy in the universe. It is meant to unite us and keep us in whatever frequency of physical form we choose. Right now, it is often doing the reverse of this because on the surface of the planet there is an imbalance between masculine and feminine energy. I believe this imbalance causes much of the pain and separation we create. It is the foundation for much of our prejudice and bigotry, which expresses itself in race relations, religion, and sexual orientation. Unfortunately, it also keeps us in a lower frequency of existence. Now we are being given an opportunity for these two complementary energies to come into balance so we can move to a higher frequency.

Let us examine the Lemurians use of sexual love energy in their relationships to see if we can gain a better understanding of its true purpose. For instance, it turns out that sexual energy originally was not connected with reproduction. This came later, after the alteration of our genes occurred as we lost our direct connection to the higher realms.

The core of Lemurian civilization is the application of universal law through unity and oneness. All advanced cultures adhere to the principles of oneness (essentially, "We are all one"). Right now these are largely just words to humans. The basis of unity is the application of unconditional love, which is very rare on the surface at this time. For most of us, love seems a sentiment. We give to get. Most of our relationships are based upon duality, not oneness. And we see failure in these types of relationships all around us. Very few marriages and relationships survive long term, let alone thousands of years. So are we ready for change?

Through our taught belief systems most of us have developed a distorted view of the balance of masculine and feminine energy. But many of us now wish to change it. We are beginning to realize that neither of these energies can go forward without being balanced by its complement. Remember, the only relationship we are having is the one with our self (and all other relationships mirror that). The other is merely a reflection for us to learn from.

In truth, we cannot love another without loving our self. And we were never taught this growing up. In fact, we were often taught the opposite: that it is wrong to love yourself "too much." But if you can't give yourself love you will simply create a need for someone else to give you what you can't give yourself. The name for this is co-dependency. Co-dependent relationships are the majority of our relationships on the surface. The feminine energy is given less opportunities to be self-reliant than the masculine. A relationship founded upon need rather than oneness is diminished. The relationship becomes a power struggle of who's right, who's wrong, and who's in control. Intimacy flies out the window and duality becomes the basis of the relationship. We all know lots of examples of this in our lives and the lives of others.

When one and one equal two (not one half plus one half equals one) and two people have developed self-love and balanced the male and female energies in themselves, self-love and balance replace neediness. Then people can join in a joyous relationship with another, or be contented and fulfilled without another being present.

Adama explains that in Lemuria no one would ever enter any relationship that is not completely rewarding based upon equality, harmony, and balance. "We honor each other's divine soul plan." Though things are better on the surface, women must stop pretending that things are equal. They are not. Many women throughout the world are still deprived of basic rights and endure physical abuse. Many think of this as normal. Even in America, the land of supposed opportunity and equality, the taught behavior of putting up with abuse ("Stand by your man") still exists in many women. Unfortunately, the men are generally women's abusers. I am not for one instant asking you to blame the victim. The irony in all of this is that until we are all equal, no one is going anywhere. Both men and women need to become aware of the imbalance and remedy it. Men, especially in childhood, also must contend with abuse.

In all advanced civilizations throughout the universe "everyone considers male and female as two divine aspects of

Source, the Creator," Adama says. "It is the Divine Mother and Divine Father that are the key components which must constantly be honored in any relationship. It's not about who's in control, or right or wrong. Those are merely points of view, something we see as a waste of energy to fight over it. There's no addiction or attachment to an outcome in Lemuria."

Attachments and addictions are comfort zones in many of our relationships on the surface, and bring drama and duality into our lives. Boy do we love drama!

Of course, being without the worries of physical survival and financial issues is a huge burden Lemurians do not share with us. This takes much pressure off of Lemurian relationships that humans have to bear. Everything they need to live is free. Can you imagine: That's the way life was intended to be for us, too? Most of our relationships on the surface fail due to issues of survival. So the flow of harmony and balance is easier in Lemurian relationships. This allows more expressions of love and connection to the planet and universe itself. Adama promises this is where we are all headed...I don't know about you, but I am ready...

Sex Itself

Remember, the Lemurians are moving at a higher frequency than us, thus their bodies (which otherwise are almost the same as ours) are less physically dense. As a result, they can become much more intimate than we on the surface can. Adama explains, "When we physically unite, we join our physical and energetic bodies in the union of divine love." You might recognize the energetic body as the chakra system. And you might guess the most important chakra is the heart, which it is! In effect, the sex act itself is a "union of the physical and the divine spiritual heart merging with the Creator energy."

Some of us on the surface feel divine mergers momentarily during orgasm, but only for a few seconds and then it's gone. The Lemurian sexual experience is about sharing and maintaining that divine heart connection, which also is connected to the Creator. The Lemurians do not engage in sexual activity without deep, mutual love and never for control. But how many of us on the surface are having sex because we think we are supposed to or for control?

Having Children

"In higher civilizations," Adama explains, "there is no such thing as an unwanted pregnancy. Individuals are completely free to express themselves sexually without conceiving an unwanted child. Through telepathic thoughts/connections when a couple is prepared and ready to have a child, a soul is invited to manifest into physical form (no matter what its frequency). Initially, this happens outside the body before coming into the body." Actually, the same thing happens with humans. A soul selects its parents. It's just that the circumstances can be, and often are, different, since we are physically denser than Lemurians.

Adama says, "The entire spiritual Lemurian community welcomes the soul before it is born. And the unborn child feels completely loved and desired. Since we are larger, our babies are as well, and grow quickly within our universal wisdom and advanced knowledge. One additional advantage we have is that we know ahead of time the soul plan for each child. So when the child reaches challenging moments, such as puberty, we make sure each child receives the support and love he or she needs to activate his or her soul's plan."

It was further explained to me that when a couple decides to have a child they go to a temple for such decision making and apply for permission to receive this privilege (children are not a "right"). In advanced civilizations, only spiritually mature couples are allowed to descend a soul into physical birth. Thus receiving permission is known as a sacred event. Before actual conception there are many meetings between the soul to come and its future parents. During that time the divine soul plan is carefully studied and everyone prepares for the sacred pledge and privilege of parenting.

Adama invites me: "Let us go to Lemuria and be with a couple expecting a child."

We arrive at a small hamlet outside Telos and the couple is in the round crystalline home that their thoughts and intentions built for them. The entire neighborhood appears to be aware of the coming birth of a new community member. This is not an isolated event by any means. The entire city seems to be aware that this one new soul can make a unique difference in their culture. After conception, the gestation is only twelve weeks (reflecting the twelve star systems that seeded our planet). But a great deal happens during the sacred triad of these three months.

The couple is invited to move into one of the seven major temples (there are many smaller ones). They choose the Temple of the First Ray, which is known as the flame of the Will of God. It is hosted by an ascended master called El Morya who is assisted by Archangel Michael. It is very appropriate our couple has chosen the Temple of the First Ray since this will be their first child. The temple is filled with huge blue flame diamonds and the parents-to-be are taken to a chamber attended by blue flames angels. During their stay here, the couple will display the most divine love they are capable of expressing to each other. The child-to-come will feel this constant love throughout the pregnancy and his or her entire life. Music that elevates their being is all around them, as they submerge into the poignantly beautiful temple and chamber. Their child will know this beauty the rest of its life.

Teenage Years

The teenage years are often a challenging period for parents on the surface, so I thought it would be helpful to go into Lemurian culture and see how they handle it. Having no unwanted pregnancies helps a lot, but this is also a period of life with no judgment or shame inflicted on the teenager (unlike here on the surface). Adama explains that they understand the activation of the sexual hormones and the natural desires this creates. It is not something to be shamed or blamed. This is somewhat changing on the surface. Pregnant adolescents are no longer hidden, as they were in the fairly recent past. The double standard of male and female is slowly changing.

"When individuals reach sexual maturity they are allowed to experiment with their sexuality through what they have been taught as children," says Adama. "Their experiences are supported and supervised by the spiritual community. The young adults always have someone to process what they are experiencing. They are allowed to express with joy and pleasure all they need to with each other. The individuals will take whatever time they need to be ready for a committed relationship." And he smilingly adds, "The young Lemurians are always free to experiment and experience their sexuality as a natural part of their maturation."

Frankly, I look forward to the day when we are all in 5D format and our young people can be free to have this quality of life.

Commitment/Marriage

Who said, "It's always about being ready?" Readiness leads to commitment. Lemuria and here are pretty much the same on this one (for once). There comes a time when two individuals reach a point in their divine soul plans to mutually commit. You resonate, you have an affinity, and it just feels right. The commitment in Lemuria is for growth and expansion, not necessarily for permanence (at least at first). And this is happening more and more on the surface also.

Adama explains, "When two people get married/become committed, they marry as part of the expression of their divine soul plans. These relationships become full expressions of both souls and can last a few years or hundreds. When both feel complete in their experience together they can agree to part in a loving, supportive manner. They may thank each other for what the relationship has brought them both and remain friends for the rest of the lives."

When a couple has experienced a profound, committed marriage for hundreds or thousands of years, they gain permission from the spiritual community to become united in a sacred marriage. Thus, they become twin flames. Such relationships are eternal and they are the ones that lead to parenthood in Lemuria.

So, to review, there's the period of sexual experimentation (as much as you like), there are relationships that don't have to be permanent (and you can have as many of these as you need), and there is the one relationship that lasts forever that can lead to parenthood. And since you and your children are immortal, really this is an important choice.

Chapter 23
Questions and Answers

Now having an idea of what, why, and where Lemuria is and how I came to connect to it, let us address additional questions in order to deepen our knowledge of this remarkable Inner Earth civilization. My questions were answered by Adama, high priest and Lemurian spokesman.

There are many extraordinary temples in Lemuria. There are seven major ones that house what are called the Seven Sacred Flames, which contain tools and wisdom that will allow humans on the surface to join the Lemurians in what has been called an ascension process.

The following conversation took place in the Temple of the Second Ray, which is known as the flame of illumination and wisdom. There are many other higher beings associated with this temple, such as Buddha, Jesus, Confucius, and an ascended master known as Lord Maitreya. As I arrived in my light body, I saw a huge golden flame being attended by many angels. Adama and I sat down in golden crystal chairs in front of it.

Adama: You have too many erroneous belief systems imprinted in your soul that keep you in pain and limitation. Let us be together, as long as you need, to bring light into your hearts and souls.

Phillip: Thank you for being with us at this time. I know it is as important to you as it is to us to share as much light on Lemuria and where our world is presently, as possible. Let us begin by asking why are you making your presence known now?

Adama: This is a very special time for our planet and both our civilizations. All planets go through what is called an ascension process where they shift to a higher frequency in order to continue their growth and expansion. That time has now come for Earth. And we Lemurians who once walked upon the surface of this planet, through our love of you, wish to assist you in the process of ushering in a new golden age of love, peace, enlightenment, and true oneness. The world cannot stay the way it is and survive. So Mother Earth has already changed her frequency, thus everything within, and upon her body must shift also. You have all agreed to be here for this wonderful event. It is time for you to remember who you are and why you are here. The name of our capitol, Telos, means "communication with spirit." And we are now communicating with you. All planets are hollow and inhabited by life forms of many vibrations. The sun is also hollow. There is much truth to be revealed. So let us begin...

Phillip: So exactly how many of you are there in our hollow Earth?

Adama: There are over 120 subterranean cities within the Earth's interior, with millions of inhabitants. They can be accessed through holes at either the North Pole or the South Pole. The northern and southern lights you see in your skies are actually reflections of the Earth's central sun, which we created. There are many names for all the places and peoples, but we do not wish to overload you with all that now. Suffice to say, it is well organized. And all that information can be made available to you. Although Atlantis and Lemuria have become myths in your world, the people of both cultures are living in underground cities.

Phillip: Why have we not heard about all this before?

Adama: There are many in your world governments who know all about this and keep it from you in order to continue to control you. We have not come forward because your world has not been ready to receive us and we cannot interfere with your freedom of will and choice. If we come too early, there are many who will try to destroy us. But our being revealed is happening sooner rather than later, since many of you are now ready.

Phillip: There is a lot of corruption in world governments on the surface. What is the core issue?

Adama: The governments you have on the surface reflect the consciousness of the people they govern. The people have largely given their power away due to a lack of interest or feeling nothing can be done. It's not your leaders, it's you. In Lemuria we have highly-evolved individuals as our governmental and spiritual leaders. Stand in your power and make another choice.

Phillip: In keeping with changing government leaders, what do you Lemurians think about our President Obama? [*Note: This book was published in 2011—author*]

Adama: The entire planet shifted its consciousness 1 percent on the night he was elected. That is huge. His divine plan includes assisting in making the necessary shifts possible to move your world into unity, equality, harmony, and balance. There were many things about the office of the president he did not know until he got there. Most world leaders are at the mercy of the hidden forces that control your world. Your current president's intention is to reduce and/or eliminate the power of these hidden forces. It's no easy job. They are powerful and have been in place for thousands of years. Most people are completely unaware of them and consider any discussion of them as conspiracy theories. You surface people are largely asleep on this major issue. Wake up! Other enlightened leaders are being sent. We are hopeful they will be accepted.

Phillip: Do these hidden forces apply in the other major aspects of our world like religions and corporations?

Adama: Of course. Religions were the first governments and became fairly corrupted early on. Jesus, aka Lord Sananda, who we in Lemuria work with closely, never intended the creation of what became humankind's version of Christianity. He wished his primary teaching ("Love one another") to be purely made available to all.

Your corporations reflect the structure of your governments and religions. And the three—religion, business, and government—control your world. It's time for a new world creation filled with truth, transparency, and authentic leaders. This is not to say you don't have some good people in places of power, you do. But they are largely handicapped by the existing systems. You the people can choose to change the system.

Phillip: What's happening with the planet with all these manmade and natural disasters occurring?

Adama: Please know, dear people of the surface, that your Mother Earth has had enough of your abuse. She is a living being who has been largely ignored and been patient long enough. The natural disasters are her way of getting your attention but they go ignored most of the time. Do you need entire continents to sink (it has happened before) to understand? The air, water, and natural resources are her vital organs that make life possible for her and you. They are not a limitless supply to be bought and sold for profit. All the elements on the planet (plants, minerals, animals) are connected and have a right to be here. They are not here for your exclusive use and abuse. Human-made disasters can show you the same consciousness needed as the natural ones. Be aware all of these will increase until you shift your consciousness and behavior.

Phillip: Are the financial shifts and changes taking place reflecting a larger picture?

Adama: Yes, they are. The forces that control the world's finances (largely unseen) know that what they have been doing for a long time no longer will work in the future of the new world. They know light forces are in place to replace greed and separation with abundance and unity for all. So you will continue to see stops and starts of the old, until the old collapses and a new economy is created.

Phillip: What will that new economy look like?

Adama: It will be based on truth and reality, not myth and fiction. Most of the world's money supply is based on inflated credit. Most money is an I.O.U., not real money. You will return to a precious metal economy, based on things that are real from Mother Earth, not human-made fiction. Economies that reflect the balance and structure of the Earth will maintain and sustain the Earth and those living on its surface. This means some of these precious metals must go back to serving the Earth, not just humankind. Eventually you will become as we Lemurians, not needing money at all. You will be able to create everything you need through the power of manifestation.

Phillip: What was it like to have your entire civilization physically destroyed over night?

Adama: We knew for many hundreds of years this would take place, that there would be an ending to our great continent, and that we were not to interfere with the destruction. Out of the destruction would come creation. The spiritual leaders throughout the land prepared the people as best they could. They stayed with the people and went down with them. Most were sleeping when some 350 million of us perished. Many of you were there, including you. As horrible as it was, we were allowed to save the jewels of wisdom of our civilization and bring them underground to our home beneath Mount Shasta. Our enlightenments are now available to you on the surface so you do not have to experience what we did. And now we can advance together into our divine plans...

Phillip: What was the cause of the destruction?

Adama: It was two powerful civilizations not agreeing on how life should be, and one trying to control the other. One was an assertive masculine energy, the Atlantean civilization, the other a receptive feminine energy, the Lemurian civilization. In the end, both were destroyed. War never works.

Phillip: Please explain some more the importance of our knowing one another now.

Adama: In order for this planet and all upon it to continue to ascend in consciousness, the entire planet must be united and join into one light from below (us) and one light from above (you). That's why we are connecting with you at this time. Knowing us now will prepare you for what is to come (us). Books like this help greatly in revealing our existence further (for those ready to receive it).

Phillip: What is like to be immortal and why do you do it?

Adama: All advanced civilizations are immortal. Only lower-vibration civilizations have life and death cycles like yours. When you live a very long time you can apply your experiences to your civilizations. When you have limited life cycles like yours you forget from lifetime to lifetime what you learned. It is limiting. This limited cycle is coming to an end for you. You'll be amazed how natural it will feel to live forever (you already do you just don't consciously experience it). The best part of being immortal is your conscious connection to the Creator.

Phillip: We live in the third dimension and you live in the fifth dimension. How many dimensions are there?

Adama: There are an infinite number of dimensions reaching toward the Creator who is forever expanding. So the Creator is always allowing us to rise to higher frequencies, as it does the same. For the moment, we all have enough to be/ do to achieve unity on this planet by both our civilizations achieving a higher frequency than the one you live in now.

Phillip: Why did you pick to live under Mount Shasta?

Adama: The atmosphere of the planet was largely interrupted by the nuclear warfare between Atlantis and Lemuria. There were also other beings from outer space on the surface and within the Earth. We needed privacy and non-interference from the others. Mount Shasta gave us privacy and protection to advance into who we are today. It's a new concept to you, but most planets are lived from within. When our continent existed, Mount Shasta had always been a beacon of galactic communication and a remaining part of our homeland. So it felt very natural to go there.

Phillip: Why have you not made your presence known before now? We could have used your help.

Adama: We went underground so we could evolve without any negative interference. We had enough war and destruction in our time on the surface. If we had revealed ourselves sooner your world would have seen us as the enemy. You were not ready. By universal law we were not allowed to interfere with your affairs. You have your own path to follow, as we have ours. Now that we have advanced to the level we have, we can share it with you. If we had not done what we did, you may not have a way back home. So we did what we did for love, for both of us.

Phillip: We know you are immortal and taller than us. Are there any other major physical differences?

Adama: Even though we feel as physical as you do our bodies are much lighter due to our higher vibration. We experience many different sensations in our bodies you will experience when you shift. Our having sex is more of a connection with the Creator experience than an orgasm. We have eliminated disease and can repair and replace organs and body parts at will. We can become invisible by shifting our vibration. This allows us to travel to higher frequencies. This is an ability you should not develop until you raise your consciousness. Can you imagine if your criminals could become invisible?

Phillip: Can you explain how I and others are able to connect with you?

Adama: It is part of an individual's divine soul plan to be able to do so. They usually spend many lifetimes to prepare for this. Basically, they remove themselves from themselves and let go and we come into their being. There are conscious channels that stay awake and trance channels that have to be totally removed from their bodies to receive messages. More and more of you are connecting to your telepathic and astral projection gifts and connecting with frequencies beyond your own. Humankind has done this from the beginning. Most of your advancements were a result of such connections. It's actually a very natural part of your being. Simply trust you can...

Phillip: Is it true you don't need money in Lemuria?

Adama: We have no need for money. We create our own homes through the power of manifestation and all foods and commodities are free or bartered. There is no profit gained at the expense of another, for we are truly one. We believe in the rights of all to live in peace and abundance, with justice for all. We do not need to own everything and share what we have. Your system of money on the surface has made you all slaves to taxes and making money for many things you do not need.

Phillip: What are the Seven Sacred Flames? And how do they relate to ascension?

Adama: The Seven Sacred Flames are a process one must go through to shift frequencies—for you from 3D to 5D; this is called ascension. You ascend from one vibration to another.

The planets and the universe are in a constant state of ascension, shifting to higher and higher frequencies, ever toward the light. These flames, also called rays, are a great gift to humankind. Without them you would have no way to get back to your true home, directly connected to the Creator. In Lemuria, we have temples dedicated to these flames with many ascended masters and other beings maintaining these unfed flames. We have kept these flames for us and now for you. Remember ascension is the main purpose of your many lifetimes on Earth.

Phillip: How did you create a sun inside the Earth?

Adama: Our sun is not as big as yours. It reflects all the light we need. This light is a crystal we brought from another planet and it will burn brightly for millions of years. All light radiates life rays and creates life. The crystal and our thoughts create all the light we need.

Phillip: Where do your water and air come from?

Adama: We have Inner Earth oceans, which flow through the Earth creating streams and lakes, not unlike on the surface. We harness ocean and lake energy to create our atmosphere underground. Before surface air became so polluted, we used to have openings to the surface for air. We now produce all our own pure air. Someday soon we shall share our crystal technologies, which will clean your oceans, other bodies of water, and air.

Phillip: How do you create perfect weather?

Adama: Your thoughts and consciousness creates all the negative weather on the surface. Our atmosphere is protected by the content of our thoughts which is always in harmony with the planet and the Creator. Thus, our weather is perfect. As you are experiencing more love and light on the surface your weather will shift. Have you ever paid attention to where you have bad weather and connect that weather to the thoughts or conditions of that area? Begin to pay attention to this. Reliable weather has allowed us to evolve more quickly. We can use our talents and gifts and inspirations and not have to wait for bad weather to pass. How many opportunities do you think you have lost on the surface due to bad weather?

Phillip: Is it true you have living crystal libraries in Lemuria?

Adama: Yes, we have wonderful living libraries within crystalline platforms. You can go to any of them and experience firsthand any history you wish. These libraries are filled with the truth of this planet's history that no one on the surface knows. Much of your history is not true. True history is an effective way to learn and grow and expand. These are one of many technologies that we have that will amaze and delight you.

Phillip: Are there really space ships coming in and out of Mount Shasta?

Adama: Of course, we take many explorations into outer space and also monitor conditions on this planet from space. Once you know there is more to life than what you just see now, the entire universe will open for you. You will see oneness and the beauty of the universe. We have the ability to make our space ships invisible to keep your military away from them. There are many people in your world who know all about us and our space-faring abilities. Your governments have kept the reality of UFOs away from you in order to control you. Suppose you knew for a fact there were advanced civilizations all around you. How would you and your governments feel about that? Are you and they ready to accept this truth? Not see it as a threat?

Phillip: What do you eat?

Adama: You on the surface largely eat dead foods that contain little or no life force. No wonder you are sick so often and die so young. We only eat live food, vegetables, fruits, grains, and nuts. And we do not destroy the plants in the process. There is no eating meat, thus no killing of animals to eat them. We have special areas where our organic hydroponic gardens produce all we need. We don't freeze, can, or process our food. Our advanced technology allows us to produce large quantities in efficient areas. We use everything and discard nothing never burying anything in our soil. The Earth and soil are alive and we honor and protect them. You vibrate according to the light portion contained in what your body assimilates. You maintain and sustain your body by the light you consume, what you eat.

Phillip: Do you have sex the same way we do?

Adama: Not quite. Our bodies are less dense than yours so we connect with our partner on a higher level. It is a complete union with each other through divine love and the Creator. Our relationships and sexual expression reflects a more evolved understanding of love and sex. Your relationships on the surface are often based upon duality consciousness. We have learned that our partner is a mirror of our self from whom to learn. We come together with a balance of the masculine and feminine energies. When this balance is in place the perfect relationship always shows up. Then a divine union with your twin flame of your heart will appear, reflecting your higher self. We have several levels of relationships that allow complete sexual freedom until a couple may choose commitment leading towards parenthood. We have the same sex organs and never dishonor them. It's revealing in your slang language on the surface you often use the names of your sexual organs as curse words.

Phillip: Do you have children the same way we do?

Adama: Not exactly. Much more responsibility and preparation comes into play before a couple can have a child.

There are no children having children or unwanted pregnancies here. Since our bodies are less dense our gestation period is one third of yours. A couple must be in a committed relationship (remember we are immortal and bringing another soul into physical form is a well thought out, planned event). When the couple is ready to commit to a child they have the spiritual training and support of their temple and community. In fact, most of the pregnancy is spent in a temple where the couple and child-to-come are in a loving and supportive environment. The child receives this level of divine love throughout their childhood and adulthood. The actual physical aspects of the pregnancy are very similar to yours, reflecting a complete balance of the male and female energies.

Phillip: What do you wear down there?

Adama: Not much, since our weather is perfect. We have no shame associated with our physical bodies so nudity is a non-issue. For eons robes and loose-fitting clothing has been used.

Phillip: You have spoken a great deal about light. Can you please explain further the principles of light?

Adama: You are composed of many layers of light, the densest of which is your physical body. You have other bodies that are not physical (light bodies), which support your physical body. All this vibrating light (energy) is what you are. Everything is composed of energy and light. You came from light and will return to light. There's nowhere else to be, to go. You are an eternal light being having a human experience at this moment. And you've had many of these human experiences in preparation to return to the light as an immortal light being.

Phillip: What do you mean it is always "now" in Lemuria?

Adama: Because now is really all there is. Your mental body creates the past and future, which we no longer need.

Universal law has taught us to always be in the moment of now. Now is your contact with your divinity. Life is meant to be lived in the present moment. Think about all the time you have wasted being concerned about what happened or is going to happen. It takes away much of the joy of life. The now allows you to take full advantage of all the forces coming together to create growth and expansion.

Phillip: What exactly is universal law?

Adama: The purpose of universal law is to maintain oneness throughout the universe. All advanced civilizations enforce this law, which requires equality, peace, harmony, and balance in all expressions of life. This law establishes divine order and maintains it. The law comes from the mind, love, and will of the Creator.

Phillip: So, who or what is the Creator?

Adama: The Creator is love that creates, transforms, heals, and harmonizes all things. It is the highest consciousness, and through its ever-expanding wisdom it creates the elements necessary to manifest seen and unseen reality everywhere. You are an individualized, unique, unlimited expression of the Creator experiencing itself. Your religions have largely personified and misrepresented the Creator. Since it is love, it cannot judge, condemn, or punish you. That is control. The Creator is an unconditionally loving force that knows you and it are one. The Creator is trust that only exists in the heart, not the mind. The divine union of you and all that is being spoken of here is the Creator.

Phillip: How do you transport yourselves inside Earth?

Adama: Through our advanced technology we use crystal and electromagnetic energies. It's the same technology we used when we were on the surface. Nothing better has come along. It's clean, and free. We have a major tunnel system using this technology. These will be shared with you when we join. We can also travel telepathically through our thoughts and astral project anywhere on or off the planet. Thoughts are light, and light is energy, and energy manifests matter as it becomes denser. You will soon experience the unlimited freedom this creates...

Phillip: When do you come to the surface?

Adama: There are many openings that only Lemurians know about, which allow us to come and go rather often. We are constantly checking conditions on the surface. More and more we are revealing ourselves to light workers on the surface. There are many surface people living near Mount Shasta who are there to stay in contact with us. You are one of those who came home to visit us. Many more will follow as the time draws near for our reunion. Many tunnels are being prepared for you to come to us and us to you.

Phillip: When you come to the surface, where do you expect to stay?

Adama: There is more time needed for the surface to become less dense so we may come up in larger numbers. We plan to bring all our technology with us that we know will delight and amaze you. Many light workers are being contacted to gain permission for us to stay in their homes. If you would like for us to be with you, simply let me know through your thoughts...

Phillip: What is the significance of the recent natural events that have been taking place on Earth?

Adama: This is a very special time for your planet. It has changed frequencies in order to move forward in its evolution. Thus, everything within and upon the planet needs to shift also (this includes you). This is the ascension process. So things are changing rapidly and significant cataclysms will continue to take place. Preparations and messages from many sources, like us, are coming to you now. Allow them to connect you to your higher selves and the light. We have been waiting many thousands of years for this ascension to take place. Mother Earth has sacrificed much for us below and you above. The end of that time has come. The time for transition into light is here.

Phillip: The alternative media has been talking about government cover-ups of chemical and biological warfare. Many think this is all conspiracy theory thinking. What light can you shed on these matters?

Adama: First and foremost, biological and chemical warfare is real and so are the cover-ups, and most of the people on the surface are completely unaware of these. We check these conditions regularly (chem-trails in your skies, land and ocean mines buried all over your planet). Many of your diseases (HIV) are manmade and have been released on purpose. These same measures took place when the Atlanteans and Lemurians were on the surface. We are saddened that this behavior is repeating itself...attempting to destroy the Earth and her peoples again. We ask you not to turn to fear, but to choose ascension into another frequency where these 3D dramas cannot harm you. We tell you these things not to upset you but to make you aware of the truth. The truth will set you free to make choices that serve your highest good.

Phillip: It's really difficult for many to believe, understand, and accept what you are saying about our government cover-ups and control of the people. Can you please explain further about this?

Adama: Throughout the planet's history, human beings have been controlled by other beings from other galaxies (ETs) and advanced civilizations here. Your genes and DNA have even been altered by them in an attempt to control you for their purposes, but they are now being repaired and additional genes are being activated. We know this sounds far out for most of you. But for those of you who can resonate with this truth, we ask that you begin to make other choices in empowering yourselves. We had this same thing happen with our time on the surface. The assertive masculine energy, the Atlanteans, often tried to control us and others with gene manipulations and enslavement. This was the major reason for our destructive wars with them.

What's happening to you is not new. Your wars and even the events of 9/11 were recent examples of governments creating situations to control the populations for the benefit of a hidden few controlling the many. The terrorist is within yourselves, not outside of you. The dark forces that are creating these events are ancient. But their time of control is coming to an end and they know it. But they are putting up a fight to the finish. They have been in power for a long time and do not wish to give it up. But give up power they will, for we are all destined to return to the light.

Phillip: Why was I led to create the journey to Mount Shasta, and what was its purpose?

Adama: It was in your divine plan to do so in this lifetime. You were once an important part of our civilization in Lemuria. You still are. Along with many others, you chose and were chosen to assist in revealing to the surface world that we exist and for what purpose. Your entire life has been a preparation for this. The actual physical trip to our home, Mount Shasta, was to open an energetic gateway between our world below and your world above and beyond, and to assist in balancing the masculine and the feminine energies (to balance giving and receiving). You also opened additional vortices and performed specific rituals, as guided by Archangel Michael, who was instrumental in the creation of Lemuria. The creation of these new vortices and the opening of the Lemurian Gateway allowed the rebooting and activation of certain crystalline technology within the mountain. The energy from these activations will allow Mount Shasta to become an even stronger beacon in assisting the planet and its inhabitants to make a shift into a higher frequency of existence. Each member of your expedition was very different from the others, because you represented proxies for humankind.

Phillip: What prevents us from coming to Lemuria now?

Adama: Your consciousness and frequency prevents you from coming to Lemuria now. When you reach a critical mass of consciousness concerning immortality, that's when we shall join in balance and harmony. If you came down now it would interfere with our frequency. Remember, you are not told of our existence when your government knows. And your governments are working to keep you in their control. Things are labeled top secret. But soon your cyberspace communication will break through this barrier. When this happens and more people on the surface accept us in their consciousness, we shall more and more come forward.

Phillip: What do you consider to be one of the most important missions of your civilization?

Adama: It is an essential part of Lemuria's divine soul plan to care for this planet until you on the surface can. We shall join together and bring the light of ascension into the entire Mother Earth, to assist in moving the planet and all her inhabitants into a higher, more evolved frequency of existence (which is your destiny as much as hers). Everyone who ever lived on Earth has returned for this amazing event of Earth's transition into the light. That's why there are so many people on the Earth now. Our light has never stopped being sent to the surface, this is the main mission of our remaining here. As below, so above...

Phillip: If some on the surface were once in 5D Lemurian experience, why are we still in 3D now?

Adama: Because only a few Lemurians were given dispensation by the Creator to move down from 5D to 4D after the 3D destruction of our continent (due to the abuse of our wisdom). Some 25,000 Lemurians were allowed to be reduced into 4D reality and to work their way back now to 5D reality. Humans on the surface are descendants and reincarnated souls from the original 3D population that remained and are now being given the opportunity through ascension to regain 5D reality. You who remained in 3D chose to do so in order to be part of this process. This process will ensure that you never lose your higher connection or abuse it again. And that you step into your divine soul plan as master teachers of the universe. The universe awaits you, and thanks you for your great contribution to all civilizations.

Phillip: Who are the light workers and what do they do?

Adama: The light workers are individuals and groups committed to assisting the Earth to transitioning into light, moving into a higher frequency. These people receive large volumes of light from below and from above, which supports the planet and increases the people's consciousness, mirroring universal consciousness. And this consciousness travels at the speed of light, consuming lower frequencies all over the planet. Light workers are being born at increasingly faster rates. Children (indigos, rainbow, and crystalline children) are coming into the earthly plane fully equipped for the task at hand, which is to bring humankind into oneness.

Phillip: What is your hope for humankind?

Adama: Our hope (and promise) for humankind is for you to live as immortal beings (like us) and to grow and expand in consciousness in an ever-expanding universe always toward the Creator within each of you. For you are the Creator experiencing itself.

Phillip: What is love?

Adama: Love is the highest vibration and frequency (energy) in the universe. Thus, it is the building block of everything. Everything is maintained and sustained by the love. Without love there is no creation, only destruction. Love will always bring our thoughts and emotions into oneness. The organ of love is your heart. Your heart knows that love is all there is. Everything else is the absence of love. We are all here to learn to love of the self first and foremost.

Phillip: There surely are going to be people who have difficulty believing what is said here because of where it came from. Can I believe the message if I don't believe the messenger exists? Can you briefly discuss the difference between beliefs and truths?

Adama: At one time you believed your Earth was flat and that the sun revolved around the Earth. And those who said otherwise were punished or killed. At one time you believed (or in many cases were forced to believe) that religion was the only true path to God. Beliefs come from your mental body, often representing control, and they can change. Knowing comes from the heart, and truth does not change or wish to control. Your acceptance of truth can change. You may now believe that Lemuria inside the Earth, within another frequency, does not exist. Because you can't see it, your mind can't believe it...like the flat Earth and revolving sun. You just haven't arrived at the truth yet.

There is actually very little truth you do know about your world. And new truths are soon to be revealed that will amaze and delight you. You will come to have a deeper knowing of what we say here. Through acceptance of not-knowing, you can arrive at the possibility and probability of truth. For the moment, focus on the message if you can't accept the messenger. You have killed or not believed many important messengers throughout your Earth's history. Killing them did not make them untrue.

Phillip: There has been a lot of talk about crystals and their importance in your advanced civilization. Can you please tell us more about crystals?

Adama: In most advanced civilizations, crystals are the main source of energy and are used in every aspect of our lives (transportation, healing, communication, travel, building, information storage, and so on). What you are aware of in your world about crystals is rather limited. Crystals, like animals and plants and you, are conscious living beings. They are a fundamental part of the structure of the universe. The core of this planet is a crystalline grid that is the heart of the Earth and has received ascension activation. So, in effect, the crystalline heart of the planet is powering all the shifts that are taking place now. Crystalline technologies are powering your advanced computer communications, as well. The first radios were called crystals because the crystal inside the radio was the receiver.

There is an important difference between your crystalline structure and ours. Since we live in a higher frequency, our crystals are lighter, clearer, and more luminous, and more able to absorb and store light. We can create crystals through our thoughts, and they can take unlimited shapes and frequencies to meet our applications. The use of crystalline energy is limitless. Your world is changing dramatically and quickly as the result of crystalline technology. When we introduce you to our level of crystalline ability all things will become possible.

Phillip: Consciousness appears to be an important part of advanced civilizations. What are the basics of consciousness?

Adama: The teaching of consciousness has filled entire libraries and continues to do so. So in a limited amount of space let me say this: Consciousness is a unique choice and path for each individual who chooses it. Consciousness is a heightened awareness and understanding of yourself (self-mastery), which reflects beyond you a total understanding life. It is an ever-expanding process that unfolds according to the level of readiness and commitment you are willing to put into it. It is about knowing who you are and why you are here. It is about knowing through your heart your purpose (your divine soul plan), which is to be expressed through your talents and gifts; and by choosing to give these to the world. Developing higher consciousness involves moving from the "me" to the "we."

Phillip: Thank you, Adama, for this time together. Your answers to my questions will hopefully give readers more insight into the Lemurian civilization and your purpose in assisting us to grow and expand into a higher state of being.

Epilogue
Going Home

As I was on the plane flying back to the East Coast from California and looking down on Mount Shasta, my heart was filled with excitement, gratitude, and joy for what had transpired there on my homecoming journey. Would anyone believe it? Did that even matter? I would simply tell the truth for those ready to resonate with it. I knew I had a class filled with students waiting for my return to learn all about the Seven Sacred Flames and my adventure upon the mountain.

My second day back in Florida would begin the ascension class. I'd developed the teacher's guide before I left, and the class would be filled to capacity. Yes, there were people ready for a new truth, a way to free themselves from themselves and to choose another existence altogether. They resonated with the promise of living with equality, harmony, and balance in a loving world. And this wasn't just some pipe dream fiction for another time in some far-off, distant future. We were being given the exact tools we needed to be and do what was necessary now.

A few hours before the class begin, I decided to make a quick stop at my favorite thrift shop and used bookstore, where the journey had begun with books falling on my feet. I went there to find some cushions for our students' chairs. As soon as I arrived, there was the familiar inner voice from before, which came in and urged me, "Walk over to the used book section."

"Oh no!" I exclaimed, with a smile. What books would fall on me now...?

෯ೲ෯

I wrote the last words of this book on my birthday, the same day I also chose to spread my late parents' ashes at our lake home. This book was the greatest gift I could have received, and I am so pleased now to give it to you—after all, balancing the energy of giving and receiving was the purpose of the trip. As I released my loving parents, I fully embraced my new reality and life.

Resources

Phillip Elton Collins
The Angel News Network
TheAngelNewsNetwork.com

The Modern Day Mystery School
Fort Lauderdale, Florida
TheModernDayMysterySchool.com

Books

The Second Coming by Joel D. Anastasi (iUniverse). Order via: GabrielSecondComing.com.

Journey of the Awakened Heart by Jeff Fasano with Stephanie Gunning (The Angel News Network). Order via: TheAngelNewsNetwork.com.

The Seven Sacred Flames and *Telos, volumes 1–3,* by Aurelia Louise Jones (Mount Shasta Light Publishing). Order via: MSLPublishing.com.

Telos and *Messages from the Hollow Earth* by Dianne Robbins (Dianne Robbins/Inner Earth Books). Order via: DianneRobbins.com.

You Are a Spirit by Kayhan Ghodsi and Stephanie Gunning (YAAS Press). Order via: YaasPress.com.

Crystals

The Crystal Room, Mount Shasta
CrystalsMtShasta.com

Sacred Seed Crystals, Mount Shasta
SacredSeedCrystals.com

Mount Shasta Travel
Berryvale Grocery &Café
Berryvale.com

Heart of Shasta Retreat Vacation Rentals:
www.perfectplaces.com/vacation rentals/24131

Shasta Vortex Adventures
ShastaVortex.com

Websites
Children of Light (Archangel Gabriel/Robert Baker)
ChildrenofLight.com

Dianne Robbins/Inner Earth Books
DianneRobbins.com

Lemurian Awakening (Kata)
LemurianAwakening.com

Telos Worldwide Foundation (Australia, France, Israel, Japan, United States)
Telosinfo.org

About the Author

Rev. **Phillip Elton Collins,** co-founder and marketing director of The Angel News Network and co-founder of The Modern Day Mystery School in Fort Lauderdale, Florida, is a healer, workshop leader, and business/life coach. His professional background is a multi-dimensional mixture, which includes being a bureau chief and reporter for his hometown newspaper, *The Tampa Tribune;* a media planner/buyer, account executive, and creative advertising executive for Young & Rubicam, New York; and director of marketing for three successful commercial TV production companies (Fairbanks Films, of which he was also founder; Ridley Scott & Associates; Industrial Light & Magic Commercials/Lucasfilm Ltd.), representing some of the industry's most talented film directors worldwide; thousands of hours of clinical healing arts therapy and teaching experiences; and the ability to connect with unseen realms throughout our world and universe. Phillip is a minister ordained by Sanctuary of the Beloved Church, Priesthood and Order of Melchizedek. He holds undergraduate degrees from Stetson University and the University of Florida, Gainesville, and a certificate in film production from New York University. Phillip brings multifaceted skills, talents, and gifts into everything he does. In the middle of his sixth decade on this planet, Phillip and his husband, James, presently reside in Fort Lauderdale, Florida, and New York City.

Made in the USA
Charleston, SC
27 March 2015

Intestinal Bacteria and Health

An Introductory Narrative

Tomotari MITSUOKA PhD

Professor of Biomedical Science
The University of Tokyo
Head of Laboratory for
Intestinal Flora, Frontier Research Program RIKEN, Saitama

Translated by
  Syoko WATANABE MSc, PhD
  W.C.T. LEUNG MSc, MEd, PhD

HARCOURT BRACE JOVANOVICH JAPAN
Tokyo, Japan

CHONAISAIKIN NO HANASHI (Intestinal Bacteria and Health)
by Tomotari Mitsuoka

Copyright © 1978 by Tomotari Mitsuoka

Originally published in Japanese by
Iwanami Shoten, Publisher, Tokyo in 1978

HARCOURT BRACE JOVANOVICH JAPAN, INC.
Ichibancho Central Bldg., 22-1, Ichibancho, Chiyoda-ku, Tokyo 102

ISBN4-8337-6507-1

Printed in Japan
90 91 92 93 9 8 7 6 5 4 3 2 1

Contents

Contents

v

Preface

Our intestinal tract while bacteria-free when we are in the mother's womb becomes inhabited by numerous bacteria soon after birth. These bacteria are called "intestinal bacteria," and the population they form, "the intestinal bacterial flora," or "intestinal flora" in short. On the other hand, a group of related bacteria including coliform bacteria, shigellae and salmonellae are sometimes called enteric bacteria; the proper designation of this group is the family *Enterobacteriaceae*.

The cultivation of the intestinal bacteria has been an extremely difficult task. Although the well known coliform bacteria are easily cultured, the number of these bacteria in the feces of healthy subjects is only in the range of 10^5–10^8/gram feces. Yet, when the feces are examined directly under microscope, the intestinal bacteria can be enumerated to be more than 10^{11} per gram (a hundred trillion). For this reason, it had been assumed that most of the bacteria excreted in the feces were dead bacteria. This was a big misunderstanding.

Since about ten years ago, new culture methods for the intestinal bacteria have finally been developed. Due to these new techniques, it was discovered that bacteria that had not been cultured until then were present alive in feces in numbers more than 1000 times that of the coliform bacteria. From then on, research in this field has been activated and new findings have been discovered one after another.

These viable bacteria which inhabit and exert their sphere of activity in the intestine number tens of trillions per gram of intestinal content in the large intestine, comprising over a hundred species; while maintaining either symbiotic or antagonistic relationship with each other, they perpetually divide in the intestine. And, some of them are useful bacteria to the host (referring to the human or animal in which the intestinal bacteria reside); some invade into tissues of the host causing damage or producing harmful substances. The number of varieties of enzymes in the intestinal bacteria is more than that found in the liver. For these reasons, the intestinal bacteria exert a great influence on our body, and, whether we can have good health depends to a large extent on the type of intestinal flora we carry.

Recently, the relationship of diet to the high incidence of large bowel cancer in Western countries has received public attention. It has been suggested that the intestinal bacteria may play a role in this relationship. An interest in the intestinal flora has at last been raised.

In this book, the intestinal bacteria will be discussed based on our own research and on the research of others in and outside Japan. The first chapter reviews the historical events concerning the research on intestinal bacteria. The second chapter describes the efforts that have been put into the culturing of the intestinal bacteria. The third chapter describes the kinds of bacteria that reside in the intestine. The fourth chapter discusses the composition of the intestinal flora, their mode of living and the factors that influence the balance. The fifth chapter deals with the relationships of the intestinal bacteria to health and disease in man. Frankly speaking, the aspects that I am going to discuss in this book include many that are not yet fully understood or are still uncertain. Despite that, I would like to make use of this opportunity to convey, as correctly as possible, the knowledge on the characters and roles of the intestinal bacteria which, in spite of bearing profound relationship incessantly to our daily life, are still to this date not known to the general public. It would be my greatest pleasure for the concern in this field to be increased.

I The History of Research in Intestinal Bacteria

Micrograph of human fecal samples.
Left: a fecal sample of a breast-fed infant, in which one type of bacteria dominate. Right: a fecal sample of an adult, in which bacteria of different shapes and sizes exist.

Discovery of Intestinal Bacteria

The first person who discovered minute organisms that are invisible to the naked eye was a Dutch, Antony van Leeuwenhoek (Fig. 1). This amateur scientist was born in 1632 in Delft, south-west of Amsterdam. While earning a living as a draper, he had made microscopes as a hobby: he painstakingly ground covex lens the size of a pinhead and with an extremely short focal distance, and then inserted the lens between two metal plates. Using these microscopes, he enjoyed observing whatever interested him for about fifty years until his death

Figure 1. Antony von Leeuwenhoek.

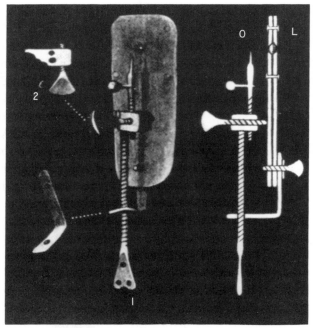

Figure 2. The microscope made by Leeuwenhoek.
(From Burnet and Sharp)
L: Lens I, and 2: Screw for focusing, O: Pin to place specimen

at the age of ninety-one. His hand-made microscope is known to have a magnifying power of about 150 times (Fig. 2).

With these microscopes, he discovered microorganisms which nobody had seen before and made accurate sketches. Among them, cocci, rods, spirilla, spirochetes and spore-forming rods were drawn in detail. In 1681, he discovered bacteria and protozoa in the feces for the first time in the world.

Although Leeuwenhoek's discoveries were marveled by the people at the time, most of his observations could not be confirmed due to the more inferior microscopes used by others. The popular microscopes of those days were compound microscopes with double magnifying mechanism, such as those used today. They were much poorer in resolving power than the simple microscopes of Leeuwenhoek with a single lens which he perfected with his excellent skills and patience. For that reason, microscopic studies of microorganisms, which had been pioneered by Leeuwenhoek, did not start in earnest until the end of the nineteenth century when optical microscopes were substantially improved in terms of higher resolving power and correction of astigmatism, two hundred years after Leeuwenhoek's discovery.

The Theory of Spontaneous Generation

The discovery of microorganisms by Leeuwenhoek again spurred interest as to how the numerous microorganisms in nature were generated. In 1665, an Italian physician, Francesco Redi, had already disproved the myth of spontaneous generation according to which maggots could be generated spontaneously from meat. He placed meat in a jar and covered it with double-layers of clean gauze and proved that no maggots were generated. Thus, the theory of spontaneous generation of animals and plants had begun to lose its foundation. However, it was far more difficult to prove that microorganisms were not spontaneously generated. Even though a jar was covered with double-layered gauze in a manner as in Redi's experiment, numerous microorganisms were generated as could be observed under microscope. This finding again encouraged believers in spontaneous generation.

In 1749, an English priest, Needham, reported the appearance of microorganisms even when broth was well boiled in a covered jar. Fifteen years later, in 1764, an Italian scientist, Spallanzani pointed out that no organisms were generated if the beef broth was boiled thoroughly in a flask which was then sealed. Although Spallanzani's experiment was splendid, it was not sufficient to refute Needham's counterargument.

On the other hand, a chemist, Gay-Lussac claimed that foods in heated and sealed containers were well preserved because the oxygen essential for the growth of microorganisms had been excluded from the containers. His claim was well received by believers in spontaneous generation. It was just the end of the eighteenth century, when oxygen was discovered as a gas and revealed to be an essential element for living animals.

In 1837 however, Schwann, a German scientist, proved that microorganisms were not generated in the broth when air was blown into the boiled soup through a red-hot coiled tube. Furthermore, in 1854, Schroeder used, in place of the heated coiled tube, a long test tube with a cotton plug through which incoming air was filtered, and showed that no microorganisms were generated. Thus, the arguments on the theory of spontaneous generation left, as by-products, techniques that prevent contamination by microorganisms from the air, such as the use of cotton plugs and sterilization by heating at 130°C, which have since become basic microbiological techniques. Finally, Pasteur (Fig. 3) performed experiments that ended the argument once and for all.

First, Pasteur passed a large volume of air through a tube plugged with a nitrocellulose cotton filter. He then recovered the cotton plug and dissolved it in a mixture of alcohol and

Figure 3. Louis Pasteur.

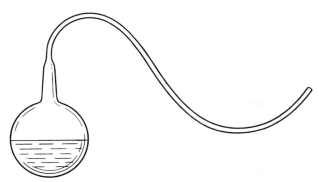

Figure 4. Swan-necked flask.

ether. When the fine particles that precipitated were collected and observed under microscope, many fungal spores and microorganisms in round or oval shapes were observed. From this experiment, Pasteur concluded that the bacteria that grew in rotten materials were derived from those present in air.

Subsequently, he performed the experiment with the famous swan-neck shaped flask (Fig. 4). He prepared a flask with a long, narrow winding neck. The broth in the flask was thoroughly boiled so that the air inside was replaced with steam. Upon cooling, although unfiltered air could freely enter the opening through the long neck into the flask, the germs in the air were stopped at the long, curved neck and failed to reach the broth. Thus, the broth remained free of microorganisms as long as the flask stayed intact. In the case the swan-neck tube was broken so that an upward-pointing opening was formed, microorganisms again appeared in the broth.

His experiment completely rejected the concept since Needham that air itself was responsible for the generation of living organisms in the broth and thus put an end to the arguments on spontaneous generation.

Cause of Fermentation

Louis Pasteur, originally a chemist, was engaged in the investigation of the optical characteristics of tartaric acid. He observed a phenomenon that the optical resonance of tartaric acid synthesized in the laboratory was different from that produced by natural fermentation, and had become interested in fermentation processes.

In 1857, Pasteur was the professor in chemistry at the University of Lille. In those days, the manufacture of alcohol from sugar beets was the prevailing industry in Lille. However, occasionally, the fermentation of sugar beets went wrong and the products were spoilt or turned sour. The manufacturers who suffered great loss asked Pasteur for help. Pasteur carefully examined the microorganisms in fermentation tanks under microscope. He found that numerous yeasts were present in normal alcohol fermentation products while microorganisms other than yeasts were predominant in the spoilt products: in fermentation that turned sour, sugar underwent lactic acid fermentation and turned to lactic acid, which also led to the complete alteration of the microbial population (to lactic acid bacteria) in the tank. With this, he experimentally demonstrated that each of the various types of fermentation, such as alcohol fermentation, lactic acid fermentation and butyric acid fermentation, occurred due to the action of a specific microorganism. Thus, Pasteur made a historic contribution to microbiology by opening a "functional" approach of studying microorganisms in their involvement in life phenomena, in contrast to the "natural history" approach initiated by Leeuwenhoek, in which microorganisms were objects of descriptive records for satisfying curiosity.

Development of the Pure Culture Technique

In his fermentation studies, Pasteur developed a technique to cultivate microorganisms in a liquid medium in a glass container. Using this technique it was relatively easy to obtain a pure culture of bacteria from samples of fermentation products which contained a small variety of bacteria. However, it was not as easy to isolate pure cultures of bacteria from samples of feces, sputum or vomit, which contained a large

Figure 5. Robert Koch.

variety of different bacteria. It was Robert Koch (1843–1910) (Fig. 5), a German physician, who established the pure culture technique.

Koch first experimented with sterilized potato slices placed in a sterilized glass container with a lid as a medium to culture bacteria, but soon found that not many kinds of bacteria grew on the potato medium. He then devised a jelly-like medium by adding gelatin to meat broth (Fig. 6). By spreading bacteria-containing material on this gelatin medium and incubating it, isolated growths of bacteria known as colonies are developed, which are visible to the naked eye. By transferring a part of a colony to fresh medium using a wire loop

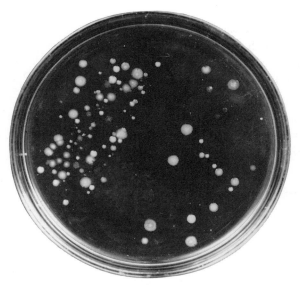

Figure 6. The pure culture technique devised by Koch.
A single bacterium proliferates and forms a colony which is visible
with the naked eye.

sterilized by flame and incubating, repeating the procedures
if necessary, one kind of bacteria in pure growth can be obtained. This is the so-called pure culture technique which made
it possible to obtain pure culture easily and substantially from
a sample containing a mixture of various microorganisms.
Later, agar was used in place of gelatin and thus the agar medium commonly used today was developed. Without this pure
culture technique developed by Koch, research on bacteria
could never have flourished to its present form. This is the
reason why Koch's contribution is given the highest esteem
in the field of microbiology.

Furthermore, using this pure culture technique, Koch established the concept that bacteria could be distinguished into species, which are unchangeable. Such misinterpretation at the time that the harmless *Bacillus subtilis* in soil and the strongly pathogenic *Bacillus anthracis* were essentially the same organism which were changeable freely under different environmental conditions was fundamentally corrected. Thus, Koch established a foundation also in the field of bacterial classification.

Principles for Distinguishing Pathogenic Bacteria

In 1882, on the basis of the pure-culture technique and the concept of distinctive species, Koch identified the causative bacteria of tuberculosis which was a much feared disease in those days. Using cultivation and staining techniques, he confirmed that one kind of bacilli, which he named tubercle bacilli, was always isolated from the lesions of patients suffering from tuberculosis. He finally published an uncontradictable thesis, "Etiology of tuberculosis."

In this thesis, he advocated the famous Koch's postulates that in order to establish that a specific bacteria is the pathogenic agent for a specific disease, certain conditions must be fulfilled. The conditions are: (1) The specific organism must be present in all cases of the disease. (2) The organisms must be isolated and grown in pure culture in the laboratory. (3) The pure culture must produce the same disease when inoculated into a susceptible animal.

Since then, within two decades, the etiological bacteria of most of the major infections in man and animals have been discovered and described. These discoveries were made in pursuance of Koch's method and by people who studied under him. Among the pathogens discovered at that time, those related to intestinal infections included cholera vibrios, typhoid bacilli and dysentery bacilli.

Research in Intestinal Bacteria

The systematic study of bacteria normally inhabiting the intestine originated from research related to infantile malnutrition and gastroenteritis. Escherich, a professor in pediatrics at the University of Vienna, isolated the coliform bacteria (*Escherichia coli*) from the feces of breast-fed infants and considered them the most predominant bacteria in the intestine of infants. He smeared infant fecal specimens on glass slides, and by observing the stained smears under microscope he could distinguish the difference between breast-fed and bottle-fed infants. This might be the first systematic investigation on the intestinal flora.

In 1899, Tissier in Pasteur's laboratory found that the most predominant bacteria in the intestine of breast-fed infants were anaerobic lactic acid bacteria and named them *Bacillus bifidus*. Since then these bacterium have always been discussed as ones which play a key role in the field of infantile nutrition in pediatrics.

On the other hand, in 1900, Moro at the University of Graz in Austria found a different kind of lactic acid bacteria in the feces of bottle-fed infants, and named them *Bacillus acidophilus*. Thus, the two representative intestinal lactic acid bacteria were discovered almost at the same time.

However, the most remarkable achievement by Moro was his ecological study on intestinal bacteria. He investigated the distribution and mode of colonization of bacteria in various sites of the infantile intestine and pointed out that normal intestinal bacteria play a preventive role against invasion by pathogenic bacteria. He also proposed the idea of endogenous intestinal infection such as the case of the coliform bacteria: while being normal inhabitants in the large intestine, they would cause abnormalities when migrated up to the small intestine. From around this time, the relationship between the normal intestinal bacteria and intestinal infection caused by exogenous pathogenic bacteria had been investigated in infants and experimental animals. Yet, the normal intestinal bacteria discussed in those days were limited to coliform bacteria and enterococci.

In Japan, the study of Rokuzo Kobayashi at Keio University (1887–1969) on experimental typhoid infection from the viewpoint of intestinal flora against *Salmonella typhi* spanned the period from 1934 to 1944. He pointed out that the intestinal flora had a decisive effect on the establishment of infection by exogenous bacteria, using the expression "formation of an organized unit by the symbiotic relationship between the intestinal mucosa and the intestinal flora." Kobayashi's study has been continued by Taizo Ushiba and Shogo Sasaki and others who studied under him.

On the other hand, René Dubos (1901–) who was born in France and is now living in the United States has investigated the interaction between infectious diseases and environmental factors such as host and intestinal bacteria during the course of his study on infectious diseases caused by pathogenic bacteria.

At the beginning of the 1900's, Metchnikoff, a Russian biologist who lived the latter half of his life in France advocated that aging or premature death was caused by intestinal putrefaction and could be prevented by taking sour milk, the so-called "longevity-without-aging by taking yoghurt" theory. However, it was not until much later that the intestinal flora of adults actually attracted attention.

During the period of 1933 to 1935, Eggerth in the United States overthrew the common sense of that time by reporting that anaerobic bacteria were far more dominant in number than aerobic bacteria, such as coliform bacteria in the intestines of human adult. He isolated and named many new species of anaerobic bacteria. Yet, the concept that coliform bacteria and acidophilic bacilli were the predominant intestinal bacteria was so strongly supported that Eggerth's discovery was not appreciated for the next twenty years.

Development of Germfree Rearing System

From the time when the coliform bacteria were discovered, there had already been much argument as to whether the intestinal bacteria were beneficial or otherwise. In 1885, Pasteur proposed the theory of usefulness of the intestinal bacteria, that the intestinal bacteria might be indispensable for the survival of animals and that without the intestinal bacteria life could not be sustained.

In the next year, Nencki in Berlin built up a counterargument, and soon with Nuttal and Thierfelder advocated the theory of uselessness of the intestinal bacteria. In order to substantiate their argument, they attempted to establish a germfree rearing system. However, with the techniques of those days satisfactory results could not be obtained.

It was in 1945, about half a century later, that the development of a perfect germfree rearing system was finally accomplished by Reyniers and his associates of the University of Notre Dame in the United States. Germfree mammals including rats, mice and guinea pigs could be successfully reared for generations by this system. Also in Japan, in 1957, Masazumi Miyakawa and his associates at the University of Nagoya succeeded in germfree rearing of guinea pigs for 305 days.

Owing to the successful development of the germfree rearing system, it was revealed that animals could survive without intestinal bacteria if sufficient nutrients were supplied. Furthermore, as a result of the various investigations using germfree animals, relations of the intestinal bacteria with nutrition, immunity, infection and carcinogenesis have been elucidated one after the other. These investigations revealed several important facts which evidently showed the interrelationship between the intestinal bacteria and host animals. Some of these facts are that germfree animals had a longer life span than conventional animals, and while liver cancer occurred in conventional animals fed with cycads, it never occurred in germfree animals, and that the development of tissues responsible for self-defense mechanism was poorer in germfree animals than in conventional animals.

Discovery of Antibiotics

In 1941, Florey and his associates opened the way for the practical use of penicillin which had been discovered by Alexander Fleming in 1928. Then in 1944, Selman A. Waksman discovered streptomycin from actinomyces in soil. Thus, the era of antibiotics began.

In 1950, Stockstad in the United States happened to observe that the growth of animals was promoted when a small amount of antibiotics was supplemented in the feed for piglets and chicks. The mechanism of growth promotion was not clearly elucidated. However, judging from the facts that the antibiotics have to be taken orally to be effective, and that no effects are observed with germfree animals, it was assumed that the antibiotics might change the balance of the intestinal flora in a way that promotes animal growth. Here again the influence of normal intestinal bacteria on host animals was addressed.

New Research Trends

In 1957, Haenel in Potsdam, East Germany, demonstrated that bifidobacteria were the predominant bacteria in the intestine of adults. In the next year, my associates and I reported that various species of anaerobic bacteria constituted the predominant bacterial population in the intestines of animals. Thus, the trend in research on intestinal bacteria had extended from research that centers solely on aerobic bacteria such as colibacilli and enterococci to one that attaches importance to the overall function of the intestinal flora which includes the anaerobic bacteria. The anaerobic bacteria which had been neglected since the discovery by Eggerth had gradually attracted attention in regards to their numbers and functions in the intestinal tract.

In 1963, we found that the anaerobic roll tube method which had been developed by Hungate in the United States for the cultivation of cellulose decomposing bacteria in the rumen of cows or sheep was applicable for the cultivation of the intestinal bacteria. The culture recovery rate of bacteria from the

intestines of animals or humans was markedly elevated so that various species of anaerobic bacteria which had previously not been isolated were discovered and reported. Thus, we pointed out that this kind of method was indispensable for research on intestinal flora.

Soon, similar observations were reported in the United States and England and modifications of Hungate's method were attempted. In the United States and Europe, anaerobic glove box methods were developed. We devised the new "plate-in-bottle" method. While it was once thought that the intestinal bacteria consisted mainly of dead bacteria, these developments in anaerobic culture techniques enabled their cultivation with relative ease. This momentous development in methodology further facilitated research in intestinal bacteria, which had been triggered by the above-mentioned development of germ-free rearing systems and the discovery of antibiotics.

Reconsideration of the Classification of Bacteria

It has to be pointed out that there was another factor which prevented the development of research in the intestinal flora. That is the confusion in the classification of bacteria.

Classification of the lactic acid bacteria which had been discovered almost simultaneously by Tissier and Moro was in confusion for more than half a century. At one time, bifidobacteria were considered identical to *Lactobacillus acidophilus*. At another time, *L. acidophilus* which is an indigenous intestinal species was put together with *L. bulgaricus* which is for yoghurt making. The reason for the confusion was that the bacterial classification was an artificial scheme making use of criteria that were optionally chosen for convenience in usage, such as the disease caused or products of fermentation, which was greatly diverted from the natural biological point of view. It was particularly true with lactic acid bacteria which has an extensive scope of application.

In recent years, there was a movement to clear up the confusion in bacterial classification in the International Union of Microbiological Society. Today, a committee composed of taxonomists from all over the world has been set up for each group of bacteria. The committee determines the most appropriate classification and nomenclature for individual organisms. The confusion in classification of lactic acid bacteria including *L. acidophilus* has been solved by this international taxonomic committee.

As for the bifidobacteria, in 1963, G. Reuter in Berlin suggested the classification for those of human origin; and then in 1969 Mitsuoka proposed the classification for those derived from animals. These were approved by the international taxonomic committee and thus ended once and for all the confusion which had continued for over half a century. Today, classification of anaerobic bacteria has started. Thus, the development in the classification of the intestinal bacteria during the last decade had a significant effect on the development of ecological studies of the intestinal flora.

II Cultivation of Intestinal Bacteria

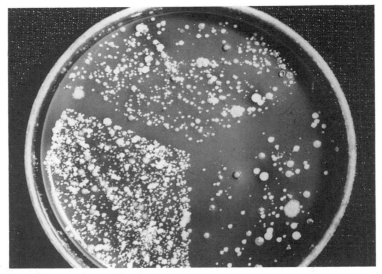

Culture of intestinal content.
After a certain period of incubation, various bacteria grow to form colonies.

Microscopic Observation of Intestinal Contents

Since bacteria are as small as around one micrometer (μm, 1/1,000 mm), they are invisible to the naked eye which has a visible limit of about 0.1 mm (Fig. 7). Consequently, the microscope is needed to observe the shape or structure of bacteria.

Leeuwenhoek observed the world of microorganisms under a simple microscope with a single convex lens having a very short focal distance. Today, a complex microscope equipped with three different sets of lenses, a condenser, an objective lens and an eyepiece is routinely used in light microscopy in the laboratory. The resolving power, which is the shortest distance between two adjacent points that can be distinguished as separate entities, of the light microscope is about 0.2 μm. This length is equivalent to the size of the smallest bacteria. Accordingly, most virus particles (0.025–0.25 μm in diameter) cannot be seen with the light microscope.

In order to observe bacteria in a normal living condition, a drop of the liquid in which bacteria are suspended is placed on a glass slide and the drop is covered with a cover slide. The thin film of liquid pressed between the two glass slides is then examined. However, in order to observe the bacteria in the liquid, it is necessary to create a contrast between the bacteria and the surrounding liquid. Phase-contrast microscopy is used for this purpose.

Since the contrast between the living bacteria and the surrounding liquid is poor, the bacteria can be treated with dyes which bind to whole cells or selectively to specific cell compositions to intensify the contrast. Various staining methods have been developed for the purposes of elucidating intracellular structure or chemical characteristics. For example, stain-

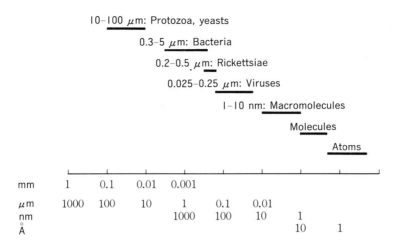

Figure 7.   Relative sizes and dimensions of micro-organ isms, molecules and atoms.

ing specific to DNA (deoxyribonucleic acid) can give information on the structure and location of the nuclear material.

Gram staining which was developed by Christian Gram in Denmark is the most widely used bacterial staining technique for taxonomical purpose. It differentiates bacteria into two groups according to their difference in composition of the outer layer of the bacterial cell. In this process, first, the bacterial smear on a glass slide is fixed by heat, stained with a crystal violet solution and then with an iodine solution and thereafter destained quickly with alcohol. Bacterial cells which are not decolorized and are stained dark purple-blue are gram-positive. Gram-negative bacterial cells which are decolorized are counter-stained with safranin.

For enumeration of bacteria in the intestinal content, one

gram of specimen is weighed out and a 1:10 dilution is prepared with a diluent. Further serial 10-fold dilutions, 1:100, 1:1000 and 1:10000, are prepared. After a drop of crystal violet is added to the suspension, 0.01 ml of the bacterial suspension is placed on a Petroff-Houser counting chamber. The chamber is ruled into squares each of which has an area of 1/400 mm^2; when it is covered with a cover glass, a space of 1/50 mm thickness is formed between the two glasses, so that the volume over a square is 1/20,000 mm^3 or 0.00005 mm^3. Bacteria observed in each ruled square, preferably at a density of 50 to 100 cells a square, are counted and multiplied by the dilution factors to obtain the bacterial count per gram of the sample.

The number of bacteria in one gram of healthy adult feces enumerated by the above-mentioned method is in the range of 3 to 5×10^{11}. If one supposes the average mass of a single bacterium to be one cubic micrometer (1 μm^3) and the feces consisting solely of bacteria, the number of bacteria in one gram of feces would be 1×10^{12}. That is to say, as much as one-third to one-fourth of the fecal mass is made of bacteria.

Next, 0.01 ml of the bacterial suspension prepared in the same manner as described above is placed on a ruled space of 1 cm^2 on a glass slide, dried and then gram-stained. The bacteria are then examined for the number, shape and size under microscope. Together with food debris and exfoliated intestinal cells, gram-positive and gram-negative bacteria in different sizes and shapes, rods, cocci, spirals or spore-bearing can be observed. Furthermore, by counting the cell numbers within a known area, the number of bacteria per gram feces can be estimated.

In the days when Tissier first discovered bifidobacteria in the feces of breast-fed infants, microscopic examination of gram-stained feces was a means of health check in the field of pediatrics. This was based on the experience that gram-positive bifidus bacilli were present like a pure culture in the feces of breast-fed infants while many gram-positive cocci and gram-negative colibacilli were mixed with gram-positive bacilli in the feces of bottle-fed infants, and that gram-negative bacilli were fully predominant in the feces of infants with diarrhea.

Although direct observation of the fecal content under microscope is essential in examining the total number and the number of species of bacteria in the intestine, by itself, it is not sufficient to determine the species of individual intestinal bacteria.

Discrepancy Between Cultivation and Microscopic Observation

Since bacteria are so small there is a limitation to the amount of information one can obtain by observing one individual bacteria. Therefore, in general, bacteria are cultured and their characteristics are investigated as a group. In order to investigate the ecology and the role of intestinal bacteria, isolation and cultivation, by which individual bacteria in the intestinal content are obtained as separate pure cultures, are the starting point of the study.

Firstly, when feces from a healthy adult is smeared and spread on a nutrient agar medium which is widely used in bacteriological study (an agar medium supplemented with meat extract, peptone and salt, pH 7.4) and then incubated, one or several kinds of coliform bacteria (*E. coli*) colonies which are grayish-white and 2–3 mm in diameter, and enterococci (a kind of streptococci) colonies which are rather transparent and about 1 mm in diameter are the only ones generally observed. By this method, however, the number of bacteria per gram of the intestinal content cannot be estimated.

Next, the fecal sample is diluted ten-fold stepwise with a diluent and then 0.05 ml of each of the dilutions: $1/10$, $1/10^3$, $1/10^5$ and $1/10^7$, is placed on one portion of a quarterly divided nutrient agar medium, spread with an L-shaped glass rod and then incubated. In general, at dilutions lower than $1/10^5$, colonies of coliform bacteria and enterococci as mentioned above appear on the agar. The number of bacteria in the feces can be calculated from the number of colonies thus obtained. For both coliform bacteria and enterococci, the number per gram feces is usually between 10^5 and 10^8. This figure is far less than that estimated from direct observation under microscope. Escherich obtained coliform bacteria colonies by cultivation in the same manner as this. Since then it had been believed that the discrepancy between the bacterial counts estimated from direct observation and cultivation on agar medium was due to the fact that most of the bacteria in the fecal sample were dead and thus could not form colonies when cultivated.

However, in recent years it has been proved that when *E. coli* is administered to a germfree mouse, the number of *E. coli* in the feces estimated by direct microscopic observation is the same as that estimated from culturing on agar medium. This showed that all the 10^{11} bacteria which were present in the intestine were viable.

Furthermore, careful microscopic observation of the feces of humans and animals reveals the presence of a number of bacteria with morphologies which cannot be found in the colonies obtained after cultivation. Also, by modifying the medium and cultivation method, bacteria other than *E. coli* and enterococci, such as lactobacilli and bifidobacteria, can be isolated. From these observations, it is evident that in the intestine bacteria exist in numbers which far exceed that of *E. coli*, that cannot be cultivated in an ordinary manner.

The environmental conditions in the intestine are quite different from those generally created in glass containers in the laboratory. Especially in the large intestine, since oxygen in the intestinal content is consumed by bacteria which require oxygen (aerobic bacteria), the atmospheric condition in the large intestine is total lack of oxygen (anaerobic). The degree of anaerobiosis as indicated by the oxidation-reduction potential is in the range of -200 to -250 mV.

Furthermore, the intestinal content has a complex chemical composition, made up of digested food components, digestive fluids, bile juice, mucous and humoral components as well as metabolic products by the intestinal bacteria. It is very complicated even from the nutritional point of view. In the large intestine, the bacteria that require and depend on these conditions for growth thrive and predominate. These are also the bacteria that are extremely difficult to cultivate in the laboratory.

Improvement of Anaerobic Culture Method

Since the old days, bacteria which are moderately anaerobic have been cultured on medium put inside a sealed container in which is placed oxygen-removing chemicals such as yellow phosphorus, steel wool soaked in an acidic copper sulfate solution, pyrogallol, or oxygen-absorbing agents such as platinum catalyst and hydrogen. By using this method, non-fastidious anaerobic bacteria can be cultured, but intestinal bacteria which require strictly anaerobic conditions cannot grow.

In 1950, Hungate in the United States developed a very important method for the isolation and cultivation of cellulose degrading bacteria in the rumen of cows and sheep (Fig. 8). His anaerobic roll tube method provided environmental conditions in the test tube similar to that in the rumen. The culture medium contained 40% of an extract of the rumen content to which was added salts with a composition similar to saliva, cellulose, cysteine and agar. In order to prevent the penetration of air, all operations from preparation of the medium to inoculation of samples were carried out under the blowing of oxygen-free carbon dioxide gas. Using this method, cellulose degrading bacteria in the rumen, which had never been cultivated were isolated for the first time.

The physical and chemical features of the intestinal content are very similar to those of the rumen content. Accordingly, my associate and I attempted to apply Hungate's method for isolation and cultivation of the intestinal bacteria. As expected, bacteria which had never been isolated before were isolated one after another. The total number of bacteria per gram feces estimated by Hungate's method was marked compared to that obtained by the conventional culture method, and it approached that obtained by direct microscopic observation.

Hungate's method required the formation of a membrane of agar medium on the inner wall of a test tube, in which colonies were formed. Therefore, isolation of the colonies was

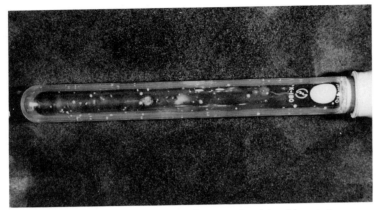

Figure 8. Anaerobic roll tube method by Hungate.

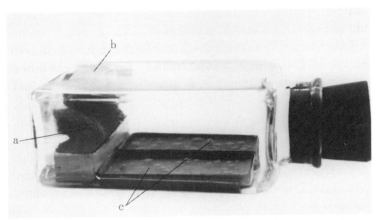

Figure 9. The "Plate-in-Bottle" anaerobic method.
(a) Steel wool covered with reduced copper (b) Tissue paper
(c) Medium

much more difficult than in the case where ordinary petri dishes with a flat surface were used. We therefore applied the principle of Hungate's method but tried to find a way of obtaining single colonies on a flat agar plate medium, and finally succeeded in devising the plate-in-bottle method (Fig. 9). In this method, medium prepared in a similar manner as in Hungate's method is dispensed aseptically, under carbon dioxide, in two stainless steel plates (c) placed in a sterilized bottle. Then, in order to remove any trace amount of oxygen remaining in the bottle, steel wool (a) covered with a film of reduced copper (formed by soaking in acid copper sulfate solution) is placed in a stainless steel vessel placed at the back of the bottle, and tissue paper (c) is inserted to adsorb moisture. The bottle is sealed tightly with a butyl gum stopper and kept in a 37°C incubator for one or two days for drying the surface of the agar medium. Then the bottle is opened for inoculation of samples, performed under constant blowing of carbon dioxide gas. By this method, colonies of bacteria which require strictly anaerobic conditions as in the intestine can be obtained on the surface of the agar plate more easily and reliably as compared to the conventional anaerobic roll tube method.

On the other hand, in the United States or in England, a method using an air-tight vinyl or plastic chamber as shown in Fig. 10 was developed. In the chamber, the air is replaced with a gas mixture consisting of 80% nitrogen, 10% carbon dioxide and 10% hydrogen, and the remaining trace amount of oxygen is removed by a platinum catalyst. Inoculation of samples on growth media is done inside the chamber using the attached neoprene gloves. This is called the anaerobic glove box method. Thus, during the last twenty years, technology in anaerobic cultivation has been improved remarkably.

Figure 10. Anaerobic glove box culture system.

Choice of Media

It is impossible to have all intestinal bacteria which have different characteristics grow on one kind of medium at the same time. A medium which is suitable for the growth of a certain bacteria may not be suited to another bacteria, or a certain bacteria may grow in advance and suppress the growth of another bacteria. In short, there is no one medium which is suitable for the growth of all bacteria. For that reason, in the investigation of the intestinal flora, multiple numbers of media with different functions have to be used.

A non-selective medium allows the growth of as many bacteria present in a sample as possible and is not for the purpose of cultivating specific kinds of bacteria. The compositions of the media for cultivating the most predominant bacteria in the intestine are similar to those for cultivating rumen bacteria. The M10 medium which is developed by Coldwell and Bryant in the United States is an example of such medium. In the cases of chickens, mice or rats, extracts of the feces of the animals have to be added to the M10 medium. This is because some bacteria require specific substrates in the feces as nutrient sources.

Furthermore, for bacteria which require rich nutrients, such as lactic acid bacteria in the intestine, media containing liver extract, yeast extract, tomato juice, specific peptone, sugar, and others are used. On the other hand, for bacteria which thrive on poorer nutrients, media containing relatively low nutrition are prepared by, for example, reducing the amount of sugars or omitting liver extract or tomato juice.

In the cases where the samples contain a large number of bacteria, such as intestinal contents, growth of the bacteria present in small numbers is likely to be suppressed by the predominating bacteria, and cannot be detected. In these cases, if growth conditions of the desired bacteria are known, chemicals can be added to the medium to inhibit the growth of the other bacteria, or physical conditions of the medium can be adjusted to promote solely the growth of the desired bacteria. Such media that selectively isolate only the desired bacteria are called selective media. For investigation of the intestinal flora, different kinds of selective media for coliform bacteria, lactic acid bacteria, bifidobacteria, bacteroides, eubacteria, Welch's bacilli, veillonella, enterococci, yeasts, etc. are used (Table 1). Thus, the fluctuations of all the bacterial groups, from the major ones to the minor ones can be studied.

Table 1.   Media and Culture Method Used for Cultivation of Intestinal Bacteria.

	Media	Bacteria expected to grow	Culture method	Incubation (days)
Non-selective media	M IO	Fastidious anaerobes	Plate-in-bottle method	3–5
	EG	Ordinary anaerobes	Steel-wool anaerobic culture method with CO_2 gas	2–3
	BL	Lactic acid bacteria, coliform bacteria, enterococci		
	TS	Aerobes	Aerobic culture	1–2
Selective media	BS	Bifidobacteria	Steel-wool anaerobic culture method with CO_2 gas	2–4
	CS	Eubacteria		
	NBGT	Bacteroides		
	NN	Welch's bacilli		
	Modified VS	Veillonellae		
	Modified LBS	Lactobacilli		
	TATAC	Enterococci	Aerobic culture	2
	DHL	Enterobacteria		1
	PEES	Staphylococci		1–2
	P	Yeasts, molds		

Sampling of Specimens

The most frequently used specimens in the study of the intestinal flora are naturally excreted feces. Since some intestinal bacteria can multiply on standing at room temperature and some are so sensitive to oxygen that they are soon killed on exposure to air, it is necessary to start cultivation as soon as possible so as not to change the balance of the intestinal flora. When immediate cultivation is not possible, the sample should be placed in a transport medium to avoid contact with air and cooled on ice.

When fecal samples are used, it is desirable to take the whole feces excreted into a vinyl bag, and the air in the bag is replaced with carbon dioxide gas by repeatedly deflating and inflating the bag with carbon dioxide gas. The opening of the vinyl bag is tightly sealed with a rubber band, and then the feces inside are thoroughly mixed. A part of the feces is used as a sample.

However, in addition to the feces, materials from various sites of the intestinal tract are occasionally required for research on intestinal flora. This is because the intestinal flora in the small intestine cannot be studied by merely investigating the fecal samples. For this purpose, various techniques have been developed.

The most widely used method is by a long plastic tube. A soft vinyl tube, non-X-ray transmissible, and 2–3 mm in inner diameter, is inserted into the intestine. The position of the tip of the tube in the intestine is located radiologically. The intestinal content at a particular site is then sampled by sucking through the tube.

Swallowing a capsule is another method of sampling. In this method, a tightly closed capsule is swallowed and a hole in the capsule is opened for a certain period of time as it passes down the intestinal tract, thus sampling at a particular site. The opening and shutting of the hole of the capsule may be controlled by sending a signal to the capsule from outside using a high-frequency oscillator or by measuring time by the trickling of silicon oil through a small opening from one vessel to another.

Occasionally, samples are taken from the intestine with a syringe during an abdominal operation. Direct samples may be collected from various sites of the intestine of individuals who died suddenly.

However, there are problems associated with each method, for example: swallowing induces pain in the tube method, bacteria sampled in the capsule at the upper part of the intestine may proliferate to some extent before the capsule is recovered by excretion, samples collected during surgical operation cannot be considered as normal samples.

Examination of the Intestinal Bacterial Flora

The practical steps from cultivation of the samples to identification of the bacteria are as follows (Fig. 11). A sample is quickly weighed on a balance, and put into a ten-fold volume of an anaerobic diluent in a tube. The tube is gassed with carbon dioxide, stopped with a butyl gum stopper and then thoroughly mixed by hand to form a homogeneous suspension. Alternately, a 10-fold dilution of the sample can be prepared under oxygen-free atmospheric conditions using a mixer. With continuous blowing of carbon dioxide gas, further serial dilutions, 10^2, 10^3 and up to 10^8, are prepared, and 0.05 ml of each dilution is pipetted on various kinds of selec-

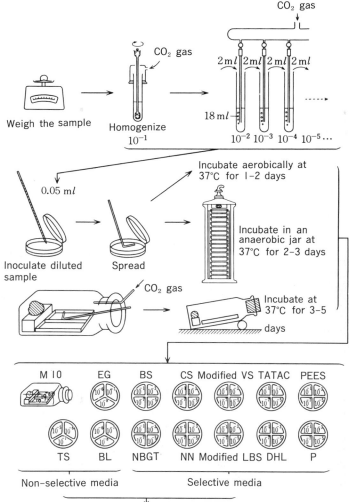

Figure 11.   Steps to cultivate the intestinal bacteria.

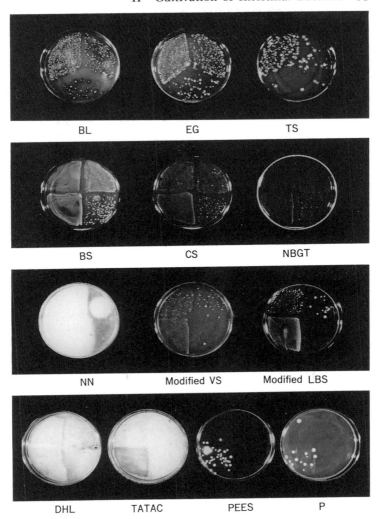

Figure 12. After a certain period of time, colonies of the intestinal bacteria are formed on each medium.

tive media and spread with a L-shaped glass rod. Incubation is carried out separately under anaerobic and aerobic conditions.

After a fixed period of incubation, colonies are formed on the respective selective media. Colonies of different bacteria have different characteristic features (Fig. 12). By experience, bacteria can be roughly identified simply by observing the colonies.

Colonies are carefully observed, and the number of colonies is counted. Part of the colony is smeared on a glass slide and stained, such as by Gram's method. By observing under microscope, bacteria are divided into groups depending on the staining characteristics, shapes, sizes, and so on.

For identification of bacteria to the level of species, individual colonies are transferred to fresh media for further purification and then the bacteria are identified by procedures as will be described in the next chapter. In order to elucidate the functions of individual bacterial species, metabolic activities are examined *in vitro*, or animal experiments are conducted. In this way, the ecology and roles of the intestinal bacteria are studied.

III Classification of Intestinal Bacteria

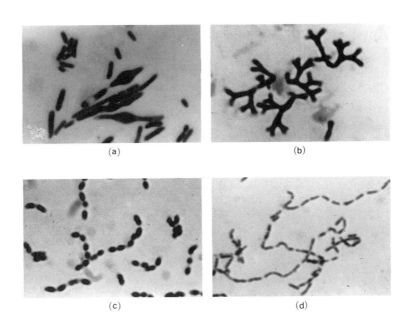

(a) (b)

(c) (d)

Intestinal bacteria are isolated and classified.
(a) Bacteroides (b) Bifidobacteria (c) Anaerobic streptococci
(d) Eubacteria

Significance of Classification

After cultivating the bacteria in the feces or intestinal content, what has to be done next is to identify the bacteria isolated. This work is important for ecological study, such as identifying the origin, features and habitats of the intestinal bacteria, or the effects of food or drugs on the bacteria. Identification of the bacteria is also essential in studying the roles of the intestinal bacteria in the human or animal body.

Names of bacteria are like codes. Given the same species of bacteria, anyone who follows a set procedure of characterization should give it the same name. This set procedure, called identification, is based on classification. Ecology is the science of analysis of an individual or a population of organisms under a certain environment, in which the concepts of the individual and population are also based on classification. Thus, taxonomy can be said to be the foundation of biology.

Basis of Classification of Living Organisms

Classification of living organisms is substantially different from that of stamps or books. Organisms have evolved through a long period of history. The basis of the classification of living organisms is to search for the natural correlations between organisms by following the trace of evolutionary process, that is the phyletic line. This classification is called natural classification or phylogenetic classification.

It is far from easy to trace the evolutionary pathways of bacteria. Even in higher living organisms, the trace of evolution, which is sometimes found in the form of fossils, has mostly vanished. Consequently, in the case of higher living organisms, many morphological or other characteristics are evaluated on the extent they indicate evolutionary traits, and from the result of this evaluation, classification is carried out.

In biological classification, the hierarchical arrangement in descending order is as follows: kingdom, phylum, class, order, family, tribe, genus and species.

"Species" is the basic grouping unit of living organisms. In higher living organisms, the boundary of the species is judged by the capability of interbreeding.

Difficulty in Classification of Bacteria

The difficulties in classification of bacteria differ from those in classification of higher living organisms. Firstly, morphological characteristics that are useful for discrimination among higher animals or plants are extremely limited, since the bacteria, being single-cell organisms, are very small and furthermore simple in structure. In addition, bacteria which normally multiply by binary fission have no complicated ontogenesis as seen in higher living organisms. Moreover, since there is no mating in bacteria, it is not possible to determine species judging by the capability of interbreeding as in the case of higher living organisms. Accordingly, "species" in bacteriology is loosely applied to organisms that possess a common set of constant characters. From these reasons, it is extremely difficult to classify bacteria by characteristics that bear phylogenetic relationship.

There is another reason for the confusion in classification of bacteria. It is that many researchers in pathological bacteriology or applied bacteriology had paid attention to the roles of bacteria, such as pathogenicity or production of specific substances, and were not at all interested in a classification system based on the natural phylogenetic relationships of organisms. As a result, they tried to devise classification schemes for practical use only, in which criteria for identification were peculiar and artificial, based merely on arbitrariness and subjectiveness, and had nothing to do with those used in classification of higher living organisms. For instance, new species were assigned solely on the basis of the production of a certain substance or the cause of a certain disease. It cannot not be denied that this approach hindered the establishment of phylogenetic classification in bacteriology.

Classification of Bacteria

The morphological characteristics of bacteria are important in classification as is also true for higher living organisms. Characteristics such as shapes, e.g. cocci, rods or spirals, sizes, the number and attachment site of flagellae, mobility due to flagellae, formation and shape of spores, mode of division and staining property are used today in basic classification. Features of colonies and the mode and appearance of growth in a liquid medium are also included in morphological characteristics.

Other standards for classification of bacteria include physiological characteristics, such as growth temperature, oxygen requirement, growth pH, growth in hypertonic solution, production of acids from various sugars, nitrate reduction, hydrogen sulfate production, gelatin hydrolysis, utilization of carbon and nitrogen compounds, decarbonation and deamination of amino acids, catalase reaction, nutrient requirements and other various biochemical properties.

Serological classification is another method. Antibodies are produced in animals that have been injected with a certain bacteria. These antibodies which react specifically with the injected bacteria are used to test similarities of other bacteria.

Furthermore, ecological features such as site of residence, distribution, parasitic property and pathogenesis are examined. This way of classifying bacteria by examining a large number of characteristics is a traditional approach to classification.

Recently newly developed techniques have been introduced for the classification of bacteria. One of them is numerical taxonomy, in which as many characteristics as possible are examined in the same manner as in the traditional classification and the results are calculated by computer to determine similarities among bacterial species. The problem of this classification is that each character is given equal weight disregarding its relative value in evolutionary terms.

Another classification is based on the genetic make up of bacteria. In this so-called molecular biological classification, the number and sequence of the four types of bases in the bacterial chromosome (DNA), namely adenine (A), guanine (G), thymine (T) and cytosine (C), are compared to determine similarities among bacteria.

DNA is known to form an antiparallel double helix in which the base sequences are complementary to each other, that is, hydrogen bonds are formed strictly between A and T and between G and C. Accordingly, the number of A + G is the same as that of C + T. Since each species of bacteria has a specific G + C versus A + T ratio, similarities among bacteria can be estimated by chemically analyzing the base composition of bacterial DNA. This method is called DNA base composition ratio analysis.

On the other hand, the extent of homology in DNA base sequence between two bacteria is analyzed by DNA hybridization. In this method, DNA from one strain of bacteria is heated lightly to separate it into single strands and the thymine is radiolabelled. The DNA from another strain of bacteria is also turned into single strands. After being broken into small fragments the two DNA preparations are mixed and cooled together. The portions of DNA having complementary base sequences will reanneal to form double strands. Thus, the similarity of the two strains of bacteria can be estimated by the extent of DNA hybridization. More work has to be done to perfect these techniques of genetic analysis. Yet, they are highly significant in that the phylogenetic relationship is being pursued practically in bacterial classification.

Other methods of classification include comparative biochemical methods such as analysis of the chemical composition of the cell wall and the difference in enzyme proteins.

Individual taxonomists could freely choose any one of the above-mentioned methods to establish a system of classification of bacteria. However, I believe that the ideal system is one that searches for the evolutionary process since bacteria are living organisms. For this purpose, I have established a systematic classification scheme. Firstly a large number of features are examined as in traditional classification. Then, taking also into consideration other information such as distribution and range of mutation, a rough classification system is developed. Differentiation within species or conformation of species designation is performed by genetic means such as DNA base ratio analysis or DNA hybridization. Finally, numerical classification may also be attempted to check the taxa established. Modifications are made, if necessary, and thus the classification system is completed.

International Committee on Systematic Bacteriology

As described above, much confusion existed in bacterial classification because bacteria were admitted as new species based solely on the fact that they caused a new type of disease or produced a new substance, even though bacteria with the same characteristics had already been reported.

In order to solve this kind of problem, the International Committee on Systematic Bacteriology and Subcommittees on Taxonomy for individual bacterial groups were made within the International Association of Microbiological Societies. Today, the most appropriate ways of classification and nomenclature of individual microorganisms are discussed and determined by the members of these committees consisting of taxonomists from all over the world.

Bacteria possess scientific names and common names. Scientific names are Latin or latinized and named according to the binomial system of nomenclature, consisting of the name of the genus followed by a single specific epithet. For example, "colibacilli" is a common name and *"Escherichia coli"* is a scientific name consisting of the name of the genus *Escherichia* and the specific epithet *coli*. The scientific names must be provided by the International Code of Nomenclature of Bacteria. Once a scientific name is published in accordance with the rules, this name is the correct name and has priority. It is not possible to change the name even if it is found not appropriate to express the characteristics of the bacterium. This rule is also important in preventing the misuse of synonyms.

In order to obtain international approval, the type strain of a species or subspecies proposed must be designated and deposited at an internationally recognized Type Culture Collections for registration and preservation. If not deposited, the strain will not be approved even if it is named according to the Code of Nomenclature. In this way, classified type strains are eternally stored in Type Culture Collections so that they can be obtained whenever requested not only for research on taxonomy but also for research in various fields or practical utilization.

The International Committee on Systematic Bacteriology is preparing the Approved Lists of Bacterial Names, in which names validly published in accordance with the Rules of the International Code of Nomenclature of Bacteria are listed. After January 1980, much confusion in the bacterial names will be avoided.

Gram-positive and Gram-negative Bacteria

Today, bacteria, once classified into cryptogamous plants, are classified as prokaryotes in which DNA is not enclosed by a nucleus membrane.

Owing to the development of electron microscopy, detailed structures of cells can be observed. Plants, metazoa, protozoa, eumycetes and algae except cyanophyta are revealed to be eukaryotic organisms in which DNA is located in nuclei surrounded by a nucleus membrane.

Among the prokaryotes, bacteria are divided into three groups on the basis of their differences in the cell boundary. Mycoplasmas do not possess a cell wall outside the cytoplas-

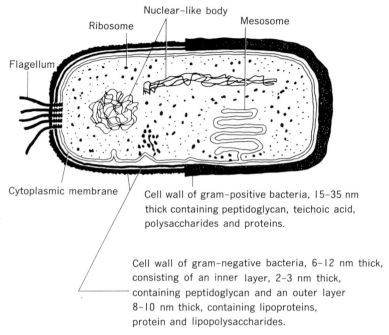

Figure 13.   Schematic structure of a bacterial cell.

mic membrane; gram-positive bacteria have a single-layered cell wall outside the cytoplasmic membrane and gram-negative bacteria possess a cell wall consisting of at least two layers of different structures (Fig. 13). The cell wall of gram-positive bacteria is as thick as 15 to 35 μm, and contains peptidoglycan as the main polymer, as well as polysaccharides and teichoic acid. The cell wall of gram-negative bacteria consists of a thin and dense 2–3 nm thick inner layer containing peptidoglycan, and a 8–10 nm thick outer layer containing proteins, lipopolysaccharides, and lipoproteins. The lipoproteins

are called endotoxins because they exert toxicity when injected into animals.

One of the theories that explains the principle of Gram's
stain is that gram-positive bacteria which are stained dark violet
with Gram's reagents contain an RNA (ribonucleic acid)-
magnesium-protein complex that forms a colored compound
with crystal violet and iodine, which cannot be destained with
alcohol. Bacterial cells consist of about 70–85% water, and
the remaining component is 50% protein, 20% cell wall component, 10% fat, 15% RNA and 5% DNA.

Shape and Arrangement of Bacterial Cells

Bacteria are generally measured in micrometers (μm). They
measure approximately 0.3 to 1.5 μm in width and are grouped
into cocci and bacilli from their shapes (Fig. 14).

The cocci are spheres and include those that separate from
each other immediately after cell division, namely the
monococci, and those that form cell groups after the division,
namely, diplococci, tetracocci, sarcinae and streptococci. Cocci
have diameters ranging from 0.6 to 1.0 μm.

Bacilli are cylindrical bacteria which have a variety of shapes
and sizes. For example, *Bacillus megaterium* are as large as
1.0–1.4 μm in width and 3.0–8.0 μm in length; *E. coli* and
Salmonella typhi are about 0.5 μm in width and 2.0–3.0 μm
in length; and one of the smallest bacteria, *Haemophilus in-
fluenzae*, measures 0.25 μm in width and 1.25 μm in length.
From their shapes, bacteria are grouped into short rods, long
rods, V-, Y-, or L- shaped coryneforms, filamentous bacilli,
curved or short spiral-shaped spirilla, and long, multiple-
spiraled spirochetes.

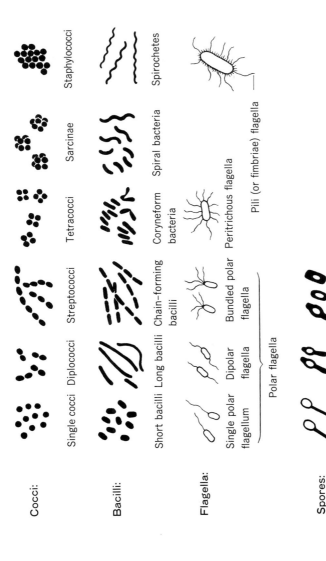

Figure 14.   Morphological classification of bacteria.

Some bacteria have flagellae and show characteristic motility. Flagella protrude from the cytoplasm and are grouped depending on the number and the position of attachment to the bacteria: single polar flagella, bundled polar flagellae, bipolar flagellae, and peritrichous flagellae in which flagellae are evenly distributed over the entire surface of the cell.

Pili are much thinner and shorter than flagella, generally distributed over the surface of the cells in numbers as many as several thousands and are thought to play a role in the attachment of the bacteria onto mucous or other objects.

Furthermore, some bacilli produce spores which are resistant to adverse environmental conditions. The shapes and location of the spores are generally specific to individual bacterial species so that they are used for identification of bacteria. Spores are described according to their locations in the cells, i.e. central, subterminal and terminal.

Grouping of Intestinal Bacteria

Intestinal bacteria can be roughly grouped according to the characteristics such as gram-staining, cocci or rods, spore formation, anaerobic or aerobic, arrangement and fine structure, features of colony, metabolic products from glucose, etc. (Fig. 15). Such grouping is based on classification systems established after many year of experience, and is used to "identify" unknown bacteria by matching their characteristics with those of bacteria already classified and named.

This rough grouping is convenient for examining the general balance of the intestinal flora. Taxonomically, this grouping provides identification to the levels of family and genus. For detailed research in intestinal bacteria, classification down to the level of species or subspecies is occasionally required. For these purposes, individual strains are isolated to obtain individual pure cultures and are subjected to examination of biochemical properties such as sugar decomposition, or physiological properties such as growth temperature, in order to identify the bacteria to the level of subspecies. In a sample of feces from a person, there exist about 15 groups of bacteria at the level of genus or family. These are further divided into 70 to 80 species, and, in some individuals, more than 100 species. In the appendix, the family, genus and species of the major bacteria isolated from the intestine of healthy and sick individuals are given. The grouping shown in Fig. 15 will be referred to in the following description on the ecology and roles of the intestinal bacteria. Fig. 16 shows bacteria isolated from the intestine.

Lactic Acid Bacteria and Putrefactive Bacteria

The above-described grouping of the intestinal bacteria is based on bacterial taxonomy. Separately, the intestinal bacteria may be grouped based on their roles, i.e. lactic acid bacteria and putrefactive bacteria, pathogenic bacteria and non-pathogenic bacteria or vitamin-producing bacteria and vitamin-consuming bacteria.

Lactic acid bacteria consume a large amount of carbohydrates to produce acids, particularly lactic acid, in abundance, and are not capable of decomposing proteins to cause putrefaction. They are obligatory or strictly anaerobic and grow preferably in the presence of little or no oxygen. Lactic acid bacteria which produce mainly lactic acid in sugar fermentation are called homo-fermentative and those which produce acetic acid,

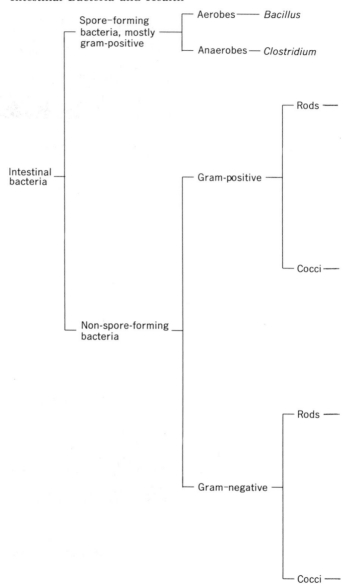

Figure 15. Grouping of intestinal bacteria.

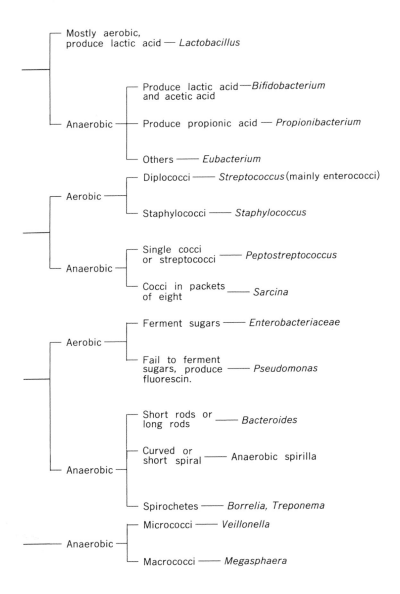

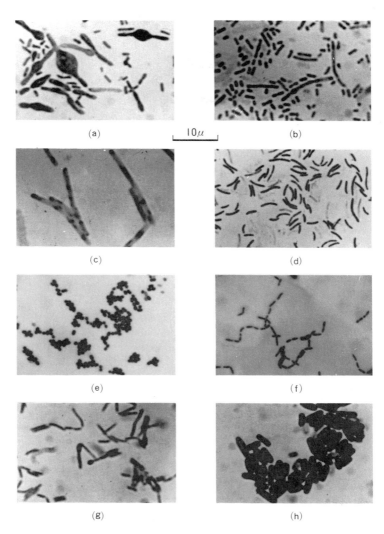

Figure 16. Bacteria isolated from the intestine.
(a), (b) and (c) *Bacteroides*   (d) Anaerobic spirilla
(e) *Peptostreptococcus*   (f) *Eubacterium*

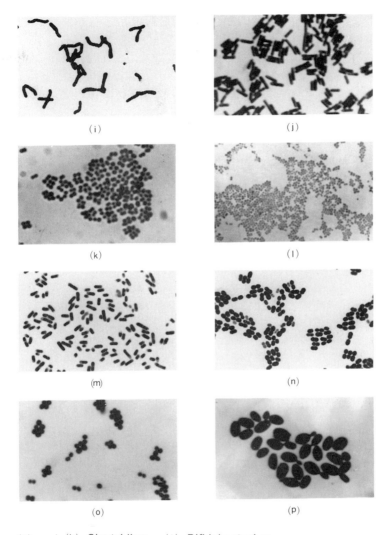

(i)

(j)

(k)

(l)

(m)

(n)

(o)

(p)

(g) and (h) *Clostridium* (i) *Bifidobacterium*
(j) *Lactobacillus* (k) *Megasphaera* (l) *Veillonella*
(m) *E. coli* (n) *Streptococcus* (o) Yeasts

ethanol and/or carbon dioxide gas, etc. besides lactic acid are called hetero-fermentative.

The lactic acid bacteria include *Streptococcus*, *Pediococcus*, *Leuconostoc*, *Lactobacillus*, *Bifidobacterium* as shown in Table 2. Lactic acid bacteria are distributed widely in nature, such as in the intestine and vagina of human and animals and in agricultural products. They are also extensively utilized in the production of foods such as yoghurt, lactic acid beverage, cheese, fermented butter, miso (bean paste), soy sauce, sake, pickles and salami sausage, and in pharmaceuticals such as lactic acid bacteria preparation and as additives in animal feed.

Lactic acid bacteria provide characteristic tastes or aromas in dairy products: *Lactobacillus bulgaricus*, *L. jugurti*, *Streptococcus thermophilus*, *S. lactis*, etc. are used for the manufacture of yoghurt, *L. jugurti*, *L. casei*, *L. acidophilus*, etc. for lactic acid beverage, *L. casei*, *S. cremoris*, *L. helveticus* and *S. lactis* for cheese, and *S. lactis* for fermented butter.

In the process of pickle-making, *L. plantarum*, *L. brevis*, *Leuconostoc mesenteroides* and enterococci grow predominately. During the maturation of salami sausage, *Pediococcus* and unidentified lactobacilli proliferate. Thus, specific kinds of lactic acid bacteria are involved in certain types of food processing.

On the other hand, the lactic acid bacteria which colonize in the intestine of human and animals are indigenous to the intestine and different from the lactic acid bacteria found in food. The most predominating lactic acid bacteria in the human intestine are various species of bifidobacteria. The other lactic acid bacteria that colonize in the human intestine are enterococci such as *Streptococcus faecalis* and *S. faecium* and

Table 2. Kinds, Distribution and Uses of Lactic Acid.

	Bacteria Strains	Major distribution and uses
Cocci	*Streptococcus*	
	S. *lactis*	
	S. *cremoris*	Butter, cheese, yoghurt
	S. *thermophilus*	
	Enterococcus	Intestine; Probiotics, feed additives
	S. *mutans*	Dental-caries-producing bacteria
	Pediococcus	
	P. *cerevisiae*	Salami sausage
	P. *halophilus*	Soy sauce
	Leuconostoc	
	L. *mesenteroides*	Fermented foods
	L. *citrovorum*	
Rods	*Lactobacillus*	
	L. *bulgaricus*	Yoghurt, fermented milk drinks
	L. *jugurti*	
	L. *helveticus*	Cheese
	L. *plantarum*	Fermented foods
	L. *brevis*	
	L. *casei*	Mouth; Cheese, fermented milk drinks
	L. *acidophilus*	Intestine and vagina; Fermented milk drinks, probiotics, feed additives
	L. *salivarius*	
	L. *fermentum*	Intestine and vagina
	Unidentified	Salami, sausage, sour dough
	Bifidobacterium	
	B. *bifidum*	Intestine of infants and adults; Fermented milk drinks, probiotics
	B. *longum*	
	B. *infantis*	Intestine of infants; Fermented milk drinks, probiotics
	B. *breve*	
	B. *adolescentis*	Intestine of adults
	B. *animalis*	
	B. *thermophilum*	Intestine of animals
	B. *pseudolongum*	
	B. *indicum*	Intestine of honey bees
	B. *asteroides*	

lactobacilli such as *L. acidophilus*, *L. salivarius* and *L. fermentum*. In many animals, lactobacilli are the predominant bacteria in the intestine. However, detailed investigations reveal that these lactobacilli are taxonomically different from those found in the human intestine.

Thus, by investigation of lactic acid bacteria to the level of species or subspecies, they are revealed to specifically inhabit various ecosystems.

Putrefactive bacteria are those that decompose proteins and produce foul-smelling substances such as ammonia, amines, indole, phenols and mercaptane. They include many kinds of anaerobic bacteria such as *Bacteroides*, *Peptostreptococcus*, *Clostridium* and *Veillonella*. Other putrefactive bacteria are those that cause diarrhea or enteritis or produce toxins, such as *E. coli, Pseudomonas aeruginosa*, *Proteus*, *Staphylococcus*, some strains of *Bacillus* and enterococci, *Shigella*, *Salmonella*, *Vibrio cholerae* and *Vibrio parahaemolyticus*.

Other intestinal bacteria include certain strains of *Eubacterium*, *Ruminococcus* and *Coprococcus* and *Clostridium* (*C. butyricum*) that produce acetic acid and butyric acid rather than lactic acid, and are not capable of decomposing proteins.

IV Ecology of Intestinal Bacteria

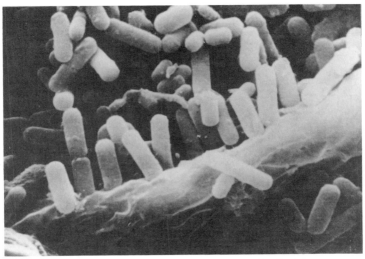

Bacteria colonizing on the stomach wall of the rat.
(D. S. Savage)

1. Structure and Function of the Alimentary Tract

The Alimentary Tract and Annexed Organs

The alimentary tract of man is a winding tube extending from the mouth to the anus, measuring as long as nine meters for an adult (Fig. 17). The buccal cavity and the esophagus together measures about 40 cm and is the portion situated above the diaphagm and the stomach. The rest of the alimentary tract, the stomach, the small intestine and large intestine are all packed in the abdomen.

The stomach is swollen like a bag and the inner volume is as small as about 30 m*l* for a newborn baby, and as large as 1.2–1.4 *l* for an adult.

The stomach consists of the cardia which is the entrance from the duodenum, the fundus which is the bulged part slightly above the cardiac level, the body of the stomach and the pylorus which is the exit.

The pyloric valve, made of sphincter muscle, is located at the transit portion between the stomach and the small intestine. The small intestine, divided into the duodenum, the jejunum and the ileum in descending order, is a winding tract, about six meters in length. The diameter is about 4–6 cm at the beginning and gradually narrows to about 2.5–3 cm at the end. The duodenum is so called because its length is about twelve fingers' breadth. The jejunum which occupies about two-fifths of the rest of the small intestine is located in the upper left central part of the abdomen. The ileum, the remaining part, is located mainly in the lower right position of the

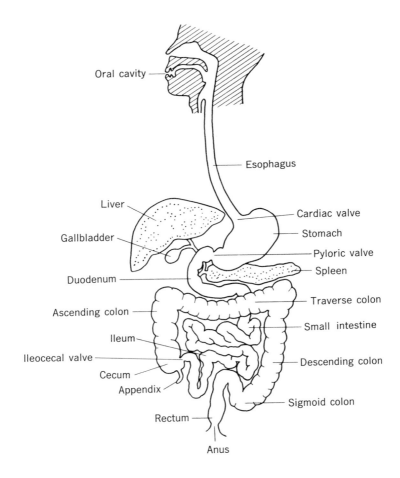

Figure 17. Human alimentary tract.

abdomen. The ileocecal valve, made of sphincter muscle, marks the end of the small intestine which meets with the large intestine at a right angle.

Passing through the ileocecal valve, the diameter of the intestinal tract is abruptly enlarged to 5–8 cm: here, the large intestine, about 1.5 m in length, begins. The initial part of the large intestine is the cecum which is about 5 cm long and the widest in the large intestine. Extruding from the left posterior wall of the cecum is the appendix, 6–7 cm long and as wide as a pencil. Extending upwards from the cecum is the colon consisting of the ascending colon on the right, the traverse colon curving under the liver, the descending colon on the left running down below the spleen, and the sigmoid colon curving in an S-shape near the iliac bone. Then it enters the pelvis to form the rectum which ends at the anus.

The salivary glands, liver and spleen that are annexed to the alimentary tract excrete various digestive fluids through ducts into the alimentary tract to help digestion.

Among the salivary glands, the labial glands, lingual glands, booker glands and palatine glands that are distributed in the buccal cavity range in size from that of a red bean to a rice grain, and excrete a mixture of saliva and mucus. The parotid gland, submandibular gland and sublingual gland manufacture saliva containing digestive enzymes, alpha-amylase and mucin, which are secreted through ducts into the mouth.

The pancreas is a long, slightly red, grayish white organ situated behind the stomach. It consists of an exocrine part from which the digestive juice, pancreatic juice, is secreted and an endocrine part from which hormones such as insulin and glucagon are secreted. The pancreatic juice is secreted into the duodenum through a duct.

The liver is the largest organ in the body weighing more than one kilogram in an adult. It is situated in the upper part of the abdominal cavity immediately below the diaphragm and is divided into a left and a right portion. In the liver, glucose that has been absorbed in the intestine is converted into glycogen to be stored in the liver or muscles, amino acids are built into proteins specific to humans, and various vitamins are stored. Harmful substances originating from food or medicines, or toxic substances produced by bacteria in the intestine are transformed into harmless forms. This is the detoxication function of the liver. It is also here that the bile juice that is important as a digestive juice is produced.

An egg-plant shaped organ, the gallbladder is connected via the cystic duct to the common hepatic duct as it emerges from the liver. In the gallbladder, the bile juice is temporarily stored while being concentrated by absorption of water and electrolytes, and mixed with mucus secreted from the wall. The common hepatic duct merges with the pancreatic duct and opens together into the duodenum, through which bile and a part of the detoxicated substances are excreted into the intestine.

Mucosa in the Alimentary Tract

The inner wall of the stomach is covered entirely with mucous membrane with gastric folds. The gastric mucosa consists of one layer of cylindrical epithelial cells. Numerous small cavities, called gastric pits, are found on the mucosa, which form the gastric glands. The gastric glands are divided into cardiac glands, fundal glands and pyloric glands depending on their sites.

The cardiac glands are distributed in the cardiac area and secrete mucus. The fundal glands are distributed in the main part of the stomach, and produce and secrete pepsinogen, hydrochloric acid, mucus and serotonin. The pyloric glands are distributed only in the pyloric area and excrete mucus, anti-pernicious-anemia-factor and a digestive hormone, gastrin.

The interior surface of the intestine, particularly of the jejunum, is made of many circular folds. The mucous membrane of the intestine also comprises one layer of cylindrical epithelial cells, like that of the gastric mucosa. On the surface of the mucous membrane, there are numerous fine protrusions, called villi, which give the intestinal surface a velvet-like appearance (Fig. 18). The surface of the villus cells is covered with brush-like microvilli, about 600 a cell, so that the surface area of the intestine is further enlarged for absorption.

Observation by electron microscopy at high magnification shows a fine fibrous structure called glycocalyx which forms a fluffy layer covering the surface of the microvilli. The glycocalyx is made of glycoproteins produced in the epithelial cells and contains acidic mucopolysaccharides such as sialic acid and uronic acid. It is negatively charged and plays an important role in the attachment of bacteria, digestive enzymes and their products, to the mucosa, and in the transportation of substances into the cells.

The duodenal and intestinal glands are situated in the pits of the intestinal mucosa. The duodenal glands are found only in the area of the duodenum. They are complex tubular glands situated deep in the mucosa and excrete alkaline mucus that neutralizes the acidic digestive gruel passed down from the stomach.

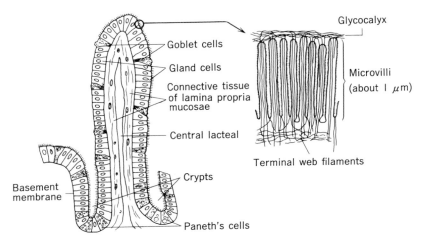

Figure 18. Structure of the villus in the small intestine.

On the contrary, the intestinal glands are simple tubular structures, called crypts. They are pits situated in the mucosa and are distributed all over the small intestine. The glands are continuous with the epithelial cells that form the villi as shown in Fig. 18. The cells at the base of the intestinal glands constantly divide and differentiate and move up to become the villus epithelial cells, and thus replenish the villus cells.

Other cell types distributed in the intestinal mucosa are Paneth's cells that excrete enzymes, goblet cells that excrete mucus, and cells that excrete serotonin and digestive hormones.

The mucosa of the large intestine has no circular folds or villi. The intestinal glands that are densely distributed on the mucosa penetrate deeper than those of the small intestine. There are many goblet cells. At the end of the colon, the mucosa is of the stratified squamous type so as to withstand the wear and tear by the passage of the feces.

Digestion and Absorption

Digestion and absorption is smoothly controlled by nervous and endocrine systems that coordinate various tissues and organs. While the stomach and the salivary glands are susceptible to control by the autonomic nervous system, secretion of pancreatic juice and bile are controlled mainly by the endocrine system. However, the nervous system and endocrine system are closely correlated, as the effect of nervous control is enhanced by gastrointestinal hormones and the effect of gastrointestinal hormones in turn is augmented by the nervous control.

Gastrointestinal hormones are produced mainly in the stomach, duodenum and jejunum in response to stimulation from food ingestion and digested gruel. The hormones are endocrinally excreted into the blood, and act on the gastrointestinal tract, pancreas and liver, effecting the control of digestive juice secretion or movement of the gastrointestinal tract. Furthermore, gastrointestinal hormones stimulate secretion of insulin and glucagon so that digested and absorbed nutrients are effectively processed in the body.

Ingested food is broken up finely in the mouth by chewing, well mixed with saliva and swallowed. The esophagus helps deglutition of food into the stomach. In the stomach, the food mass is warmed to body temperature and made into a homogenized waterly gruel. Digestion of starch proceedes to some extent by the α-amylase originating from the saliva. Furthermore, pepsinogen secreted in the stomach is changed into pepsin by the gastric acid. The food mass is further finely mashed, and fats and sugars are dispersed, ready for the major digestion to be started in the small intestine. The content in the stomach is passed into the small intestine a little at a time.

In humans, two to three liters of gastric juice is secreted a day. The gastric juice contains hydrochloric acid, pepsin and mucus. The pH inside the stomach varies during the day depending on the ingestion of food. The pH is as low as 1–2 at night time when the stomach is empty. Immediately after breakfast, the pH increases up to 5–6 and gradually decreases down to the range of 1–3 as the stomach content gradually enters the small intestine. The pH of the stomach content is markedly affected by the amount of food ingested and the time of its retention in the stomach.

The food mass then reaches the duodenum where it is mixed with pancreatic juice, bile and intestinal juice that are excreted there. Substantial digestion begins by the actions of the digestive enzymes. In the jejunum and ileum, a large volume of intestinal juice is excreted, and digestion is more or less completed here. The information of food is perceived sensitively by the duodenal mucosa and, as a result, gastrointestinal hormones which are excreted in the blood stimulate the excretion of pancreatic juice and bile, and the excretory function and movement of the stomach are efficiently controlled.

The pancreatic juice contains bicarbonate salts that render the pH in the intestine alkaline so as to activate the functions of α-amylase, lipase and trypsin. By the actions of these enzymes, digestion of sugars, lipids and proteins is carried out.

On the other hand, the ingestion of food stimulates the discharge of bile juice into the duodenum via the common bile duct. About 30 minutes after ingestion, the gallbladder contracts strongly due to the action of gastrointestinal hormones and concentrated bile juice is excreted. The bile juice contains bile salts which are strong surface-active agents and essential for digestion and absorption of fats and fat-soluble vitamins in the intestine. Bile salts and fatty acids combine to form water-soluble complexes (micelles) which stimulate digestion and absorption of monoglycerides and fats. Furthermore, the bile is important in the excretion of bile pigments, cholesterols, medicines and toxic substances.

Consequently, the nutrients digested in the small intestine are absorbed effectively through the intestinal villi with the aid of segmentation movement and peristalsis of the intestine. The undigested substances are passed into the large intestine. Water and electrolytes are absorbed in the first half of the large intestine, then the remaining mass is formed into feces which are accumulated temporarily and then excreted outside the body.

2. Formation of Intestinal Flora

Development of Intestinal Flora

The human being stays in the womb for a period of about one percent of his whole life. In the womb, the fetus is protected from bacterial invasion by the mother's own resistance. The fetal body is formed by repeated cell divisions from a fertilized egg. The fetus, in which the immune system is hardly developed, can only grow soundly in a germfree environment inside the womb.

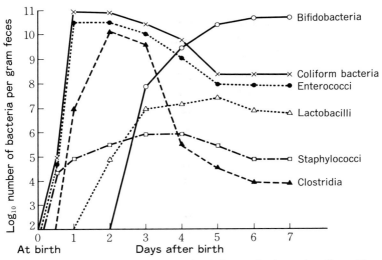

Figure 19. Change in intestinal flora during the first 7 days after birth.

However, from the very moment of birth, the bacteria start to proliferate on the mucosa of skin, respiratory and alimentary tract (Fig. 19). The intestinal content of the baby at birth, which is excreted as meconium within a day or so, is a sticky, greenish-brown or black mass and almost free of bacteria when observed under microscope. Within 24 hours after birth, however, the feces of most newborn babies contain a variety of bacteria such as coliform bacteria, enterococci, lactobacilli, putrefactive bacteria (e.g. clostridia) and staphylococci in various proportions, forming a chaotic microbial flora. The bacterial count is as high as over 10^{11} per gram feces. In 3–4 days after birth, bifidobacteria start to proliferate, and the numbers of the previous occupants, namely, coliform bacteria, enterococci and putrefactive bacteria, gradually decrease. Around the fifth day, bifidobacteria become dominant, the numbers of coliform bacteria and enterococci decrease down to about one hundredth that of bifidobacteria, and the number of putrefactive bacteria is even lower. Thus, a well balanced stabilized bacterial flora with predominating bifidobacteria is established in the intestine of newborn babies.

Where Do the Intestinal Bacteria Come from?

Where do the intestinal bacteria that populate the intestine of the newborn baby come from? There have been a number of arguments on this matter for years. Some of the speculations are: that the intestinal bacteria are acquired in the birth canal at the time of birth, that they originate from air, that they are attached onto the mother's breast and ingested while nursing, that fecal bacteria are always present on the fingers of the mothers and nurses and are transmitted to the babies.

Babies are delivered through the birth canal except when delivered by Cesarean section. A number of bacteria are consistently living in the vagina of the mother. Particularly in the latter period of pregnancy, lactobacilli proliferate and become almost like a pure culture. Furthermore, bacteria which originate from the feces, such as coliform bacteria and enterococci, can be commonly detected in the environment into which the baby is born, such as the air and the fingers of mothers and nurses. Hence, it appears that these bacteria may gain access to the small intestine of the newborn babies by any one of these routes.

However, as will be mentioned later, it is recently found that the bifidobacteria that become predominant in the infant's intestine at around the fifth day after birth are different from those found in the intestine of the mother. The bifidobacteria found in the infant's intestine are specific species. Consequently the speculation that the intestinal bacteria of infants originate from those of mothers seems unreasonable.

Another speculation is that the bifidobacteria specific to infants are grown in the colostrum, the milk first excreted after delivery. However, despite careful examination of the skin of the mother's breast and breast milk, there is no evidence that the infant-type bifidobacteria proliferate in the breast. The adult-type bifidobacteria are found, though, probably as a result of contamination by the mother herself.

Werner at the University of Bonn in West Germany and Crociani at the University of Bologna in Italy independently investigated whether the infant-type bifidobacteria are present amongst the lactobacilli found in the vaginal discharge of pregnant women. The result revealed that about one fourth of the women investigated had bifidobacteria in the vagina and that half of them had bifidobacteria of the infant-type. That is to say, approximately one tenth of pregnant women harbor the infant-type bifidobacteria, which suggests that they are one of the probable sources of the bifidobacteria found in the intestine of infants.

However, this evidence is not sufficient to explain the origin of bifidobacteria found in the intestine of babies delivered by Cesarean section or babies from mothers who have no infant-type bifidobacteria in the vagina. Thus, the question is not totally answered. Mitsuoka speculates the following.

At birth, the birth canal is one probable opportunity for bacterial contamination. However, immediately after birth, all the surroundings can be sources of contamination, and bacteria may often be transmitted from previously born babies via the hands of nurses. Furthermore, it cannot be ruled out that the infant-type bifidobacteria may harbor in small numbers in the intestine of mothers. Thus, bacteria from the birth canal and from the environment may gain access into the intestine of the newborn baby via the mouth or the anus, and then the bacteria that are best adapted to the intestinal environment of the neonate colonize and proliferate.

Route of Invasion of the Intestinal Bacteria

Then, from where in the body do the bacteria gain access into the intestine of infant? In order to answer this question, bacteriological examinations of the mouth and anus of infants immediately after birth have been conducted by various researchers. As a result, some scholars suggested that bifidobacteria enter from the anus on the basis of the facts that bifidobacteria were not always found in the mouth of infant immediately after birth and that bifidobacteria were found in the meconium before they were found in the mouth.

On the other hand, some scholars advocated that bifidobacteria enter not from the anus but from the mouth. This is based on the following evidence. In the newborn baby who had imperforate anus, bifidobacteria were found proliferating in the intestine at the time of surgery four days after birth. Also, in the intestine of a newborn baby who died one day after birth, bifidobacteria had been growing in the duodenum, jejunum and ileum but not at all in the rectum. The argument was that if the bifidobacteria had entered by the anus, bacterial growth would have to take place against the peristalsis and that bifidobacteria would not have been found in the upper intestinal tract at such an early stage of life.

After all, the major mode of entrance for bifidobacteria may be through the mouth, though the anus is still a probable alternative.

Breast Feeding and Bottle Feeding

It has been demonstrated statistically that breast-fed infants are apt to be less susceptible to maldigestion, shigellosis and colds than bottle-fed infants, and, even if affected, have a very low mortality rate. Today, the quality of artificial milk formula is highly improved but yet this disadvantageous tendency remains. The cause of the difference in morbidity and mortality has not yet been clearly defined but is considered to be due to the presence of substances in the mother's milk that confers resistance to infections or the difference in the intestinal flora between breast-fed infants and bottle-fed infants.

The feces of breast-fed infants is light yellow and has little smell, while the feces of bottle-fed infants is yellowish brown and smells strongly. This is because in the feces of breast-fed infants, bile pigments are not decomposed by the intestinal bacteria, thus retaining a light yellow color, and putrefactive substances are produced in small amount, thus imparting little smell.

When the feces of breast-fed infants is spread on a slide glass, gram-stained and examined microscopically, slightly curved gram-positive bacilli are observed in almost a pure state. In the feces of bottle-fed infants, other than the gram-positive bacilli, gram-negative bacilli and gram-positive cocci are observed in rather large numbers.

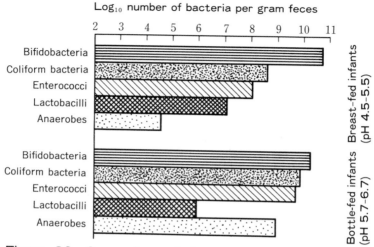

Figure 20. Comparison of the intestinal flora between breast-fed infants and bottle-fed infants.

Next, bacterial counts are compared by the cultivation method. As shown in Fig. 20, in the feces of breast-fed infants, bifidobacteria are found to be predominant, at a level of 10^{10} to 10^{11} per gram feces, coliform bacteria and enterococci are at a level of 10^8 per gram feces and anaerobic bacteria including putrefactive bacteria such as bacteroides are found in small numbers, if at all. The pH of the feces of breast-fed infants is low, in the range of 4.5 to 5.5.

The feces of bottle-fed infants have a different pattern. Although in most cases bifidobacteria are predominant resembling the feces of breast-fed infants, in some infants bifidobacteria are not isolated at all. However, the numbers of aerobic bacteria such as coliform bacteria and enterococci are about 10 times those found in the feces of breast-fed infants. The numbers of bifidobacteria and aerobic bacteria are nearly the same. Anaerobic bacteria such as bacteroides are found more frequently and in larger numbers. The pH of the feces is near neutral, in the range of 5.7 to 6.7.

Another characteristic difference between the feces of breast-fed infants and those of bottle-fed infants is the oxidation-reduction potential. The feces of the former show a lower degree of anaerobiosis than those of the latter, which may explain why the number of bacteroides which require high anaerobiosis is much less in the feces of breast-fed infants than in those of bottle-fed infants.

Bifidus Factors

Since bifidobacteria were first discovered, it was believed that there were some substances in the mother's milk which stimulate the growth of bifidobacteria, the so called bifidus factors, which explained why bifidobacteria dominated overwhelmingly the fecal flora of breast-fed infants. Consequently, many researchers attempted to isolate bifidus factors from human milk or other materials.

Some reports of bifidus factors isolated are as follows. György and his associates at the University of Pennsylvania isolated a polysaccharide that contained N-acetyl-glucosamine, L-fructose, D-galactose and acetic acid. Raynaud and his associates at the Pasteur Institute isolated a certain kind of peptide. Petuely at the University of Graz in Austria reported on lactulose in which the glucose portion of lactose is substituted by fructose. Tamura at the University of Tokyo isolated 4'-phosphopanthotein-S-sulfonic acid. Other substances that are reported to stimulate growth of bifidobacteria in growth medium include autolysis products of yeast, pepsin, pancreatin, papain, peptone, liver extract, malt extract and vitamin C. All these so called bifidus factors, however, share no common characteristics. Today, it is known that cultivation of bifidobacteria is not as difficult as once thought and the research on bifidus factors has rather declined.

As already mentioned, the intestinal flora of breast-fed infants appears to be characterized by small numbers of aerobic bacteria such as coliform bacteria and enterococci and anaerobic bacteria such as bacteroides rather than by the predominating bifidobacteria. In this connection, Willis in Britain proposed the following. In the intestine of the breast-fed infants, bifidobacteria convert lactose in milk to lactic acid and acetic acid, thereby lowering the pH of the intestine. Since the human milk has a buffering capacity of only about 1/3 that of cow's milk, the acidic intestinal pH is maintained, which is favorable for the growth of bifidobacteria but inhibitory for the growth of coliforms and putrefactive bacteria.

Bifidobacteria of Infants

As shown in Table 3, there are a variety of species of bifidobacteria, and specific species inhabit different hosts, such as human infants, human adults and other animals.

The human infant-type bifidobacteria include *B. infantis, B. breve*, infant-type *B. bifidum* and infant-type *B. longum*. The human adult-type bifidobacteria include *B. adolescentis*, adult-type *B. bifidum* and adult-type *B. longum*. The major animal-type bifidobacteria are *B. thermophilum, B. pseudolongum, B. animalis, B. indicum* and *B. asteroides*, etc.

Table 3. Species and Distribution of Bifidobacteria.

	Human infant	Human adult	Monkey	Dog	Pig	Chicken	Cattle, Sheep	Mouse, Rat	Guinea pig	Honey bee
B. bifidum	○	○								
B. longum	○	○								
B. infantis	○									
B. breve	○									
B. adolescentis			○	○	○					
B. thermophilum					○	○	○			
B. pseudolongum				○	○	○	○	○		
B. animalis							○	○	○	
B. indicum									○	
B. asteroides										○

From the intestine of infants, adult-type bifidobacteria are often isolated along with infant-type bifidobacteria probably due to the contamination of the adult-type bifidobacteria from mothers and nurses. However, in the intestine of adults, infant-type bifidobacteria, particularly *B. infantis* and *B. breve*, are very rarely found.

No agreement has been reached about the difference between bifidobacteria found in breast-fed infants and those found in bottle-fed infants. Dehnert at the University of Heidelberg reported in 1957 that bifidobacteria of group IV (*B. infantis* ss. *lactentis*) according to his classification were specific to breast-fed infants. Petuely in Austria in 1965 and Haenel in East Germany in 1970 confirmed this finding.

However, Reuter at the Free University of Berlin and my research group could not isolate this strain despite extensive investigation of the feces from breast-fed infants. Furthermore, Seelinger and Werner at the University of Bonn in 1962 reported that *B. breve* is the specific strain for breast-fed infants. Yet, there has been no agreement regarding whether bifidobacterium strains specific for breast-fed infants exist. Viewing the discrepancies between these reports, it should be noted that species and types of bifidobacteria harbored by infants are markedly affected by the bifidobacteria present in the environment surrounding the infants.

Our survey on babies delivered in three maternity hospitals in Tokyo revealed that different types of bifidobacteria are found specifically in individual hospitals. This is probably because the bifidobacteria of specific types are spread from one infant to another by hands of nurses or utensils within the individual hospitals.

These observations suggest that Dehnert's group IV bifidobacteria which had been thought to be specific to breast-fed infants may be one which happened to be widespread in that particular environment at that time.

From Weaning to Adult Age

At weaning when milk-diet is changed to mixed diet, the infant intestinal flora changes to one similar to that of adults. Anaerobic bacteria such as *Bacteroides*, the most predominating bacteria in the intestine of adults, *Eubacterium*, and anaerobic streptococci become dominant in the intestine of infants. After weaning, the intestinal flora is almost identical to that of adults. At the same time, bifidobacteria change

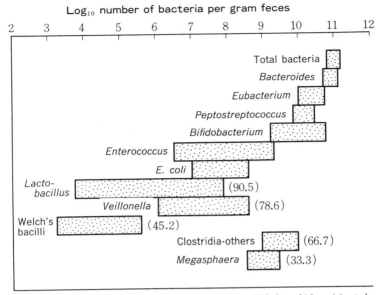

Figure 21. Intestinal flora of human adults (42 subjects). Figures in parentheses are detection rates. Detection rates are 100 % where figures are not shown.

from the infant-type to the adult type. Weaning is thus a period of big change for the intestinal flora.

After weaning, the intestinal flora is stable as far as the individual remains healthy. Fig. 21 shows the results of an investigation of the fecal flora of 42 adults in my laboratory at the age range of 24–42. As shown clearly, the most predominating bacteria were anaerobic bacteria such as *Bacteroides*, *Eubacterium* and *Peptostreptococcus*, and bifidobacteria. These two goups of predominating bacteria have counts in the range of 10^9–10^{11} per gram intestinal content and are

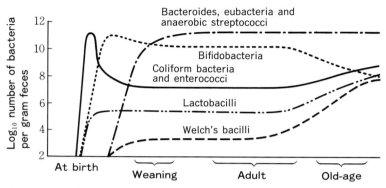

Figure 22. Change in intestinal flora with age.

well balanced with each other. On the other hand, the numbers of coliform bacteria, enterococci, *Lactobacillus* and *Veillonella* were as low as 10^5–10^8 and never exceed this range.
Welch's bacilli, *Staphylococcus* and yeast were less frequently found and at a level as low as less than 10^5.

The balance of the intestinal flora is often disturbed when
one gets old. This is demonstrated by comparing the intestinal flora of young adults in our laboratory with the elderly
(65–85 years old). The detection rate and the average number of bifidobacteria in the feces of the elderly were both low.
On the other hand, Welch's bacilli, which were infrequently
harbored by the young adults and in small numbers, were detected at a rate as high as 92% in the elderly and the average
bacterial count was markedly high. Furthermore, the number of lactobacilli also increased. Fig. 22 shows the change
in the intestinal flora with age. The reason and effect of the
change will be discussed later.

Intestinal Flora of Different Parts of the Alimentary Tract

Let us examine how the intestinal flora differs from site to site in the alimentary tract (Fig. 23). Firstly, as many as 10^7 bacteria per ml are found in the saliva. These are a mixture of bacteria that have grown on the surface or root of the teeth and on the surface of the soft tissue, and bacteria contained in food. They vary depending on age, the number of dental caries and dental hygiene. The major bacteria are aerobic bacteria such as *Streptococcus* and *Lactobacillus* and anaerobic bacteria such as *Veillonella, Fusobacterium, Propionibacterium, Bacteroides, Peptostreptococcus* and *Leptotrichia*. The numbers of aerobic bacteria and anaerobic bacteria are about the same. Furthermore, *Neisseria, Staphylococcus, Spirochaetaceae, Vibrio*, yeasts, *Mycoplasma* and *Bifidobacterium* are found in small numbers. However, coliform bacteria which are considered to be fecal in origin are rarely found.

The saliva containing these bacteria is swallowed with the food and passed through the esophagus to reach the stomach. The empty stomach has a pH as low as less than 3.0 due to gastric acid secretion. Only a small number of microorganisms inhabit the stomach, namely, acid tolerant bacteria such as lactobacilli and streptococci and yeasts, at a level of 10^2–10^3 per gram gastric content. When food is brought into the stomach, it is warmed to body temperature and the pH of the gastric content is raised to 4.0. As a result, bacteria proliferate to a level of 10^4–10^8 per gram gastric content. The microorganisms which grow in the stomach in these conditions are the inhabitant microorganisms, such as lactobacilli

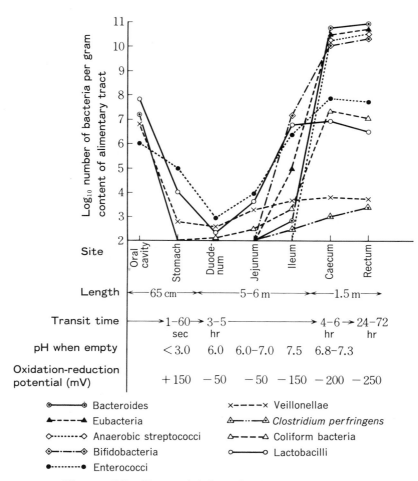

Figure 23. Bacterial flora in the alimentary tract.

and yeasts, and bacteria from the mouth and ingested food, such as streptococci, *Bacteroides*, *Bifidobacterium*, *Veillonella*, *Fusobacterium*, coliform bacteria, *Bacillus* and *Staphylococcus*. However, as the pH of the stomach content drops due to mixing with the gastric juice, the acid-sensitive bacteria die so that the total bacterial count in the content decreases. Thus, the stomach is a barrier to the bacteria that enter the body with food. The food mass together with the bacteria is sent to the small intestine through the pyloric valve.

When empty of food, the upper part of the small intestine harbors lactobacilli, yeast and veillonellae at a level as low as less than 10^4 per gram content. When the food mass enters the small intestine from the stomach it carries bacteria also in small numbers due to the low pH of the gastric juice. Bacteria do not grow well here in the upper intestine due to chemical factors such as bile juice discharged into the duodenum and lysozyme and mucus secreted from the intestinal mucosa, and the physical factor, peristalsis. Therefore, the bacteria found in this area are limited to streptococci, lactobacilli and *Veillonella*. The small numbers of *Bacteroides*, coliform bacteria and *Eubacterium* which are sometimes detected are considered to be transit bacteria originating from the buccal cavity.

In the lower part of the intestine, the number of bacteria increases rapidly. This is because the content is neutralized by the intestinal juice and the transit speed is lowered. The total number of bacteria is as many as 10^5–10^7 per gram content even when empty of food. The bacterial flora here consists of a mixture of bacteria including those found in the upper small intestine such as lactobacilli, streptococci and *Veillonella*, and those predominating in the large intestine, such as *Bac-*

teroides, *Bifidobacterium*, *Eubacterium* and anaerobic streptococci. The number of the bacteria in the lower part of the ileum is as high as 10^7 per gram content. Once the digested food passes through the ileocecal valve into the cecum, the transit speed is suddenly lowered and the total number of bacteria abruptly increases. In this site, as many as 10^{10} bacteria per gram content constantly colonize, which grow even further utilizing the intestinal content from the small intestine as growth medium. The bacterial flora is almost the same as that of the feces, comprising predominately anaerobic bacteria, such as *Bacteroides*, *Bifidobacterium*, *Eubacterium* and *Clostridium*, with the minor groups such as coliform bacteria, streptococci (including enterococci), lactobacilli, *Veillonella* and staphylococci in numbers as small as 10^5–10^8 per gram content.

In the upper part of the large intestine, water and electrolytes in the fluid content sent from the small intestine are absorbed, and in the lower half, the feces is formed and stored temporarily. Below the traverse colon peristalsis occurs only once or twice a day. With the stimulation of intake of food, sudden strong peristalsis occurs from the traverse colon to the sigmoid colon thereby sending the content in the large intestine to the rectum for excretion.

The time required for food to pass through the intestinal tract varies depending on the quality and quantity of food, movement of the large intestine, capability of absorption, psychological conditions and physical exercise. In general, the average transit time is in the range of 24 and 72 hours; namely, food reaches the duodenum from the stomach in 3–5 hours, to the ileocecal sites in another 4–6 hours and then to the sigmoid colon in a further 12–16 hours.

Individual Patterns of Intestinal Flora

It is understood that in humans, the patterns of intestinal flora vary depending on age and sites in the body. Yet, individuals of the same age do not necessarily have common patterns of the intestinal flora. The fecal flora of six men in my laboratory was investigated in detail, seven samples were collected from each individual over a period of two months. The findings show that the patterns of intestinal bacteria, like facial features, are different from one individual to another, and the individual patterns remain rather consistent. Patterns of the intestinal flora of three subjects, A, B and C, are compared in Fig. 24. As evident from the figure, the number of *Bifidobacterium* was always high in subject C but in subject B it was about one hundredth that of subject C, while the number of enterococci was always high in subject B but in subject C it was only 1/10,000 that of subject B. Furthermore, *Veillonella* was not found at all in subject A but was consistently found in subjects B and C at levels of about 10^9 and 10^6 per gram feces, respectively. *Megasphaera* was also found in subjects A and C at the level of 10^9 per gram feces, but not at all in subject B. Similarly, lactobacilli were always found in subjects A and B at levels as high as 10^6–10^8 per gram feces, but were almost absent in subject C. Furthermore, it was revealed that the patterns of the intestinal flora are rather stable. Day-to-day variations in the predominating bacterial populations were remarkedly small while those in the minor bacterial populations were rather drastic.

The possible causes of the difference in pattern of the intestinal flora are physical conditions of the digestive tract such as peristalsis and excretion of gastric juice or bile acids, and eating habits. However, the intimate biological relationship between the host and the bacteria inhabiting the intestine, that is, the adaptation and acclimatization of the intestinal bacteria to the intestinal mucosa is an important factor that should not be neglected.

As described above, bifidobacteria in newborn babies have

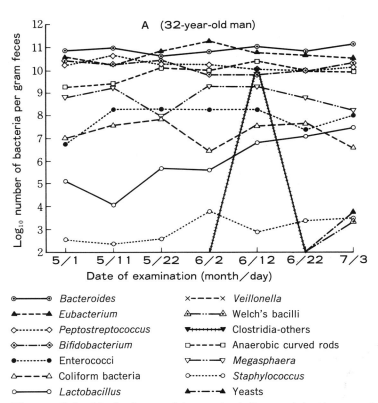

Figure 24. Variations of intestinal flora with time and individual differences.

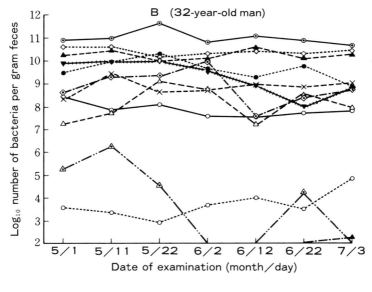

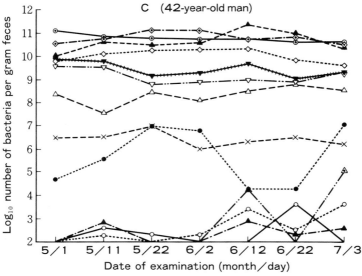

group-specificity, namely, the babies delivered in the same hospital have the same strain or type of bifidobacteria. This tendency is often observed as an "epidemic" phenomenon in the intestinal bacteria, both pathogenic and non-pathogenic.

Intestinal Flora of Animals

Animals and humans are different in the structure and physiology of the alimentary tract and dietary habits. The human, monkey, pig, chicken, mouse, rat and hamster are omnivorous, the dog and cat are carnivorous, and the rabbit, guinea pig, horse and cattle are herbivorous. As shown in Fig. 25, the patterns of the intestinal flora are different from animal to animal.

A feature commonly observed in the intestinal flora of the human (adult) and many animals is that anaerobic bacteria such as *Bacteroides, Eubacterium* and *Peptostreptococcus* comprise the predominating populations. In addition, in many animal species, lactic acid bacteria such as bifidobacteria or lactobacilli are included in the predominating populations.

The bacterial flora of the monkey is similar to that of human. The number of *Bifidobacterium* and lactobacilli in the monkey intestine is higher than that in the human intestine. Spirochetes inhabiting deep in the intestinal mucosa are often observed.

The bacterial flora of the chicken cecum is very complicated and resembles that of the monkey except that the number of lactobacilli is high. The pig has less bifidobacteria but more coliform bacteria and enterococci than the dog.

The mouse, rat, hamster and guinea pig belong to the same group. In the intestine of these animals, lactobacilli and

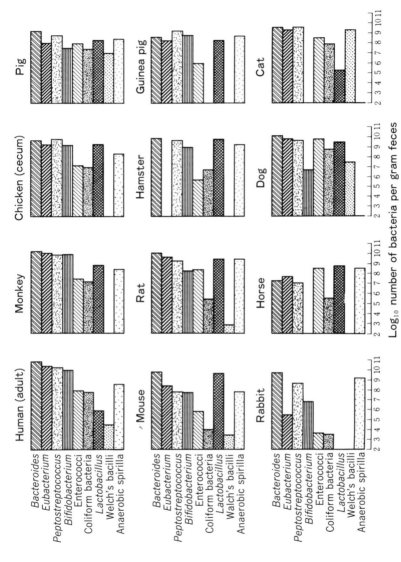

Figure 25. Fecal flora of various animals.

anaerobic bacteria are dominant with fusiform bacteria specific to rodents being the most prevalent. The numbers of coliform bacteria and enterococci are higher in the rat and hamster than in the mouse. The intestinal flora of the hamster contains a higher number of bifidobacteria than that of the mouse or rat and rather resembles that of the guinea pig. In the intestine of the guinea pig, like in the human and monkey, bifidobacteria predominate and outnumber lactobacilli.

In the intestine of the rat, lactobacilli are rarely detected, bifidobacteria are not present in abundance, and, as in the horse intestine, anaerobic spirilla characteristic of the herbivores are most prevalent. In the horse intestine, enterococci and lactobacilli are also dominant populations.

In the intestine of the dog and cat, Welch's bacilli are one of the dominant bacteria due to carnivorous habits, the number of the coliform bacteria is increased while that of lactobacilli is decreased. Especially in the cat intestine, Welch's bacilli are the most prevalent.

The process of the establishment of the intestinal flora from birth in animals, such as the pig, chicken, rat and mouse, is similar to that observed in human.

The bacteria that first appear in the intestine are those which are ubiquitous and flourish easily, such as coliform bacteria, enterococci and Welch's bacilli. Accordingly, when animals are reared in a clean environment, the appearance of these bacteria is delayed. Soon, in many animal species, lactobacilli appear and then the numbers of coliform bacteria, enterococci and Welch's bacilli decrease while bifidobacteria and lactobacilli become dominant. This change may be closely related to the start of normal secretion in the host's stomach.

The anaerobic bacteria such as *Bacteroides, Eubacterium*

and anaerobic streptococci prevail in the large intestine of the mature animal. They start to appear and colonize in the intestine at the time of partial weaning in mammalians and 3–4 weeks after hatching in chickens. Thus the intestinal floras of matured animals are established. It is very interesting that for most of the animal species, a common process is observed in the establishment of the intestinal flora. The coliform bacteria and enterococci, which dominate immediately after birth and therefore should be the ones that grow easily in the intestine, cannot prevail in the latter stage of life. This clearly demonstrates that the coexistence with the host is a prerequisite in establishing the intestinal flora. Then, in ill health, an abnormal situation that coliform bacteria dominate in number over bifidobacteria and lactobacilli can be seen. In other words, it may be inevitable that coliform bacteria are destined not to predominate in the intestine of healthy animals.

3. Mode of Colonization of Intestinal Bacteria

Proliferation Rate of Intestinal Bacteria

When coliform bacteria (*E. coli*) are inoculated in a medium in a test tube and incubated at 37°C, the bacteria undergo cell division once every 20–30 minutes. The number of bacteria reaches about 10^9/ml at full growth and then decreases due to cell death caused by metabolites produced by the cells.

The bacterial growth in the intestine, however, is known to be considerably slower than that in the test tube. Gibbons and Kapsimalis reported that cell division of the intestinal bacteria occurred 0.5–1.4 times a day for hamsters and guinea pigs and 3.5–5.1 times a day for mice. *E. coli*, which grows fast *in vitro*, has been reported to undergo cell division only 1.2 times a day when transferred to the alimentary tract of germfree mice. Meynell and Sabbaiah reported that bacterial cell division occurred once in about 6 hours in the large intestine of mice. In all these reports, the bacterial growth in the intestine was considerably slower than that in a test tube.

Nevertheless, the intestinal tract is a kind of continuous culture vessel in which constant numbers of bacteria inhabit given sites of the intestine at any time. At each site, the bacteria, while multiplying by utilizing the nutrients reaching them from above, are being passed down the intestinal tract simultaneously. When the rate of increase by cell division equals that of decrease by being carried away, an equilibrium state is maintained.

Resident Bacteria and Transient Bacteria

The group of bacteria living in the intestine of a healthy subject is called the "normal intestinal (bacterial) flora." Detailed investigation of the normal intestinal flora revealed that some of the bacteria live for a long time in the intestine, but some appear only for a few days. The former are called resident bacteria and the latter, transient bacteria.

The resident bacteria that colonize in humans have been established through the long evolutionary history of humans and comprise those bacteria that are most adapted and trained to have a symbiotic relationship with the host. They can therefore be considered as the native bacteria. Moreover, the bacteria which colonize in animals vary with the animal species, and even within the same animal species, they are specific to individuals. Because of their highly specific relationships with the host animals, the bacteria are often called indigenous bacteria. The resident bacteria in the human intestine include the most predominating bacteria such as *Bifidobacterium*, *Bacteroides*, *Eubacterium* and *Peptostreptococcus* and the less abundant groups such as coliform bacteria and enterococci. Different animal species and individuals harbor different indigenous species and types of resident bacteria.

On the other hand, the transient bacteria gain access into the intestine with ingested food but cannot inhabit there and are soon eliminated from the body due to the defense mechanism of the host or the power of the predominating resident bacteria. The transit bacteria include many foreign bacteria such as those that grow in food, e.g. lactobacilli, enterococci, coliform bacteria, *Bacillus*, staphylococci, and pathogenic bacteria, e.g. *Shigella*, *Vibrio cholerae* and *Salmonella*.

Thus, an equilibrium is established in the intestine between the host and the intestinal bacteria, which results in the formation of a normal intestinal bacterial flora. However, the equilibrium is by no means permanent and may be disturbed by various factors as will be mentioned later. An unbalanced bacterial flora may sometimes cause acute diseases, or may insidiously cause chronic malignant diseases.

Colonization in the Mucosa

Then, how do the intestinal bacteria colonize in the intestinal mucosa? The recent developments of the scanning electron microscope and transmission electron microscope have made it possible to observe the mode of colonization of the intestinal bacteria in the intestinal mucosa of animals such as mice, albino rats and chickens.

In the gastric mucosa of mice and rats, the indigenous lactobacilli inhabit the non-secretory epithelium while yeasts inhabit the secretory epithelium. At the epithelium of the crop of chickens, lactobacilli indigenous to chicken live but none of the lactobacilli derived from other mammalians can colonize. These associations between the indigenous lactobacilli and mucous membranes are so strong that they are not easily affected by feed or rearing methods.

In the duodenum, the intestinal bacteria can hardly live probably due to rapid transit of the digestive content, regeneration and degradation of mucous epithelial cells and secretion of the intestinal juice. Various bacteria live in the jejunum and ileum. The height of the villi in the small intestine is about 1 mm and the depth of the crypts is about 0.4 mm. The epithelial cells of the villi are one of the cells that have the most rapid turnover rate in the body. They are actively generated at the base of the crypts and gradually move up the villi, reaching the tip in a day or two, where they are shed into the intestinal lumen. The intestinal bacteria multiply at the same time of epithelial cell division and successively attach themselves to the newly generated cells.

In the large intestine, a large number of bacteria inhabit the intestinal lumen. Gram-positive bacilli, cocci, fusiform bacteria and yeasts are covered with mucin and appear as a thick layer closely attached to the mucous epithelia.

Fuller and Brooker revealed that occasionally the adhesion of bacteria to the mucous surface is mediated by an acid mucopolysaccharide layer located outside the cell wall of the bacteria. In the case of *E. coli*, it is believed that a layer of polysaccharide made of branched sugar molecules extends from the surface of the bacteria and surrounds the bacteria forming a felt-like glycocalyx. This glycocalyx then binds specifically to the mucous epithelia via lectin, a simple protein, and the glycocalyx that extend from the surface of the microvilli. The properties of the glycocalyx of the intestinal mucosa are known to be affected by viral infection and aging. The increased susceptibility to bacterial infections during viral infections and old age may be explained by the changes of properties of the glycocalyx.

In mice, the attachment of fusiform bacteria to the colon via a long thread-like substance can be observed. On the other hand, thread-like bacteria adhere to the epithelium of the small intestine by sticking into holes of the epithelium. In this case, certain changes are said to occur on the membrane of the mucous cells.

Ecotypes of Lactic Acid Bacteria

Next, let us examine the correlation between classification and ecology of the lactic acid bacteria. When bifidobacteria isolated from the intestine of humans and animals were characterized and classified, it was revealed that there were differences in the species of bifidobacteria found in humans and animals. Apart from a few strains isolated from monkeys and dogs, the bifidobacteria isolated from the intestine of animals had never been isolated from the human intestine. They were thus classified as new species, and named *B. thermophilum*, *B. pseudolongum* and *B. animalis*. Monkeys harbor *B. adolescentis* which is also isolated from humans. Dogs have

B. pseudolongum that is specific to animals, as well as *B. adolescentis*. Pigs and chickens have *B. thermophilum* and *B. pseudolongum*; cows, sheep, mice and albino rats have *B. animalis* and *B. pseudolongum*; guinea pigs have *B. animalis*; and honey bees have *B. indicum* and *B. asteroides*.

A similar phenomenon is observed with another important lactic acid bacteria, the *Lactobacillus*, in the animal intestine. The major species of *Lactobacillus* isolated from the intestine are *L. acidophilus*, *L. salivarius*, and *L. fermentum*. These species cannot be isolated from foods such as yoghurt, pickles and salami sausages. The kinds of lactobacilli inhabiting the intestine are different from those that grow naturally in foods, except in the cases when they are isolated from the intestine and utilized in certain foods. Detailed investigation of *L. acidophilus* revealed the difference in types of the bacteria in different animal species. For example, pig-type lactobacilli inhabit the pig intestine, and human-type bifidobacteria are rarely found. Similar situations exist in the intestines of chickens and mice.

Viewing these observations from a different point of view, among the various lactic acid bacteria that gained access into the human or animal body, only the species or types that are selected to be the most suitable for the host during a long history of evolution can inhabit the intestine. Accordingly, most of the lactic acid bacteria contained in ordinary foods hardly colonize in the intestine when ingested. This is something to be taken into consideration when lactic acid bacteria preparations and lactic acid bacteria drinks are prepared for the purpose of implanting the lactic acid bacteria in the intestine by oral administration.

Colonization Experiment

The following experiment was carried out to find out why the lactic acid bacteria colonizing in the intestine have animal species specificity.

Firstly, the change in the composition of the intestinal flora was examined in 14 mice which were divided into two groups, one was fed human milk and the other cow's milk. Next, human-type bifidobacteria were administered to see whether they could colonize in the intestine of these mice (Fig. 26).

In the feces of the mice fed with an ordinary commercial feed, *Bacteroides*, fusiform bacteria and lactobacilli were the most dominant bacteria followed by anaerobic streptococci. *B. pseudolongum* and *B. animalis* were both detected at a level of 10^7–10^8 per gram feces. Enterococci and coliform bacteria were found in small numbers.

When human infant-type bifidobacteria, *B. breve*, and human adult-type bifidobacteria, *B. adolescentis*, (about 10^8 viable bacteria per mouse) were administered to these mice, the bacteria could not live in the intestine and soon disappeared.

Next, these mice were divided into two groups, seven mice each, one was fed human milk only and the other cow's milk only. After two weeks of feeding, the animal-type bifidobacteria, *B. pseudolongum* and *B. animalis*, markedly increased in number and became the predominant bacteria. In other words, feeding of either human or cow's milk to mice stimulated the growth of the indigenous animal-type bifidobacteria inhabiting the mouse intestine.

After one week, when the human-type bifidobacteria previously administered were given again, they inhabited the

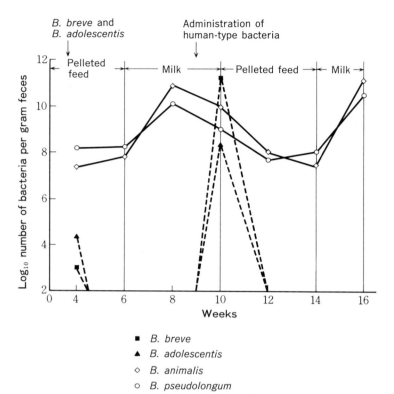

- ■ *B. breve*
- ▲ *B. adolescentis*
- ◇ *B. animalis*
- ○ *B. pseudolongum*

Figure 26. Experimental colonization of human-type bifidobacteria in mice.

intestine of mice, and, together with the animal-type bifidobacteria, became the most predominating bacteria.

However, when milk feeding was discontinued and was replaced with commercial feed, the human-type bifidobacteria soon disappeared and at the same time the numbers of the animal-type bifidobacteria decreased. After feeding with commercial feed for four weeks, the animals were fed again with either human milk or cow's milk. After two days, bifidobac-teria became predominant but none of the human-type bi-fidobacteria were detected. From these observations it was thought that probably the environment of the intestine of the mice fed with the commercial feed was not appropriate for the growth of the human-type bifidobacteria so that they dis-appeared all together from the intestine. As a matter of fact, it seemed that bacteria other than bifidobacteria were respon-sible for expelling the human-type bifidobacteria from the in-testine of mice. To prove this hypothesis, a separate experiment was carried out using germfree mice.

Human-type bifidobacteria, *B. breve*, were orally inocu-lated into germfree mice reared on germfree feed and water. The bifidobacteria grew as well in the intestine of the mice as in a test tube with a medium. After the human-type bi-fidobacteria had well colonized, *B. animalis* and *B. pseudolon-gum* isolated from mice were administered. These bifidobac-teria inhabited well together with the human-type bifidobac-teria previously administered.

Next, the mice were administered, in succession, with bac-teria such as *E. coli*, enterococci, *Staphylococcus, Clostridi-um, Bacillus, Lactobacillus, Peptostreptococcus, Eubacterium, Bacteroides* and fusiform bacteria and yeast. Yet, the human-type bifidobacteria only slightly decreased in number but was by no means eliminated from the intestine. Therefore none of the bacteria administered could eliminate the human-type bifidobacteria.

In the next step, the cecal content taken from conventional mice was orally administered to the mice to which various bac-teria had been given. Two days after the administration, the human-type bifidobacteria completely disappeared from the fecal flora; the growth of *E. coli* was suppressed to a level similar to that in the intestine of conventional mice. This experiment suggests that unknown bacteria in the intestine of conventional mice interfere with the inhabitation of human-type bifidobacteria in the mouse intestine. Furthermore, the growth of coliform bacteria in the intestine of conventional mice is similarly inhibited by certain bacteria.

Similar observations were also made in experiments with germfree chickens. *Lactobacillus acidophilus* isolated from the human intestine, or *L. casei* derived from dairy food, when orally given to germfree chickins, proliferated well in the intestine. When *L. acidophilus* or enterococci, isolated from the intestine of chickens, were administered additionally, the human-type lactobacilli that proliferated previously were readily eliminated from the chicken intestine. It is evident that in the human intestine also, various factors such as food composition, physical function, antagonism and synergism between the intestinal bacteria, intertwine in a complicated manner and determime whether a particular bacteria can colonize in the intestine.

4. Factors Influencing Intestinal Flora

Physical Condition of Host

It is quite natural that the structure and functions of the alimentary tract influence the balance of the intestinal flora. The pH in the alimentary tract affects the kinds of intestinal bacteria that can inhabit it. Generally, in low pH, only a few kinds of lactic acid bacteria and yeasts can grow. Particularly in the stomach where the pH is extremely low, the variety and number of bacteria are limited. Gastric acid acts as a barrier to stop invasion of pathogenic bacteria entering the alimentary tract. In the stomach of an achlorhydria patient, a large number of bacteria are consistently present. In a person whose stomach has been resected due to, for example, gastric ulcer, the small intestine is colonized with bacteria that are detectable normally in the large intestine of healthy subjects, such as coliform bacteria, *Proteus*, Welch's bacilli and *Pseudomonas aureus*.

Peristalsis in the intestine serves an important function in conveying the intestinal content. Where the rate of bacterial growth is slower than that of the peristaltic movement, the number of bacteria present becomes small. This is the reason why the numbers of bacteria in the upper and middle parts of the small intestine are relatively small.

The intestinal bacteria are also affected by enzymes, mucus and bile juice that are secreted or discharged in the intestinal lumen. Bile acids, a major component of the bile juice exert complicated actions on intestinal bacteria. They are bactericidal to certain intestinal bacteria, have no affect on enterococci, slightly suppress the growth of gram-negative bacteria and promote the growth of *Bacteroides fragilis*, the dominant bacteria in the large intestine. For this reason, the bile acids are important in the control of the balance of the intestinal flora in the small and large intestines.

Certain kinds of bacteria utilize mucin, a kind of polysaccharide secreted from salivary glands, as a carbon source. It is common to observe indigenous intestinal bacteria forming colonies in mucin on the surface of the intestinal mucosa or in the intestinal lumen.

Stress due to, for example, intense emotional disturbance causes cessation of the peristalic movement and poor secretion of gastric acid and intestinal juice. As a result, the balance of the intestinal flora is disturbed. In 1976, Holdeman and his associates investigated the intestinal flora of three astronauts who were on the Skylab of NASA. They reported that the intestinal floras of the astronauts were altered, in which the anaerobic bacteria *Peptostreptococcus productus* completely disappeared and the number of *Bacteroides thetaiotaomicron* increased.

When animals are reared under overcrowded conditions, at extremely high or low temperatures, in high humidity, or in strong wind, the balance of the intestinal flora is disturbed, which results in delayed growth of the animals. Addition of antibiotics to the feed of the animals reared under these conditions reportedly prevents growth delay. In man as well, it is likely that various kinds of stress indirectly affect the intestinal flora, which further deteriorates the conditions of the body. With age, all the physiological functions become weak. This affects the balance of the intestinal bacteria; bifidobacteria decrease in number or even disappear; at the same time, the numbers of Welch's bacilli and *Proteus* which produce harmful substances in the intestine increase. These phenomena further accelerate aging.

Furthermore, abnormal changes in the intestinal flora were observed in the cases of liver cirrhosis, chronic kidney inflammation, cancer, constipation, cold, vaccination and radiation therapy. In most of these cases, the number of bifidobacteria decreases, while that of *E. coli*, enterococci, staphylococci, or Welch's bacilli increases.

Bacterial overgrowth in the small intestine is occasionally

observed in cases such as colds, acute gastro-enteritis, jejunal diverticulosis, diabetes, tropical sprue and carcinomatous stricture. These seem to be related to abnormal peristalsis, among other causes. When bacteria that normally inhabit the large intestine proliferate in the small intestine, competition for nutrients occurs between the host and the bacteria. Also, bacterial metabolites are increased, toxins are produced by Welch's bacilli, coliform bacteria, staphylococci, etc. Pathogenic bacteria may invade from the mucous epithelia to the lamina propria mucosae, causing abnormal excretion of water and electrolytes which results in diarrhea.

Host Immunity

Antibodies to certain intestinal bacteria are found in the serum and intestinal secretions from humans and animals. For example, when *Vibrio cholerae* invades and colonizes in the mucosa of the small intestine, antibodies against these bacteria are soon produced in the body of the host and excreted into the intestine. The growth of the cholera vibrios is then suppressed and the bacteria are eliminated from the body. On the other hand, it is often observed that some indigenous intestinal bacteria possess antigens common to the intestinal mucosa and mucus of the host. These observations suggest that the surface antigens of the indigenous bacteria in the intestine resemble those of the host so closely that they are recognized as "self" by the immune system of the host. This is another reason why indigenous bacteria in the intestine are not eliminated by the host.

Phagocytic cells such as macrophages and polymorphonuclear leukocytes which are situated in the lamina propria mucosae in the intestine are discharged into the intestine to completely eliminate pathogens invading from outside. It is interesting that, among the epithelial cells of the small intestine, Paneth's cells located at the base of the crypts are functionally and structurally phagocytic so as to eliminate bacteria intruding deeply into the crypts. Thus, bacteria are not normally observed in the base of the crypts.

It is known that the number of bacteria in the intestine of patients with immunoglobulin deficiency is higher than that in the intestine of healthy subjects. This also demonstrates that the antibodies that are excreted in the intestine are important in controlling the intestinal flora and to prevent the growth of pathogens.

Diet

It is easy to speculate that the balance of the intestinal flora may easily be affected by food. However, in practice, the influence of food has not yet been clearly demonstrated. Due to problems such as balance of the diet composition, eating habit, age, methods and techniques in the investigation of the intestinal flora, etc., no unanimous conclusion has been reached.

When a large amount of lactose is fed to mice every day, the number of lactobacilli decreases and the number of bifidobacteria markedly increases 10–20 days after the start of feeding. A similar phenomenon is observed with sucrose.

Many researchers have pointed out that the intestinal flora is altered by change in diet only when the change is extreme. Recently, the relationship between diet and the intestinal flora has attracted public attention since correlations between diet and carcinogenesis are statistically demonstrated. However, no consensus in opinion has been reached.

Hill et al. (1971) in England examined the fecal flora of adults in England, United States, Uganda, India and Japan. They reported that in the feces of the adults in the United States and England where incidences of colon and breast cancer are high, the number of *Bacteroides* was 10 times higher than that in the feces of the other populations. The numbers of coliform bacteria, enterococci and *Eubacterium* were high in the feces of the Japanese and Indians. However, Finegold et al. and Moore et al. in the United States examined the difference in the intestinal floras of subjects fed Japanese and western diets and reported that they could not confirm the data of Hill et al. Finegold et al. reported that in the feces of subjects fed a Japanese diet, the numbers of enterococci, a *Eubacterium* species and *Peptostreptococcus* were higher than those in the subjects fed the western diet. Also, we investigated the influence of Japanese diet and western diet on the balance of the intestinal flora. About one month after the switch from Japanese diet to western diet, no remarkable changes of the intestinal flora at genus level could be detected, though some important changes might have been found at the level of species or subspecies. Variation among individuals was larger than that due to the difference in diet.

Interaction Between Intestinal Bacteria

There have been many investigations on antagonistic relationships among bacteria, in which a certain bacteria affect the survivability or growth of another. Competition for essential nutrients is one type of antagonistic interaction. It is not clearly known how many nutrients are consumed by the intestinal bacteria. There is a report saying that in the case of rats, about 10% of calories ingested by the host is utilized by the intestinal bacteria.

Change in pH and oxidation-reduction potential, production of hydrogen peroxide, hydrogen sulfide, organic acids and antibiotics are factors which may adversely affect the growth of bacteria. Meynell et al. (1963) reported that ordinary mice were not easily infected by *Salmonella* probably because a combined action of low oxidation-reduction potential and high concentration of volatile fatty acids in the cecum prevents the growth of *Salmonella*. Furthermore, since the fatty acids exert the highest bactericidal activity in their dissociated forms, the pH of the environment affects the activity. The inhibitory effect of the fatty acids against bacteria also depends on the number of carbons. Formic acid and acetic acid are known to be effective against *Shigella*.

Conjugated bile acids, the major components of bile juice excreted in the intestine, are deconjugated by the intestinal bacteria and further transformed into secondary bile acids which prevent the growth of a certain type of bacteria.

Hydrogen sulfide, produced by anaerobic bacteria, is known to suppress the growth of *E. coli*. This may partly explain the fact that the number of *E. coli* in the large intestine of humans and animals is less than one thousandth of anaerobic bacteria.

Synergism between the intestinal bacteria as well as antagonism is well known. In the symbiotic relationship, one bacteria renders the environment beneficial for another bacteria by producing essential nutrients, or changing the oxidation-reduction potential or pH. Sometimes substances that cannot be utilized by one party alone are utilized jointly by sharing complementary enzyme actions. For example, *E. coli* strains A and B, both require isoleucine for growth and grow well when cultured together in an isoleucine-free medium. In this case, strain A produces ketonic acid which strain B cannot make, but strain B has the enzyme, which strain A does not have, for transamination of the ketonic acid into isoleucine. Thus, the two strains together synthesize isoleucine in the medium in a symbiotic manner.

After the growth of aerobic bacteria, an anaerobic environment is produced. In the upper part of the alimentary tract, aerobic bacteria grow and oxygen is consumed. On descending the tract, the environment becomes more anaerobic, and anaerobic bacteria become predominant in the lower part of the alimentary tract. This phenomenon is another example of synergism.

Bacteriocins are another example of bacterial interaction. Bacteriocins are proteins produced by certain strains of bacteria and act only against closely related bacteria. Colicin, a bacteriocin produced by certain species of *Enterobacteriaceae*, acts on *E. coli*. The bacteria which produce colicin are not affected by colicin. In susceptible bacteria, colicin is absorbed at a specific site of the cell wall, blocks oxidative phosphorylation and inhibits synthesis of DNA, RNA, proteins, etc. to kill the bacteria. Other examples of bacteriocins are pyocin produced by *Pseudomonas aeruginosa* and megacins produced by *Bacillus megaterium*. Bacteriocin production is mediated by a DNA fragment which can be transferred from one bacterium to another, for example, from *E. coli* to *Shigella* or *Salmonella*.

Antibiotics

The administration of antibiotics disturbs the balance of intestinal flora. The changes vary depending on the type of antibiotics, dose, frequency, method and period of administration or age of the subject, and the effect is different from one individual to another. It has been proved experimentally using animals that administration of antibiotics reduces the numbers of normal intestinal bacteria so that the barrier against invading bacteria is removed, which results in increased susceptibility to intestinal infection by *Salmonella enteritidis*. When mice which had been orally given streptomycin were challenged with less than ten streptomycin-resistant *Salmonella*, about 50% of the animals were infected; whereas control mice not given streptomycin were infected only when as many as more than 10^6 of *Salmonella* were administered. Thus, the disturbance of the intestinal flora weakens the resistance to infection.

Recently it was reported that chickens which were receiving a certain kind of antibiotics commonly used as a feed additive excreted salmonellae in the feces in larger number and for longer period than chickens which received no antibiotics. This phenomenon also demonstrates that certain intestinal bacteria are eliminated by the antibiotics so that salmonellae which are suppressed in the intestine of ordinary chickens can colonize and proliferate.

An example of the serious effect of administration of antibiotics is the so-called bacterial replacement symptom which often occurs during antibiotic treatment. In this symptom, microorganisms that are considered to have low pathogenicity, such as streptococci, *Staphylococcus aureus*, *Proteus*, yeasts and molds, multiply in various parts of the body and cause fever, vomiting, abdominal pain, diarrhea and vitamin deficiency. These are the results of the disturbance of normal intestinal flora, that is caused by administration of antibiotics. When the balance of the intestinal flora is disturbed for some reason or when the defense ability of the subject is weakened, these bacteria, which have dormant pathogenicity but normally not causing diseases, exhibit virulence.

Food Contaminated with Bacteria

It has been reported that patients hospitalized in the same hospital have the same serotype of *E. coli* in the feces. This is due to the transmission of the same type of *E. coli* from patient to patient in the hospital. Cook et al. (1970) reported that food provided in hospital was contaminated with a large number of *E. coli* in the same ways as school meals or food provided in company canteens, while contamination with *E. coli* is very rare in meals cooked at home.

These data show that the fluctuation of *E. coli* population in the feces is directly related to the number of *E. coli* in food ingested. That is, when a large volume of food, for example, in a restaurant is contaminated by *E. coli* through the hands of cooking personnel, the bacteria that have grown in the food are ingested and then excreted in the feces. Experimentally, it has also been shown that *Pseudomonas aeruginosa* were temporarily excreted in the feces of volunteers who had ingested more than 10^6 of the bacteria, occasionally for a period of over 7 days.

It is reported that healthy individuals living in India and Guatemala carry more bacteria in the small intestine than those living in a moderate climate. This probably reflects the fact that there are more chances in these countries to ingest contaminated food. Furthermore, the variety and number of bacteria in the stomach and small intestine of animals are about 100 times those of humans. This may be related to the fact that some animals are coprophagous. Dubos in the United States reported that the fecal floras of mice, 7 males and 5 females, that were delivered by Cesarean section and reared in a clean environment were much simpler than those of mice reared in an ordinary environment. No *E. coli*, *Proteus*, *Staphylococcus aureus* or *Clostridium* were detected; lactobacilli were predominant, and enterococci and lactose nonfermentative bacteria of *Enterobacteriaceae* were found in small numbers.

V Intestinal Flora and Human Health

A system for rearing germfree chicken.
(a) Feed bag (b) Water supply (c) Air filtering device
(d) Inlet for sterilized egg (e) Air inlet (f) Feed
(g) Water (h) Sterilization test medium

Hypothesis on Interrelationship Between Intestinal Flora and Host

As already mentioned, a large number of bacteria inhabit the human intestine soon after birth, and from then, there is not a single moment in man's life in which he is not associated with the intestinal bacteria. Among the bacteria that enter through the mouth, those that are adapted to colonize in the human intestine form the intestinal flora and maintain a certain balance. The relationship between humans and the bacteria can be said to be a pattern of existence acquired through the long biological history, in which symbiosis is a primary requirement. In the intestine of an individual, as many as a hundred trillion bacteria comprising 100 species are present. The bacteria grow utilizing food components ingested daily and substances secreted or excreted into the intestine. Particularly in the area from the lower part of the small intestine to the large intestine, various kinds of substances are produced. The varieties of enzymes possessed by the intestinal bacteria are much more abundant than those found in the liver. However, unlike the liver enzymes which always function for the benefit of the body, the enzymes of the intestinal bacteria do not always work to the advantage of man. Thus, there are two sides of the intestinal bacteria to the host, beneficial and harmful.

From the end of the last century, there were arguments regarding the relationship between the intestinal bacteria and human health: whether the intestinal flora is essential for the living of humans or whether they contribute in the prevention of infections. However, it was not until recently that these arguments were substantially taken up, partly because it had

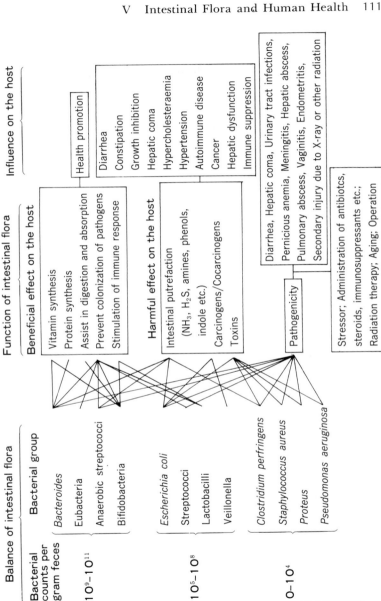

Figure 27.   Interrelationships   between   intestinal   flora   and   the   human   body.

not been possible to cultivate the most predominant intestinal bacteria.

About ten years ago, when I found that special anaerobic bacteria previously impossible to culture were isolated and cultured in numbers as many as 1,000–100,000 times that of *E. coli* or enterococci and that the bacteria comprised about one-third of the fecal mass, I made a hypothetic scheme (Fig. 27) to show the possible life-long effects of the intestinal flora on human health.

The hypothetic scheme is briefly explained as follows. There are two kinds of bacteria in the intestine, beneficial and harmful. In healthy subjects, they are well balanced. Beneficial bacteria play useful roles in the aspects of nutrition and prevention of infections, but some of them are potentially pathogenic, exert virulence when the resistance of host is weakened and invade into various organs to cause infections and gastroenteritis. However, more importantly, some intestinal bacteria produce substances that are harmful to the host, such as putrefactive products, toxins and carcinogenic substances. These substances may not have an immediate detrimental effect on the host but they are thought to be a cause of aging, promoting cancer, liver disease, arteriosclerosis, and reduce immunity. Yet, little is known regarding which intestinal bacteria are responsible for these effects. In this chapter, the ways in which intestinal bacteria are involved in human health and disease will be discussed.

1. Intestinal Flora and Nutrition

Development of Germfree Rearing System

The idea of raising animals in an environment entirely free from bacteria had first come to Pasteur's mind in 1885. He thought that the intestinal flora was important and indispensable for the survival of animals. He suggested to his young researchers to raise small animals such as rabbits, guinea pigs, dogs and chickens immediately after birth in a germfree environment with sterilized feed.

Nuttal and Thierfelder, both of the University of Berlin, built a counterargument to Pasteur's idea and started trying to rear germfree animals in 1894 for the first time in the world. They advocated that nutrients were readily transformed into absorbable forms by enzymes in the alimentary tract, without the aid of intestinal bacteria, and that, instead, the intestinal bacteria transformed proteins into useless or rather harmful substances such as aromatic unsaturated fatty acids, phenol, cresol, indole, skatole, carbon dioxide, hydrogen, methane and hydrogen sulfide. They succeeded in rearing germfree guinea pigs, though for a short period of time, and concluded that if purely animal-derived feed was supplied, the intestinal bacteria are not indispensable for the survival of animals.

After that, rearing of germfree animals was attempted, for example, with chickens by Schottelius (1895) and Cohendy (1912), with goats by Küster (1912) and with guinea pigs by Glimstedt (1933). Some succeeded in rearing for a period of several months. However, it was Reyniers and his associates of the University of Notre Dame in the United States who succeeded in rearing higher animals in the germfree state and breeding them successively for several generations. In 1945, the second generation of germfree rats were born in their laboratory, which proved that animals were able to grow and breed in the absence of the intestinal bacteria. Thus, the arguments, since Pasteur, on whether the intestinal bacteria are indispensable for the survival of the animals ended.

Germfree rearing of chickens, mice, guinea pigs, rabbits, dogs, quails, monkeys, cows, cats, pigs, etc. was successfully achieved. In Japan, in 1942, Akazawa at Chiba Medical School attempted the rearing of germfree chickens, and in 1957, Miyakawa at Nagoya University succeeded in rearing germfree guinea pigs for 305 days. The success of the germfree rearing system was largely due to the development of rubber, filtering material, bactericidal agents, etc. and improvement of feed.

Today, germfree mice and germfree albino rats can be easily reared in large numbers in a convenient rearing device, a vinyl isolator. The rearing method using the vinyl isolator is explained as follows.

A vinyl isolator is a transparent chamber which is kept inflated with constant blowing of sterilized air as shown in Fig. 28. Two percent peracetic acid (a bactericidal agent) is sprayed through a small spraying hole into the chamber for complete sterilization prior to use. Air delivered by a ventilator is filtered through an autoclaved glass filter installed at the inlet of the chamber so that air completely free of bacteria is blown into the chamber. Waste air is exhausted through an outlet with a similar filter. All operations are done through neoprene gloves installed at the side of the chamber. Insertion and removal of animals, utensils, apparatus and feed are carried

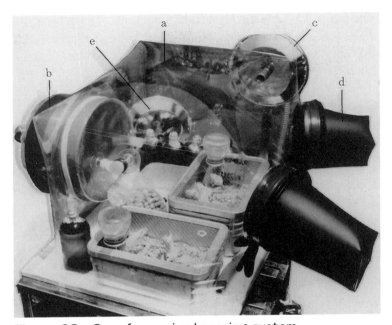

Figure 28. Germfree animal rearing system.
(Vinyl isolator)
(a) Vinyl chamber   (b) Sterile lock   (c) Air filter   (d) Neoprene
glove   (e) Air exhaust

out through a sterile lock also installed at the side of the chamber.

To obtain germfree animals from a conventional animal, Cesarean section is performed on a mother at full-term pregnancy. The full-term fetuses together with the uterus are extracted, passed through a tank filled with an antiseptic solution into the vinyl isolator where the animals are taken out by opening the uterus. The newborn animals inside the chamber are rubbed down with gauze to stimulate spontaneous respiration.

They are hand fed with sterile artificial milk. These animals, males and females, grow to maturity and mate inside the sterile chamber so that sterile offspring are reproduced for generations. To establish a different line of germfree mice, the offspring of the desired lineage are brought into the chamber in the manner as described above, and breast-fed by mother mice of a different line, which has been already established. In this case, no artificial feeding is needed.

Characteristics of the Alimentary Tract of Germfree Animals

Humans and animals living in the natural environment carry bacteria on the mucosa and skin which are open to the exterior as well as in the alimentary tract and are accordingly affected by these bacteria. By comparing conventional and germfree animals, the effects of bacteria can be elucidated. There are no substantial differences between the conventional and germfree animals regarding the organs that are not normally accessible to bacteria. However, the weight (relative to the body weight) of organs that are closely related to bacteria, such as respiratory organs, thymus gland, spleen and lymph nodes are significantly lighter in germfree animals than in conventional animals. The ceca of rodents and chickens are heavier in germfree animals than in conventional animals.

In germfree animals, the mucosa facing the outside is thin in general, and the rates of shedding and regeneration of the mucous epithelial cells are rather low. In the small intestine, the wall is thin and light, and the lymphatic system in the lamina propria mucosae is underdeveloped. However, when germfree animals are administered bacteria such as Welch's bacilli, enterococci and *E. coli*, the intestinal wall thickens. Furthermore, the life span of epithelial cells of the small intestine is as long as 4 days in germfree mice, while it is only 2 days in conventional mice.

The cecum of the germfree rodent is extremely enlarged and its weight is nearly four times that of the conventional rodent. This enlargement of the cecum is due to the retaining of content with a large amount of water. When the germfree animal is administered the intestinal content of the conventional animal, the cecum soon becomes small. When a large amount of antibiotics are given orally to the conventional animal, the intestinal flora is changed and the cecum is enlarged. However, it is not clearly known which bacteria are responsible for these phenomena.

Digestion

Most of the researchers who work with germfree animals do not think that the intestinal bacteria play an important role in digestion of host. However, the intestinal bacteria may have something to do with improvement of digestion or with utilization of substances which cannot be otherwise digested by enzymes secreted in the human alimentary tract.

In the stomach and small intestine of healthy humans, the number of bacteria is small so that direct involvement of the bacteria in digestion is the least probable. However, in the area from the lower part of the small intestine to the large intestine, where bacteria actively prevail, substances which are not digestible and absorbable in the small intestine are partly decomposed by the bacteria. For example, the intestinal bacteria decompose a part of dietary fiber contained in food, which is believed to be indigestible in the human intestine, such as cellulose, inulin, pectin, *Konjak* mannan, arginine, chitin and agar, into organic acids such as butyric and lactic acid, methane, carbon dioxide and hydrogen gases. Organic acids are absorbed and used as an energy source. In the horse, the colon is enormous and it is where fibers such as straw ingested as feed are digested. Similarly the colon of pigs is fairly large and a part of the fibers are digested here by the intestinal bacteria and utilized.

In addition, enzymes, mucosa and shed epithelial cells discharged into the intestine are decomposed to some extent in the area from the lower intestine to the large intestine. The resultant metabolites are also absorbed.

Vitamins

Germfree rats fed folic acid-free feed suffer from folic acid deficiency, while conventional animals fed on the same diet do not. This demonstrates that in the conventional animals, folic acid is synthesized by the intestinal bacteria and utilized by the host. In order to study this phenomenon in more detail, various kinds of the intestinal bacteria are administered to germfree animals; administration of bacteria of *Enterobacteriaceae* such as *E. coli* and a certain species of *Clostridium* prevents the folic acid deficiency. It is likely that in the human intestine folic acid is synthesized by the intestinal bacteria and utilized.

Rodents have a habit, called coprophagy, to eat their own feces immediately after excretion. It is known that by feeding on the feces, they utilize vitamins synthesized in the intestine such as vitamins B_2, B_6 and B_{12}, pantothenic acid and biotin.

Rats fed a vitamin K-deficient diet suffer from deficiency but recover when they are brought into the conventional environmental conditions. Otherwise, the vitamin K deficiency can be cured by colonization of the intestine by either *E. coli* or *Micrococcus*.

Vitamin B_1 is known to be synthesized by the intestinal bacteria. However, when radiolabelled vitamin B_1 precursor is given to rats, very little synthesized B_1 is found in organs in the body, in spite of active synthesis of vitamin B_1 in the cecum. This experiment suggests that vitamin B_1 synthesized in the intestine is not very utilized by mice.

On the other hand, some intestinal bacteria decompose vitamins. Some people suffer from beriberi despite sufficient intake of vitamin B_1. This is due to the proliferation of aneurinase producing bacteria which decompose vitamin B_1 in their intestine. These bacteria are also isolated from the feces.

Germfree guinea pigs fed a diet without vitamin C could survive as long as 50 days, while conventional guinea pigs fed the same diet died in 25 days. The conventional animals died earlier probably due to vitamin C degradation by the intestinal bacteria.

Similarly, conventional rats fed a diet without vitamin A die within 20–50 days, while germfree animals fed the same diet survive for 250–270 days. This entails that vitamin A requirements of germfree rats and conventional animals are different due to the presence or absence of the intestinal bacteria.

Thus, vitamins synthesized by the intestinal bacteria are partly absorbed. On the other hand, vitamins are also decomposed or consumed by the intestinal bacteria. Furthermore, there are complications related to malabsorption of vitamins which will be discussed next.

Interference of Absorption

By comparing germfree and conventional animals it has been shown that intestinal bacteria cause slight inflammation of the intestinal mucosa, which slightly affects the function of the intestine. A study on xylose absorption in the intestine showed that absorption is better in germfree animals than in conventional animals. Absorption of glucose, sodium ion, cholesterin and fats is also reported to be more effective in germfree animals.

In healthy man, only a small number of bacteria, mainly gram-positive facultative anaerobic bacteria such as lactic acid bacteria and streptococci are harbored in the small intestine. Bacterial overgrowth occurs in the small intestine when gastric functions are abnormal, for example, after gastrectomy or in hypoacidity, or when peristalsis is irregular, or when intestinal content is retained in blind-loop syndromes including intestinal stricture, fistulae and jejunodiverticuli. In these cases, bacteria which are normally found only in the large intestine proliferate in the small intestine. As a result, harmful substances are accumulated in the small intestine, which may cause malabsorption or diarrhea.

When bacteria such as enterococci, clostridia, bifidobacteria, coliform bacteria and bacteroides proliferate abnormally in the small intestine, bile acids which are the major component of the bile juice are deconjugated so that micelle formation of fat is hindered, which results in fat malabsorption. At the same time, long chain saturated fatty acids and enterotoxins produced by the intestinal bacteria induce diarrhea. In the colon, the amount of free bile acids increases and water and electrolytes are secreted, which may also result in diarrhea. In addition, diarrhea is also said to be caused by the production of hydroxy-fatty acids, a component of castor oil, from fat by the intestinal bacteria. In fact, various strains of clostridia, bacteroides, bifidobacteria and coliform bacteria have the capability to transform oleic acid into 10-hydroxy-stearic acid.

When bile acids are deconjugated to free bile acids by the bacteria in the small intestine, or when a large amount of organic acids are produced by bacterial fermentation, transportation in the intestinal mucosa is disturbed, which results in the obstruction of glucose absorption.

It is well known that abnormal bacterial growth in the small intestine causes malabsorption of vitamin B_{12}, which results in megalocytic anemia (pernicious anemia). However, the way in which the intestinal bacteria interfere with vitamin B_{12} absorption is not yet clearly understood. In this connection, there are three hypotheses. The first one is that the intestinal bacteria take up B_{12}. The second one is that intestinal bacteria decompose an intrinsic factor which is a mucoprotein secreted from the cell wall of the pyloric part of the stomach. Normally, this factor forms a complex with B_{12}, and as the complex is brought to the lower part of the ileum, B_{12} alone is absorbed into the blood by binding to a receptor on the microvillus. When the intrinsic factor is destroyed, B_{12} absorption cannot take place. The third hypothesis is that a certain kind of bacterial toxin damages the B_{12} receptor on the microvilli. However, viewing the various investigations so far, the most probable reason is that the intestinal bacteria consume B_{12}. Thus, abnormalities in the bacterial flora in the small intestine are associated with malabsorptions of fats, proteins, carbohydrates and vitamins.

Story of Highlanders of Papua New Guinea

There is a mystery associated with the natives living in the highlands of Papua New Guinea. Their diet consists mainly of sweet potatoes (96.4%) and rarely fish or meat. In spite of their protein-deficient diet, they are all in good health, are sturdily built and hard working. While their average nitrogen intake is about two grams a day (equivalent to 10–15 grams of protein), the total nitrogen excretion from the feces and urine amounts to about twice that ingested. Consequently, a question arises as to the source of the excess nitrogen excreted. One hypothesis is that nitrogen ingested with air is synthesized by the intestinal bacteria into proteins which are utilized by the body. In 1970, Bergersen and Hipsley, Australian scientists, investigated the fecal bacteria of these Papuan natives. They isolated strains of bacteria which synthesized protein from nitrogen gas (nitrogen fixation), belonging to the genera *Klebsiella*, *Enterobacter* and others. Incidentally, these bacteria are also isolated from pigs and guinea pigs. At present only data on aerobic bacteria are available. Investigation on aerobic bacteria has not been completed. It was speculated that these nitrogen-fixing bacteria might synthesize protein from atmospheric nitrogen which reaches the intestine with food ingested, and then man takes up this protein as nutrient. Assuming that to be true, the common knowledge that man cannot survive without ingesting protein as food has to be reconsidered.

Papuan highlanders have festivals in good seasons of the year, from April to September, in which they kill pigs and then enjoy eating, singing and dancing. On these occasions, a symptom called "pig belly" which is severe necrotic enteritis often occurs. This disease has a rather high mortality rate. A large number of Welch's bacilli are found in the small intestine of the patients and therefore speculated as the cause of the disease. It is likely that overeating of pork meat by the highlanders who are not used to taking much animal protein causes a sudden proliferation of Welch's bacilli that leads to necrotic enteritis. In other words, this is a response of the body which is under the influence of the intestinal flora that has been adapted to a low protein diet against the abrupt overgrowth of the pathogenic Welch's bacilli which are almost alien to the body. The intestinal floras of the highlanders are probably quite different from those of ours; however, little is known on this aspect.

Protein Synthesis

In Japan, there is a form of diet somewhat similar to that of Papuan tribes. Food taken by practicing priests in Zen temples is considerably lower in protein than that taken by ordinary people. In this case, the intestinal bacteria may synthesize proteins from gaseous nitrogen or nitrogen compounds other than food proteins, such as ammonia and nitrates; and the resulting proteins may be digested and absorbed.

A legendary hermit in an old story who was said to live on mist might have been utilizing air as a protein source. When mice are starved for about three days, the color of the intestinal content suddenly turns chocolate-like; the balance of the intestinal flora alters and the number of bacteria decreases. When humans are starved, chocolate-colored feces are also excreted on the third day of starvation; and then a state of so-called "*satori*" (spiritual awakening in Zen) is experienced. At this time, the intestinal flora might also change drastically, and the bacteria which utilize nitrogen in air might appear in this stage.

The stomach of the cattle or sheep consists of four chambers. The first chamber, the rumen, is as large as 200–300 litters. Food ingested by the cow is first sent to the rumen and then returned to the mouth to be ruminated. Cellulose contained in grass is converted by cellulose-utilizing bacteria in the rumen into organic acids such as formic, acetic, propionic, butyric, lactic and succinic acid and hydrogen, carbon dioxide gas, methane and others. The organic acids are absorbed and become energy source for the cattle.

On the other hand, in the rumen, urea that is excreted with the saliva is transformed into ammonia by the bacteria in the rumen. The ammonium is then used by ammonia-utilizing bacteria for growth and synthesized into bacterial protein. Some of these bacteria are eaten up by protozoa so that the bacterial protein is converted into protozoal protein. The bacteria and protozoas are soon passed to the fourth chamber, killed by the gastric acid and digested into amino acids by proteinases in the stomach. Then the amino acids are absorbed and utilized for the synthesis of cattle's own protein. In order to cut expenses of cattle's feeds, a part of the protein in the feeds are replaced by urea. This is based on the fact that the first chamber of the cattle's stomach acts as a fermentation tank in which the transformation by bacteria occurs, i.e. urea → ammonia → microbial proteins.

Is it possible that similar phenomena happen in the human or pig which has a single stomach? Among the herbivorous animals, the horse has an extremely huge colon, and the rabbit has a markedly large sac-like cecum. In these structures cellulose is digested by the intestinal bacteria like that in the cattle's rumen. The pig also has a large colon in which more than 10^{10} bacteria per gram content thrivie. Many of these bacteria prefer amino acids as a nitrogen source. In other words, ammonia is a satisfactory nitrogen source for the bacteria residing in the pig colon, and proteins are not essential. In the pig fed an ordinary feed, ammonia is produced by the intestinal bacteria from proteins in the feed or from urea that is produced by detoxication in the liver and excreted into the intestine. Therefore in the pig intestine, a process similar to that in the cattle's rumen takes place. Consequently, if proteins in the feed could be partly replaced by ammonia and urea, economization of protein source can be achieved. The investigation in this field has been conducted jointly by S. Namioka at Hokkaido University and ourselves.

Growth Promoting Action of Antibiotics

Soon after World War II, it was discovered that the growth of chickens and pigs is stimulated when the animals are fed a feed supplemented with a small amount of antibiotics. This phenomenon can be commonly observed with various antibacterial substances such as antibiotics, sulfonamides drugs, organic arsenic compounds and copper sulfate. Similar phenomena are observed also with experimental animals such as mice and rats as well as with humans.

These growth promoting effects are most clearly demonstrated when oral administration of antibiotics to animals is started immediately after birth. Moreover, the effect is particularly remarkable when the rearing environment is not hygienic and the feed is nutritionally inferior. In contrast, no effect is observed in germfree animals or in animals which are reared under highly hygienic conditions. From these observations, it is highly probable that the growth promoting effect of the antibiotics is due to the suppression in the intestine of a certain kind of bacteria that have a harmful effect on growth, and improvement of the balance of the intestinal flora. Many reports pointed out that the number of Welch's bacilli in the intestine decreases when feeds are supplemented with antibiotics. Furthermore, the growth of chickens is said to be delayed when Welch's bacilli are harboring in the intestine. Also it is known that residence of clostridia in the intestine delays weight gain in mice. However, not all the growth promoting effects by antibiotics administration can be explained by these findings. Many questions regarding changes in the intestinal flora remain unanswered.

Antibiotics may help prevent infections in animals and thereby promote growth of animals. Adverse environmental conditions such as high or low temperatures, high humidity or dryness; undesirable rearing conditions such as overcrowding and insufficient ventilation, abrupt changes in feed or nutritional deficiencies are stresses to animals. This leads to the disturbance of the balance of the intestinal flora and proliferation of harmful bacteria, or infection by pathogenic bacteria in sites other than the intestine; which results in interference of growth of the animals. By addition of a trace amount of antibiotics, as little as 10–50 mg per kg feed, the balance of the intestinal flora becomes normal and weight gain and feed efficiency are improved. These effects can be due to the decrease in incidence of diseases.

It has been confirmed that when antibiotics are given to animals, certain kinds of intestinal bacteria that produce harmful substances are suppressed and thus the amounts of ammonia, various amines, hydrogen sulfate, phenol compounds and others decrease. As a result, the intestinal wall becomes thinner so that nutrients are absorbed more efficiently. Toxic substances produced in the intestine are normally absorbed and detoxicated in the liver. Energy is needed for this detoxication process. Visek (1969) in the United States reported that the energy required for detoxication of ammonia in the liver can be saved by the use of feeds supplemented with antibiotics, so that animal growth is promoted. However, the mechanism of the growth promotion by antibiotics does not seem to be so simple; rather, various factors are involved and interrelated in the phenomena described above.

2. Intestinal Flora and Immunity

Mechanisms of Immunity

Immunity is an important function in the protection of individuals from infections by viruses or bacteria. This function is shared by lymphatic tissues located all over the body. Three kinds of cells, lymphocytes, plasma cells and macrophages play major roles.

Immune response is to distinguish self and non-self and to react by, for example, producing antibody against a foreign substance which is harmful to the body. The antibody is made specifically corresponding to the chemical structure of the foreign substance. The immune system comprises a receptor part which receives immunological stimulation and a reaction part in which specific antibodies are produced. Substances which stimulate antibody production are called antigens. In order to effectively stimulate antibody production, the antigens must be organic molecules having a size over a certain range and with a specified structure. However, some of the small molecules can act as antigens to stimulate antibody production by binding with larger molecules in the body, such as proteins and peptides.

An antigen that enters the body is firstly engulfed by macrophages and processed into a form appropriate for stimulation of antibody production. The antigenic information is transmitted to two types of lymphocytes, T-cells (thymus-derived cells) and B-cells (bone marrow-derived cells). The B-lymphocytes which received the information begin to divide and proliferate. Some are differentiated into antibody-producing cells and others are turned into memory cells which remain in the body for a long time to be ready for immediate response in the case of re-challenge by the same antigen.

There are two types of immune responses. One is the so-called humoral immunity in which immunoglobulins (antibodies), a kind of protein molecule, are produced mainly by plasma cells and discharged in the blood and lymphatic fluids. The other is called cell-mediated immunity in which lymphocytes play major roles. Delayed allergy reactions such as tuberculin reaction, immunity of cancer and rejection reaction in tissue implantations are mostly due to the cell-mediated immune response.

Both T-cells and B-cells are derived from stem cells in the

bone marrow. In the case of T-cells which play major roles in cell-mediated immunity, cells from the bone marrow enter the thymus gland where they divide repeatedly; part of these cells differentiate into lymphocytes having the capability to undergo immune response and are then discharged into peripheral tissues. B-cells are lymphocytes that are discharged directly from the bone marrow into the periphery. B-cells are present in the spleen and in the peripheral lymphatic tissues such as lymph nodes in which they differentiate by the stimulation of antigens, proliferate and are transformed into plasma cells that produce antibodies for humoral immunity.

T-cells and B-cells work together to control the antibody production. In particular, T-cells can either help or suppress the antibody production by B-cells; these T-cells are called helper T-cells or suppresser T-cells, respectively.

In humoral immunity in which immunoglobulin antibodies in the blood and lymphatic fluids play major roles, bacteria are bound to the corresponding antibodies and complements produced in the liver so that the resultant complexes are readily engulfed and digested by macrophages, rendering them harmless.

Immunoglobulins in the blood consist largely of IgG, IgM and IgA and a small amount of IgD and IgE. IgG antibodies are the major immunoglobulins, comprising 77% of the total antibodies, and contain most of the antibodies against bacteria. IgM antibodies appear in the early stage of the immune response and contain natural antibodies such as blood group antibodies. IgA antibodies are secreted from the mucosa of the respiratory and intestinal tracts and are thus important for the prevention of infections. IgE antibodies are easily bound to cells containing histamine, such as mast cells and basophilic leukocytes. When antigens bind to IgE antibodies, histamine is discharged. As a result, atopic reactions such as asthma and urticaria occur.

Immune responses mediated by thymus-derived T-cells are referred to as cell-mediated immunity; examples of cell-mediated immunity include rejection reaction in transplantation, delayed hypersensitivity, cancer immunity, immunity against intracellular parasitic pathogens such as viruses, tubercle bacilli and fungi. In this type of immune response, lymphocytes that are specifically sensitized by the stimulation of an antigen proliferate and then bind the antigen again so that various activating factors called lymphokines are secreted to effect various forms of reactions.

Stimulation of Immunity by Intestinal Bacteria

How are the intestinal bacteria involved in the immune system in the body?

Germfree animals having no bacteria in the intestine receive much less antigen stimulation than conventional animals, and the tissues responsible for the defense mechanism, such as thymic lymph nodes, the spleen and bone marrow are poorly developed. Moreover, the number of antibody-producing cells in germfree animals is only about 1/3 that of conventional animals. However, in the case where germfree animals are exposed to an ordinary environment from an early stage of life, the lymphatic tissues are well developed within several days and the animals gradually acquire resistance like conventional animals.

The inhabitation of bacteria in the intestine of newborn animals stimulates various factors which affect the defense mechanisms in the body, e.g. local antigenic reactions on the mucosa, thickening of the intestinal wall, stimulation of the reticuloendothelial system, production of immunoglobulin, increase in the amount of properdin-complement complex, and enhancement of bactericidal activity of the blood.

By antigenic stimulation by the intestinal bacteria, antibodies against the intestinal bacteria are produced and can be detected in the body. Secretary immunoglobulins, IgA, are also excreted in the intestine and play an important role in preventing intestinal infections by pathogenic bacteria. Furthermore, the IgA antibodies probably affect colonization of normal intestinal bacteria. This presumption is also supported by the fact that in the case of malabsorption syndromes due to bacterial overgrowth in the small intestine, IgA secretion in the intestine is suppressed.

When bacteria are colonized in the intestine of germfree animals, the animals acquire resistance to various pathogens such as *Salmonella typhi* and *Vibrio cholerae*. However, in order to acquire resistance equivalent to that of conventional animals, colonization of many kinds of bacteria are required. This indicates that the kinds of bacteria that inhabit the intestine affect the immunological activities of the host animals.

Another important factor which affects the resistance of the host is the bacterial endotoxin. Endotoxins are produced by decomposition of the cells of gram-negative bacteria such as *E. coli* and *Bacteroides*. When these endotoxins which are lipopolysaccharides are injected to animals, ulcers are formed in the stomach or duodenum. Endotoxins of *E. coli* are known to be related to the manifestation of certain respiratory diseases, and ulcers caused by stress and pyelitis. Furthermore, the reticuloendothelial system in the intestine is either suppressed or activated by bacterial endotoxin depending on the amount of endotoxin and the duration of contact with the toxin.

In humans and animals, the incidence of cancer increases with age. One explanation is that the capability of producing lymphocytes in the thymus is diminished with age. As already mentioned, the balance of the intestinal flora changes with age in humans and animals. In humans, the number of bifidobacteria decreases while the number of Welch's bacilli increases. It is probable that the decrease in the number of bifidobacteria may diminish the stimulation of immunological activity, or toxins produced by Welch's bacilli may act as immunosuppressants. If the balance of the intestinal flora at a young age can be maintained, superior immunological capabilities may be maintained so that cancer due to aging may be suppressed. However, more investigations and discussions have to be devoted in these regards.

One aspect which has also to be pointed out here is that the stimulation of specific or non-specific immune mechanisms by the intestinal bacteria is not necessarily always beneficial to the host. Sometimes, a given intestinal bacteria possess antigen in common with other antigens. In the case when common antigen is shared with pathogenic bacteria immune responses are advantageous in preventing infection. However, in other cases, sensitization of immune cells may occur, which triggers autoimmune diseases such as asthma and rheumatism, and finally cause diminution of the defense mechanism. This is a problem which should be addressed in discussing the relationships between the intestinal flora and immunity.

Inhibition of Growth of Foreign Bacteria

The stable normal intestinal flora colonizing on the intestinal epithelial mucosa protects the host from intestinal infections by various pathogenic bacteria. In an outbreak of cholera, dysentery or typhoid, there are differences in the degree of sickness presented in individuals even though the same causative food or drink was taken. Some individuals fall ill, some do not but stay as carriers; in others, pathogenic bacteria are not even detected in the intestine. Although this individual difference may partly be explained by the difference in physical strength of the individuals, the difference in the intestinal flora seems to be ultimately responsible. This was demonstrated by animal experiments in which salmonella, shigella or cholera vibrios were fed to animals to cause intestinal infections.

Ushiba of Keio University found that when normal mice were orally administered a large number of *Salmonella enteritidis*, only some of the animals became sick and died. However, when streptomycin was given in advance to the animals, the mortality was increased. Furthermore, when streptomycin and erythromycin were given together to the animals in advance, all the animals died from the infection. Among the intestinal bacteria, gram-negative bacteria were mainly eliminated by the administration of streptomycin, and gram-positive bacteria were eliminated by the administration of erythromycin. This experiment clearly demonstrated that by the elimination of most of the intestinal bacteria by administration of the two antibiotics, the animals were rendered more susceptible to *S. enteritis* infection. Thus the low morbidity and mortality in the animals without any treatment was attributed to the normal intestinal bacteria which prevented the growth of the foreign pathogenic bacteria.

Later, Sasaki of Tokai University investigated this phenomenon further and found that among the normal intestinal bacteria, the numbers of lactobacilli and enterococci were decreased by the administration of streptomycin, and that when enterococci derived from mice were given along with streptomycin and erythromycin, the infection rate was again decreased. It was thus concluded that the enterococci worked to the advantage in preventing infection by *S. enteritidis*.

When Welch's bacilli are orally administered to conventional guinea pigs, the spores of the Welch's bacilli are soon eliminated from the intestine. However, when Welch's bacilli are given to germfree guinea pigs, the bacteria proliferate in the intestine and the animals die. Similarly, germfree guinea pigs are infected by shigellae leading to death while conventional guinea pigs are not infected by shigellae. However, when coliform bacteria are allowed to colonize in the intestine of germfree guinea pigs in advance, the animals are no longer susceptible to shigellae. When conventional mice and guinea pigs are administered antibiotics first and then fed cholera vibrios or shigellae, these bacteria colonize well in the intestine. However, when *E. coli* is administered afterwards, the vibrios and shigellae are soon eliminated from the intestine.

Similar phenomena are also observed in humans during antibiotics treatment, in which the intestinal flora is disturbed and part of the normal bacteria diminish or disappear, so that bacteria that cannot normally grow in the intestine, such as staphylococci and yeast overgrow to cause enteritis. Several possible mechanisms by which intestinal flora prevents the invasion by pathogenic bacteria have been suggested. They include the accumulation of acetic acid, propionic acid, butyric acid and lactic acid produced by the normal intestinal bacteria; decrease in pH or oxidation-reduction potential; production of antibiotics by the normal intestinal bacteria; and production of secondary bile acids. Furthermore, competition for nutrients and space in the intestinal mucosal has been reported. Nevertheless, no perfect explanation has been reached so far.

Local immunity of host animals is also related to the prevention of infections by intestinal pathogens. By experimentally infecting mice with *V. cholerae*, Freter of the University of Michigan recognized that two mechanisms are involved in preventing infections. One is that local antibodies, including secretory IgA, interfere with the adhesion of cholera vibrios to the intestinal mucosa. The other mechanism is by the cooperation of the mucosa and antibodies, which results in bacteristatic or bactericidal effects on cholera vibrios. While these types of defense mechanisms act mainly on bacteria which colonize on the intestinal mucosa, antagonism among bacteria affects the bacteria living in the intestinal lumen. It is probable that these two mechanisms cooperatively control the growth of the pathogenic bacteria in the intestine.

The following is the results of the study by Freter and his associates, which lead to the conclusions described above. When germfree mice were fed cholera vibrios only, 10^9–10^{10} vibrios per gram content was found in the cecum. When the animals were previously immunized by oral or other routes, the number of vibrios decreased to about one third. However, when antagonistic bacteria were given before the administration of cholera vibrios, only 10^5–10^8 vibrios per gram cecum content was found. Furthermore, when these animals had been actively immunized with cholera vaccines in advance before administering the antagonistic bacteria and vibrios, the number of bacteria was significantly decreased by 1/5–1/60 of that in non-immunized animals. These observations evidently demonstrated that local immunity was considerably enhanced when combined with bacterial antagonism.

However, this local immunity is thought to be effective only for the suppression of growth of invading bacteria which are pathogenic to humans, such as shigellae, cholera vibrios and pathogenic *E. coli*, and not to the normal intestinal bacteria. This was also demonstrated by the report of Kenny et al. (1974) in which mice were orally administered a streptomycin-resistant strain of *E. coli*, O-128, which is a member of the normal intestinal bacteria. Even when the same strain was used to induce local immunization in these mice, no suppression in growth of the *E. coli* could be observed.

Another interesting observation was obtained in an experiment in which germfree mice were infected with *V. cholerae* alone and the antigenic characters of the vibrios isolated in the feces were monitored for a long period of time. It was found that the vibrios changed their antigenicity as soon as the host animals acquired immunity against the given vibrios. This appearance of mutants is considered to be an adaptation of bacteria to shelter themselves from the immunological attack by the host.

Recently, Freter et al. found that the intestinal bacteria affected the quantity and quality of antibodies discharged into the intestine and that only secretary IgA antibodies were found in the intestine of germfree mice which had been immunized locally or parenterally, while considerable amounts of IgM and IgG as well as IgA were found in the intestine of conventional mice which had been similarly immunized.

Viewing the experimental data by Freter and other researchers regarding the relationships between immunity and the normal intestinal bacteria, it can be concluded that the intestinal flora itself is affected by the local immune system in the intestine, and at the same time cooperates with the immune system in the elimination of foreign invaders. However, the local immune system is in turn affected to some extent by the intestinal flora.

3. Metabolism of Intestinal Flora and Disease

Life Span and Aging

In the beginning of this century, a Russian biologist, Elie Metchnikoff (1845–1916) first advocated that the intestinal bacteria affect aging. He thought that aging in man is the process of chronic intoxication caused by putrefactive intestinal bacteria and that life could be prolonged by preventing such putrefaction in the intestine. He noticed that many centenarians lived in a Bulgarian region where a large amount of yoghurt was consumed. He believed that lactobacilli (*L. bulgaricus*) in the yoghurt established themselves in the intestine and eliminated putrefying bacteria, preventing putrefaction. He himself made yoghurt and consumed it regularly. This is the principle of the famous "Metchnikoff's longevity-without-aging theory."

Afterwards, however, the lactobacilli which were suggested by Metchnikoff to be beneficial were shown not able to colonize in the intestine and accordingly his theory was dismissed an unfounded idea. Thus, at the time, people were aware of the possible effects of putrefactive products in the intestine on health and aging but these ideas were not substantially proved.

Recently, owing to the development of germfree rearing systems, it was revealed that germfree mice live much longer than conventional animals. Gordon and his associates (1966) conducted an experiment that compared the life span of mice using 300 each of germfree and conventional animals. They used 12-week-old mice taking into account the fact that younger mice might die due to reasons other than aging. The results showed that male and female germfree mice lived for an average of 723 days and 681 days, respectively, while male and female conventional mice lived for an average of 480 days and 518 days, respectively. Thus, germfree mice have a life span 1.5 times longer than conventional mice. In germfree mice, the males lived longer than the females while the opposite was true for conventional mice.

Another experiment was conducted by Walburg and Cosgrobe (1967) to compare the life span of mice using 41 germfree mice and 44 conventional mice. Their results were that male and female germfree mice lived for an average of 536 days and 547 days, respectively, while male and female conventional mice lived for an average of 546 days and 535 days, respectively. Thus, according to these raw data there was no difference in life span between the germfree and conventional mice. However, when correction was made by subtracting the number of deaths due to volvulus associated with enlargement of the cecum, which is common in germfree mice, the average life span of the germfree mice was 586 days; that is, about 8% longer than that of the conventional mice. Although these two experiments showed some discrepancy due to differences in the mouse strains, the age at start of experiment, and feed, they sufficiently demonstrate that germfree mice live longer than conventional animals if one compares the remaining life span after maturity of the animals. Findings common to these two experiments are that many germfree mice died of volvulus due to enlargement of the cecum while many conventional mice died of inflammation, and incidences of degeneration of vital organs and cancer were the same in both germfree and conventional animals.

In humans, over a trillion bacteria inhabit the intestine soon after birth. In breast-fed infants, bifidobacteria predominate, with coliform bacteria and enterococci constituting the minorities; and accordingly no putrefaction occurs. However, in the intestine of bottle-fed and mixed-fed infants, putrefactive bacteria such as coliform bacteria and anaerobic bacteria appear together with bifidobacteria. After weaning, the number of anaerobic putrefactive bacteria abruptly increases. And thereafter, throughout the life, foods and drugs which are ingested and substances that are secreted by the body are constantly transformed into various substances by the intestinal bacteria. Some of these substances are harmful as shown in Fig. 29, and they are produced in large amounts particularly in the lower part of the small intestine and the large intestine. Some of these harmful substances are absorbed and in the long run become a burden to the host, causing various distresses such as cancer and aging. With age, harmful bacteria tend to dominate and the amount of harmful substances produced in the intestine increases, which enhances aging. If one considers the environmental factor to be an important

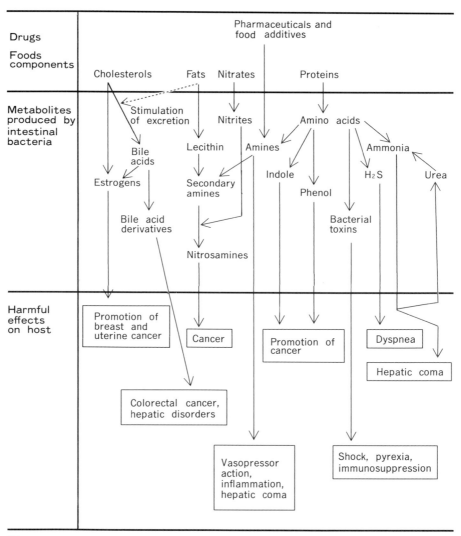

Figure 29. Harmful substances produced by intestinal bacteria.

cause of human diseases, the significance of the harmful substances that are continually produced in the intestine is very great indeed.

Diet and Cancer

Statistical data demonstrate that incidences of most of the cancers are related to environmental factors. These relationships have become more clear owing to the world-wide progress in epidemiological investigations on the types and rates of various cancers in relation to race, diet, smoking habits, occupations, regional factors such as air pollution and quality of soil, immigration, etc. Particularly, the relationship between diet and cancer has recently been elucidated and has attracted public attention.

It is shown epidemiologically that the incidence of large bowel cancer, especially colon cancer, is low in countries where incidence of stomach cancer is high. In Japan and Chile where the incidence of stomach cancer is the highest in the world, the incidence of colon cancer is conversely the lowest. On the contrary, in the United States, northwestern Europe, New Zealand and Canada, the incidence of stomach cancer is about one third that of Japan whereas the incidence of colon cancer is five times that of Japan (Fig. 30). A similar tendency is also found between the incidences of breast cancer in Japan and the United States. However, in the case of American-born Japanese, the second and the third generations of Japanese immigrants to California and Hawaii, the incidence of stomach cancer decreases and the incidences of colon and breast cancer are as high as those of Americans. Thus, these differences in the incidences of various cancers have been shown to be due

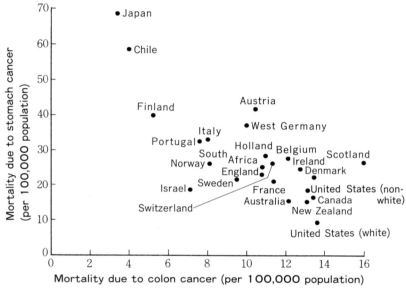

Figure 30. Correlation between mortalities due to colon cancer and stomach cancer in different countries (E. L. Wynder).

to the difference in the daily diet and not to the difference in race. With the recent change in diet of the Japanese from traditional Japanese to western type, the incidence of stomach cancer has decreased and the incidences of colon, breast and lung cancer have conversely increased. Thus, the correlation between diet and cancer is again verified.

It is necessary to consider the interrelationships among diet, intestinal bacteria and cancer. Diet of Americans and north-western Europeans differs from that of Japanese mainly in the amount of meat and fat intake, which is high in the former diet and very low in the latter diet (Figs. 31 and 32). Conse-

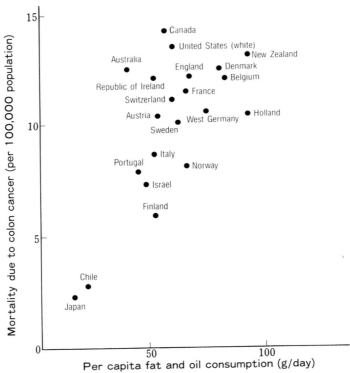

Figure 31. Colon cancer mortality and dietary fat and oil consumption (E. L. Wynder).

quently, it is speculated that meat and fat may be related to the high incidences of colon and breast cancer. However, no carcinogenic substance can be detected in meat or fat alone. One speculation is that nutrients contained in meat such as protein, fats or cholesterol may be converted into carcinogens or co-carcinogens by the intestinal bacteria. Another specu-

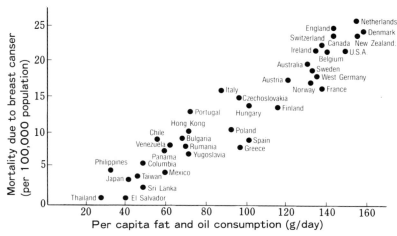

Figure 32. Breast cancer mortality and dietary fat and oil consumption (K. K. Carroll).

lation is that the bile juice which is abundantly secreted when a large amount of fat is ingested may be converted into carcinogenic substances by the intestinal bacteria. These are still hypotheses and are not yet proven. However, recent studies have shown them highly probable. Let us examine now how the intestinal bacteria convert food components and intestinal secretions, and how these conversions affect the body.

Ammonia

Proteins in ingested food are decomposed by digestive enzymes in the stomach and small intestine into amino acids and then absorbed. However, some of the proteins are deaminated and converted by certain kinds of intestinal bacteria into ammonia. On the other hand, urea which is produced from the detoxication of ammonia in the liver is partly discharged in the intestine. This urea is transformed by urease of certain intestinal bacteria into ammonia and carbon dioxide gas. The intestinal bacteria which are able to deaminate a wide range of amino acids are species of the *Enterobacteriaceae*, such as *E. coli, Proteus, Klebsiella, Salmonella* and *Shigella, Clostridium* and *Staphylococcus*. Some enterococci, lactobacilli and bacteroides are capable of deaminating limited kinds of amino acids. On the other hand, the intestinal bacteria which transform urea into ammonia include aerobic bacteria such as *Proteus* and *Pseudomonas aeruginosa* and many kinds of anaerobic bacteria. An animal experiment showed that the amounts of ammonia detected in the alimentary tract of pigs were 197 and 650 mg/l of digestive content in the stomach and colon, respectively. The amounts varied depending on the amino acid composition of the proteins in feed, sites in the intestine and environmental conditions. Particularly, when antibiotics were fed orally, the amount of ammonia in the intestine sharply decreased. This was due to the reduction of ammonia-producing bacteria by the action of antibiotics. Furthermore, the amount of ammonia in the intestine of germ-free animals is much smaller than that of conventional animals.

In healthy man, ammonia produced in the intestine is absorbed through the intestinal wall and immediately detoxicated into urea in the liver, and then the urea is excreted in the urine or discharged into the intestine. The urea that is discharged into the intestine is again transformed by the action of intestinal bacteria into ammonia which returns to the liver. This is the so-called enterohepatic circulation of ammonia.

In cases of severe hepatic diseases such as liver cirrhosis where the detoxicating capacity of the liver is impaired, ammonia reaches the brain through the blood and causes the life-threatening condition of hepatic comma. Antibiotics, lactulose or lactic acid bacteria preparations are administered to patients with hepatic comma for the purpose of suppressing the production and absorption of ammonia in the intestine. When lactulose is administered, the numbers of lactic acid bacteria such as bifidobacteria, enterococci and lactobacilli increase, which renders the intestine acidic, thereby interfering with ammonia absorption. At the same time, the transit time of the digestive content is shortened, which has the effect of lowering the ammonia concentration in the blood so as to relieve the symptom. Lactic acid bacteria preparations also increase the number of lactic acid bacteria in the intestine and suppress the production and absorption of ammonia.

Amines

On the other hand, amino acids are decarboxylated by bacterial decarboxylase into various putrefactive products (Fig. 33). The representative amine-producing bacteria in the intestine include *Enterobacteriaceae* such as *E. coli*, *Salmonella*, *Shigella* and *Proteus*, and *Clostridium* species including Welch's bacilli. Also, bacteroides and bifidobacteria produce amines from lysine, arginine and ornithine.

When animals are fed antibiotics, the amount of amines in the feces and urine decreases. The amount of amines in the intestine is much smaller in germfree animals than in conventional animals. Thus, it is evident that most of the amines are produced by the intestinal bacteria.

Many of the amines are harmful and even a trace amount can affect the body. Histamine lowers the blood pressure by

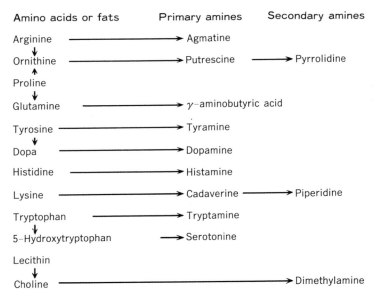

Figure 33. Production of amines by intestinal bacteria.

enlarging blood vessels and causes inflammatory reactions by promoting leukocyte chemotaxis; tyramine raises the blood pressure; cadaverine and putrescine are diamines that slightly raise the blood pressure; monoamines decrease the blood pressure; and agmatine has an insulin-like activity.

Amines produced in the intestine are absorbed and brought via the portal vein into the liver and detoxicated. In the case of liver cirrhosis, the detoxicating capacity of the liver is impaired, amines circulate to various part of the body and occasionally cause hepatic comma. Histamine stimulates secretion of gastric acid and causes inflammation, which may result in a digestive ulcer in patients with cirrhosis. When a large amount of tyrosine is administered to young mice, they are killed by the tyramine produced, since the detoxication capacity of the liver is not sufficiently developed.

Ornithine and lysine are transformed into primary amines, putrescine and cadaverine, and further transformed into secondary amines, pyrrolidine and piperidine, respectively. These secondary amines are excreted in the urine. Although not an amino acid, lecithin which is contained in abundance in soy beans and egg yolks is transformed to choline and then to a secondary amine, dimethylamine. The intestinal bacteria which exhibit high activity in this reaction are *E. coli*, enterococci and clostridia including Welch's bacilli. Also, bacteroides, bifidobacteria and *Eubacterium* have this capability. The most abundant form of secondary amines excreted in the urine of man is dimethylamine, an average of 20 mg a day, about 50% of which are produced by the intestinal bacteria. The amounts of piperidine and pyrrolidine excreted daily are about 0.8 mg and 0.4 mg, respectively. When antibiotics are administered, dimethylamine excretion in the urine decreases by 20%. The amount of dimethylamine excreted in the urine of germfree pigs, albino rats and mice is about 50% that of the corresponding conventional animals. Thus, it is evident that the intestinal bacteria play an important role in the production of the secondary amines in the body.

Nitrosoamines

Amines which are contained in food or produced in the intestine are transformed to nitrosoamines in the stomach and intestine when combined with nitrites. Nitrosoamines are strongly carcinogenic. Since the optimal pH for nitrosoamine formation is 3.4, the stomach is the most preferable site for this reaction. However, some of the coliform bacteria, enterococci, clostridia, bacteroides and bifidobacteria are known to produce nitrosoamines at nearly neutral pH, around 6.5. On the other hand, the fairly high concentration of nitrate in vegetables and drinking water is readily reduced to nitrite by bacteria in the alimentary tract. Nitrites are also contained in processed meat or fish products such as ham and sausages as color stabilizer. It has been believed that both nitrates and nitrites are readily absorbed and excreted in the urine and therefore do not reach the lower part of the intestine. However, it has been recently reported that nitrates are excreted from the intestinal mucosa with mucous and that nitroso-compounds are isolated from human feces.

Today, nitrosoamines attract public attention in relation to cancer in man, particularly stomach cancer. It is distinctly shown statistically that the incidence of stomach cancer is high in Japan and Columbia. The reason is not clearly known but there is a high possibility that food is responsible. In Columbia, the nitrate concentration in drinking water is high. Moreover the incidence of gastric cancer is high in patients with hypoacidity and achlorhydria. In the stomach of such patients more bacteria proliferate than in that of healthy individuals. The connection with stomach cancer is likely to be as follows. Firstly secondary amines are produced by bacteria in the stomach. Nitrite is formed separately by reduction of nitrate present in saliva, vegetables or drinking water. The amines and nitrites are then combined chemically to form nitrosoamines which are carcinogenic.

In the large intestine where the largest number of bacteria is harbored, the concentration of secondary amines is high, and the transit of the intestinal content is slow, so that nitrosoamines may be produced in large quantities if nitrites are provided. Lysine and arginine which are the source of secondary amines are present in abundance in animal proteins; lecithin and choline which are the source of dimethylamine, a secondary amine, are contained in animal fats. Therefore, when meat is consumed, the amount of secondary amines increases and if nitrite is available, nitrosoamines are formed. In consequence, the correlations among food, intestinal bacteria and nitrosoamines have been intensively investigated from the viewpoint of the etiology of colon and bladder cancer.

In mice that are fed nitrate together with pyridine or pyrrolidine, nitrosoamines are detected in urine; but nitrosoamines are not detected when mice are fed either nitrate or secondary amine alone. Nitrosoamine production by infected bacteria is observed in the bladder of patients with urinary tract infection. Most of the pathogens found in urinary tract infection, such as pathogenic *E. coli*, *Pseudomonas aureus, Klebsiella pneumonia* and *Proteus*, have the capability to transform secondary amines into nitrosoamines. Nitrosoamine production in the bladder by pathogenic bacteria has been verified in experimental cystitis in mice, which suggests possible involvement of nitrosoamine production in the etiology of bladder cancer.

Phenols

The amount of phenol compounds in the urine increases with the increase in the amount of protein in diet. This is because tyrosine and phenylalanine in food are transformed into phenol by the action of intestinal bacteria. *E. coli* and some strains of *Clostridium* are known to have the capability of this transformation; other intestinal bacteria, however, have not been investigated in this regard.

Phenol compounds produced in the intestine are brought into the liver and detoxicated or conjugated to some extent. The resultant products are circulated in the body and excreted in the urine. The phenol derivatives have been suspected to be related to carcinogenesis in man. In mice whose skin had been painted an appropriate co-carcinogen in advance, the application of a small amount of phenol, 2-ethylphenol or p-cresol on the skin promoted the formation of malignant and benign skin tumors. Dimethylbenzanthracene causes liver cancer when administered to conventional newborn mice but the same treatment in newborn germfree mice of the same lineage does not result in cancer formation. In germfree mice, incidences of malignant lymphosarcoma, breast, uterus and ovarian cancer are low, which is another demonstration that the intestinal bacteria produce carcinogenic or co-carcinogenic substances. In the intestine, various kinds of phenol compounds are produced from substances other than tyrosine. These compounds cause problems particularly in patients with cirrhosis whose liver functions are impaired.

Tryptophane

Tryptophane is an essential amino acid which is contained in relative large amounts in animal protein. Tryptophane is decomposed by the intestinal bacteria and converted into amines, such as tryptamine and serotonin, and ammonia as mentioned above; as well as to indole, indoxyl, skatole, 3-hydroxykynurenine, and 3-hydroxyanthranilic acid. Some of them are absorbed and further transformed.

Some of the tryptophane metabolites are reported to be carcinogenic or promote carcinogenesis. When mice are given feed containing a carcinogenic agent, 2-acetylaminofluorene and supplemented with tryptophane, the incidence of bladder cancer is 100%. Moreover, when indole is added in place of tryptophane, the same result is obtained. When various tryptophane metabolites are directly injected into the bladder, they exert carcinogenic effects. Oral or subcutaneous administration of indole is also known to cause malignant tumor of the lymphatic tissues or leukemia. Furthermore, it has been demonstrated that the administration of indole to hamsters which had been fed with 2-acetylaminofluorene accelerated the onset of bladder cancer.

The intestinal bacteria which produce indole in the intestine are *E. coli, Proteus* and some strains of *Bacteroides and Clostridium*.

Azo Food Dyes

Azo compounds are derivatives of aromatic amines and are widely used as artificial colorings and dyes in food and cosmetics, and as medicament. However, when these compounds are used for a long period of time, they may induce chronic intoxications, or even carcinogenic effects.

Azo compounds had long since been found to be reduced by intestinal bacteria when the principle of action of prontosil, a kind of sulfonamide, was elucidated. Prontosil shows no antibacterial action in vitro and exerts its effect only when it is reduced in the intestine into sulfanilamide (Fig. 34). When absorbed, azo compounds are reduced to aromatic amine

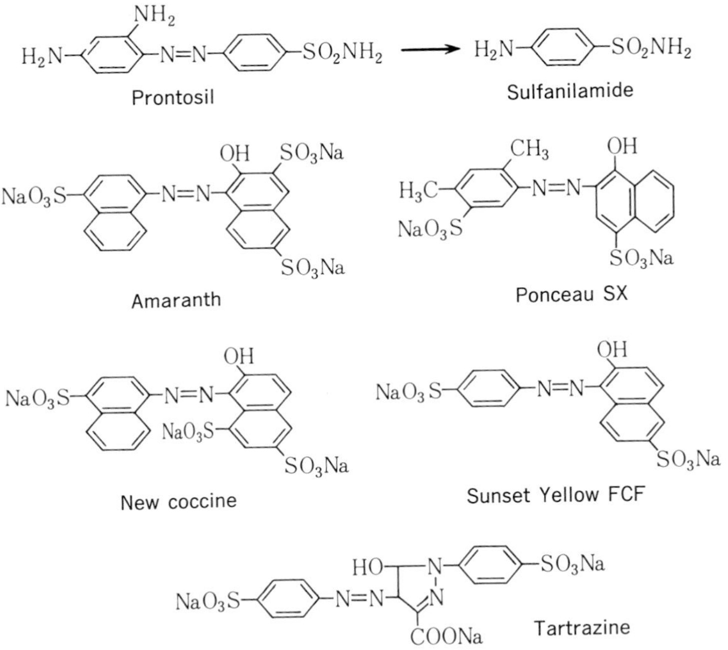

Figure 34. Chemical structure of prontosil and azo dyes.

derivatives in the liver; when not absorbed, they are reduced into aromatic amine derivatives by the bacteria in the intestine. Azo compounds are used as dyes. Amongst them, there are four kinds of azo food dyes which have sulfonyl groups, are water soluble, less absorbable, and are excreted promptly. The examples of such food colorings are amaranth, Ponceau SX, new coccine and Sunset Yellow FCF (Fig. 34). They are mainly reduced by the intestinal bacteria into aromatic amines. In rats, these reactions occur at the end of the ileum and in the cecum.

Another azo food dye, tartrazine (Fig. 34), is characterized by having a pyrazole ring instead of the naphthalin ring possessed by the other food colorings. When tartrazine is being reduced in the intestines, the azo ring is opened to form sulfanilic acid. Substances produced by decomposition of the azo food dyes, particularly tartrazine, are involved in hypersensitivity such as asthma, purpura and urticaria. However, the mechanism of their involvement is not at all understood. One possibility is that a reduced compound of tartrazine, aminopyrazolone, is absorbed, oxidized in the liver into iminoquinone or 4,5-dihydroxy derivatives which are antigenic proteins that react readily with NH_2-groups or SH-groups of proteins. Another possible adverse effect of azo dyes is that aromatic amines which are formed by reduction of the azo food dyes by intestinal bacteria are carried to the liver where they might be transformed into toxic and carcinogenic substances. These possibilities must be taken into consideration in evaluation of the safety of food additives.

Cycad Nuts

People living in the south Pacific islands such as Guam commonly eat cycad nuts. In these areas, the incidence of amyotrophic lateral sclerosis is high. There is a speculation that the ingestion of cycad seeds may be responsible for this high incidence. When rats were experimentally fed cycad nuts, no neurotic disorders were observed but a high incidence of cancer of the liver and kidney resulted. A glucoside, cycasin, which is contained in cycad nuts, is revealed to be the causative substance. However, when cycad nuts were given to germfree rats, no cancer occurred. Laqueur et al. demonstrated that cycasin enters the intestine and is hydrolyzed by beta-glucosidase of the intestinal bacteria to methylazooxymethanol which has carcinogenic properties; this substance is absorbed through the intestinal wall and transformed by the tissue enzymes into diazomethane, thereby exerting strong carcinogenic effects. When administered by means other than the oral route, cycasin is excreted in the urine as such and does not exhibit toxicity. That is to say, without the action of the intestinal bacteria, cycasin is not toxic. Individual difference in the degree of toxic effect exhibited in rats given the same dose of cycasin can be explained by the difference in the intestinal flora of individual animals.

The effect of cycasin was observed in germfree rats that had been colonized with one kind of bacteria bearing β-glucosidase, such as enterococci or *L. salivarius*. Germfree rats which had been colonized with enterococci suffered from severe liver disorders and all died, while those colonized with *L. salivarius* suffered from mere moderate intoxications. This may be explained by the fact that, although both enterococci and lactobacilli have β-glucosidase activity, the activity of the former is stronger than that of the latter.

The target organs on which cycasin exerts the carcinogenic effect vary depending on the animal species, age, sex, dosage, and period and method of administration. When cycasin is administered into the stomach of mature albino rats, carcinoma is formed mainly on the intestinal mucous membrane. Administration directly into the rectum causes cancer formation in the large intestine, or, in colectomized animals, in the small intestine.

Various kinds of glucosides other than cycasin are widely distributed in plants, and some are used as medicaments, e.g.

cascara or senna as cathartic agents. In all the cases, the gluco-sides are not pharmaceutically active as they are. They exert effects only when the active aglycons are released by hydrol-ysis by bacteria in the intestine. However, when aglycons are taken orally directly, they may lose activity in the stomach due to acid or in the small intestine. Therefore it is important that the medicaments are allowed to pass through the stomach and small intestine in the form of glucosides and then the ac-tivity of intestinal bacteria in the large intestine is employed to transform them into pharmacologically active forms.

A wide range of the intestinal bacteria such as coliform bac-teria, enterococci, lactobacilli, clostridia, bacteroides and bi-fidobacteria have β-glucosidase activity.

Toxic substances ingested with food and drugs and a part of toxic substances produced by the intestinal bacteria are ab-sorbed and deconjugated with glucuronic acid in the liver and thus detoxicated as glucuronide conjugates. A part of these is excreted in the urine and a part is discharged together with bile into the intestine. The glucuronide conjugates discharged in the intestine are deconjugated by β-glucuronidase of the intestinal bacteria and absorbed and returned to the liver. Due to this so-called enterohepatic circulation, toxic substances are not easily completely excreted out of the body. In the case where the toxic substance is carcinogenic, retention of such substance in the body may cause cancer. Among the intesti-nal bacteria, coliform bacteria, Welch's bacilli and some strains of bacteroides have the strongest β-glucuronidase activity; ac-cordingly, proliferation of these bacteria in the intestine af-fects detoxication capacity of the body. Some scholars consider that the high incidence of large bowel cancer in the United States and north-western European countries is due to the high-protein high-fat diet which increases the β-glucuronidase activity in the intestine and in turn interferes with the excretion of carcinogens, co-carcinogens.

Bile Acids

In the liver, bile acids such as cholic acid and chenodeoxycholic acid are synthesized from cholesterol. These are then conjugated with glycine or taurine to form conjugated bile acids which are discharged as bile. These conjugated bile acids are involved in digestion and absorption of fats in the upper part of the small intestine. Some of the conjugated bile acids are deconjugated by the action of the intestinal bacteria to form free bile acids some of which are further converted into secondary bile acids by the 7α-dehydroxylation reaction, such as deoxycholic acid from cholic acid and lithocholic acid from chenodeoxycholic acid. Some of the free bile acids are transformed into keto-bile acids by oxidation-reduction at positions C-3, C-7 and C-12. Approximately 95% of the bile acids excreted in the bile are re-absorbed, returned to the liver, reconjugated and then excreted again in the intestine as bile. Bile acids which are not re-absorbed move to the large intestine and are then metabolized by the intestinal bacteria.

Deconjugation is carried out by the action of most strains of enterococci, clostridia, bifidobacteria and bacteroides; 7α-dehydroxylation is effected by the action of limited strains of coliform bacteria, veillonellae, bacteroides, clostridia and enterococci.

When a large amount of fat is ingested, bile is excreted in abundance for digestion and absorption of the fat. Consequently the amount of bile acids in the intestine increases. The secondary bile acids produced by the actions of intestinal bacteria, such as lithocholic acid, deoxycholic acid, apocholic acid and 3β-acetoxy-bisnor-Δ^5-cholenic acid, are speculated to be carcinogenic or promote carcinogenesis.

When deoxycholic acid or lithocholic acid are heated at 330°C, a strongly carcinogenic substance, 20-methylchoranthrene, is synthesized. It is not sure yet whether this substance is actually formed in the intestine. The amount of deoxycholic acid is high in the feces of people in areas where the incidence of large bowel cancer is high. Deoxycholic acid which is weakly carcinogenic is found consistently and in a high concentration in the intestine of individuals who take a high-fat diet; this eating habit may induce large bowel cancer in the long run. Furthermore, deoxycholic acid might be further transformed by the intestinal bacteria into a more carcinogenic substance; this is another serious problem to be considered.

Cholesterol

Cholesterol is transformed by the intestinal bacteria in the large intestine; more than 50% is transformed into coprostanol and 5–10% into coprostanone.

Coprostanol is less absorbable than cholesterol. Therefore the amount of cholesterol in the body depends on the intestinal flora. Bacteroides, bifidobacteria and some strains of clostridia have the capability of transforming cholesterol into coprostanol but coliform bacteria and enterococci do not possess such capability. In bottle-fed infants, the serum cholesterol level is low when lactobacilli in the intestine predominate, which suggests that the intestinal bacteria play an important role in cholesterol metabolism in the host.

It is known that the incidence of naturally occurring breast cancer is high in experimental animals fed a high-fat diet. Also breast cancer is induced in rats injected with estrogens. Moreover, it has been shown *in vitro* that some of the intestinal bacteria synthesize estrogens although it is still not proven whether this happens in the intestine. If this really occurs in the intestine, the western-type high-cholesterol diet might be responsible for the high incidence of breast cancer.

Sodium Cyclamate

Since 1969, the use of sodium cyclamate as a non-nutritive sweetener has been banned in Japan. However, there are still arguments regarding its toxicity and carcinogenicity.

According to the experiments of Draser et al. (1972) and Renwick and Williams (1972), in which sodium cyclamate was administered to guinea pigs, rabbits, albino rats and humans, immediately after the administration was started, sodium cyclamate was excreted as such and no changes were observed. However, when animals were given feed supplemented with sodium cyclamate for a long period of time, sodium cyclamate was gradually converted into cyclohexylamine and excreted. This is the phenomenon of adaptation (of bacterial flora) to cyclamate metabolism. This adaptation occurred earlier in rats than in guinea pigs and rabbits. When sodium cyclamate was administered to three human subjects, conversion of sodium cyclamate into cyclohexylamine was observed within 10 days in one individual but the transformation was not observed in the other two even 30 days after the administration. This metabolizing ability can be induced only if cyclamate is administered orally and is lost when administration is interrupted. This shows that cyclamate is converted into cyclohexylamine in the intestinal tract only. Furthermore, when the feces or intestinal content from animals which have been given feed supplemented with cyclamate is cultivated anaerobically *in vitro* in a medium containing sodium cyclamate, cyclohexylamine is formed. On the other hand, when the content of colon or rectum of these animals thus reared was successively subcultured in 10 times volume of a medium without cyclamate, the metabolizing activity disappeared after the third subculture. However, when cyclamate was included in the medium, the activity was retained to some extent.

The intestinal floras of the animals and human subjects that had been given cyclamate were examined. There were almost no changes in that of humans. However, in the intestine of rats, the number of clostridia increased from 10^3 per gram content to $10^7–10^8$ per gram content. These strains of clostridia were isolated and shown to have the capability of transforming cyclamate to cyclohexylamine. One out of ten strains of *Enterobacteriaceae* had this capability but ten strains each of enterococci, bacteroides and bifidobacteria had no such activity. In the feces of the human subjects who excreted cyclohexylamine, only enterococci were shown to have this activity.

Thus, the metabolizing ability from cyclamate to cyclohexylamine varies with animal species and from individual to individual in the same species. These differences may reflect the differences in the detailed constitutions of the intestinal flora. The toxicity of cyclamate lies in the causation of bladder cancer when cyclohexylamine is excreted in the urine. It follows that individuals who harbor the intestinal bacteria having the capability of cyclohexylamine formation may stand a higher chance of bladder cancer.

As mentioned above, the metabolism of the intestinal bacteria plays important roles in the manifestation of drug efficacy and toxicity. Accordingly, in the determination of the effects or toxicity of drugs, agricultural chemicals or food additives, the intestinal flora of the experimental animals used has to be taken into consideration.

Detoxication by the Intestinal Bacteria

What has been discussed up to now is that many intestinal bacteria produce toxic substances. However, on the other hand, among the intestinal bacteria, some have the ability to detoxicate certain kinds of toxic substances.

Rowland and Grasso (1975) in England reported that nitrosamines were decomposed by intestinal bacteria. Nitrosamines such as diphenylnitrosamine and dimethylnitrosamine were decomposed into the corresponding secondary amines, nitrate and an unknown volatile substance *in vitro* by coliform bacteria, lactobacilli, bifidobacteria, enterococci, bacteroides and others. When the concentration of nitrosamine in the reaction mixture was as low as less than 50 micromoles, about 55% of diphenylnitrosamine, about 30% of nitrosopyrrolidine and about 4% of dimethylnitrosamine were decomposed. The decomposing activity varied with the bacterial species; the activity was highest in lactobacilli and coliform bacteria. Bacterial strains which decomposed diphenylnitrosamine did not decompose dimethylnitrosamine, which suggests that the decomposing mechanisms for these two nitrosamines are not the same.

Benzopyrene, a polycyclic aromatic carbohydrate and a known strong carcinogen, is decomposed by the action of the intestinal bacteria such as *Pseudomonas, E. coli* and *Bacillus*. Like the reactions of benzopyrene-decomposing enzymes in the liver and intestinal mucosa of mammalian animals, the breakdown of benzopyrene by bacteria requires molecular oxygen and is accelerated by cyanide. However, it is not yet known whether these benzopyrene-decomposing strains can survive in the intestine of mammalians or how effective they are in the actual decomposition of carcinogenic substances contained in food.

Hydroxyacetylaminofluorene, a carcinogenic amine, is well-known to be dehydrogenated by the action of *E. coli*. Also it is revealed that hydroxy-4-acetylaminobiphenyl is reduced by anaerobic streptococci and *Bacteroides fragilis* into 4-acetylaminobiphenyl. These facts suggest that toxic or carcinogenic substances excreted in the intestine as glucuronic acid conjugate compounds may be hydrolyzed by intestinal bacteria and further reduced into nontoxic substances.

Here I would like to describe an experimental study of our laboratory using germfree mice. The incidence of liver cancer occurred in about 39% of the germfree animals during the rearing period of one year; while in conventional animals of the same lineage the incidence of liver cancer was 85%. Then, germfree mice were colonized separately with one or more kinds of bacteria isolated from human feces and bred to produce a new generation of mice which were also observed for one year. The incidence of liver cancer varied markedly depending on the kind(s) of bacteria that had colonized in the parent mice. An incidence of 100% which is higher than that of conventional mice was observed in some second generation mice. It is probable that the kind and amount of co-carcinogens produced in the intestine are dependent on the kind of bacteria colonized in the intestine. Another interesting observation was that when *Lactobacillus acidophilus* was colonized in combination with other bacteria, the incidence of liver cancer was reduced by 40% as compared with the animals without the lactobacilli, which suggests that lactobacilli detoxicate co-carcinogens produced by other bacteria so that the occurrence of liver cancer is delayed. In the human intestine also, it is likely that some bacteria are involved in the production of harmful substances while others function to detoxicate the harmful substances, thus composing a complicated intertwining ecological system. This further demonstrates the importance of the balance of the intestinal flora.

Production of Intestinal Gas

In healthy man, about 400 to 2000 ml of gas is released daily from the rectum. Abdominal distention which is often experienced soon after eating is due to the passing of excessive gas in the intestine to the rectum. The volume of the gas produced in the intestine varies tremendously depending on food. Particularly, bean-rich diet increases the volume of the wind: the average volume of wind released in an hour increased from 15 ml to 176 ml in five men who experimentally took 56% of the total calories from soy beans. In general, about 100 ml of gas is constantly present in the intestine, according to measurements by various means.

The composition of the gas in the alimentary tract differs from site to site. The composition of the gas in the stomach resembles that of air (78% nitrogen and 21% oxygen): according to one source, it contains 79% nitrogen, 17% oxygen and 4% carbon dioxide gas. On the other hand, the composition of the wind is very variable, generally containing less than 2% oxygen with the rest being nitrogen, carbon dioxide, hydrogen and methane. Levitt of the University of Minnesota reported that the composition of the wind differs tremendously from individual to individual; the common composition is 23–80% nitrogen, 0.1–2.3% oxygen, 0.06–47% hydrogen, 0–26% methane and 5.1–29% carbon dioxide. He suggests that the individual differences depend on the volume of air ingested with food and saliva and on the intestinal flora.

Hydrogen and methane in the intestine are produced solely by the intestinal bacteria. This is evident from the facts that cells in man are not capable of producing these gases by any metabolic pathways and that these gases are not detected in the intestine of germfree animals.

Coliform bacteria and various kinds of anaerobic bacteria produce hydrogen *in vitro*; however, it is not known which bacteria are mainly responsible for the hydrogen produced in the intestine. It is possible that coliform bacteria produce hydrogen in the intestine. However, when rats are given neomycin to suppress coliform bacteria, hydrogen production in the intestine is instead increased to 3–6 times that of control mice, which suggests that the hydrogen produced by coliform bacteria is not likely to be a major source of hydrogen in the intestine of conventional animals. Although hydrogen production in the human intestine takes place normally in the colon, when the intestinal bacteria proliferate abnormally in the small intestine, hydrogen is also detected in the small intestine.

Hydrogen is mainly produced from food by the intestinal

bacteria. Hydrogen production is very low during fasting, but when a small amount of carbohydrate is directly inserted into the colon using a tube, hydrogen production rapidly increases. Among the daily food compositions, stachyose and raffinose contained in beans are not digested or absorbed in the small intestine, and reach the large intestine where they are decomposed by the intestinal bacteria to produce hydrogen.

Gases in the intestine can be exchanged freely with gases in the blood in the intestinal mucosa; the direction of the movement is determined by the partial pressure. Neither hydrogen nor methane originally exists in the blood; part of these gases in the intestine is absorbed through the intestinal wall into the blood, brought into the lung and then discharged finally in the breath. The hydrogen concentration in the breath is affected by factors such as blood circulation of the intestinal wall, surface area of the intestinal mucosa and the hydrogen concentration in the intestine. One report stated that the hydrogen concentration in the breath was about 14%. Based on these facts it is therefore possible to estimate the approximate volume of the intestinal gas by a breath analysis.

Since methane-producing bacteria require strict anaerobiosis, methane is produced solely in the colon. In the intestine of infants, methane cannot be detected before two years of age while hydrogen can be detected within 48 hours after birth. From the age of ten, the methane content of the intestine becomes similar to that of an adult. Regarding methane production, men can be divided into 2 groups: methane-producers and non-producers. About two thirds of adults are non-methane-producers; less than 1.8 ppm of methane is detected in the breath. The rest are methane-producers; the average methane concentration in the breath is 23 ppm. Methane production seems to be a stable feature, which suggests that methane production in the intestine does not depend on the food composition but rather by whether methane-producing bacteria are harbored in the intestine. It seems that there is a family trait: families which harbor methane-producing intestinal bacteria and those which do not, although the reason is not known. This suggests that the composition of the intestinal flora is strongly affected by genetic and environmental factors after birth. The daily amount of methane produced is relatively stable whereas the amount of hydrogen produced is markedly influenced by diets.

Carbon dioxide gas in the intestine is produced by 3 sources: diffusion from the blood into the intestinal tract, neutralization of acid by bicarbonate and intestinal bacteria. Carbon dioxide gas diffuses between the blood and the intestine to reach an equilibrium. In the upper part of the small intestine, carbon dioxide gas is discharged by the neutralization of hydrochloric acid by bicarbonate. The volume of carbon dioxide gas discharged into the small intestine, as calculated from the volume of the gastric acid excreted in the stomach, is 2200 m*l* daily. The volume of carbon dioxide gas produced by the neutralization of acids produced as a result of fat and protein digestion is estimated to be about 3000 m*l*. Carbon dioxide gas produced by these routes is mostly absorbed in the small intestine. Carbon dioxide gas in the wind seems to be produced by fermentation by the intestinal bacteria, similar to hydrogen. Some forms of fermentation produce carbon dioxide directly and some produce organic acids which generate carbon dioxide on neutralization with carbonate.

Oxygen and nitrogen gases seem to be derived from air ingested with food and saliva. Oxygen in the intestine is utilized by the intestinal flora, which results in an extremely low oxygen concentration in the intestine. Nitrogen concentration is the highest of the gas compositions in the intestine. Apart from that derived from air, a part of nitrogen is produced by the intestinal bacteria and by diffusion from the blood. The diffusion of nitrogen from the blood occurs when the partial pressure of nitrogen decreases as the volume of carbon dioxide, hydrogen and methane increases. Occasionally, nitrogen fixation by the intestinal bacteria occurs.

The above-mentioned gases, hydrogen, methane, nitrogen, carbon dioxide and oxygen, are all odorless, but gases with offensive odor, such as ammonia, hydrogen sulfide, indole, skatole, volatile amines and volatile fatty acids, are also contained in the wind. Although the total concentration of these constituents is less than 1%, they are sufficient to be a source of unpleasant smell to the sensitive human nose which can detect odor at a concentration of one part per hundred million.

Thus, the composition and volume of gases accumulated in the intestine vary depending on the volume of air ingested with food and saliva, the amounts of oligosaccharides and nitrogen compounds in food which reach the large intestine undigested, and the kind and numbers of the intestinal bacteria which act on these substances. Therefore, the quality and volume of the wind can be changed to some extent by controlling the diet. In the case of lactose-intolerance, gas formation in the intestine can be reduced by taking sour milk which has a lower lactose content as compared to ordinary milk. However, methane production is a family trait, it is almost impossible to eliminate methane-producing bacteria. Patients who complain of bowel distention, excessive wind breaking or abdominal pain often have disorders in digestive functions such as abnormal peristalsis. Patients with aerophagia, who constantly ingest air with saliva may have some abnormalities in the body, which should be carefully checked.

Opportunistic Infections

Opportunistic infections are caused by bacteria which are normally harmless in their normal habitats. These bacteria turn virulent and cause abscesses or infections when patients become less resistant, for example, in the late stage of cancer or nutritionally deficient for some reasons. Many of such causative bacteria, such as *E. coli, Klebsiella, Proteus, Staphylococcus, Pseudomonas aureus, Bacteroides, Peptostreptococcus* and *Clostridium*, are ordinarily found in the intestine and are weakly pathogenic.

Opportunistic infections occur often when the balance of the intestinal bacteria is disturbed by the use of antibiotics and the normal indigenous bacteria are replaced by a population which is antibiotic resistant, and when the immunity of the body is reduced by the use of steroid hormones or immunosuppressants or by radiation therapy. Opportunistic infections occur also in patients after a big surgical operation, with leukemia, cancer in the late stage, severe diabetes mellitus or arterial sclerosis. Moreover opportunistic infections are difficult to cure partly due to the physical weakness of the patient, and in the worst cases, they are fatal.

There are two types of infection routes. One is by intestinal bacteria excreted outside the body, which contaminate food, water, clothes, linens, air or utensils in the hospital causing infections. The other one is by the bacteria colonizing in the intestine, which directly invade the blood or lymph vessels and enter other tissues to cause infections such as pneumonia, cystitis, meningitis, peritonitis, cholangitis, abscesses in the brain, lung, liver or kidney and septicemia. In healthy subjects, the intestinal mucosa acts as a barrier that prevents penetration of bacteria, and even if some bacteria penetrate, they are soon killed by the defense mechanisms of the body. In the case of cancer, ulcer or enteritis, the intestinal bacteria can easily invade the blood stream and then cause infections.

The incidence of opportunistic infections due to the intestinal bacteria has been increasing probably because of the proliferation of drug-resistant bacteria due to the extensive use of antibiotics, the frequent use of chemotherapeutic agents for cancer, steroid hormones and immunosuppressants and the increased frequency of major surgical operations.

4. Diarrheal Enteritis

What is Diarrhea?

When the functions of the alimentary tract, such as gastric acid production and peristalsis, are normal, digestion and absorption proceed normally, and normal feces are passed. When these functions are impeded, watery or liquid feces are excreted. Sometimes abnormal constituents such as mucous are mixed with the fecal content. Furthermore, when inflammation occurs in the alimentary tract, the excretion of pus or blood components in the feces is often seen.

Although there are many causes of diarrhea, they can be broadly divided into two categories. One consists of those caused by the actions of pathogenic microorganisms or their toxins. The other, also called non-specific diarrheas, are complications of diseases unrelated to intestinal infections, such as indigestion, retention of feces in the intestine, mercury poisoning, uremia and food allergy.

The pathogenic bacteria that cause diarrhea include *Vibrio cholerae, Shigella, Salmonella, E. coli, Vibrio parahaemolyticus, Clostridium perfringens* (Welch's bacilli), *Clostridium botulinum, Bacillus cereus, Proteus, Pseudomonas aeruginosa,* enterococci and *Yersinia.*

Proliferation of the Causative Bacteria

Before the causative bacteria can exert their actions in the intestine, they must, first of all, proliferate in the intestine. However, in the intestine, especially the small intestine, peristalsis occurs incessantly towards the direction of the colon, and the villi of the mucosal epithelium move continually. Due to these constant movements, bacteria cannot normally stay put, but are carried towards the large intestine. Therefore, the first step in the causation of diarrhea is the attachment of the bacteria to the intestine, by adhering to the intestinal mucosa. The mechanism of adhesion for some bacteria is said to be via the surface O-antigen polysaccharide of the bacteria. The molecular structure of the base determinant of the O-antigen is common for all *Shigella* species including *S. flexneri,* as well as the invasive types of pathogenic *E. coli.*

The mode of attachment of *Salmonella* and the other types of *E. coli* to the intestine is not yet clearly understood. In the case of *S. typhimurium,* the piliated form is more infective than the non-piliated form. Pili are appendages of bacteria, totally distinct from the flagellae. The special antigens on the pili are known to play an important role in attachment.

Next, the causative bacteria proliferate. In diarrheal diseases due to *V. cholerae, Shigella, Salmonella* and *E. coli,* the number of the causative bacteria in the feces is normally 10^7–10^9 per gram feces. By monitoring the quantitative change it is possible to assess whether active enteritis or a carrier state exists in a patient. Another change which occurs in the intestinal flora is the marked decrease of anaerobic bacteria. In patients suffering from acute cholera, the number of anaerobic bacteria is reduced to less than 10^5 per gram feces. This is probably because the rapid transit of the intestinal content through the large intestine results in the formation of an aerobic environment which is adverse to the anaerobic bacteria.

During acute diarrhea caused by pathogenic bacteria such as *V. cholerae* and *E. coli,* the causative bacteria colonize and multiply in the small intestine, while members of the intestinal flora that normally inhabit only the large intestine also proliferate.

The Mechanisms of the Causation of Diarrhea

When *V. cholerae* or *E. coli* causes diarrhea, the bacteria proliferate in the intestine and produce enterotoxin which acts on the intestinal mucosa of the small intestine, causing abnormalities in water and ion transport. As a result, the amount of water exuded into the intestinal lumen is larger than that absorbed in the large intestine, thereby causing diarrhea. Bacteria that produce enterotoxins and cause diarrhea include *E. coli* and most of the members of the *Enterobacteriaceae, Aeromonas, P. aeruginosa,* and the spore-forming bacteria including Welch's bacilli and certain strains of *Bacillus cereus*. The spore-forming bacteria enter the intestine with food, the spores germinate, and when spores are being formed again, enterotoxin is released, causing diarrhea. *V. parahaemolyticus*, the important causative bacteria of acute gastroenteritis, is also thought to induce diarrhea by the action of an enterotoxin.

In contrast, enteric pathogens such as *Shigella*, some *E. coli* strains and *S. typhimurium* possess enteroinvasive properties. Firstly, they invade and penetrate the epithelial cells of the intestine, especially the large intestine, then proliferate and cause damage to the mucosa. The degree of damage caused to the mucosa depends on the species or types of the bacteria, and ranges from slight inflammation to ulcer formation.

When enteroinvasive *E. coli* invades the large intestine, not only that abnormalities in water transport and morphology of mucosal epithelial cells can be seen in the large intestine, in some instances, abnormal water and ion transport can also be observed in the small intestine although bacterial invasion and morphological change cannot be detected in this site. From these, it is thought that when enteroinvasive pathogenic bacteria infect the large intestine, abnormalities in the large intestinal mucosa give rise to symptoms of dysentery while abnormal water secretion from the small intestinal mucosa causes diarrhea which commonly occurs in this type of infection.

Cholera

Cholera toxin, a kind of enterotoxin produced by *V. cholerae* causes abnormal secretion of water and ions from the cytoplasm of the small intestinal mucosal cells into the intestinal lumen, resulting in copious loss of body fluids. The heavy secretion of mucous from the goblet cells of the mucosal epithelium is due to functional change in the epithelial cells, and not organic disorders. Cholera toxin is most active in the duodenum and jejunum, moderate in the ileum and has no action at all in the colon. In the acute phase of cholera, the vibrios proliferate in profusion from the stomach to the anus. However, 4–8 days after the onset of the disease when the symptoms are subsiding, the bacteria also start to disappear. At this time, if antibiotics are given, the disappearance of the bacteria is accelerated and recovery is enhanced.

When *V. cholerae* is administered to adult mice and guinea pigs, diarrhea does not occur. However, if the animals have been fasted or given antibiotics in advance, they come down with cholera. This is another proof that the normal intestinal bacteria protect the host against infection by *V. cholerae*.

Diarrhea Due to *E. coli*

It has been known for 40 years that certain strains of *E. coli* can cause acute diarrhea. These strains are called pathogenic *E. coli,* and are distinguished from the ordinary *E. coli* strains by serological typing. They are often isolated from the stomach and duodenum of infants who suffer from acute diarrhea. These strains when taken in large doses by healthy adults also cause diarrhea, thus confirming that they are also causative agents of adult diarrhea. In such cases, however, multiplication of the *E. coli* in the upper part of the small intestine is a prerequisite; direct introduction of the bacteria into the large intestine does not result in diarrhea.

From experiments of administering *E. coli* to volunteers, it was shown that symptoms of diarrhea did not appear immediately after administration of the bacteria; a lag interval of up to 6 days was observed. It was also reported that in one infant, the pathogenic *E. coli* serotype 055 was carried in the intestine for 7 days before the onset of diarrhea.

As with cholera toxin, *E. coli* enterotoxin is more active in the jejunum than in the ileum. Also, the bacteria grow throughout the whole intestinal tract at the time of diarrhea.

The pathogenic *E. coli* commonly isolated in infantile diarrhea is not always successfully detected in sporadic cases of diarrhea in older children and adults. In these non-infantile cases, other *E. coli* strains unassociated with any specific serotype proliferate instead. This shows a possible association of "non-pathogenic" strains of *E. coli* with diarrhea.

The research on tropical diarrhea in India revealed that *E. coli* was present as the predominant bacteria in the feces of about half of the patients with diarrhea. Furthermore, it was observed that the *E. coli* grew right up to the upper part of the small intestine. In these cases, the *E. coli* strains isolated were not pathogenic. Although whether an *E. coli* strain is pathogenic or non-pathogenic is determined by the ability to produce enterotoxin, the roles that non-pathogenic strains of *E. coli* play in diarrhea await further investigations.

Food Poisoning

Food poisoning is an illness with acute gastroenteritis as the major symptom, caused by the ingestion of food containing harmful microorganisms or harmful substances. Food poisoning may be caused by bacteria (bacterial food poisoning), or natural poisons such as that found in poisonous mushrooms and globe-fish, or poisonous chemicals such as mercury and arsenic (chemical food poisoning). Bacterial food poisoning, often referred to simply as food poisoning is classified according to the mode of occurrence, namely, infection- or intoxication-type. In the infection-type food poisoning, pathogenic bacteria such as *Salmonella,* pathogenic *E. coli, V. parahaemolyticus* or Welch's bacilli are ingested together with food, and cause food poisoning by either proliferating in the gastrointestinal tract or exerting direct action of the toxin on the intestine. In intoxication-type food poisoning, bacteria such as *Cl. botulinum* and *Staphylococcus aureus* grow in food and produce toxins or harmful metabolites which are ingested together with the food, resulting in food poisoning. Therefore, in the infection-type, a considerable number of viable bacteria must be present to cause food poisoning; whereas in the intoxication-type, it does not matter whether the bacteria are present, as long as the toxin produced remains intact in the food, food poisoning can occur. In other words, if the bacteria causing food poisoning are already present in food, heat treatment which kills the causative bacteria is effective in preventing infection-type food poisoning, whereas the only way to prevent the intoxication-type is by destroying and inactivating the preformed toxins. Although botulism toxin is destroyed at 80° C for 15 min so that heat treatment is effective in preventing food poisoning, other toxins such as that of *S. aureus* are resistant to ordinary heat treatment so that heating is an ineffective preventive measure should the food already contain the preformed toxin.

Apart from the intoxication-type food poisoning due to *Cl. botulinum* and *S. aureus, Proteus* and other bacteria proliferate in the flesh of fish such as mackerel pike, yellow tail, bonito and sardine, producing amines such as histamine as putrefactive products. Upon ingestion, they cause allergy-like rashes similar to urticaria. This is the so-called allergy-like food poisoning.

According to the statistics of the Japanese Ministry of Health and Welfare in 1969, the most common causative bacteria of bacterial food poisoning is *V. parahaemolyticus,* constituting 56.6%; next come *S. aureus,* 20.3 %, *Salmonella,* 15.8%; and pathogenic *E. coli,* 3.7 %. Regarding the types of causative food, fish and shellfish and their processed products constitute the majority, 303 cases, then in descending order, complexly treated food (74 cases), cereals and their processed products (44 cases), desserts (29 cases), meats and meat products (27 cases), eggs and their processed products (20 cases), vegetables and their processed products (20 cases), and milk and dairy products (2 cases). Furthermore, on the relation between food poisoning and the seasons, the incidences of bacterial food poisoning increase drastically from July to September when temperature and humidity are both high; over 70% of the annual total occur during this period.

Diarrhea of Unknown Etiology

In diarrheas that occur once in a while in our daily life, it is relatively rare to isolate the causative bacteria discussed so far. Even if bacteriological investigations are conducted, the majority will be diagnosed as unknown etiology. In these cases, however, an imbalance in the intestinal bacterial flora as compared to healthy subjects can often be observed. Bacteria such as *E. coli,* enterococci, *Klebsiella, Aerobacter, Proteus, P. aer-*

uginosa which are present in small numbers in the feces of healthy subjects, become abnormally abundant in cases of traveler's diarrhea, summer diarrhea, epidemic infantile diarrhea in hospital, and amebic dysentery. Recently, it has been demonstrated that many of these bacteria produce toxins. Although based on these facts alone it is not sufficient to decide conclusively that these bacteria are causative agents of diarrhea, they deserve special attention as important factors relating to diarrhea.

It may also be possible to explain the diarrhea which frequently accompanies antibiotic treatment as due to the disturbance in the balance of the intestinal flora.

It has been reported that in around 70% of cases where the causative bacteria cannot be isolated, the bacteria which are normally seen only in the large intestine proliferate in the upper part of the small intestine. This is also thought to be one cause of diarrhea. At times when the physiological functions of the body are out of order due to, for example, cold, emotional stress and influenza, it is conceivable that abnormal growth of intestinal bacteria occurs in the small intestine.

Diarrhea can also be related to the digestion and absorption of carbohydrates in food. If undigested carbohydrates reach the large intestine, they are fermented by the bacteria in the large intestine, which results in the production of organic acids such as lactic, formic, acetic, propionic and butyric acid. These organic acids stimulate the intestinal mucosa and increase the osmotic pressure inside the intestine causing diarrhea. Individuals who have no lactose-decomposing enzymes experience diarrhea by drinking milk, a condition called lactose intolerance.

5. Longevity and Intestinal Bacteria

Metchnikoff

Elie Metchnikoff (Fig. 35), a Russian biologist, was born in 1845 the youngest child of a landlord on the prairie of Kharkov in Little Russia. He majored in Zoology at the University of Kharkov and became a lecturer at the University of Odessa at the age of 22. There he commenced his research in comparative biology. In 1883, he went to Sicily and established his own laboratory in Messina, where he conducted research on biology and developed the idea of the famous theory on phagocytes. For this work, he was awarded the Nobel Prize in 1908. In 1886, he was invited to become the director of a bacteriological research institute which was established in Odessa, and thus he returned to Russia. He resigned one year later due to the failure in the manufacture of the anthrax vaccine. In 1888, he left Russia and through the goodwill of Pasteur, was given a laboratory in the Pasteur Institute. There he made a lot of contributions in the areas of immunology, toxins and syphilis, and became the deputy director of the Institute in 1904.

Towards the end of the 19th century. Metchnikoff turned his attention to aging as an extension of his work on phagocytes. The basic idea was that aging was caused by chronic intoxication due to toxins produced by intestinal bacteria, and, to prevent aging and perhaps also arteriosclerosis, it was necessary to remove the harmful bacteria from the intestine. This, he thought, might be achieved by diet therapy, introducing lactic acid bacteria into the intestine. Supported by the fact

Figure 35. Elie Metchnikoff.

that longevity was common in a Bulgarian region where yoghurt was the daily food, he made yoghurt and consumed it every day regularly to demonstrate its beneficial effect on health, and recommended it to the people around him. This is the so-called "Metchnikoff's longevity-without-aging theory". Due to his theory, yoghurt had gained popularity not only in Europe but all over the world.

Although this episode provided an opportunity for the research on intestinal bacteria, the complexity of the intestinal flora presented a big obstacle. Metchnikoff died in 1916, of arteriosclerosis complicated by uremia, at the age of 71. After that, it was discovered that *L. bulgaricus*, a species of lactic acid bacteria present in the yoghurt recommended by Metchnikoff could not grow in the intestine. Metchnikoff's theory was thus dismissed and forgotten. The research on the relationship between intestinal bacteria and aging did not proceed any further.

Types of Dairy Products with Lactic Acid Bacteria

Today, about half a century after the death of Metchnikoff, yoghurt and other lactic acid bacteria-containing drinks have once again attracted attention.

After *L. bulgaricus* present in yoghurt was found not able to inhabit the intestine, *L. acidophilus*, originally a resident bacteria of the intestine, was used to produce fermented milk products (milk fermented by the addition of lactic acid bacteria). Products such as "Acidophilus Milk," "Reform Yoghurt," "Bioghurt," "Aco Yoghurt" were marketed in the United States and Europe. However, regarding these products, various criticisms were raised such as that the lactic acid bacteria used was not *L. acidophilus* taxonomically, and that after being cultured in the milk, the bacteria lost their capability to proliferate in the intestine. Anyway, the arguments on whether the lactic acid bacteria in these products or fermented milk products could colonize in the intestine continued for some time.

In recent years, it has been recognized that bifidobacteria are important lactic acid bacteria in the intestine of both adults and infants. Therefore fermented milk products made from bifidobacteria have appeared in the Japanese and European market.

Therefore, among the various products of yoghurt and fermented milk-based drinks, the types and numbers of lactic acid bacteria used are different, and the proportions of milk constituent also vary. In Japan, the constituents of these kinds of products are determined by an ordinance of the Ministry of Health and Welfare. The classification will be briefly discussed here.

"Fermented milk" is prepared by fermenting milk (cow's, buffalo's, goat's, sheep's or horse's milk) by lactic acid bacteria or yeasts. Since this product is made from whole milk or skimmed milk as such, the non-fat solid content (solid content excluding fats) should be over 8.0%, and the number of lactic acid bacteria or yeasts should exceed 10^7 per ml. Yoghurt is the representative of this type of product. Other examples include Kefir, Kumiss, Acidophilus milk and Bioghurt.

Fermented milk drinks are produced by adding sweetening, flavours, etc. to the fermented milk base. Those that contain over 3% of non-fat solid content, and over 10^7 per ml of lactic acid bacteria or yeasts are classified into "fermented milk drinks." These drinks may contain live lactic acid bacteria or may be pasteurized. The lactic acid bacteria-containing beverages that contain less than 3% of non-fat solid content, and over 10^6 per ml of lactic acid bacteria or yeasts are classified into "food with milk as the main raw material, lactic acid bacteria drink" or simply "lactobacillus milk drinks."

Although the respective components of the fermented milk, fermented milk drinks and lactobacillus milk drinks are legally determined, the bacterial species used are not governed by any ministerial ordinance. Apart from the *L. bulgaricus* and *S. thermophilus*, the so-called yoghurt bacteria, *L. acidophilus, L. casei* and bifidobacteria are also being used.

The Effects of Fermented Milk

From the past there have been numerous reports on the medical effectiveness of yoghurt and other fermented milk. Many reports have indicated that yoghurt is effective in conditions such as loss of appetite, diarrhea, constipation, tympanites, liver diseases, and nephritis. Acidophilus milk has also been reported to be effective in the treatment of diarrhea, constipation, stomatitis and dermatitis. However, among these reports, some were clinical cases without the inclusion of controls, others provided scanty supporting data on the characteristics of the bacterial strain used, quantity of bacteria, colonizing property of the bacteria in the intestine, and intestinal flora. While it cannot be denied that some degree of efficacy must have resulted, it cannot be assumed that all the conclusions reached were correct.

In recent years, it has been reported that lactic acid bacteria such as *L. bulgaricus* and *L. acidophilus* produce antibiotics. Also, when yoghurt was given to mice that had been transplanted with Erlich's peritoneal cancer cells, the multiplication of the cancer cells was somewhat suppressed. The effective component was shown to be the bacterial cell component of the lactic acid bacteria.

However, is the fermented milk really effective? If so, what are the mechanisms of action? So far, it seems that the discussion on the effectiveness of fermented milk has been centered on the multiplication of the lactic acid bacteria in the intestine. Yet, it is known that *L. bulgaricus* and *L. jugurti* contained in yoghurt do not survive in the intestine. Also, it has become clear that other lactic acid bacteria, too, when taken by mouth, do not multiply readily in the intestine. Then, it is not possible to explain the effectiveness of fermented milk if only the viable lactic acid bacteria are addressed. Here, the effects of fermented milk will be discussed under four categories:

(1) effects due to the base material, the milk component,
(2) effects of substances produced and released by the activities of the lactic acid bacteria,
(3) effects due to the bacterial cellular components, and
(4) effects due to the viable lactic acid bacteria.

(1) Substances in milk that are useful to our body, such as proteins, lactose, vitamins, fats and minerals are provided in fermented milk, in much the same way as in natural milk.

(2) The lactic acid produced by lactic acid bacteria is said to reduce gastric acid secretion, stimulate peristalsis and prevent putrefaction in the intestine. A part of the lactic acid combines chemically with calcium to form lactic acid-calcium complex which is a more easily absorbable form. Part of the milk proteins is digested by the lactic acid bacteria to peptones and peptides which are more easily utilized, and consequently improves liver function and stimulates intestinal secretion. Also, trace amounts of active substances may be produced which may promote or maintain a healthy balance of the intestinal flora or may improve intestinal metabolism.

(3) In the case when the lactic acid bacteria are killed by gastric juice or bile, or when pasteurized fermented milk drinks are taken, the cellular components released from the dead bacteria are absorbed. They have stimulatory effect on the immune system, augment the anti-cancer immunity and promote liver function, and may be associated with detoxication of harmful substances in the intestine.

(4) If the viable lactic acid bacteria reach the intestine and

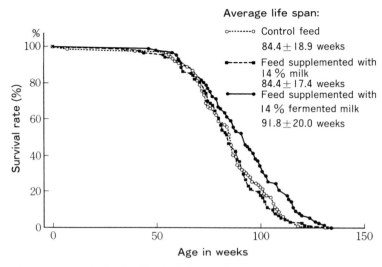

Figure 36. Effect of administration of pasteurized fermented milk on life span of mice.

succeed to multiply there, the substances produced during growth may improve the balance of the intestinal flora, and as in (3) may play a role in the detoxication of harmful substances produced by other bacteria.

In our laboratory, in order to verify the effectiveness of fermented milk, we used sterilized fermented milk as a starting experiment. The purposes of killing of the lactic acid bacteria in advance are to simulate the situation that *L. bulgaricus* in fermented milk products is killed in the intestine, and to eliminate the effect of live bacteria. Three experimental groups, 90 mice each, are given normal feed, or feed supplemented with 14% milk, or feed supplemented with 14% sterilized fermented milk. The life span of the 3 groups of mice are compared in Fig. 36. While the groups fed normal feed and feed supplemented with milk lived for an average period of 84.9 and 84.4 weeks, respectively, the group given feed supplemented with sterilized fermented milk lived for an average of 91.8 weeks, 7 weeks longer than the other two groups. From these results, it can be discussed that the fermentation products or cellular components of the lactic acid bacteria in the sterilized fermented milk have some beneficial effects on the host. Although the efficacy of fermented milk producks is still not completely understood, it will not be too long before the mechanism of action will be elucidated.

Villages of Longevity in the World

There are some places in the world that are known to be countries or villages of longevity. If we examine the number of people who live over 100 years (centenarians), the country that has the most centenarians is the Soviet Union, 137 per 1,000,000 population, which far exceeds the figure of 32 per 1,000,000 population for the United States. In the Caucasus area of the Soviet Union, the number of centenarians is especially high, 45 per 100,000 population, according to the survey of 1959. Bulgaria is famous as a country of longevity, with the number of centenarians being 51.8 per 1,000,000 population. In the Smolyan area in the south of Bulgaria, which is known for the number of people enjoying longevity, the number of centenarians reached 318.3 per 1,000,000 population, according to the survey of 1965. In Japan, according to the statistics of 1976, the number of centenarians was 113 for men, and 553 for women, totaling 666, or 5.6 per 1,000,000 population. Although the average life expectancy in Japan is the top in the world, the number of centenarians is rather low among the developed countries.

Diets in the Villages of Longevity

Professor Leaf of Harvard University conducted a study on the villages of longevity in the world ("Youth in Old Age" by Alexander Leaf and John Lannois: McGraw-Hill Book Company, 1975). He surveyed the eating habits of the adults with an average age of 55 living at Hunza in Cashmere. Their diet is a plain one, consisting of mainly wheat, barley, millet and beans. In the summer they eat plenty of vegetables such as tomato, chili, red pepper, egg plant and bottle gourd, and also dry and store vegetables for winter. In the winter they eat potato, turnip, dried vegetable, fruit and almond. The daily food intake contains on average 1,923 Cal, 50 g protein, and 35 g fat. Comparing to the average daily intake by a 55-64-year-old American, which is 2,422 Cal, 98 g protein, 121 g fat, and 227 g carbohydrate, the diet in Hunza is considerably lower in calorific value, protein and fat. Particularly, the consumption of meat and dairy products is low, not exceeding 1% of the total intake.

Professor C. Bella investigated the nutritional intake of the elderly in Bilcabamba in Peru, South America. Their daily food intake contains on average 1,200 Cal, 35–38 g protein, 12–19 g fat, and 200–300 g carbohydrate. The protein and fat intake which is even lower than that in Hunza is mainly of vegetable origin; the daily animal protein intake is as little as 12 g. The inhabitants here are engaged mainly in agriculture, concurrent with stock farming. They take a mainly vegetation diet: the staple food is cereal, eaten with boiled potato, maize and beans, and a considerable amount of greens, carrot, pumpkin and green pepper.

In contrast to the diets in Hunza and Bilcabamba, that in Caucasus is not necessarily of low-calorie and low-cholesterol. The elderly here takes 1700–1900 Cal per day, with most people consuming milk, vegetables, meat, fruits and others. About 70% of the amount of food taken is vegetarian while the rest consists of dairy products and a small quantity of meat. Among the total protein taken, 70–90% is from dairy products such as yoghurt, milk, butter and cheese. Sunflower seeds which contain high quality vegetable oil are eaten as snack. Kvas, a kind of beer made from home-made wine and left over brown bread is drunk modestly. Vegetables and fruit are eaten in abundance. The staple food is brown bread made from rye, gruel made from buckwheat grains, unpeeled potatoes, and gruel of roughly ground maize.

Shoji Kondo (Tohoku University) has reported on a long-term on-site study in villages of longevity and villages of short life in Japan. He pointed out that while villages of longevity in the rest of the world are mainly mountain villages, the villages of longevity in Japan are located in offshore islands or coastal areas in the southwest. In Yamashiro Hot-spring, Kaneno Village, Komatsu Town and Hisatsune Village in Ishikawa Prefecture, the reason that women live longer than men is due to the man-dominating society such that women have to eat cereals as the staple food. Among the offshore islands of Hokkaido, Tamaura Village on Okushiri Island is a village of long life, and is famous as a fish market for herring. Farming plots are found only in this village, and the villagers while eating plenty of fish also eat a lot of carrot, pumpkin and greens. Consequently, animal protein and vegetables are taken in good balance. On the contrary, in the other villages where only fish and white rice are eaten, the incidences of heart and liver diseases are high and people have shorter lives.

In Kunizaki Village in Ise, Mie Prefecture, the woman divers of the Shima Peninsula live a very long life. As rice cannot be grown in this village, wheat and sweet potatoes grown in the fields are eaten as staple food. Also, soy bean, sesame, vegetables, fish, shellfish and seaweed are taken sufficiently. In summary, the conditions existing in villages of short life in Japan are: only rice eaten as the staple food, and in excess amount, insufficient vegetables, and overeating of fish. On the other hand, the conditions existing in villages of longevity are: regular eating of meat, fish, egg or soy beans, consumption of plenty of vegetables such as carrots and sweet potatoes, and seaweeds; and in places where rice is not available, the eating of wheat, soy bean and potatoes as the staple food.

Reviewing the combined results of these investigations on the eating habits in villages of longevity in the world, a few common points can be extracted. Firstly, the diet in any village of longevity is plain, consists of abundant wheat, soy bean, oat, maize, cereals such as buckwheat, beans and potatoes. Moreover, the total calories and protein content are always low, that is, there is no overeating. Also, plentiful vegetables and fruits are eaten. Therefore, together with vitamins A, C, D, E and minerals present in these foods, indigestible materials such as dietary fibers and seaweeds are taken abundantly, and the diet is well balanced. In addition, characteristic food is taken daily in some places, such as kumiss and yoghurt eaten by people in Caucasus and Bulgaria, and sea weeds eaten by villagers of longevity in Japan. Additional facts that must not be omitted are that in all these places, people who live to a great age live in a land with unpolluted air and mild climate, keep early hours, work appropriately and have little stress.

The Effects of Indigestible Substances

Cereals, potatoes, beans, seaweeds, vegetables and fruits contain indigestible polysaccharides such as cellulose, hemicellulose, lignin, pectin, inulin, *Konjak* mannan, alginic acid and carrageenan. Recently, these kinds of food have become popular again due to the dietary fibers they contain. The reason is that the incidence of large bowel cancer in the United States and northwestern Europe has increased by about ten times compared with that in the past; also, arteriosclerosis has become the first cause of death, the incidence of which is about 10 times that of Japan. The cause of these serious situations is thought to be the high-protein, high-fat, low-fiber diet of the western countries.

The effectiveness and the cause and effect relationship of indigestible substances in the prevention of arteriosclerosis are not yet definitely elucidated. A number of possible effects can be considered.

One is that when dietary fibers that are difficult to digest are added to food, the amount of feces excreted is increased by 2–3 times. Thus the concentration of carcinogenic or harmful substances produced by intestinal bacteria is diluted, their action on the intestinal wall is also weakened and they are soon excreted outside the body.

In addition, when these undigested substances enter the large intestine, they are utilized by the intestinal bacteria, and broken down to organic acids such as butyric and lactic acid, and gases such as methane, carbon dioxide and hydrogen. The organic acids stimulate the intestine, promoting peristalsis, which helps to excrete harmful substances more rapidly. This efficacy has been proved by giving feed supplemented with cellulose to animals that had been administered ^{65}Zn. The absorption of ^{65}Zn from the intestine decreased with the increase of cellulose supplemented.

Furthermore, dietary fibers have been shown to lower cholesterol level in blood, and moderate the actions of toxic materials administered. The mechanism is not fully understood. However, it has been demonstrated that dietary fibers have the ability to soak up water, cholesterol and toxic materials. If this happens in the intestine, the absorption of these harmful substances by the body is hindered and they are excreted out of the body together with the fibers. When pectin, *Konjak* powder or seaweed is given to mice in advance, the onset of intoxication symptoms due to cadmium, PCB or azo food dyes is considerably delayed. The alginic acid contained in seaweed is also effective in lowering blood pressure. Attention has been drawn to the fact that the Bantu tribe in Africa who eat a large amount of fiber-containing food daily has markedly lower incidences of polyps of the colon, inflammatory colitis, colon cancer and arteriosclerosis compared to people of the western countries.

The other benefit conferred by indigestible food is that apart from the dietary fibers, various nutrients valuable to our body are often present in high concentrations. Examples are vitamin E in cereal germ; iodine, iron and calcium in seaweed; vitamin C and D_2 in mushrooms; and vitamin A and C in vegetables and cereal germ. The polysaccharides in mushrooms and cellular components of the lactic acid bacteria in sour milk such as yoghurt when absorbed may augment the immune functions of the body.

However, it is too hasty to assume that protection against diseases and promotion of health will happen by simply taking fiber-rich food. Excessive consumption of fibers can result in distention and rumbling in the abdomen and hindrance in absorption of minerals such as iron, copper and calcium. A balanced diet containing a suitable amount of fibers is important. There is still no consensus opinion on the appropriate amount of fibers that man should take. More investigations are needed to arrive at the conclusion as to the kinds and amount of dietary fibers that should be taken daily.

The Dream of a Healthy Long Life

Japanese who suffered from the shortage of food immediately after World War II had hoped to catch up with the eating standard of the United States. This was achieved over ten years afterwards. After that, accompanying the high degree of economic growth, the eating habits have moved gradually towards the road of westernization, and life expectancy has drastically been extended, occupying the first place in the world in 1977, exceeding that of England, the United States, Germany, France and the three Scandinavian countries. In the old days, many people died due to infectious diseases such as pneumonia, bronchitis, tuberculosis and enteritis. After the War, the improvement of public health, development of new drugs, chiefly antibiotics, the advance of medical care, as well as the marked improvement of nutrition have resulted in marked reduction of deaths due to infectious diseases. Since 1958, the number one cause of death is cerebral apoplexy followed by, in second place, cancer and in third place, heart diseases such as myocardial infarction. Hence the top three causes of death are those of chronic degenerative diseases. According to the vital statistics in 1977, deaths caused by cerebral apoplexy, cancer and heart diseases occupy 27.1, 17.3, 17.0%, respectively, of all deaths, and the three diseases together constitute 61.4%. Therefore, six out of ten deaths are due to the three chronic degenerative types.

If we compare the causes of death in Japan with those of the Western countries, the places of number one and three are reversed, that is, the number one cause of death in Western counties is heart diseases and number three, cerebral vascular diseases. However, in recent years, it is recognized that the causes of death are being drastically changed in Japan; that is, stomach cancer and cerebral apoplexy which had been prominent among Japanese are on the decline, instead, incidences of lung cancer, colon cancer and heart diseases are drastically increased. Moreover, such changes are remarkable among residents in urban areas. This is perhaps a warning on the effect of westernization of eating habits and living environment.

In recent years, there has been a reflection on the excessive use of medical drugs. The time has come to refrain from abusive use and to go back to proper usage. Also, from now on, it is important that we individuals pay attention to disease prevention and health maintenance rather than treatment of diseases. The most important factor in the acquirement of a healthy long life is the daily eating habit. There is no doubt that depending on the diet, cerebral apoplexy and heart diseases can be caused and the occurrence of cancer can be accelerated. The larger the amount of harmful substances produced in the intestine, the more health is affected. Even though this affect may not seem to happen soon, it will be expressed in the long run. This kind of affect has already started while man is still in the mother's womb. The harmful substance produced in the mother's intestine is carried to the fetus together with the nutrients. Moreover, given the same harmful substance, the affect it has during the fetal period is stronger than during later in life. It is not uncommon that the affects start to appear in adulthood. Therefore, the importance of maintaining an intestinal flora in which beneficial bacteria dominate over harmful bacteria comes into play. To achieve this, it is necessary for each individual to consider a diet that is suited to his own age, physical status and occupation.

The principle of a proper eating habit is the intake of a balanced diet. In addition, food that promotes the growth of beneficial bacteria and suppresses harmful bacteria has to be taken actively. In order to prevent obesity, arteriosclerosis and hypertension, care must be taken not to excessively consume fats and carbohydrates which result in surplus calories. Excessive salt intake has to be avoided to prevent hypertension. In addition, attention must be paid to diet that is biased towards fish and meat, which will lead to the accumulation of large amounts of harmful substances in the intestine. Appropriate amount of dietary fibers has to be taken in order to excrete the harmful substances rapidly. In old age when digestion is deteriorated, easily digestible food and calcium which is the main component of bone have to be taken sufficiently, with care being taken to include food that prevents constipation. Furthermore, vitamin E and C should be taken to remove superoxide from the body.

As the research in intestinal bacteria proceeds, in the future, it will be possible to decide an ideal balance of the intestinal flora that is essential for the healthy life of man. The intestinal flora can be checked periodically so that aging and cancer could be predicted. In addition, as a measure for their prevention, diet therapy that maintains a good balance of the intestinal flora might be designed. Furthermore, with the advance in genetic engineering techniques, bacterial strains that function best in the human body, as well as having strong colonizing power in the intestine, could be developed. These strains could then be added to food such as sour milk to be taken daily. By these means, more people might be able to enjoy longevity in good health. To achieve this, however, a lot more research will be needed.

Postscript

In 1953, after graduating from the Department of Veterinary Medicine, Faculty of Agriculture, the University of Tokyo, I entered the graduate school and became engaged in the study of intestinal bacteria. The theme was assigned to me by the honored Professor Yuichi Ochi (now, President of Azabu Veterinary Medical School). At that time infectious diarrhea was an epidemic among chickens, and Professor Ochi thought that in order to elucidate the cause of this disease, it was necessary to define clearly the actual states of the normal bacterial flora in the intestine in which diarrhea is staged. He had already published the theory on autogenous infectious diseases, and had proved by investigating many clinical cases that most infectious diseases are caused by bacteria that normally inhabit the host, and that the disease is manifested when host resistance is lowered. Furthermore, he had then accomplished his study on normal bacterial flora in the respiratory organs but had not yet set his hand on intestinal bacterial flora.

The obstacle I encountered as soon as I started the study of intestinal bacteria was the problem of the cultural method. It was a barrier that had to be overcome by all means in order to accomplish the ecological research, in which composition of the intestinal bacterial flora must be investigated as it is. I spent many years making successive improvements on the method, and the problem was finally solved fifteen years later.

195

Another problem was the work of classifying bacteria, for almost none of the bacteria newly isolated from the intestine were well-known until then. What I had to do at first was to classify lactobacilli and bifidobacteria. During that time I was actually most delighted in being able to set foot on the work of classification and devoted myself intensely to it. It was partly because I had been deeply impressed by the lectures in botany by Professor Fumio Maekawa (now, an emeritus professor of the University of Tokyo) in Seikei college on his work in classification, and had held an aspiration in that field. I had learned at his lectures that taxonomy, liable to be neglected as a science of collection, was really an important science dealing with fundamental problems of biology, and additionally was an interesting science associated with profound philosophy, and I had hoped to make taxonomy my lifework.

Thus I set about establishing classification systems, beginning with that of lactobacilli detected from the intestine followed by those of bifidobacteria and bacteroides. And by using the completed classification schemes, I investigated the intestinal bacterial floras of humans and animals under various conditions, and identified intestinal bacteria to the levels of species and subspecies. After that I elucidated the functions of each individual bacteria, and further integrated the functions of these bacteria as a group, i.e. an ecological system, which enabled me to acquire new pieces of knowledge in succession. If my study on intestinal bacteria had not been based firmly on bacterial taxonomy, all these results could not have materialized.

From 1964 to 1966 I stayed in West Germany to study under the direction of Professor Lerche, Professor Sinell, and Dr. Reuter at the Free University of Berlin, which was my long-cherished desire. This experience had a decisive influence on myself as a taxonomist. Here I learned to conduct research based on a firm foundation, which stayed unscathed even in the postwar era of Germany. This spirit of study has accompanied all my subsequent as a research scientist, exerting a great influence on the study of intestinal bacterial flora. The establishment of the classification system for bifidobacteria was actually realized during my stay in Germany.

What I wish to say here by all means is the following. After I graduated from the postgraduate school, I was able to continue my research at The Institute of Physical and Chemical Research (RIKEN), Tokyo, a most extraordinary place in the world, which is liberal and blessed with circumstances conducive to research. I believe that it was by being at this place that I could grow and develop without reserve the small bud that had just formed in the study of intestinal bacteria. I am filled with a deep sense of gratitude for those who have educated and encouraged me in the last 20 years in my pursuance on the subject "Classification and Ecology of Intestinal Bacterial Flora," a study which is considered remarkably basic in nature.

The importance of medical bacteriology which has solved many problems of infectious diseases appears to be increasing as a science in the investigation of the causes of chronic degenerative diseases such as cancer, to take preventive measures and subsequently to maintain human health. These problems cannot be solved without interdisciplinary cooperation among various fields such as physiology, biochemistry, pathology, dietetics and clinical medicine. The problem of intestinal bacteria is the central theme of such investigations. Fortunately, the methodology and taxonomic system for the study of intestinal bacteria have now been almost completely established, and it is expected that results of practical applications in this field will be yielded in the near future.

For writing this book I have referred to many reports in the literature and books both Japanese and foreign, including also those in areas different from my own. I would like to express my gratitude here.

I also owe my deep appreciation to the following people who encouraged and assisted me in writing this book and took troubles to publish it; Mr. Tamiki Ono, Mr. Yoichiro Goto and all the staff of Iwanami Shoten.

1978   Tomotari Mitsuoka

Appendix

List of Intestinal Bacteria and Other Related Bacteria

Spirochaetaceae
  Treponema
  Borrelia

Pseudomonadaceae
  Pseudomonas
    P. aeruginosa

Enterobacteriaceae
  Escherichia
    E. coli
  Salmonella
    S. typhi
    S. enteritidis
    S. typhimurium
  Shigella
    S. dysenteriae
    S. flexneri
    S. sonnei
  Klebsiella
    K. pneumoniae
  Proteus
  Yersinia

    Y. enterocolitica

Vibrionaceae
  Vibrio
    V. cholerae
    V. parahaemolytica

Bacteroidaceae
  Bacteroides
    B. fragilis
    B. thetaiotaomicron
    B. melaninogenicus
    B. oralis
    B. ruminicola
  Fusobacterium
    F. necrophorum
    F. nucleatum
    F. varium

Anaerobic spirilla
  Desulfomonas
  Succinimonas
  Butyrivibrio
  Selenomonas

Veillonellaceae
  Veillonella
  Megasphaera

Micrococcaceae
  Staphylococcus
    S. aureus
    S. epidermidis

Streptococcaceae
  Streptococcus
    Enterococci
    (*S. faecalis,*
    S. faecium, etc.)
    S. mutans
    S. lactis
  Leuconostoc
    L. mesenteroides
    L. citrovorum
  Pediococcus

Anaerobic streptococci
  Peptococcus
  Peptostreptococcus
  Ruminococcus
  Coprococcus
  Sarcina

Bacillaceae
  Bacillus
    B. subtilis
    B. cereus
  Clostridium
    C. perfringens

    C. butyricum
    C. botulinum

Lactobacillaceae
  Lactobacillus
    L. bulgaricus
    L. jugurti
    L. helveticus
    L. acidophilus
    L. salivarius
    L. casei
    L. plantarum
    L. brevis

Propionibacteriaceae
  Propionibacterium
    P. acnes
  Eubacterium
    E. aerofaciens
    E. rectale

Actinomycetaceae
  Bifidobacterium
    B. bifidum
    B. infantis
    B. breve
    B. longum
    B. adolescentis
    B. animalis
    B. pseudolongum
    B. thermophilum
    B. indicum
    B. asteroides

Index